CONTENTS

MATERIAL CONNECTIONS IN THE ANCIENT MEDITERRANEAN

Mobility, Materiality and Mediterranean Identities

Edited by
Peter van Dommelen
and A. Bernard Knapp

Routledge
Taylor & Francis Group

LONDON AND NEW YORK

First published 2010
by Routledge
2 Park Square, Milton Park, Abingdon, Oxon OX14 4RN

Simultaneously published in the USA and Canada
by Routledge
270 Madison Ave, New York, NY 10016

Routledge is an imprint of the Taylor & Francis Group, an informa business

© 2010 Peter van Dommelen and A. Bernard Knapp for selection and
editorial matter; individual chapters, their contributors

The right of Peter van Dommelen and A. Bernard Knapp to be identified as
author of this work has been asserted by them in accordance with sections 77
and 78 of the Copyright, Designs and Patents Act 1988

Typeset in Adobe Garamond Pro by
Bookcraft Ltd, Stroud, Gloucestershire

Printed and bound in Great Britain by
CPI Antony Rowe, Chippenham, Wiltshire

British Library Cataloguing in Publication Data
A catalogue record for this book is available from the British Library

Library of Congress Cataloging in Publication Data
A catalog record for this book has been requested

ISBN 13: 978-0-415-58668-9 (hbk)

ISBN 13: 978-0-415-58669-6 (pbk)

ISBN 13: 978-0-203-84211-9 (eb)

FIGURES

The following are reproduced with kind permission of the copyright holders. While every effort has been made to trace copyright holders and obtain permission, this has not been possible in all cases. Any omissions brought to our attention will be remedied in future editions.

Book cover: Popular representation of a material connection in action. The scene is set in Iron Age west central Sardinia (Gulf of Oristano), showing Phoenician traders and Nuragic islanders exchanging material goods. Mural on the central square of Terralba (OR), Sardinia, commissioned by the local council and realised under the auspices of the local cultural association, SELAS. As is customary with Sardinian *murales*, the work is anonymous and undated (reproduced with permission; photo P. van Dommelen).

TABLES

CONTRIBUTORS

Carlos Cañete holds a PhD from the University of Málaga (Spain). He has worked at the School of Arabic Studies in Granada (Spain) and is currently an honorary lecturer at the University of Málaga. His research focuses mainly on the historiography of archaeological and anthropological studies in Africa and the Mediterranean, on which he has published several articles. He also participates in archaeological projects investigating the pre-Roman colonial presence in *Lixus* (Larache, Morocco) and seventeenth-century Jesuit settlements in the Lake Tana region of Ethiopia.

Marina Gkiasta has studied at the universities of Athens (BA), Sussex, University College London (MA) and Leiden (PhD), and has worked on several research projects in Greece and England. She has a long experience of fieldwork in Greece, England and Italy and is particularly interested in landscape archaeology, Aegean prehistory, social psychology and the method and theory of archaeological practice. Her most recent publication, *The Historiography of Landscape Research in Crete* (2008), explores the theoretical and methodological frameworks of archaeological interpretation based on landscape studies, from the onset of the discipline up to the present day.

Jeremy Hayne is currently studying for a PhD at Glasgow University's Department of Archaeology. His interests include the prehistoric Iron Age and how identities were formed in periods of migration and colonisation. Drawing on anthropological and postcolonial theory, he is researching identity, islandness, hybridisation and connectivity of the peoples of the Tyrrhenian and western Mediterranean Iron Age by careful examination of their material culture. He has excavated at Iron Age sites in Scotland and the north of England as well as in Sardinia, where he works as part of the Terralba Rural Settlement Project and at the Iron Age site of Sant'Imbenia.

Sarah Janes received her PhD from the University of Glasgow in 2008, with a thesis entitled 'The Cypro-Geometric Horizon, a View from Below: Identity and Social Change in the Mortuary Record'. She is currently an Honorary Research Associate in the Department of Archaeology, University of Glasgow. She has been involved in several survey and excavation projects in Cyprus, including the Troodos Archaeological and Environmental Survey Project (TAESP), and recently has worked in Egypt on the North Karnak Survey Project. Her main research interests involve issues related to mortuary archaeology and identity, especially in Cyprus and the eastern Mediterranean, with an ongoing interest in survey methodology, computer applications in archaeological research, Cypriot Iron Age pottery, Archaic sanctuaries and terracotta figurines.

Alicia Jiménez is a postdoctoral researcher at the Spanish National Research Council (CSIC, Instituto de Historia in Madrid). She is the author of *Imagines hibridae. Una aproximación postcolonialista al estudio de las necrópolis de la Bética* (2008) and co-editor (with M.P. García-Bellido and A. Mostalac) of *Del imperium de Pompeyo a la auctoritas de Augusto. Homenaje a Michael Grant* (2008). Her research interests include archaeological theory and the transition between the Iron Age and the Roman period in the Iberian Peninsula, with a special interest in topics like social change and colonisation, material culture in public and private contexts and the interaction between the past and the present in the creation of contemporary 'myths of origins' in Spain.

A. Bernard Knapp is Professor Emeritus of Mediterranean Archaeology at the University of Glasgow (Scotland). His research interests include island archaeologies and identities in the eastern Mediterranean, where he has conducted long-term fieldwork in Cyprus. He recently published *Prehistoric and Protohistoric Cyprus: Identity, Insularity, and Connectivity* (2008) and co-edits the *Journal of Mediterranean Archaeology*.

Maria Kostoglou is a specialist in the archaeometallurgy of the Greek Iron Age. Her research interests include the study of technology and society in the first millennium BC Mediterranean, the application of analytical techniques in archaeology and the use of museum collections for object-based learning and research in archaeology. Her publications include *Iron and Steel in Ancient Greece: Artefacts, Technology and Social Change in Aegean Thrace from Classical to Roman Times* (2008), 'Iron and steel currency bars in Ancient Greece', *Mediterranean Archaeology and Archaeometry* 3 (2003) and a number of technical reports including 'Metal working debris from the excavations in Bahrain', in T. Insoll (2006), *The Land of Enki in the Islamic Era: Pearls, Palms and Religious Identity in Bahrain*.

Damià Ramis is an archaeologist involved in research associated with projects at the University of Glasgow (Department of Archaeology) and the University of the Balearic Islands (Department of Earth Sciences). He received his PhD in prehistory from the Universidad Nacional de Educación a Distancia, Madrid, in 2006. His dissertation research focused on a review of the chronology of the earliest human settlement in the Balearic Islands and on the faunal analyses of the earliest sites in Mallorca, including the extinction of the endemic fauna. The main results of this work were published in the *Journal of Archaeological Science*, the *Proceedings of the Prehistoric Society* and the *Journal of Mediterranean Archaeology*. Currently he co-directs long-term excavation projects at the Iron Age necropolis of Son

Real (Santa Margalida) and at the Bronze and Iron Age site of S'Hospitalet Vell (Manacor) on Mallorca. He is also involved – with participation in fieldwork and faunal analysis – in other excavation projects on Mallorca, Menorca and Cabrera that cover everything from the early Bronze Age to late Antiquity.

Corinna Riva is Lecturer in Mediterranean Archaeology at University College London. She received her PhD in Etruscan archaeology from the University of Cambridge in 2001. From 2000 to 2005 she held a Junior Research Fellowship at St John's College, Oxford and served as Lecturer in Mediterranean Archaeology in the Department of Archaeology, University of Glasgow in 2005–6. Her research interests cover Iron Age Italy and the first millennium BC in the central Mediterranean. She is co-director of the Upper Esino Valley Survey project (Marche, Italy). She has co-edited (with Nicholas Vella) *Debating Orientalization: Multidisciplinary Approaches to Change in the Ancient Mediterranean* (2006), and (with G. Bradley and E. Isayev) *Ancient Italy: Regions without Boundaries* (2008). Her own book *The Urbanization of Etruria* was published in 2010.

Michael Rowlands is Professor of Anthropology at University College London. His research interests include theoretical approaches to the study of material culture and cultural heritage with a strong regional focus on West and Central Africa today and in the recent past. His current interests relate to reinvestigating questions of 'cultural spread' and transformation in spaces that conventional concepts of social theory have tended to neglect. He is also interested in issues of duration and ontology that question the strong ethnocentrism that still dominates much archaeological theorising. In identifying phenomena that escape description, he raises the possibility of developing alternatives to mundane explanations of things. He has co-edited (with Ferdinand de Jong) *Reclaiming Heritage* (2007) and (with Christopher Tilley *et al.*) the *Handbook of Material Culture* (2006).

Anthony Russell is a research student in the Department of Archaeology at the University of Glasgow. He is currently writing his PhD dissertation, entitled 'Cultural Encounters in the Central Mediterranean between 1450 and 900 BC: Insularity, Connectivity and Islanders' Identities', under the supervision of Professors A.B. Knapp and P. van Dommelen. He won the 2008 Byvanck Award with the paper 'Deconstructing Ashdoda: migration, hybridisation and the Philistine identity', *BABesch* 84 (2009).

Jaime Vives-Ferrándiz holds a PhD in archaeology from the University of Valencia (Spain) and has been Curator in the Museum of Prehistory of Valencia since 2004. His principal field of research is eastern Iberia during the first millennium BC. He is especially interested in postcolonial perspectives on colonial situations and exchange relations, as is shown in his book *Negociando encuentros* (2005). He presently directs a research project funded by the Ministerio de Ciencia e Innovación (Spain) on the materiality of social life in Iberian settlements and co-directs fieldwork at the settlement of La Bastida de les Alcusses (Valencia, Spain).

Peter van Dommelen is Professor of Mediterranean Archaeology at the University of Glasgow (Scotland), where he has taught since 1997. His research interests include colonialism and rural organisation in the west Mediterranean and he conducts long-term fieldwork on the island of Sardinia; in collaboration with the University of Valencia he is currently engaged in a series of site surveys and excavations of Punic farmsteads in the Terralba district of west central Sardinia. He has published (with Carlos Gómez Bellard) *Rural Landscapes of the Punic World* (2008) and co-edits the *Journal of Mediterranean Archaeology*. He also serves on the editorial board of *World Archaeology*.

PREFACE

The *Material Connections* project developed out of discussions between ourselves and our various involvements in and collaboration with the research of the contributors to this volume. Although the wide range of regions and periods covered by these research projects might at first sight suggest otherwise, we noted manifold connections between them and we realised the potential of combining a wide variety of regional and chronological contexts within a coherent theoretical and methodological framework. An additional interesting variable was the diverse national and academic backgrounds of the contributors.

Thanks to the award of an AHRC Workshop Grant (AH/G00109X/1), it finally became possible to bring the whole group together in one place, not just once but twice. The first occasion was at the 14th Annual Meeting of the European Association of Archaeologists in Malta, where we organised a half-day session under the title 'Material Connections' (20 September 2008). The session was well attended and sparked quite a few reactions, not least owing to Mike Rowlands's insightful closing comments; all this was discussed further at a separate project meeting in Malta. The prolonged joint presence in Malta also offered all of us a valuable opportunity to explore and deepen the connections between our research agendas. At the same time, it enabled us to broaden the scope of the conference session and to bring in two additional participants.

Following the discussions in Malta, we elaborated our introductory presentation into a substantial discussion of what we saw – and still see – as the rationale for and the theoretical underpinnings of the *Material Connections* project. We presented this statement to all project members as the starting point for further discussion, which was to be held in Glasgow. All contributors developed their conference presentations into substantial papers over the ensuing winter, and these were circulated well ahead of the Glasgow workshop on 19 and 20 March 2009. On that occasion, no papers were presented formally but each one was introduced for discussion by one of the other project members, with about one hour devoted to each paper. A round-table debate introduced by Mike Rowlands as well as numerous discussions on the side strengthened the multiple relations between the project's members and their research, and helped further to integrate the papers.

The next step was to produce the present volume and to this end, we finalised our introductory paper, which is published here as Chapter 1, and we provided further feedback as well as practical guidelines. The final versions of these chapters were eventually submitted during the summer of 2009.

In addition, we have established a website at http://materialconnections.arts. gla.ac.uk that offers information about the project and has allowed its members to communicate and exchange information. While it is obvious that this book could not have been produced without the support of the AHRC workshop grant, we are also indebted to Nick Vella (Department of Archaeology, University of Malta), who kindly provided crucial assistance for the Maltese stage of the project, despite his already overcommitted diary as EAA conference co-organiser. In Glasgow, the Department of Archaeology provided space and all kinds of practical support for the workshop, for which we thank in particular Dr Jeremy Huggett and Mrs Pauline McLachlan.

Peter van Dommelen and A. Bernard Knapp
Glasgow, March 2010.

1

MATERIAL CONNECTIONS
Mobility, materiality and Mediterranean identities

A. Bernard Knapp and Peter van Dommelen

Introduction

The movement of people and objects has always stood at the heart of endeavours to understand the course and processes of human history. In the Mediterranean, evidence of such movements is particularly abundant, and issues like colonialism, migration and exchange have played prominent roles in archaeological, historical and anthropological discussions (e.g. Ward and Joukowsky 1992; Knapp and Cherry 1994; van Dommelen 1998). Moreover, because migration and colonisation processes have linked the Mediterranean to temperate Europe in both the distant and recent past, the region occupies a critical place in the formulation of modern European identities (e.g. Renfrew 1994; Dietler 2005; Hamilakis 2007).

European perceptions of the Mediterranean, however, whether popular or scholarly, have long been framed by a one-sided focus on the classical Mediterranean – often in exclusively colonialist Greek or Roman terms (e.g. Abulafia 2003; Harris 2005). In the wake of global decolonisation and large-scale migration in the past half century, such long-standing attitudes increasingly are called into question. Ingrained assumptions about the Hellenic roots of European civilisation, for instance, and outdated perceptions of how the classical world and its material representations may inform contemporary practices in modern (but now mostly postcolonial) contexts have thus come under intense scrutiny (e.g. van Dommelen 1997; Dietler 2005).

Preliminary studies, past and recent, have suggested that material connections in the widest sense of the term – i.e. processes such as long-distance and prolonged migrations, hybrid practices and object diasporas – may have been far more prevalent than generally accepted (Frankenstein and Rowlands 1978; Frankenstein 1979; Tronchetti and van Dommelen 2005; Vives-Ferrándiz 2008; Voskos and Knapp 2008). Conversely, bounded cultures and well-defined populations with readily distinct identities may have been far less common than usually assumed (Figure 1.1). If so, extensive and detailed analyses of ancient migrations and connectivities are not just warranted but crucial for a better understanding of the formation of prehistoric

Figure 1.1 Monumental Nuragic Iron Age head of a warrior from the site of Monte Prama in west central Sardinia, which offers a good example of local hybrid practices and Mediterranean-wide material connections (Tronchetti and van Dommelen 2005; drawing by Erick van Driel, Leiden).

and early historic Mediterranean identities, and for developing more realistic insights into the emergence of what we recognise as European cultural diversity.

Accordingly, Mediterranean colonial occupations, migrations and all manner of social exchanges in the past now demand more meaningful and effectively theorised representations. Such work is essential if we wish to develop fresh cultural and historical understandings of how factors such as materiality, mobility, hybridisation, co-presence and conflict impact(ed) on the formation of identity and subjectivity, whether past or present.

With the contributors to this book we therefore embrace a new subject of enquiry, the social identity of prehistoric and historic Mediterranean peoples, and consider how materiality, migration, colonial encounters, hybridisation and connectivity or insularity influence those identities. Our main resource is the material culture that people used throughout their lives: this allows us to look well beyond the rather narrow focus on archival, epigraphic and literary written evidence. An approach

2

based in materiality also provides far greater time-depth that enables us to venture deep into prehistory and to adopt a truly long-term perspective in examining how mobility (migrations, colonial encounters, trade/exchange) impacted on the prehistoric and historic inhabitants of the Mediterranean. The case studies in this volume are intended to amplify the ways that Mediterranean scholars have looked at the objects and subjects of their studies. Adopting a material and diachronic, socio-historical approach, the authors examine contacts among various Mediterranean islands – the Balearics, Sardinia, Crete, Cyprus – and their nearby shores to explore the social and cultural impact of migratory, colonial and exchange encounters.

Conceptualising contacts

Mediterranean studies typically are characterised by an acute 'hyper-specialisation' (Cherry 2004: 235–6) that discourages comparative research of the many material, cultural and socio-economic features and trends that overlap and interconnect in this region. Moreover, because much current fieldwork and research in the Mediterranean are typically concluded on a local or at most a regional scale and lack systematic comparison of distinctive cultural developments in different regions (cf. Alcock and Cherry 2004), there is ample scope for new perspectives on studying material culture. Engaging the themes of materiality, mobility and identity with the study of a wide range of objects and ideas should breathe new life into current theoretical and methodological approaches, facilitating new dialogues and understandings of transregional and trans-cultural practices in the Mediterranean.

Migratory movements and colonial encounters have long constituted prominent themes in Mediterranean and classical studies, but scholarly attention has remained largely focused on the colonisers' expansion and achievements (e.g. Boardman 1980; Tsetskhladze 2006). The local inhabitants of these colonised regions were considered simply as passive objects in these colonial situations, if they were given any attention at all. Only in recent years have their active involvement in and contribution to the colonial process been highlighted. In contrast, because recent accounts have tended to emphasise indigenous accomplishments and local resistance to the colonisers, few studies offer detailed examination of specific colonial situations that go beyond these stereotypical, binary oppositions to delve into the complex and dynamic contexts of social and cultural interaction (cf. van Dommelen 2002; Vives-Ferrándiz 2008).

The general insistence on using the term 'colonisation' rather than 'colonialism' further underscores a widespread reluctance to engage Mediterranean contact situations in cross-cultural comparisons (Dietler 2009: 20–3). One recent volume on *Ancient Colonizations* (Hurst and Owen 2005) is even reluctant to compare Greek colonialism with other colonial expansions, to consider the Greek 'overseas settlements' as colonial in any way or to explore questions of terminology (Owen 2005: 17: cf. Osborne 1998). Overall, alternative postcolonial perspectives on these contact and colonial situations have largely been avoided in the study of 'ancient colonisation' in the first millennium BC (van Dommelen 2006; Osborne 2008).

Within the wider Mediterranean world, archaeologists typically look at identity one-dimensionally, i.e. as ethnic identity, class identity or gender identity (e.g. Morgan 1991; Cornell and Lomas 1997; Hitchcock 1998). Other scholars use the terms 'identity' and 'ethnicity' interchangeably, or else assume that a close relation exists between material culture and ethnicity (e.g. Emberling 1997; Frankel 2000). Identity, however, is a broad, encompassing concept that incorporates categories such as age, sexuality, class and gender, as well as ethnicity (Díaz-Andreu *et al.* 2005). Discourses on identity involve not just individuals but broader social groupings, be they antagonistic or cooperative. Yet identity is not simply a by-product of belonging to a household, neighbourhood or community, nor do individual people 'possess' identity. Instead, it must be seen as a transitory, even unstable relation of *difference* (Meskell 2001).

The lesson that archaeologists can learn from the social sciences is that self-ascribed identities, whether individual or collective, are not primordial and fixed, but emerge and change in diverse circumstances: socio-political, historical, economic, contextual and – in the case of the Mediterranean's seas and mountainous islands – geographical. Given the loosely defined concepts of the Mediterranean (see further below), and the limited research conducted on island identities within the Mediterranean region (cf. Robb 2001; Constantakopoulou 2005; Knapp 2008), the geographical scale needs to fit the problem (Morris 2003: 45), and our conceptual tools need to be refined in order to gain new perspectives (Figure 1.2). Focusing on difference, symbolism, boundaries and representation as distinguishable features of the Mediterranean material record should enable archaeologists to recognise practices shared by social groups as well as individuals, and thus help to unravel the tangled web people of that region spun around their identities.

While studies of ancient objects and materials have long been the mainstay of Mediterranean archaeology, the emergence of material culture studies (e.g. Buchli 2004; Tilley *et al.* 2006) has gone largely unnoticed in the very same field. For many archaeologists working in the Mediterranean, classifying objects remains an aim in itself; even when categories of objects are mapped onto social, political or ethnic relations, the latter typically are derived directly from other (written) sources. Studying archaeological data from a social perspective, however, as advocated by material culture studies, opens up new avenues of research to examine the ways in which people were using objects, to explore how objects framed and shaped people's life worlds and how their own physicality (their bodies) was intimately entangled with other 'things'.

Studying material culture is an interdisciplinary undertaking by its very nature, as objects are always examined in their wider context. This context may be scientific, when their material make-up is analysed, or it may be social and cultural, when the ways in which objects are perceived and used come under scrutiny. The notion of materiality lies at the heart of endeavours to explore objects as an integral dimension of culture and to demonstrate that human behaviour or social existence cannot be understood fully without taking into account the role of objects (e.g. DeMarrais *et al.* 2005; Meskell 2005). In short, adopting a material culture perspective for

Figure 1.2 The so-called 'Temples' of late Neolithic Malta, like this one at Ḥaġar Qim on the south coast of the island, offer a fine example of spectacular island developments.

studying the social and cultural meetings and mixings of people and objects in the Mediterranean enables us to focus on the materiality of migratory, colonial and other cultural encounters and their role in restructuring existing identities and formulating new, hybrid identities.

Material connections

From the viewpoint of material culture, the critical element of mobility resides in the co-presence of both people and objects in a specific context – as a result of their movements. In other words, the actual physical encounters that take place between different people, or between those people and objects old or new, oblige us to acknowledge the existence of these encounters and to come to terms with their significance. Depending on the nature and intensity of the meeting, people will seek ways – both physical and conceptual – to fit new people and/or new objects into their existing lives, often by developing new hybrid practices in which old and new items as well as traditions can be accommodated. Regardless of whether people themselves arrived

5

in a new place or encountered other people or objects coming from elsewhere, the process of constructing a new world, literally and mentally, holds the key to understanding mobility and the ensuing engagements that result in the restructuring of existing identities and/or the formulation of new, hybrid identities (van Dommelen 2006; Voskos and Knapp 2008).

Because of the diversity in the materials, landscapes and histories of the regions involved in these case studies, the methodology we describe here is intended to be inclusive and general rather than exclusive and specific. The basic material evidence investigated throughout the volume constitutes specific objects – e.g. figurines, metal objects, pottery, monumental architecture, mortuary remains, floral or faunal data – that played a critical role in cultural encounters (Figure 1.3). A key question guiding these studies is whether and to what extent the items concerned were involved in facilitating contacts between two or more social groups or, alternatively, in creating distance between them. The notion of the 'social biography' of objects provides the conceptual tool for assessing the perception, use and meaning of these objects in diverse contexts of migration, colonisation or hybridisation (Kopytoff 1986; Gosden and Marshall 1999). A parallel line of investigation focuses on the landscapes and seascapes in which the cultural and social encounters took place and in which objects both old and new were hybridised, integrated or created anew. Because

Figure 1.3
Cypriot female figurine (Type A, bird-faced) holding an infant, thirteenth century BC (Cyprus Museum, Nicosia; no. 1934/IV-27/23; courtesy of the Director of the Department of Antiquities, Cyprus).

of the prominence and propinquity of the sea throughout the Mediterranean, the authors pay particular attention to the maritime dimension of mobility and the actual encounters. We thus seek to gain an insight into how an ideology of the sea impacts on individual or group identities, and on the diverse social, material and ideological exchanges linking different parts of the Mediterranean world.

All contributors explore how 'things' mediate the experience of Mediterranean peoples, and how these experiences were – and are – shaped and informed by long-term collective memories of movement, migration, colonisation or localisation. Although based on different islands and coastal regions, all research is linked thematically and examines how materialised landscapes, seascapes and 'memory-scapes' impacted on Mediterranean identities. In these long-term interactive and interrelated spaces, the modern and the ancient constantly inform and predict each other. This diachronic perspective provides important insights into how new senses of place are created and how new identities are forged.

The contributors to this volume investigate the movements and encounters of people in both the ancient and modern Mediterranean. They draw upon the key concept of materiality in formulating new perspectives on mobility and identity in the Mediterranean, applying experiences and interdisciplinary insight from archaeology, anthropology and classics. The intention is not just to interrogate existing viewpoints, but actively to unlock and explore new ways of thinking about:

- how the dynamics of materiality, including object diasporas and transmissions, offer insights into migratory and colonial experiences;
- how factors such as mobility, travel, communication and hybridisation impact on colonial and local identities and subjectivities.

This volume is thus intended to propose a coherent alternative methodology to the ways in which Mediterranean scholars have looked at the objects and subjects of their studies. Adopting a diachronic, socio-historical approach, the contributors examine contacts between various Mediterranean islands and their nearby continental shores to explore and assess:

- how Mediterranean peoples used material culture to establish, maintain or alter their identities, especially during periods of transition, cultural encounter and change;
- how, in general, mobility, connectivity or insularity, and the Mediterranean Sea itself, along with colonialism, migration and hybridisation more specifically, influenced trans-regional and local subjectivities and identities;
- how recent colonial encounters can enhance understanding of materiality, mobility and identity as formative experiences embedded in territorial expansion or cultural transitions.

To pursue these three aims, the following interlinked themes structure the various case studies, to different extents and with different emphases in each chapter:

- **Materiality:** highlighting the material dimensions of cultural encounters and social contexts and focusing on the role of material culture in identity formation and long-term cultural transmission.
- **Mobility:** considering hybridisation, connectivity and insularity, along with modes of travel and communication, as mechanisms that served to establish, motivate or modify diasporic, trans-regional and local identities.
- **Contact, conflict and co-presence:** exploring various contexts in which people of diverse cultural backgrounds met and interacted. Such contacts range from fleeting encounters to long-term shared settlement, whether harmonious or hostile. The common denominator was the physical co-presence of people in a particular context and the socio-cultural dynamics created in the course of their interactions.
- **Identity:** examining how the social identity of Mediterranean islanders and coastal dwellers emerged or changed in diverse cultural encounters and during periods of major social discontinuity or reorganisation. The intention is to determine when different types of identities are likely to be proclaimed as distinguishing features, and what kinds of materials might be employed as media for such identity statements.

Because no single society, polity or region constitutes the ideal unit of analysis, and because there may be as many social boundaries or connections within a single culture or polity as there are between different ones, these crucial issues warrant attention from a broad, comparative research perspective. The specific material and – where relevant – documentary or ethnographic evidence examined relates in equal measure to the main Mediterranean islands (Sardinia, Crete, Cyprus, the Balearics) and their nearby mainland shores (Italy, Spain, Greece, the Levant and North Africa). In chronological terms, the chapters focus on prehistoric and early historic periods (from the Early Bronze Age through the Roman period), but also include one case study that treats the historical trajectory of what has been termed 'Mediterraneanism' (Herzfeld 1987b: 64–70). Such an approach makes it possible to examine the Mediterranean world comparatively, interactively and from an interdisciplinary perspective over a time span of nearly 5,000 years.

Mediterranean definitions

While our study region might seem unproblematic, defining the Mediterranean has been a matter of debate for some time now and, presumably because of the aforementioned 'hyper-specialisation', few scholars – some archaeologists and some historians – have embraced the Mediterranean in its entirety as a coherent area for study and analysis (e.g. Morris 2003; papers in Blake and Knapp 2005). Like Braudel (1972; 2001) long before them, Horden and Purcell (2000) propose to examine the unity of the ancient Mediterranean, its connectivity within diversity. Increasingly the adoption of a comparative approach in regional archaeologies of the Mediterranean (e.g. Trigger 2003; Joffe 2004) has provided useful insights into the social, symbolic and ideological aspects of diverse cultures whose connectivity expanded and intensified throughout antiquity, and continued into and beyond the post-Roman world. In contrast, at least two Mediterranean anthropologists, Herzfeld (1984; 1987a, b) and de Pina-Cabral (1989; 1992) argue that attempts to portray Mediterranean cultural unity reveal a 'pervasive archaism', a 'Mediterraneanism' no different from what Said (1978) identified as 'Orientalism'. Thus the quest for a broad anthropological perspective on the Mediterranean is construed as an ideologically motivated discourse in which the Mediterranean is reproduced as the 'other', a category just as exotic as that of the Orient (Mitchell 2002: 4–5).

Sant Cassia (1991: 4–7), another social anthropologist, insists that the Mediterranean is no different from any other area of ethnographic focus, and that the intertwined histories of various Mediterranean cultures must be seen within the context of the shifting frames of reference that implicitly oppose 'the Mediterranean' to other categories of anthropological discourse (e.g. Europe, the Balkans, Melanesia, West Africa). For geographers, 'Mediterraneanism' (King *et al.* 1997: 6–9), is a well-established concept represented by a landscape in which the region's cultural, physical and visible aspects – the climate, the sea, the land and the vegetation – are intertwined with the human (Figure 1.4). The long traditions of rural and urban life within the Mediterranean basin, as well as its environmental diversity, recur to differing degrees

Figure 1.4   A terraced landscape with an abandoned olive grove in the Sierra Calderone hills of Valencia (Spain) that shows a typical Mediterranean landscape inscribed with both natural and cultural features.

and in different ways throughout the region: they form part of the Mediterranean *as experience* and provide a physical backdrop to any discussion of Mediterranean identity, mobility or materiality.

Mediterranean contexts and content

In spatial and chronological terms, this volume literally spans the Mediterranean, from the Levant to the Straits of Gibraltar, during formative periods that cover the millennia between the Early Bronze Age and the Roman Empire (Figure 1.5). As Braudel (1972: 148–61) pointed out long ago, the size, resources, relative isolation and different cultural traditions of the Mediterranean's main islands or island groups have often made them stand out in social and cultural terms. At the same time, because they were also situated on major routes of interaction and commerce, these islands have frequently participated in and contributed to wider Mediterranean trends and innovations, and repeatedly have been involved in mobility networks and cultural encounters (Antoniadou and Pace 2007). Herein lies a fundamental paradox: while islands in general serve as essentialising metaphors for isolation (e.g. Kirch 1986; Rainbird 1999), in the Mediterranean they are more often than not interconnected through much broader social, cultural and politico-economic interaction spheres (e.g. Broodbank 2000; Constantakopoulou 2007; Dyson and Rowland 2007).

The connectivity patterns and colonial networks that spanned most of the Mediterranean during the periods considered in this volume also link its various case studies. Each case study, moreover, is tied to one or more of the others by either spatial or chronological contiguity. The volume's interlinked themes – materiality, mobility, co-presence and identity –provide structure to each case study. These thematic links also incorporate the single case study that extends beyond antiquity, and that is included pointedly in order to explore these themes in the wider Mediterranean context, as well in the more recent past. It also extends the diachronic perspective of the volume's papers and helps to bridge the time between the recent and the ancient past. While firmly tied to the other case studies by the shared geographical and thematic focus, this historiographic study provides a key analytical counterpart to the other archaeological case studies.

The volume's contributors were asked to consider and if possible to orient their studies around the following series of questions, which were devised specifically to address current perceptions and prejudices associated with the movement of peoples in the Mediterranean. The aim is not just to interrogate existing viewpoints, but also to explore new ways of thinking about how materiality, mobility, hybridisation and co-presence impacted on diasporic, regional or local identities and subjectivities:

- how did Mediterranean peoples fashion their world and formulate their identities?
- how can the dynamics of materiality – including object diasporas and transmissions – offer insights into the experiences of migration, colonisation and hybridisation?

- what long-term material and social dynamics are involved in formulating and establishing people's identities?
- how did travel, geography and changing (diachronic) perceptions of the sea help to establish Mediterranean identities and reinforce a sense of difference?
- how do shared social practices – imprinted in material culture ranging from monuments to household tools – contribute to expressing local and trans-regional identities?
- how can factors such as insularity, connectivity and co-presence illuminate the ways that distance and 'the exotic' impacted on people, materials and memories?
- how did 'connectivities' with overseas powers – as material processes (e.g. technologies, gifts, consumption) – impact on the development of more complex social systems?
- how did local people resist foreign intervention, or appropriate colonial innovations?

The nature of mobility or the specific colonial networks in which an island or coastal region was involved are closely linked to the regional and chronological setting of each case study. Here we list the regions examined by these case studies in their approximate chronological order, even if the volume itself is thematically organised around the notions of materiality, mobility/connectivity and Mediterranean identities (Figure 1.5).

- Balearic islands (Mallorca and Menorca): because human occupation of the Balearics only occurred during the third millennium BC, much later than on most other Mediterranean islands (Ramis and Alcover 2001; Ramis *et al.* 2002), these islands offer the opportunity to explore the origins and material conditions

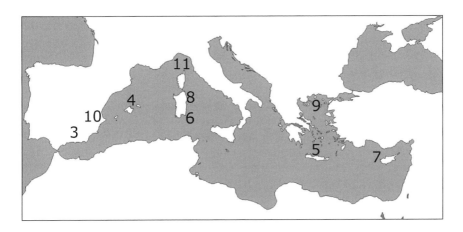

Figure 1.5   Map of the Mediterranean showing the location of the case studies presented in this volume (figures refer to chapter numbers).

of migration, exploitation and initial colonisation. Monitoring developments during the course of the Bronze Age provides further insights into local processes of identity formation.

- Crete: this study explores the variability of local identities on Bronze Age Crete (third millennium BC) through the medium of materiality and by assessing the role of landscape (Gkiasta 2008) in constructing and perpetuating social identity. The mountainous, insular landscape of Crete has played a major role both in connecting and in isolating people. Communities, their connections and their interdependent relationship with specific regions form the key themes in this study, which focuses on the basic frameworks of social life and their signatures in material objects and the landscape.

- Cyprus: this research focuses on issues of insularity, connectivity and identity during the Late Bronze and early Iron Ages (twelfth to seventh centuries BC) (Janes 2008). With the breakdown of the larger, centralised polity and the emergence of smaller, local, hybridised polities that involved native Cypriotes and incoming peoples from the Aegean and Levant, this study examines how material culture was actively involved in the multiple social and spatial dynamics – maritime interactions, migrations and colonial encounters – that occurred.

- Sardinia and southern France: the three studies that revolve around Sardinia and the nearby mainland shores examine the extent of connectivity in and around the north Tyrrhenian Sea from the end of the Late Bronze Age through the Iron Age and into the early historical period (eleventh to fifth centuries BC) (Ridgway 2000; Riva 2005). During that time, these waters were frequented by Phoenicians, Carthaginians, Greeks, Etruscans, Sardinian and other local peoples, all of whom became entangled in ever-shifting regional and intra-regional movements and colonial networks. The shifting nature of identities is also investigated in terms of people's materiality, and with respect to the dynamic encounters that ensued.

- Northern Aegean: iron technology and its products in mainland Greece and the Aegean islands during the Iron Age and Classical period are critically examined in order to explore mobility through the transfer of technological knowledge and by studying identity through the cultural milieu of iron production (Kostoglou 2008). Starting from the premise that technological processes and choices are culturally embedded, a detailed case study of interaction between the indigenous and colonial inhabitants of coastal Thrace shows that local identities may be constructed around the particular technical skills required to produce material culture, in this case iron objects.

- Spain: focusing on the eastern and southern regions of the Iberian Peninsula during the Iron Age (eighth to seventh centuries BC) and late Roman Republic and early Roman Empire (second century BC to second century AD) respectively, the two Spanish case studies both explore strategies for constructing local identities (van Dommelen 2001; Vives-Ferrándiz 2005; 2007; Jiménez 2008). The appropriation of material culture is examined in a colonial situation of contact and co-presence related to Phoenician trade on the eastern Iberian seaboard, exploring how objects were used and perceived in burial contexts to construct group and individual identities. In southern Spain, the focus is on parallel discourses that spread through different media (tombs, coins, monumental and public buildings and spaces like the *forum*) that may be associated with collective or individual identities, in order to understand how different local memories might have interacted. Special attention is given to postcolonial issues and to the modern perception of the area under study as a *mirror* of Rome in ancient times.

- Mediterraneanism: given diverse understandings of the notion of 'the Mediterranean' (Horden and Purcell 2000: 10–15; Morris 2003), this study evaluates the role of classificatory practices in configuring (early) modern perceptions of the Mediterranean and traces in detail the historical trajectory of this notion. It demonstrates in particular that scientific research and the knowledge generated were and are deeply embedded in contemporary social thought and contingent on established practices; they were certainly anything but neutral.

Conclusions

Materiality, mobility and identity represent the intellectual tools that all contributors use to different extents in order to gain insights into how Mediterranean peoples literally and conceptually constructed new worlds, time and time again. By confronting unexplored ideas and crossing traditional boundaries in a theoretically distinctive and informed manner, the volume's studies offer substantial new perspectives on issues of materiality, mobility and identity in the ancient and recent Mediterranean. Our analyses of these concepts will, we hope, breathe new life into current theoretical and methodological approaches, and facilitate new dialogues and understandings of trans-regional and trans-cultural practices.

A comparative approach enables us to cover the entire Mediterranean over an unprecedented, diachronic time span. More pertinently, it also allows us to transcend a long-standing practice in classical and Mediterranean studies, namely to ascribe innovations or differences in socio-cultural, economic and material practices to intervention by outside forces, be they travelling artisans, intrepid traders or invading armies. As long as innovation and intervention remain inadequately theorised or critiqued in Mediterranean archaeology and anthropology, this prevailing external perspective ensures that the inhabitants of various Mediterranean lands remain unseen and unheard, antithetical to history, denied their own identity – all this at a time when multi-vocality and the local invigorate and structure both historical and social scientific practice. Consigning the agents of change to vague and untheorised external forces precludes any attempt to consider how enduring factors such as mobility, contact, conflict and co-presence influenced and underlay local people's cultural and social practices, indeed their very identities, memories and ideologies.

This volume offers a novel agenda intended to pave the way for more creative, comparative work on crucial issues and questions related to materiality, mobility and identity in the Mediterranean world. Our ambition in this respect is to transform both scholarly and popular representations of how individuals, small groups and major collectivities of people in the ancient and recent Mediterranean moved across the region and interacted with other people and polities. In turn, such insights should impact on the ways in which both local people and outsiders (including modern-day developers and tourists) perceive and engage with the existing material remains and the cultural heritage of the Mediterranean.

References

Abulafia, D. (ed.) 2003 *The Mediterranean in History*. London: Thames and Hudson.

Alcock, S.E., and J.F. Cherry (eds) 2004 *Side-by-Side Survey: Comparative Regional Studies in the Mediterranean World*. Oxford: Oxbow Books.

Antoniadou, S., and A. Pace (eds) 2007 *Mediterranean Crossroads*. Athens: Pierides Foundation.

Blake, E., and A.B. Knapp (eds) 2005 *The Archaeology of Mediterranean Prehistory*. Blackwell Studies in Global Archaeology. Oxford: Blackwell.

Boardman, J. 1980 *The Greeks Overseas: Their Early Colonies and Trade*. London: Thames and Hudson (3rd edition).

Braudel, F. 1972 *The Mediterranean and the Mediterranean World in the Age of Philip II*. Volume 1. New York: Harper and Row.

Braudel, F. (ed. R. de Ayala and P. Braudel) 2001 *The Mediterranean in the Ancient World*. London: Allan Lane.

Broodbank, C. 2000 *An Island Archaeology of the Early Cyclades*. Cambridge: Cambridge University Press.

Buchli, V.A. (ed.) 2004 *Material Culture: Critical Concepts in the Social Sciences*. London: Routledge.

Cherry, J.F. 2004 Mediterranean island prehistory: what's different and what's new? In S.M. Fitzpatrick (ed.), *Voyages of Discovery: The Archaeology of Islands*, 233–48. New York and London: Praeger.

Constantakopoulou, C. 2005 Proud to be an islander: island identity in multi-polis islands in the Classical and Hellenistic Aegean. *Mediterranean Historical Review* 20: 1–34.

—— 2007 *The Dance of the Islands: Insularity, Networks, the Athenian Empire and the Aegean World*. Oxford Classical Monographs. Oxford: Oxford University Press.

Cornell, T., and K. Lomas (eds) 1997 *Gender and Ethnicity in Ancient Italy*. Accordia Specialist Studies on Italy 6. London: Accordia Research Institute.

de Pina-Cabral, J. 1989 The Mediterranean as a category of regional comparison: a critical view. *Current Anthropology* 30: 399–406.

—— 1992 The primary social unit in Mediterranean and Atlantic Europe. *Journal of Mediterranean Studies* 2: 25–41.

DeMarrais, E., C. Gosden and C. Renfrew (eds) 2005 *Rethinking Materiality: The Engagement of Mind with the Material World*. Cambridge: McDonald Institute.

Díaz-Andreu, M., S. Lucy, S. Babić and D. Edwards 2005 *The Archaeology of Identity: Approaches to Gender, Age, Status, Ethnicity and Religion*. London: Routledge.

Dietler, M. 2005 The archaeology of colonization and the colonization of archaeology: theoretical reflections on an ancient Mediterranean colonial encounter. In G. Stein (ed.), *The Archaeology of Colonial Encounters. Comparative Perspectives*, 33–68. Santa Fe: School of American Research Press; Oxford: James Curry.

—— 2009 Colonial encounters in Iberia and the western Mediterranean: an exploratory framework. In M. Dietler and C. López-Ruiz (eds), *Colonial Encounters in Ancient Iberia. Phoenicians, Greeks and Indigenous Relations*, 3–48. Chicago: University of Chicago Press.

Dyson, S.L., and R.J. Rowland, Jr 2007 *Archaeology and History in Sardinia from the Stone Age to the Middle Ages: Shepherds, Sailors, and Conquerors*. Philadelphia: University of Pennsylvania Museum of Archaeology and Anthropology.

Emberling, G. 1997 Ethnicity in complex societies: archaeological perspectives. *Journal of Archaeological Research* 5: 295–344.

Frankel, D. 2000 Migration and ethnicity in prehistoric Cyprus: technology as *habitus. European Journal of Archaeology* 3: 167–87.

Frankenstein, S. 1979 The Phoenicians in the Far West: a function of Assyrian neo-imperialism. In M. Trolle Larsen (ed.), *Power and Propaganda. A Symposium on Ancient Empires*. Mesopotamia 7: 263–94. Copenhagen: Akademisk Forlag.

Frankenstein, S., and M. Rowlands 1978 The internal structure and regional context of early Iron Age society in south west Germany. *Bulletin of the Institute of Archaeology, London* 15: 73–112.

Gkiasta, M. 2008 *The Historiography of Landscape Research on Crete*. Archaeological Studies Leiden University 16. Leiden: Leiden University Press.

Gosden, C., and Y. Marshall (eds) 1999 *The Cultural Biography of Objects = World Archaeology* 31.

Hamilakis, Y. 2007 *The Nation and its Ruins. Antiquity, Archaeology, and National Imagination in Greece*. Classical Presences. Oxford: Oxford University Press.

Harris, W.V. (ed.) 2005 *Rethinking the Mediterranean*. Oxford: Oxford University Press.

Herzfeld, M. 1984 The horns of the Mediterranean dilemma. *American Ethnologist* 11: 439–54.

—— 1987a *Anthropology through the Looking-Glass. Critical Ethnography in the Margins of Europe*. Cambridge: Cambridge University Press.

—— 1987b 'As in your own house': hospitality, ethnography, and the stereotype of Mediterranean society. In D. Gilmore (ed.), *Honor and Shame and the Unity of the Mediterranean*. American Anthropological Association Special Publication 22: 75–89. Washington, DC: AAA.

Hitchcock, L. 1999 A Near Eastern perspective on ethnicity in Minoan Crete: the further tale of conical cups. In P. Betancourt, V. Karageorghis, R. Laffineur and W.-D. Niemeier (eds), *Meletemata: Studies in Aegean Archaeology Presented to Malcolm H.Weiner as He Enters His 65th Year*. Aegaeum 20: 371–79. Liège: Histoire de l'art et archéologie de la Grèce antique, Université de Liège; Austin: Program in Aegean Scripts and Prehistory, University of Texas at Austin.

Horden, P., and N. Purcell 2000 *The Corrupting Sea: A Study of Mediterranean History*. Oxford: Blackwell.

Hurst, H., and S. Owen (eds) 2005 *Ancient Colonisations: Analogy, Similarity and Difference*. London: Duckworth.

Janes, S. 2008 The Cypro-Geometric Horizon, a View from Below: Identity and Social Change in the Mortuary Record. Unpublished PhD dissertation, Department of Archaeology, University of Glasgow.

Jiménez, A. 2008 A critical approach to the concept of resistance: new 'traditional' rituals and objects in funerary contexts of Roman *Baetica*. In C. Fenwick, M. Wiggins and D. Wythe (eds), *TRAC 2007. Proceedings of the Seventeenth Annual Theoretical Roman Archaeology Conference, London 2007*, 15–30. Oxford: Oxbow Books.

Joffe, A.H. 2004 Athens and Jerusalem in the third millennium: culture, comparison, and the evolution of social complexity. *Journal of Mediterranean Archaeology* 17: 247–67.

King, R., L. Proudfoot and B. Smith 1997 *The Mediterranean: Environment and Society*. London: Arnold.

Kirch, P.V. (ed.) 1986 *Island Societies: Archaeological Approaches to Evolution and Transformation*. Cambridge: Cambridge University Press.

Knapp, A.B. 2007 Insularity and island identity in the prehistoric Mediterranean. In S. Antoniadou and A. Pace (eds), *Mediterranean Crossroads*, 37–62. Athens: Pierides Foundation.

—— 2008 *Prehistoric and Protohistoric Cyprus: Identity, Insularity and Connectivity*. Oxford: Oxford University Press.

Knapp, A.B., and J.F. Cherry 1994 *Provenance Studies and Bronze Age Cyprus: Production, Exchange, and Politico-Economic Change*. Monographs in World Archaeology 21. Madison, WI: Prehistory Press.

Kopytoff, I. 1986 The cultural biography of things: commoditization as process. In A. Appadurai (ed.), *The Social Life of Things: Commodities in Cultural Perspective*, 64–91. Cambridge: Cambridge University Press.

Kostoglou, M. 2008 *Iron and Steel in Ancient Greece: Artefacts, Technology and Social Change in Aegean Thrace from Classical to Roman Times*. British Archaeological Reports International Series 1883. Oxford: John and Erica Hedges.

Meskell, L.M. 2001 Archaeologies of identity. In I. Hodder (ed.), *Archaeological Theory Today*, 187–213. Cambridge: Polity Press.

—— (ed.) 2005 *Archaeologies of Materiality*. Blackwell: Oxford.

Mitchell, J.P. 2002 Modernity and the Mediterranean. *Journal of Mediterranean Studies* 12: 1–21.

Morgan, C.A. 1991 Ethnicity and early Greek states: historical and material perspectives. *Proceedings of the Cambridge Philological Society* 37: 131–63.

Morris, I. 2003 Mediterraneanization. *Mediterranean Historical Review* 18 (2): 30–55.

Osborne, R. 1998 Early Greek colonization? The nature of Greek settlement in the West. In N. Fisher and H. van Wees (eds), *Archaic Greece: New Approaches and New Evidence*, 251–69. London: Duckworth.

—— 2008 Colonial cancer. *Journal of Mediterranean Archaeology* 21: 281–4.

Owen, S. 2005 Analogy, archaeology and archaic colonization. In H. Hurst and S. Owen (eds), *Ancient Colonisations: Analogy, Similarity and Difference*, 5–22. London: Duckworth.

Rainbird, P. 1999 Islands out of time: towards a critique of island archaeology. *Journal of Mediterranean Archaeology* 12: 216–34, 259–60.

Ramis, D., and J.A. Alcover 2001 Revisiting the earliest human presence in Mallorca, western Mediterranean. *Proceedings of the Prehistoric Society* 67: 261–69.

Ramis, D., J.A. Alcover, J. Coll and M. Trias 2002 The chronology of the first settlement of the Balearic Islands. *Journal of Mediterranean Archaeology* 15: 3–24.

Renfrew, A.C. 1994 The identity of Europe in prehistoric archaeology. *Journal of European Archaeology* 2: 153–73.

Ridgway, D. 2000 The first western Greeks revisited. In D. Ridgway, S. Serra Ridgway, M. Pearce, E. Herring, R. Whitehouse and J. Wilkins (eds), *Ancient Italy in its Mediterranean Setting. Studies in Honour of Ellen Macnamara*. Accordia Specialist Studies on the Mediterranean 4: 179–91. London: Accordia Research Institute.

Riva, C. 2005 The culture of urbanization in the Mediterranean *c.* 800–600 BC. In R. Osborne and B. Cunliffe (eds), *Mediterranean Urbanization 800–600 BC.* Proceedings of the British Academy 126: 203–32. London: The British Academy.

Robb, J. 2001 Island identities: ritual, travel and the creation of difference in Neolithic Malta. *European Journal of Archaeology* 4: 175–202.

Said, E.W. 1978 *Orientalism*. New York: Pantheon.

Sant Cassia, P. 1991 Authors in search of a character: personhood, agency and identity in the Mediterranean. *Journal of Mediterranean Studies* 1: 1–17.

Tilley, C., W. Keane, S. Kuechler, M. Rowlands and P. Spyer (eds) 2006 *Handbook of Material Culture*. London: Sage.

Trigger, B.G. 2003 *Understanding Early Civilizations: A Comparative Study*. Cambridge: Cambridge University Press.

Tronchetti, C., and P. van Dommelen 2005 Entangled objects and hybrid practices. Colonial contacts and elite connections at Monte Prama, Sardinia. *Journal of Mediterranean Archaeology* 18: 183–209.

Tsetskhladze, G.R. (ed.) 2006 *Greek Colonisation: An Account of Greek Colonies and Other Settlements Overseas*. Mnemosyne Supplements 193. Leiden: Brill.

van Dommelen, P. 1997 Colonial constructs: colonialism and archaeology in the Mediterranean. *World Archaeology* 28: 305–23.

—— 1998 *On Colonial Grounds: A Comparative Study of Colonialism and Rural Settlement in First Millennium BC West Central Sardinia*. Archaeological Studies Leiden University 2. Leiden: Faculty of Archaeology, Leiden University.

—— 2001 Cultural imaginings. Punic tradition and local identity in Roman Republican Sardinia. In S. Keay and N. Terrenato (eds), *Italy and the West. Comparative Issues in Romanisation*, 54–70. Oxford: Oxbow Books.

—— 2002 Ambiguous matters: colonialism and local identities in Punic Sardinia. In C. Lyons and J. Papadopoulos (eds), *The Archaeology of Colonialism. Issues and Debates*, 121–47. Los Angeles: Getty Research Institute.

van Dommelen, P. 2006 Colonial matters. Material culture and postcolonial theory in colonial situations. In C. Tilley, W. Keane, S. Kuechler, M. Rowlands and P. Spyer (eds), *Handbook of Material Culture*, 104–24. London: Sage.

Vives-Ferrándiz, J. 2005 *Negociando encuentros. Situaciones coloniales e intercambios en la costa oriental de la península Ibérica (ss. VIII–VI a.C.)*. Cuadernos de Arqueología Mediterránea 12. Barcelona: Bellaterra.

——— 2007 Colonial encounters and the negotiation of identities in south-east Iberia. In S. Antoniadou and A. Pace (eds), *Mediterranean Crossroads*, 537–62. Athens: Pierides Foundation.

——— 2008 Negotiating colonial encounters: hybrid practices and consumption in eastern Iberia (8th–6th centuries BC). *Journal of Mediterranean Archaeology* 21: 241–72.

Voskos, I., and A.B. Knapp 2008 Cyprus at the end of the Late Bronze Age: crisis and colonization, or continuity and hybridization? *American Journal of Archaeology* 112: 659–84.

Ward, W.A., and M.S. Joukowsky (eds) 1992 *The Crisis Years: The 12th Century BC. From beyond the Danube to the Tigris*. Dubuque, IA: Kendall-Hunt.

CLASSIFYING AN OXYMORON

On black boxes, materiality and identity in the scientific representation of the Mediterranean

*Carlos Cañete**

Introduction

Current study of the Mediterranean seems to be affected by a continuous dichotomy. When Horden and Purcell (2000: 39–43) stated that Braudel's (1972) *magnum opus* marked the 'end of the Mediterranean', they meant that it was increasingly difficult to study it as an intelligible unity. Since then, the notion of the Mediterranean has repeatedly been called into question as a modern construct. Herzfeld (1984; 1987) and de Pina-Cabral (1989; 1992), for example, consider any unitary perception of the region as an illusion resulting from the marginalisation of the Mediterranean vis-à-vis northern Europe, in mainly Romantic representations. The material and ideological French interests of the nineteenth and twentieth century have also been highlighted as a source of this unified image (Ruel 1991), and similar views have recently been signalled in modern art (Jirat-Wasiutynsky 2007). The Mediterranean has also been presented as a modern product of discursive hegemony, like the Orient before it (Said 1978), and the term 'Mediterraneanism' might be seen as one way of describing this situation (Knapp and Blake 2005: 2). Other scholars, however, have directed their efforts to establishing new methodological and theoretical frameworks to reassess the historical study of this region (Horden and Purcell 2000; Blake and Knapp 2005; Harris 2005).

This apparently irreconcilable dichotomy between constructivist and practical approaches makes the Mediterranean an elusive and slippery notion. It disappears under discursive scrutiny but it makes sense if used 'on the go'. The Mediterranean might therefore be considered a 'black box' as described by the French sociologist Bruno Latour (2005: 26). For him, scientific facts and theories that from the outside appear coherent in practical scientific activity are like closed black boxes. If

* I would like to express my gratitude to Kathryn Lafrenz for correcting the English text. Also thanks to Bernard Knapp, Peter van Dommelen and the other members of the *Material Connections* project for their helpful support and comments.

considered from a critical perspective, however, they appear to be contingent and dependent on their sociological trajectory – as a box that is opened. In a broad sense this scheme could be applied to all scientific productions but, in practice, this situation is more characteristic of scientific controversies (Latour 2005: 29). The only way to evaluate all the implications behind a controversy is thus to analyse its practical formation, that is, to study scientific production as it is being made. Although it is obviously impossible to analyse directly an intellectual process that took place in the past, the opportunity remains to analyse the social formation of its categories within a historical context.

The aim of this study, therefore, is to offer a brief look at that process of scientific representation of the Mediterranean. The key role of classification in modern epistemic regimes makes the 'order of things' particularly interesting for this purpose (Foucault 2004: 126–46), as the material connections established by classificatory practices throughout the Mediterranean may give us some idea of the repercussions of this process upon the formation of identities. I focus on the scientific missions that accompanied the French military exploits of the nineteenth century across the Mediterranean, as these interventions are widely regarded as fundamental for the modern scientific representation of this region (Bourguet *et al.* 1998; 1999). A closer look at the particular circumstances surrounding the processes of mobility and materiality offers interesting insights into many aspects of modern Mediterranean identities. In the concluding section I suggest how the dichotomies of these representations might be overcome.

Classification

In Latour's (2005) view, scientific practice has been an integral feature of the wider emergence of modernity from at least the seventeenth century. A key element of the new scientific inquiry was a 'strategy of purification' to separate Nature clearly from Culture. In this view, Nature is seen as universal and essential, whereas Culture is particular and contingent (Lévi-Strauss 1969: 3–11; Derrida 1978). The belief in the ability 'to liberate' reality from what is contingent, relative or subject to opinion and the feasibility of formulating universal laws, concepts or categories lies at the heart of what it is to be modern. This 'strategy of purification' and the endeavour to rationalise every aspect of reality from biological description to social administration shows the totalising nature of this epistemic-cum-political programme, as purification was thought to offer universal answers to any question about the physical world or social practices.

In contrast to this ideal image of purification – the separation between Nature and Culture, between *episteme* and *doxa* – Latour argues that the practicalities of this activity reveal a very different situation. The daily routine of rationalisation is based on social interaction in relational networks made up of both human actors and 'non-humans', such as tools, machines and concepts that help to situate and stabilise meaning. The result is that scientific, social and political representations are based on particular experiences and that they are thus inevitably and necessarily contingent, and that 'non-humans' are constantly created in the 'purification' process as supposedly impartial aides. It remains implicit, however, that those 'non-humans' are hybrid constructions that are charged with both epistemic and social values. The contingency of the relational network within which knowledge is created is therefore at the same time the source for the concentration of interests and values that form different and often opposed identities. The key role of non-humans like tools and machines during this process makes them especially interesting as makers and markers of identity (see Kostoglou's contribution to this volume).

One of the main ways in which non-humans have been integrated into this process of purification has been through the practice of classification. 'Ordering things' as the consequence of a wide-ranging *episteme* (Foucault 2004: 126–46) has imposed a grid for the description and identification of any entity that shows particular features and that redefines the world in terms of a universalised framework. The application of this classificatory grid set by the epistemic/political agenda of modernity to any aspect of the world is manifest in the widespread use of statistics and of its promotion as a means to gain social or scientific insights. The proliferation of censuses, maps and museums as efficient devices in this regard (e.g. Smith 1998) offers another example that also informs us about the connections between this practice and collective identities (Anderson 1991: 184). Following Tilley (2006), we could also define this situation as the means by which the modern agenda has objectified the world as a complex relation between the material and the social. In that case, a closer look at the 'order' of materiality, how some things were connected to others and which identities were involved, may help to evaluate the contingencies of the 'practice of purification'.

To review this process in relation to the Mediterranean, however, would be an enormous task, and I therefore concentrate on three particular fields of materiality to gain an overview of those connections: environment, human anatomy and material culture. These seem to be the ones most suitable for this purpose, because they are closely associated with the three key controlling and identity-creating devices of modernity just mentioned: the map, the census and the museum. Nevertheless I shall also consider the historical circumstances of the perceptions on the basis of which relations between things were established.

Elias (1993) has shown how the transformative impulse, from which modernity arose in Europe, emerged from the widespread adoption of the customs and interests of specific privileged social fields. This trend, whose economic dimensions Hobsbawm (1971: 26–53) has uncovered, represented the rise to power of particular groups in European society, groups that reaped the economic and symbolic benefits of the modern agenda. As a result, the self-representation of those particular social fields was adopted across society as the norm. A good example is the way in which the language of the privileged classes became the measuring-stick of the linguistic competence for the whole of France (Bourdieu 1991: 43–65).

In France, too, the reliance of the absolutist monarchy on civil servants to control the aristocracy eventually shifted the balance of power to those state officials, and it was these groups, along with those who had benefitted most from the colonial enterprise in the Americas, that came to embody the social standards of the new system.

It was their customs and interests that became the hallmarks of civilisation, and the universal projection of this image eventually turned civilisation into the standard by which French strategies would be measured.

Homi Bhabha (1994: 121–31) has demonstrated the ambiguous effect of this situation in colonial discourse, as the universalising and homogenising intentions of civilisation are constantly cancelled out by the perceived necessity to maintain the social distinctions upon which the power and self-image of the privileged groups are based. I would suggest that similar processes are at work beyond colonial situations as well, since similar ambiguities occur whenever and wherever the standards of modernity are brought into practice. Civilisation itself is therefore an ambiguous representation of modernity, as it both assimilates and rejects other regions and societies. Nonetheless it lies at the root of the hierarchy that has structured classifications and perceptions of materiality in the Mediterranean.

Explorations

The French military and political interventions in the nineteenth-century Mediterranean were rooted in the previous century, when a remarkable proliferation of scientific studies accompanied an increasing commercial and political interest in that region. The French government financed new cartographic projects and the Académie Française encouraged travellers to collect a wide range of information as systematically as possible. Travel descriptions of that time are characterised by quantified and 'useful' information and effectively marked the starting point of a systematic scientific practice in the Mediterranean (Amstrong 2005). In the wake of intense French–English competition in both continental Europe and the Mediterranean and following open conflict with the Ottoman Empire, scientific inquiry became institutionalised and militarised as the first of several major scientific expeditions was launched in Egypt, in which the sciences appeared as a complementary partner to, if not justification of military action (Silvera 1975).

After a somewhat improvised start, many high-profile researchers were enlisted as scientific members of the expedition and fieldwork took place in 1798–1801. Subsequently, in 1798 the Institut d'Egypte was established, and after years of hard work the massive twenty-volume *Description d'Egypte* was published between 1809 and 1828 (Laurens 1997: 7–9). One of the outcomes of this expedition was an explicit strategy to relate military and scientific actions. Although the universal objectives of intervention were motivated and justified by the principles of the *mission civilisatrice*, in practice they relied on specific national interests. Scientific activities also followed quite specifically the models of the École Polytechnique and the École Normale, which were both explicitly national institutions. To promote the principles of civilisation allegedly to regenerate decadent Egyptian society meant in practice the imposition of values and notions of modernity (Laurens 1997: 25–6).

In recent years there has been much debate about other interventions that replicated the knowledge–power model initiated by the exploration of Egypt and how they jointly stimulated the formation of a unified notion of the Mediterranean in accordance with French strategic and economic ambitions (Ortega 1996; Schmitz 2002; Bourguet *et al.* 1998; 1999). The model set by the explorations in Egypt (1798–1801), the Morea, as the Peloponnese was called in those days (1829–31), and Algeria (1839–42) is defined as a systematic territorial exploration which aimed to cover everything and thus included all sciences and disciplines, and which accompanied military action and was officially supported by the state. These expeditions were not a specifically Mediterranean phenomenon, as comparable missions were undertaken in Mexico (1864–7) during the French-supported empire of Maximilian I and in Senegal (1857–61) as an extension of the earlier exploration of Algeria. It is also important to note that official support of scientific research was not limited to these missions and that the Service des Missions also awarded funding to individual projects that met strategic government criteria (Heffernan 1994). As a result, the differences between the various expeditions were substantial, albeit within the limits of the shared model.

Such differences are also evident in aspects like the institutional support of the explorations, as each was commissioned by a different ministry. The circumstances that surrounded them varied no less: in the Morea, the expedition took place after hostilities had ended, while in both other cases the conflict was still ongoing. In Algeria in particular, the so-called 'nomad section' – the scientific team sent to the interior of the country – followed the military columns at a short distance.

The relationship between scientific practice and military or political intentions was no less variable: even if all three expeditions were government sponsored, there were various other agents involved in their organisation and realisation as well. Several academies, for instance, played a significant role in raising interest in the Algerian expedition at a time when most politicians remained indifferent (Dondin-Payre 1991). There are also strong indications that military–scientific connections were frequently undermined, as military control over publication was, for example, met by sustained academic opposition (Lepetit 1998; Nordman 1998). While it is clear that the military influenced a range of aspects of scientific production through, for instance, restrictions on study areas or the application of new techniques to topographic survey and excavation, the connections between official interests and academic production of knowledge may also be considered in a broader sense. The results produced by the expeditions may be related in particular to the epistemic changes behind the general introduction of statistical and territorial parameters in the administration of both France and the overseas territories, as the military and academics were in agreement about this.

It follows from this that other academic activities in the Mediterranean, which were not organised as scientific missions but still contributed to the systematic 'ordering' of materiality, could and should be considered alongside the three formal French expeditions. In Spain, for instance, no comprehensive exploration was carried out, but during the Napoleonic military occupation of the country (1808–14) the Dépôt de la Guerre (the military cartographic service) nevertheless promoted a systematic geographical study of the Iberian Peninsula. It is surely not without significance that this project was directed by Jean-Baptiste Bory de Saint-Vincent, who was to head the expeditions in the Morea and Algeria (Castañon and Quirós 2004). Both the Iberian survey and the Egyptian expedition, moreover, were motivated by the notion of restoring a lost civilisation (Bonaparte 1821: 332–3). The overall picture is therefore one of widespread interventionist mobility in the Mediterranean with the aim of imposing systematically a 'material order', one which was based on the modernist notion of civilisation and resulted in a hierarchical configuration of regional identities.

Maps

From the first intervention in Egypt, geography was defined as one of the principal axes for systematic investigation, as new means of transport transformed eighteenth-century exploratory practices from cursory maritime investigation to extensive land-based investigation and conquest. Linear marches in the tracks of military movements were abstracted and redrafted as maps and plans. Geographical information became a fundamental tool not only for military intervention but also for the entire civilising mission. The standards of the civilising principles are well illustrated by the claim that full cartographic documentation of the Peloponnese, as detailed as any in France, represented a major step towards civilisation (*Bulletin de la Société de Géographie* 1829: 146; Peytier *et al.* 1833).

The increasing importance of geographical representation as the vehicle of a wide range of knowledge reached its zenith during the Algerian expedition, when geography was to provide the parameters for all types of information collected by other disciplines (Bory de Saint-Vincent: 1823: 2). Even if this pre-eminent position was not fully realised in practice, it seems clear that geography was seen as an overarching, higher-level undertaking. This had an impact on how the environment of the Morea and Algeria was seen, as the geographic principles applied meant that a systematic and generalising view prevailed over detailed study (Broc 1981: 353). Geographical representations were also consistently related to history, as ancient geography offered a key source for cultural definitions.

This geographical gaze, however, did not result in an integrated vision of the Mediterranean as a whole but rather led more often to an emphasis on the specific characteristics of the particular territory under scrutiny. This was, for instance, the case in Spain, where the term 'Iberian Peninsula' was coined and adopted; this both emphasised the unity of the region and set it apart from the rest of Europe (Figure 2.1). This separation was based on the view that Spanish culture was peripheral to modernity and thus by extension backward if not barbaric. A similar development has been noted in the Maghreb (Thomson 1987), which may explain why, after the failed French military intervention in Spain (1808–14), geographical and historical representations were combined to emphasise the ties between the Iberian Peninsula and North Africa and to separate them from European geography and history in the process (Bory de Saint-Vincent 1823: 226–33).

The expeditions not only had an impact on spatial and geomorphological knowledge but also delimited and fragmented Mediterranean identities. The introduction of modern boundaries in particular helped to shape new countries and regions by

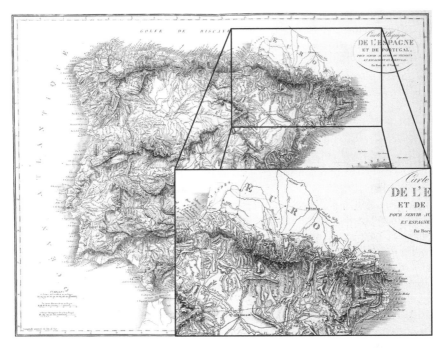

Figure 2.1   Topographical map of Spain and Portugal drawn by Bory de Saint-Vincent for his study of the Iberian Peninsula, in which he situates Europe beyond the Pyrenees (from Bory de Saint-Vincent 1823).

differentiating space. Algeria, for instance, was delimited as a country by separating it from hostile neighbours, like the Moroccan kingdom, and unproductive desert lands, while internal boundaries were drawn to administer the tribal communities (Nordman 1996: 25–39). Another example is the boundary that was drawn between, on the one hand, the new Greek state and its European sponsors, and, on the other hand, the Ottoman Orient, even if the latter was largely Mediterranean in geographical terms. These divisions were clearly crucial for the construction of identities in the eastern Mediterranean.

Just as the physical representation of these territories was not separate from the perception of nature, the regime of observations was also rather variable. The work of the exploratory commissions in particular marks a shift away from the earlier fragmented representation of nature. For example, during the eighteenth century the term 'Mediterranean' referred just as much, if not more, to any other internal sea elsewhere in the world and references like the 'Mediterranean of Colombia' and the 'Mediterranean of China' were commonplace. There is simply no trace of a naturalist definition of the Mediterranean as a unified entity in this period or in the first publications of the exploratory missions. When someone like Desmarest argued for the significance of the Mediterranean as a whole in the early nineteenth century, he did so in relation to the liminal nature of the region between Europe and Africa (Sinarellis 1998). An even more evident example is the work of René Desfontaines (1800), who was sent in 1783 by the Académie des Sciences to study the natural history of Algeria and Tunis and who gave the resulting book the striking title *Flora Atlantica*. This view owed much to the catastrophist perspective of that time, which postulated that the Mediterranean itself was the result of a dramatic irruption of the Atlantic Ocean that had imposed a boundary between Europe and Africa. Systematic botanical studies by the exploratory missions, however, gradually revealed the regularities of the Mediterranean, as descriptions of both Greece and the east coast of Spain suggest (Sinarellis 1998: 307–8; Bory de Saint-Vincent 1823: 207).

The Algerian experiences played a crucial role in this shift in perception. The preliminary work to set up the mission already pointed to the need to revaluate the notion of a natural divide between North Africa and Europe as held by Desfontaines, and it was proposed to carry out a comparative botanical study between North Africa, southern France, Spain, mainland Italy and Sicily. In addition to the scientific interest, it was also argued that such a comparison could contribute to the intensification of agricultural exploitation (Brongniart 1838: 5–6). This utilitarian vision also existed in zoology, which was limited to the study of marine species and their productivity (Duméril 1838: 3–4). Geologists noted parallel formations in Europe and the Maghreb and proposed to explore the possibilities of coal mining, while it was also suggested that fossils from the Morea, Sicily and Algeria should be carefully compared to each other (Élie de Beaumont 1838: 9–48). The results published by the mission were clear and removed any doubt about the biological continuity between the shores of the Mediterranean (Sinarellis 1998).

Bones

The impact of the Enlightenment went well beyond the promotion of scientific and utilitarian studies of the environment and included a critical revision of traditional explanations of human origins largely based on religious and narrow biblical arguments. From considering human beings as part of nature it was a small and logical step to apply the new naturalist approaches to humanity itself as well. Classification became the logic that lay behind the historical articulation of nature, including humans, and, because culture was not ignored, the classificatory practices were extended to other cultural subjects, such as languages. But physiology – the materiality of humans – increasingly became the key framework for systematically ordering societies, as racist attitudes gradually became more prominent in the social imagination. That does not mean, however, that these human classifications were taken for granted by everyone, and scholars like Buffon, for example, questioned the artificial discontinuity that classification imposed on a continuous and dynamic scenario of human development (Blanckaert 1998: 113).

By the end of eighteenth century, classification had widely been adopted as a common methodology, first and foremost by the so-called polygenists, who favoured a separate origin for each human group or community. Even the so-called monogenists, however, who insisted on a single shared origin for all humankind, could not resist classifying the world, albeit for a different reason. For them, differences developed between societies under the 'degenerative' influence of geography, climatic conditions and even social customs and as societies diverged from the original and ideal European model, a hierarchical order was created (Blanckaert 1998: 121–2). Despite the fundamentally different theoretical positions of the two approaches, their scientific methods in practice were rather similar, and classification would indeed remain a key feature of nineteenth-century European science even after the collapse of polygenism (Barnard 2004: 15–26).

Most of these ingredients were present when William Frédéric Edwards published his *Des caractères physiologiques des races humaines considérés dans leurs rapports avec l'histoire* in 1829. It was intended to offer a programmatic and state-of-the-art overview of scientific research across the board, from natural history to the history of humankind. It led eventually to the creation in 1839 of the Société Ethnologique with Edwards himself as president, and in 1859 of the Société d'Anthropologie de Paris. In this book, Edwards (1841: 101) complained that there was not sufficient evidence to provide an overview of social change through time, including of European society, but he suggested that the expeditions in Egypt and the Morea, which took place as he was writing, might substantially boost classificatory studies; he speculated in particular that the old distinction between Pelasgians and Hellenes might be confirmed and that it could contribute to finding ways for restoring classical civilisation.

The Morea expedition did not disappoint those expectations. Although its director, Bory de Saint-Vincent, initially favoured an explanation of racial mixture between contemporary Greek populations, he was eventually persuaded by what he interpreted as the expedition's evidence that at least certain 'ancient traits' had persisted in the long term. The recognition of Pelasgian physical continuity in turn paved the way for the restoration of ancient Greek glory and the installation of a democratic regime (Thomson 1998: 278–81). The Greek integration into the European self-image did not signal in and of itself, however, the demise of the anthropological Mediterranean divide. Several years earlier, Bory de Saint-Vincent (1825), as a leading polygenist, had still defended the view that no fewer than 15 different human species could be distinguished, which was by no means an uncommon position to hold at that time. Among these species, the European one was not surprisingly seen as *la plus belle*. More significant was his classification of about half the Iberian population as belonging to the 'Arabic' species, within which most people were identified as of the 'Atlantic' and 'Adamic' races, whose distribution also comprised North Africa (Bory de Saint-Vincent 1825: 288–94; Figure 2.2). In his view, the Atlantic race had migrated to the Iberian Peninsula from North Africa through an ancient connection at a time he associated with Atlantis – hence the label. By effectively classifying the Iberian Peninsula as non-European, science thus served not only to relegate most of the Spanish population to the anthropological periphery but also to justify European political and military intervention in both Spain and the Maghreb.

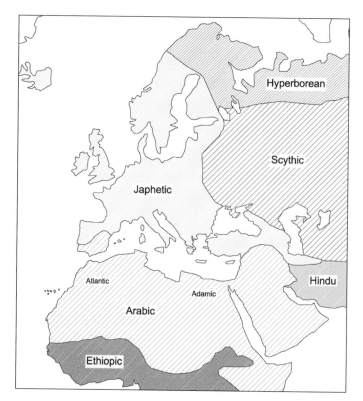

Figure 2.2   Schematic representation of the distribution map of the various human species distinguished in Europe, the Middle East and North Africa (after Bory de Saint-Vincent 1827).

It was against this background that the scientific exploration of Algeria was set up. Its aim, however, was to study Roman colonisation, which reflected the government's intention to promote archaeology and history as a means for optimising control and legitimising military intervention (Bory de Saint-Vincent 1838). The results dramatically changed the prevailing negative view of the indigenous populations of North Africa, as the linguistic variability and social differentiation documented in the Maghreb drew attention to the Berber communities, who were often confusingly referred to as 'Moors' (Pouillon 1993; Thomson 1993). As a new category of Berber was defined in opposition to Arab, it came to be seen as an adequate anthropological basis on which to build a French bridgehead across the Mediterranean (Duprat 1845: i–v).

On the basis of physical analogies, Berbers were subsequently grouped together with Iberians and Celts in an overarching class that was entirely separate from the Arab communities in the Maghreb. The anthropological results of the Algerian expedition thus transformed the Mediterranean divide and indeed bridged it by offering the justification for French intervention that the political and military authorities had been looking for. Underlying these views was the so-called assimilation model, which included the notion of 'potential civilisation' that just needed the right external conditions to be triggered (Bory de Saint-Vincent 1845). This model was propagated by many members of the Algerian expedition, many of whom also subscribed to Saint-Simonianism, a utopian political movement that defended the liberating effect of free trade and industrialisation in a united Mediterranean (Lorcin 1995: 99–106; Temime 2002; Cañete 2006).

The distinction between Arab and Berber elements and the analogy of the latter with European communities is mostly seen as a conscious endeavour to impose colonial domination. It has been suggested alternatively that these categories are not the result of conscious manipulation but that they instead extend a classification system based on the degree of (European) civilisation (Boëtsch and Ferrié 1996). As such, they can be traced back to modernity, which may thus be argued to have encouraged political and military interventions in both Europe and Africa and to have engendered anthropological notions reliant on diffusionist and migration explanations (Blaut 1993).

Stones

Material culture represented another dimension of the scientific and classificatory turn in the eighteenth century, as its study became a consistent and ever more prominent feature of the exploratory missions from the French expedition to Egypt onwards. Architectural remains in particular were widely and systematically documented and analysed as evidence of the past glory of Egypt and Greece. New methods and techniques to do so were borrowed from engineering and topography, as is for instance evident from the systematic integration of ruins in the cartographic description of the Peloponnese (Puillon-Boblaye 1835). Presumably because of their alignment with other disciplines, the material culture studies of the earlier missions initially tended to support the divided representation of the Mediterranean.

This is particularly evident during the early years of the Algerian expedition when, despite the broad objective to document the material features of Roman colonisation, only military Roman structures were recorded. As shown by the plan drawn up for the expedition, the reason for this was the prevailing view of Algeria as a region dominated by the barbaric resistance of its indigenous inhabitants, as well as being remote and far removed from the architectural splendour of Rome (Bory de Saint-Vincent 1838). It was only later that civilian architecture began to be taken into consideration, and when it was eventually related to Roman civilisation it could also contribute to a united view of the Mediterranean (Dondin-Payre 1998; Oulebsir 1998).

There existed, however, a marked contrast between the limited attention given by the expedition plan to the indigenous inhabitants of Algeria and the numerous and long-standing reports about substantial funerary monuments. These megalithic tombs included small dolmens (3–4 m in diameter), most of which were surrounded by a circle of standing stones. They were recorded mainly in the regions of Guelma and Constantine in northeast Algeria (Figure 2.3). Today the North African funerary world offers a much more complex image, extending to Tunisian examples and including rock-cut hypogaea commonly known as *haouanet*. They are now also seen as a late prehistoric phenomenon that continues well into the historic period (Ben Younes 2007; Camps 1961: 146–8; 1974: 343–45). In the nineteenth century, however, these dolmens immediately raised doubts about the limited attention given to the pre-Roman period in preliminary explorations, and in fact encouraged the study of those material elements.

In France, megalithic monuments had by then been ascribed to Celtic populations within the new discipline of prehistoric archaeology, and the morphological analogy between the Algerian and French monuments resonated strongly with existing views of invasions and migrations as the main causes of cultural change (Guyon 1846). In combination with the anthropological classification that connected European and African populations, before long it was assumed that the Celts had also migrated to North Africa, a conclusion that was used to turn the military intervention into a national issue (Féraud 1863: 215, 232–3). An alternative interpretation, however, which was supported by scholars like the Danish archaeologist Worsaae, saw migration moving from south to north, because the issue was examined in the context of the wider debate over European origins in either Africa or the Indo-European world

Figure 2.3   A dolmen in the Roknia district (Constantine, northeast Algeria) (from Reygasse 1950: 23).

(Ferrié and Boëtsch 1990). As a result of these wide-ranging discussions, the colonial experience in Algeria also impacted on the French self-image, and it is surely no coincidence that the Celtic paradigm was abandoned in the later 1860s and the more neutral label of Megalithic Culture was adopted to describe the perceived material connections between France and the Maghreb (Camps 1961: 14–20; Coye 1993). The change, however, did not entail rejection of the ethnocentric view that the North African megaliths represented the outcome of a cultural intervention by superior Europeans, even if the monuments were recognised as indigenous constructions (Bourguignat 1868 – see Figure 2.4).

The association between megalithic monuments and European communities was lent additional support by a further archaeological survey in the western Maghreb (Morocco), where numerous megalithic monuments were recorded and classified in relation to their European counterparts (Tissot 1876). In combination with the previously discussed evidence from physical anthropology and geography the net result was that Berber and European origins were increasingly conflated (Broca 1876: 393). At a political level, meanwhile, the French defeat by Prussia (1870) encouraged not only Germanic and English perceptions of the Latin race as decadent but also led France to ally itself more closely with Italy and Spain, which in turn increased the interest in Roman remains in North Africa (Litvak 1980; Lorcin 2002). As the

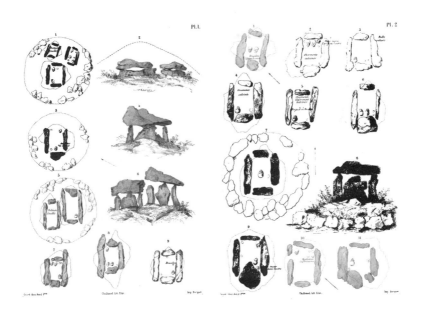

Figure 2.4   Drawings of the megalithic tombs in the Roknia district (Constantine, northeast Algeria) that were recorded by J.B. Bourguignat (1868: figures 1 and 2).

Mediterranean increasingly came to be viewed as a backward periphery, it was also more and more regarded as a single unity, which in turn may have owed much to a progressively divided understanding of Europe.

Conclusions

The material connections forged by the French exploratory missions in the Mediterranean thus raise a number of fundamental issues. The notion of the Mediterranean as a unified scientific category was (and is) first of all in no way automatic or self-evident but represented the outcome of a lengthy and complex development. The same process paradoxically also kept intact or even resurrected competing fragmented identities that were far from eliminated by the united image, as the practicalities of classification brought out its particular and contingent character.

Overall, the unified image of the Mediterranean as a scientific category is the result of a contingent order of things subjected to particular relations and representations. As Latour (1997: 173–7) argued, however, the contingent activities through which this was achieved show the inescapably particularist nature of our universals. The illusion of a clear distinction between the universal and the particular can thus be seen to lie in a permanent denial of the hybrid nature of the relational networks of humans and non-humans in which knowledge is created, as they are simultaneously universal and particular as well as natural and cultural.

In this view, the Mediterranean represents the outcome of these situations and should therefore be considered to be hybrid as well, as encompassing both natural and cultural aspects. It exists out there and it is universal; but at the same time our knowledge of it is mediated by the particularities of the relations and networks of humans and non-humans in which that knowledge is generated. This, I suggest, may provide a relatively simple explanation for the Mediterranean paradox in scholarly debates: sometimes it constitutes a clear and united entity – the black box is closed – and at other times it is more evidently a discursive construction – when the black box is open.

Integration of these hybrid notions, which have so long been relegated from our purified scientific texts, could offer a first but decisive step in resolving the current controversy and in beginning to construct a more realistic and nuanced representation of the Mediterranean region. This may already have been considered by Braudel (1972), when he systematically used paradoxes and oxymorons as a textual strategy to disarticulate a fixed and essentialist representation of the Mediterranean (Ankersmit 2003: 436).

This volume offers several examples of comparable situations, where material connections across the Mediterranean have resulted in complex, relational and hybrid manifestations of identity (see also van Dommelen 2006). In this sense, the scientific representation of the Mediterranean is just another one of those historical processes of mobility which, since prehistoric times, have connected materialities to create identities that were surely historically situated and particular but certainly not fictitious.

References

Anderson, B. 1991 *Imagined Communities*. London: Verso.

Ankersmit, F.R. 2003 *Historia y tropología: ascenso y caída de la metáfora*. Mexico City: Fondo de Cultura Económica.

Amstrong, C.D. 2005 Travel and experience in the Mediterranean of Louis XV. In W.V. Harris (ed.), *Rethinking the Mediterranean*, 236–67. Oxford: Oxford University Press.

Barnard, A. 2004 *History and Theory in Anthropology*. Cambridge: Cambridge University Press.

Ben Younes, H. 2007 Interculturality and the Punic funerary world. In D.L. Stone and L.M. Stirling (eds), *Mortuary Landscapes of North Africa*, 32–42. Toronto: Toronto University Press.

Bhabha, H.K. 1994 *The Location of Culture*. London: Routledge.

Blake, E., and A.B. Knapp (eds) 2005 *The Archaeology of Mediterranean Prehistory*. Oxford: Blackwell.

Blanckaert, C. 1998 Contre la méthode: unité de l'homme et classification dans l'anthropologie des Lumières. *Études de Lettres* 3–4: 111–26.

Blaut, J.M. 1993 *The Colonizer's Model of the World. Geographical Diffusionism and Eurocentric History*. New York: Guilford Press.

Boëtsch, G., and J.-N. Ferrié 1989 Le paradigme berbère: approche de la logique classificatoire des anthropologies français du XIXe siècle. *Bulletins et Mémoires de la Société d'Anthropologie de Paris* 3–4: 257–76.

—— 1996 Classification et pratique classificatoire dans l'anthropologie physique du nord de l'afrique. *Préhistoire Anthropologie Méditerranéennes* 5: 17–33.

Bonaparte, N. 1821 *Oeuvres de Napoléon Bonaparte*. Paris: Panckoucke.

Bory de Saint-Vincent, J.B. 1823 *Guide du voyageur en Espagne*. Paris: L. Janet.

—— 1825 Homme. In J.B. Bory de Saint-Vincent (ed.), *Dictionnaire classique d'histoire naturelle* 8 (H–Inv), 269–346. Paris: Rey et Gravier.

—— 1827 *L'homme. Essai zoologique sur le genre humain*. Paris: Le Normand Fils.

—— 1838 *Note sur la commission exploratrice et scientifique d'Algérie*. Paris: Cosson.

—— 1845 Sur l'anthropologie de l'Afrique française. *Comptes rendus hebdomadaires des séances de l'Academie des Sciences* 20: 1812–25.

Bourdieu, P. 1991 *Language and Symbolic Power*. Cambridge: Polity Press.

Bourguet, M.-N., B. Lepetit, D. Nordman and M. Sinarellis (eds) 1998 *L'invention scientifique de la Méditerranée. Egypte, Morée, Algérie*. Paris: Éditions de l'École des Hautes Études en Sciences Sociales.

Bourguet, M.-N., D. Nordman, V. Panayatopoulos and M. Sinarellis (eds) 1999 *Enquêtes en Méditerranée. Les expéditions françaises d'Egypte, de Morée et d'Algérie*. Paris: Éditions de l'École des Hautes Études en Sciences Sociales.

Bourguignat, J.-R. 1868 *Souvenirs d'une exploration scientifique dans le Nord de l'Afrique* IV. *Histoire des monuments mégalithiques de Roknia*. Paris: Challamel Ainé.

Braudel, F. 1972 *The Mediterranean and the Mediterranean World in the Age of Philip II*. New York: Harper and Row.

Broc, N. 1981 Les grandes missions scientifiques françaises au XIXe siècle (Morée, Algérie, Mexique) et leurs travaux géografiques. *Revue d'Histoire des Sciences* 34: 319–58.

Broca, P. 1876 Les peuples blonds et les monuments mégalithiques dans l'Afrique septentrionale. Les vandales en Afrique. *Revue d'Anthropologie* 5: 393–404.

Brongniart, A. 1838 Rapport concernant la botanique. *Rapports de la commission chargée de rédiger les instructions pour l'exploration scientifique de l'Algérie*, 5–6. (s.l.): (s.n).

Bulletin de la Société de Géographie 1829 Carte de Morée. *Bulletin de la Société de Géographie* 78: 145–8.

Camps, G. 1961 *Aux origines de la Berbérie. Monuments et rites funéraires protohistoriques*. Paris: Arts et métiers graphiques.

—— 1974 *Les civilisations préhistoriques de l'Afrique du Nord et du Sahara*. Paris: Doin.

Cañete, C. 2006 La antigüedad en la comisión de exploración científica de Argelia (s. XIX): variabilidad para un fin común. *alAndalus-Magreb* 13: 43–68.

Castañon, J.C., and F. Quirós 2004 La contribución de Bory de Saint-Vincent (1778–1846) al conocimiento geográfico de la Península Ibérica. Redescubrimiento de una obra cartográfica y orográfica olvidada. *Ería* 64–5: 177–205.

Coye, N. 1993 Préhistoire et protohistoire en Algérie au XIXe siècle. Les significations du document archéologique. *Cahiers d'Études Africaines* 129: 99–137.

de Pina-Cabral, J. 1989 The Mediterranean as a category of regional comparison: a critical view. *Current Anthropology* 30: 399–406.

—— 1992 The primary social unit in the Mediterranean and Atlantic Europe. *Journal of Mediterranean Studies* 2: 25–41.

Derrida, J. 1978 Structure, sign and play in the discourse of the Human Sciences. In J. Derrida, *Writing and Difference*, 278–94. London: Routledge.

Desfontaines, R.L. 1800 *Flora atlantica, sive historia plantarum, quae in atlante, agro tunetano et algeriensi crescunt*. Paris: Blanchon.

Dondin-Payre, M. 1991 Une institution méconnue: la commission d'exploration scientifique de l'Algérie. In A. Mastino (ed.), *L'Africa Romana. Atti dell'VIII convegno di studio, Cagliari, 14–16 dicembre 1990*, 239–52. Sassari: Gallizi.

—— 1998 La production d'images sur l'espace méditerranéen dans la commission d'exploration scientifique d'Algerie. Les dessins du Capitaine Delamare. In M.-N. Bourguet, B. Lepetit, D. Nordman and M. Sinarellis (eds), *L'invention scientifique de la Méditerranée: Egypte, Morée, Algérie*, 223–38. Paris: Éditions de l'École des Hautes Études en Sciences Sociales.

Duchet, M. 1995 *Anthropologie et historie au siècle des Lumières*. Paris: Albin Michel.

Duméril, A.M.C. 1838 Rapport concernant la zoologie. *Rapports de la commission chargée de rédiger les instructions pour l'exploration scientifique de l'Algérie*, 3–4. (s.l.): (s.n).

Duprat, P. 1845 *Essai historique sur les races anciennes et modernes de l'Afrique septentrionale, leurs origines, leurs mouvements et leurs transformations, depuis l'antiquité la plus reculée jusqu'à nos jours*. Paris: J. Labitte.

Edwards, W.F. 1841 *Des caractères physiologiques des races humaines considérés dans leurs rapports avec l'histoire.* Paris: Dondey-Dupré.

Elias, N. 1993 *El proceso de la civilización. Investigaciones sociogenéticas y psicogenéticas.* Mexico City: Fondo de Cultura Económica.

Élie de Deaumont, L. 1838 Rapport concernant la géologie. *Rapports de la commission chargée de rédiger les instructions pour l'exploration scientifique de l'Algérie*, 9–48. (s.l.): (s.n).

Féraud, L. 1863 Monuments dits celtiques dans la Province de Constantine. *Recueil des notices mémoires de la Société Archéologique de la Province de Constantine* 7: 214–34.

Ferrié, J.N. 1993 La naissance de l'aire culturelle méditerranéenne dans l'anthropologie physique de l'Afrique du Nord. *Cahiers d'Études Africaines* 129: 139–51.

Ferrié, J.N., and G. Boëtsch 1990 Du berbère aux yeux clairs à la race eurafricaine: la Méditerranée des anthropologues physiques. *Annuaire de l'Afrique du Nord* 28: 191–208.

Foucault, M. 2004 *Las palabras y las cosas.* Mexico City: Siglo veintiuno.

Guyon, J.-L.-G. 1846 Note sur des tombeaux d'origine inconnue situés au Ras Aconater entre Alger et Sidi Ferruch. *Comptes rendus hebdomadaires des séances de l'Académie des Sciences* 23: 816–18.

Harris, W.V. (ed.) 2005 *Rethinking the Mediterranean.* Oxford: Oxford University Press.

Heffernan, M. 1994 A state scholarship: the political geography of French international science during the nineteenth century. *Transactions of the Institute of British Geographers* 19: 21–45.

Herzfeld, M. 1984 The horns of the Mediterranean dilemma. *American Ethnologist* 11: 439–54.

—— 1987 *Anthropology through the Looking-Glass. Critical Ethnography in the Margins of Europe.* Cambridge: Cambridge University Press.

Hobsbawm, E.J. 1971 *Las revoluciones burguesas.* Madrid: Guadarrama.

Horden, P., and N. Purcell 2000 *The Corrupting Sea: A Study of Mediterranean History.* Oxford: Blackwell.

Jirat-Wasiutynsky, V. (ed.) 2007 *Modern Art and the Idea of the Mediterranean.* Toronto: University of Toronto Press.

Knapp, A.B., and E. Blake 2005 Prehistory in the Mediterranean: the connecting and corrupting sea. In E. Blake and A.B. Knapp (eds), *The Archaeology of Mediterranean Prehistory*, 1–23. Oxford: Blackwell.

Latour, B. 1997 *Nous n'avons jamais été modernes. Essai d'anthropologie symétrique.* Paris: La Découverte.

—— 2005 *La science en action. Introduction à la sociologie des sciences.* Paris: La Découverte.

Laurens, H. 1997 *L'expédition d'Egypte, 1798–1801.* Paris: Éditions du Seuil.

Lepetit, B. 1998 Missions scientifiques et expéditions militaires: remarques sur leurs modalités d'articulation. In M.-N. Bourguet, B. Lepetit, D. Nordman and M. Sinarellis (eds), *L'invention scientifique de la méditerranée: Egypte, Morée, Algérie*, 97–116. Paris: Éditions de l'École des Hautes Études en Sciences Sociales.

Lévi-Strauss, C. 1969 *The Elementary Structures of Kinship*. London: Taylor and Francis.

Litvak, L. 1980 *Latinos y anglosajones. Orígenes de una polémica*. Barcelona: Puvill.

Lorcin, P. 1995 *Imperial Identities: Stereotyping, Prejudice and Race in Colonial Algeria*. New York: I.B. Tauris.

—— 2002 Rome and France in Africa: recovering colonial Algeria's Latin past. *French Historical Studies* 25: 295–329.

Nordman, D. 1996 Problématique historique des frontières d'Europe aux frontières du Maghreb (XIXe siècle). In D. Nordman, *Profils du Maghreb. Frontières, figures et territoires (XVIIIe–XXe siècle)*, 25–39. Rabat: Publications de la Faculté des Lettres et des Sciences Humaines.

—— 1998 L'exploration scientifique de l'Algerie: le terrain et le texte. In M.-N. Bourguet, B. Lepetit, D. Nordman and M. Sinarellis (eds), *L'invention scientifique de la méditerranée: Egypte, Morée, Algérie*, 71–95. Paris: Éditions de l'École des Hautes Études en Sciences Sociales.

Olsen, B. 2006 Scenes from a troubled engagement. Post-structuralism and material culture studies. In C. Tilley, W. Keane, S. Küchler, M. Rowlands and P. Spyer (eds), *Handbook of Material Culture*, 85–103. London: Sage.

Ortega, M.L. 1996 La construcción científica del Mediterráneo: las expediciones francesas a Egipto, Morea y Argelia. *Hispania* 192: 77–92.

Oulebsir, N. 1998 Rome ou la Méditerranée? Les relevés d'architecture d'Amable Ravoisié en Algérie, 1840–1842. In M.-N. Bourguet, B. Lepetit, D. Nordman and M. Sinarellis (eds), *L'invention scientifique de la méditerranée: Egypte, Morée, Algérie*, 239–71. Paris: Éditions de l'École des Hautes Études en Sciences Sociales.

Peytier, P., E. Puillon-Boblaye and M. Servier 1833 Notice sur les opérations géodésiques exécutes en Morée, en 1829 et 1830. *Bulletin de la Société de Géographie* 118: 89–104.

Pouillon, F. 1993 Simplification ethnique en Afrique du Nord: Maures, Arabes, Berbères (XVIIIe–XXe siècles). *Cahiers d'Études Africaines* 129: 37–49.

Puillon-Boblaye, E. 1835 Extrait des recherches géographiques sur les ruines de la Morée. *Bulletin de la Société de Géographie*: 5–21.

Reygasse, M. 1950 *Monuments funéraires préislamiques de l'Afrique du Nord*. Paris: Arts et métiers graphiques.

Ruel, A. 1991 L'invention de la Méditerranée. *Vingtième siècle. Revue d'Histoire* 32(1): 7–14.

Said, E. 1978 *Orientalism*. New York: Vintage.

Schmitz, J. 2002 Territorialisation du savoir et invention de la Méditerranée. *Cahiers d'Études Africaines* 165: 143–59.

Silvera, A. 1975 Bonaparte and Talleyrand. The origins of the French expedition to Egypt in 1798. *American Journal of Arabic Studies* 3: 1–14.

Sinarellis, M. 1998 Bory de Saint-Vincent et la géographie méditerranéenne. In M.-N. Bourguet, B. Lepetit, D. Nordman and M. Sinarellis (eds), *L'invention scientifique de la méditerranée: Egypte, Morée, Algérie*, 299–310. Paris: Éditions de l'École des Hautes Études en Sciences Sociales.

Smith, A. 1998 Landscapes of power in nineteenth century Ireland. *Archaeological Dialogues* 5: 69–84

Temime, E. 2002 *Un rêve méditerranéen. Des saint-simoniens aux intellectuels des années trente*. Arles: Actes du Sud.

Thomson, A. 1987 *Barbary and Enlightenment. European Attitudes towards the Maghreb in the 18th Century*. Leiden: Brill.

———— 1993 La classification raciale de l'Afrique du Nord au début du XIXe siècle. *Cahiers d'Études Africaines* 129: 19–36.

———— 1998 Bory de Saint-Vincent et l'anthropologie de la Méditerranée. In M.-N. Bourguet, B. Lepetit, D. Nordman and M. Sinarellis (eds), *L'invention scientifique de la Méditerranée: Egypte, Morée, Algérie*, 273–87. Paris: Éditions de l'École des Hautes Études en Sciences Sociales.

Tilley, C. 2006 Objectification. In C. Tilley, W. Keane, S. Küchler, M. Rowlands and P. Spyer (eds), *Handbook of Material Culture*, 60–73. London: Sage.

Tissot, C.J. 1876 Sur les monuments mégalithiques et les populations blondes du Maroc. *Revue d'Anthropologie* 5: 385–92.

van Dommelen, P. 2006 Colonial matters. Material culture and postcolonial theory in colonial situations. In C. Tilley, W. Keane, S. Küchler, M. Rowlands and P. Spyer (eds), *Handbook of Material Culture*, 104–24. London: Sage.

3

REPRODUCING DIFFERENCE
Mimesis and colonialism in Roman *Hispania*

Alicia Jiménez[*]

Introduction

Mimesis forms a central idea in archaeological studies of cultural transformation in the Mediterranean. Explanations for resemblances in material culture from different regions have always been closely tied to the idea of copying and emulation. This concept is often implicitly associated with changes we are able to track in the material record, whether to explain the spread of techniques and ideas, to analyse processes such as 'Orientalisation', 'Hellenisation', 'Punicisation' and 'Romanisation', to theorise about the relationship between centre and periphery or to describe the path from barbarism to civilisation. Scholars studying the classical period in particular have traditionally perceived the Mediterranean as the 'natural' geographical framework within which to trace the spreading of an 'original' model to a wide network of regional replicas. It is not by chance that such histories revolve, usually quite literally, around cities situated in the middle of this sea, namely Athens and Rome. It is indeed likely that the allegedly Graeco-Roman roots of Western civilisation are at least in part to blame for the construction of a 'Mediterraneanism' in classical studies quite similar to Said's 'Orientalism' (Herzfeld 1987; de Pina-Cabral 1989; 1992, quoted in Blake and Knapp, 2005: 2; Harris 2005: 2). It is important, however, to point out that the concept of 'the Mediterranean' is just as slippery as others usually taken for granted, such as 'Europe', whose margins seem to be no easier to define in geographical or ecological terms than those of the Mediterranean. The very fact that the notion of the Mediterranean as a cultural construct makes sense both in Greek and Roman times (when the region was called the *oikoumene* or *mare nostrum*) and

---

[*] I am grateful to Peter van Dommelen for greatly improving the English and the content of this chapter with his suggestions, to Michael Rowlands, Bernard Knapp, Corinna Riva and Ana Rodríguez Mayorgas for their comments on an earlier draft of this paper and also to all the participants in the *Material Connections* seminar held at Glasgow University (March 2009) for their feedback on my presentation. I would also like to thank Juan Pimentel and Jesús Bermejo for their help during the writing of this paper. This chapter draws on research funded by the European Social Fund (*Contrato Postdoctoral* I3P; project HUM2007-64045/HIST).

in the present (Horden and Purcell 2000: 27–8) turns it into an interesting object of study within a critical and postcolonial analysis that looks beyond currently perceived frontiers between Europe and Africa, Orient and Occident or Islam and Christianity (van Dommelen 1998; 2006; Morris 2005; Vives-Ferrándiz 2006; Jiménez 2008a; see also Blake and Knapp 2005: 3). Comparing ancient and contemporary discourses on the Mediterranean is, moreover, of interest in its own right, because the notion of modern Europe as the principal heir of classical culture sits uneasily in the vast regions of North Africa that were once part of the Roman world.

The model of Rome: interpretations of mimesis

The period spanning the final centuries of the Roman Republic and the beginning of the Roman Empire (late third century BC to first century AD) is especially suited to a study of mobility, connectivity, conflict, co-presence and the role of material culture in the construction of identities during times of transition. Roman military expansion in the Mediterranean during these centuries resulted in a new model of resource exploitation largely based on intensified interactions among the provinces of the empire and supported by the establishment of Roman colonies around the sea's basin. The question of Mediterranean homogeneity or unity versus heterogeneity (Harris 2005: 20–9) is particularly critical to understanding the so-called 'Romanisation' process, as it is traditionally seen in terms of the spread of Roman material culture around the Mediterranean in the wake of the conquests. Studies of the desire to 'become Roman' or to 'stay native' in the newly created provinces by mimicking or rejecting Roman material culture have been central in the archaeological debate in the last decade or so (Woolf 1997; 1998; van Dommelen 2007; Jiménez 2008b). This may partially explain the increasing number of reviews and critiques of the centre–periphery model of transformations in material culture spreading from a metropolis or central place (Rowlands 1987; Woolf 1990). It may also account for recent debates on the utility of the term 'globalisation' for understanding the expansion of Roman material culture across the Mediterranean (Witcher 2000; Malitz 2000; Hingley 2003: 118–19; 2005; 2009; Hitchner 2008; Sweetman 2007).

The idea of mimicry as a pathway from barbarism to civilisation is not entirely original, since Plato (386a–398b) and Aristotle (3.4) had already surmised that imitation produces learning. The concept of mimesis has implicitly resurfaced in modern academic writing, in particular in evolutionist theories that regard the imitation of superior cultures – in particular Greek and Roman – as a key route for native populations to become civilised. The process of becoming Roman in *Hispania* has similarly been described as coming down to a progressively increasing number of cities with Roman legal status and the consequent gradual development of literacy and monumental display in these towns. Writing in the late second century AD, Aulus Gellius (16.13.8–9) already asserted that Roman colonies 'seem to be, in a manner of speaking, small representations [of Rome] and images of a sort'.[1] When looked at in detail, the colonies may not have had the appearance of *exact* copies of Rome, but it is true that most of them look quite similar to each other (Bispham 2006:

75). This Roman 'urban kit' – a regular grid of streets surrounded by a city wall and equipped with a *forum* or central square, temples, a *curia* or senate house and a theatre – is present even in cities that never obtained the status of colonies. Such cases have simply been explained as instances of less privileged cities that emulated the material culture of Roman colonies like *Tarraco*, *Emerita* and *Corduba*, which thus in turn became important sources of 'Romanisation' in territories far from Rome.

The notion of Roman cities abroad as *simulacra Romae* ('images', 'likeness' or 'representations' of Rome) has been carefully examined for the province of *Hispania* by Trillmich (1996; 1997; 1998). He focused on the three exceptional sites of *Corduba*, *Tarraco* and *Emerita*, the cities that had been designated as provincial capitals of *Baetica*, *Tarraconensis* and *Lusitania* under Augustus, the first emperor. He also considered the imitation of the special urban space of the Augustan *forum* in Rome (Figure 3.1). The large-scale colonisation programme implemented under Caesar and Augustus is precisely contemporary to an increasingly 'Roman appearance' of the material culture of *Hispania*. The newly constructed public squares (*fora*) of *Corduba*, *Tarraco* and *Emerita* that Trillmich analysed were unusually symbolic, because they were probably set up personally by the emperor or provincial governors and because they were the scene of a wide range of political, ritual and commercial activities.

Figure 3.1 Map of *Hispania* in Augustan times (base map courtesy of *Trabajos de Prehistoria*, http://tp.revistas.csic.es).

It is difficult to understand the meaning of the new 'piazzas' that mimicked Augustus' *forum* in provincial cities such as *Corduba*, *Tarraco*, *Emerita* or other towns outside *Hispania*, such as Arles, *Pompeii*, Vienne and Nyon without taking into consideration the special circumstances that surrounded the construction of the 'model' in the *urbs* itself. In the transitional years between the republic and the first years of the empire, Augustus built his new *forum* in Rome as part of his plan to transform a town of brick into a capital of marble that could replicate the most monumental of Hellenistic cities. It is important to note that he did not remodel the traditional old republican *forum* that was intimately associated with the tomb of the founder (Romulus) and the mythical origins of Rome; rather he decided to create a duplicate of this sacred space to promote his own ideological and iconographic programme. Much as Virgil had written around the same time a 'new Iliad' (the *Aeneid*), the new *forum* sought to connect Troy and Aeneas to the new imperial family of the *Iulii* and the new Golden Age (*aurea aetas*) of Augustus (Zanker 1987: 249–53). Augustus himself became an

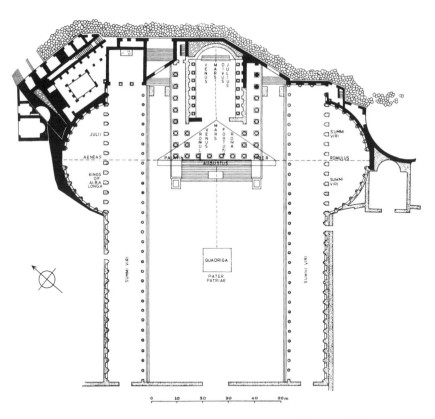

Figure 3.2 Plan of the *forum* of Augustus in Rome showing the location of the statues in the iconographic program (from Zanker 1987: figure 149, with permission).

ancestor for the Roman people when, in 2 BC, to mark the consecration of the new *forum*, he was granted by the Senate and the people of Rome the title of *pater patriae* (literally 'father of the fatherland': *Res Gestae* 35).

A fragmentary description by Ovid (5.551–70) and decades of archaeological excavations have documented the highly symbolic arrangements of this urban area (Figure 3.2). Ironically, some elements are only known to us thanks to provincial copies of this space. A temple devoted to *Mars Ultor*, the father of Romulus, the first king of Rome, overlooked the *forum*. The entrance displayed representations of the arms and armours of all the peoples defeated by Augustus. In a large apse on the left-hand (west) side of the square (Figures 3.2 and 3.3) stood a sculpture of Aeneas carrying his father Anchises and holding the hand of his son Ascanius as they fled from Troy and embarked on the journey that would eventually take them to *Latium*. Anchises holds a statuette that he has presumably saved from the destruction of the city. It represents the *di Penates*, the sacred spirits of the ancestors worshipped in domestic shrines with the *pater familias* directing the rituals. This image of Aeneas as the founding hero saving the *sacra* and transferring them to Rome after the fall of Troy constitutes a linear representation of time, origins and mythic ancestors of the Roman people. It starts with Anchises in the upper right corner of the image and follows with Aeneas and Ascanius in the bottom left, resembling family trees (*stemmata*) displayed by aristocrats in their houses, where sometimes mythical characters such as Numa (king after Romulus) held the honoured place reserved for the first ancestor (Zanker 1987: 230–55; Bettini 1988: 167–83; Rose 2008; Rodríguez Mayorgas 2010). It is worth noting that the statue displays the Trojan hero Aeneas in Roman dress: he wears Roman armour (*thoracata*) and patrician shoes that signal his role as the forefather of the *Iulii*, the imperial family. On the opposite side of the *forum*, in the east apse (Figure 3.2), there was an image of Romulus, the founder of Rome, carrying a trophy made up of the arms and armour of the enemies he had defeated. Here, ancestors played a decisive role as models to be imitated. Augustus followed the examples of virtue and piety set by Romulus and Aeneas by honouring his adoptive father Caesar after his assassination and by restoring the ancestral laws (*mores maiorum*) of ancient Rome.

The sculpture of Romulus was surrounded by a gallery of illustrious men (*summi viri*) who established a line between mythical kings of the history of Rome and forebears of the imperial family, echoing contemporary portrait galleries of famous ancestors set up by aristocrats in their houses. This parade of ancestral images probably also included some of the heroes described by Virgil in a famous passage of the *Aeneid* (6.752–859), when Aeneas descended into the underworld where his by then dead father Anchises introduced him to a series of famous Roman heroes culminating with Caesar and Augustus. In addition to all these veiled references, a colossal statue of Augustus' 'guardian spirit' (*genius*) – in fact an idealised statue of the emperor with divine attributes – was worshipped in a small chamber.

Imitations of Augustus' *forum* in the provinces included not only the main statuary programme, but also other parts of the complex discourse on Roman origins represented by that place, such as the shields or *clipei* with the images of *Jupiter Ammon*

Figure 3.3 Aeneas leaving Troy with Anchises and Ascanius. The statues of Aeneas and Romulus from the *forum* of Augustus have been lost. The best surviving reproduction of these figures are these paintings of Aeneas and Romulus that decorated the façade of the fullery of *Ulutremulus* in Pompeii (*Regio* IX 13.5). They represented the statues that stood on the façade of the building of *Eumachia* in the *forum* of the town and which imitated, in turn, the group of statues of the Augustan *forum* (from Zanker 1987: figure 156a, with permission).

on the upper floor of the porticoes. Even copies of copies present in the new *forum* were conveyed to other regions of the empire. The replicas of the Erechtheion cary-atids from the Athenian acropolis (*c.* 415 BC), which marked the grave of a hero and founder of Athens and which may be interpreted as another 'quotation' of the glorious past that linked Rome with Greece, have also been found in provincial repre-sentations of the *forum* of Augustus (Zanker 1968; 1987: 299–307; Spannagel 1999; La Rocca 2001: 184–95, Ungaro 1997; 2008; Haselberger 2007: 156–60). In fact elements of this architectonic scenario were present not only in urban spaces, but also in partial images depicted on small objects. Portrayals of the Aeneas group were particularly popular and have been found represented in wall paintings, mosaics, sculpture or on smaller artefacts like coins, medallions, gems and reliefs in stone, bronze and lead (Spannagel 1999: 90).

The town of *Emerita Augusta*, founded under the first emperor to serve as the capital of the newly created western province of *Lusitania*, offers an excellent example of the re-creation of the *forum* of Augustus outside the Italian peninsula. A group of colossal statues identified for the first time by Trillmich (1992: 28–35) as representa-tions of Aeneas with Ascanius and Anchises was located in one of the town's porticoed squares (Figure 3.4). They were found in connection with an inscription that repeats the text of a famous epigraph found in Pompeii.[2] According to common opinion, this is itself a reproduction with some variants of the honorific inscription recording his main achievements (*elogium*) that was located in the pedestal supporting the image of Aeneas in the *forum* of Augustus in Rome (de la Barrera and Trillmich 1996: 128–36). Nogales (2008) has further suggested that another fragmented sculpture found in the same area may be a representation of Romulus. The apses of the porticoes were also decorated with statues that recall the ancestral portrait galleries of Augustus' *forum*. The *clipei*, caryatids and capitals found in this space also show to what extent the *forum* of *Emerita* was not meant to be an exact copy of the Roman *forum* but a local re-creation of it, meaningful in local terms. In *Emerita* the shields with the images of *Jupiter Ammon*, placed again in the attic of the porticoes, were combined with *clipei* showing representations of Medusa. The architect of *Emerita* produced his own varia-tion of the metropolitan model of the caryatids, as we have seen, a reproduction itself of the caryatids of the Erechtheion in Athens. The capitals, inspired by those of the temple of *Mars Ultor* of Augustus' *forum*, became in turn a model in *Emerita*, acting as the source of inspiration for local artisans employing traditional techniques that produced similar pieces with a distinct style.

Comparable replicas have been found in the other provincial capitals of Hispania. The 'Romulus' statue of *Emerita* has been compared specifically to what remains of an enormous statue of a man wearing Roman armour, found in the northern *forum* of *Corduba*, the capital of the southern province of *Baetica*. Again Cordoba has yielded examples of Corinthian capitals located in the *forum* similar to those of the temple of *Mars Ultor* in Rome. The *clipei*, which combine images of *Jupiter Ammon* and Medusa, recall those of *Emerita*, but were part of the theatre of the town, not the portico of the *forum*. The same kind of *clipei* has also been recovered in a public square of *Tarraco*, the capital of *Hispania Tarraconensis* (Dupré 2004a: 55–60, 121–2,

Figure 3.4   Reconstruction of the sculpture group representing Aeneas, Anchises and Ascanius found in *Emerita Augusta* (Mérida, Spain) (from Nogales 2008: figure 3, with permission).

126–7; 2004b: 44–5, 118–22; 2004c: 49–51, 115, with previous bibliography; see also Nogales and Álvarez 2006 and Ayerbe *et al.* 2009).

Images of the ancestral myth that connected Aeneas, Augustus and the origins of the Roman people were not only displayed in Rome and abroad in public spaces connected with the cult of the emperor, such as theatres or the *forum*, but were also

45

found in the private sphere. In this realm, mimesis of official symbols was closely connected with a transformation of meaning stemming from the new context. The Aeneas group was for instance often reproduced on rings and lamps, possibly as a token of loyalty to the emperor but it could also have been read in some cases as a symbol of the sense of 'filial piety' (*pietas*). In Liguria, a freedwoman called Petronia Grata used this image on the tombstone she set up for herself and her mother, showing devotion to her similar to that of Aeneas saving his father, the household gods and his son from Troy. Petronia, however, takes over from Ascanius and appears represented as the little girl that follows Aeneas (Figure 3.5).

Figure 3.5
Funerary stone of *Petronia Grata* from *Aquae Statiellae* (Liguria), probably datable to the first half of the first century AD (from Zanker 1987: figure 163, with permission).

Meanwhile, in *Hispania*, an inhabitant of *Corduba* thought that a ceramic statu-ette of Aeneas, the hero guided by his father in his descent to the underworld, was appropriate to be included as a funerary gift in the tomb of someone who was about to begin a journey to meet his or her ancestors (Figure 3.6). In a painting from *Pompeii* or perhaps from *Stabiae*, Aeneas and Ascanius are depicted as ithyphallic apes; Anchises carries a dice box instead of the household gods; and all of them have canine features (Figure 3.7). For a Latin speaker, the image was, among other things, a visual pun on *canis* (both 'dog' and 'you sing') that would have easily brought the first line of the *Aeneid* to mind: 'I sing of arms and of the man' ('*arma virumque cano*') (Zanker 1987: 248; Kellum 1997: 174–6).

Figure 3.6 Ceramic figurine showing Aeneas and Ascanius found in Cerro Muriano (Córdoba, Spain) (from Vaquerizo 2001:165, with permission).

Figure 3.7 Caricature of Aeneas, Anchises and Ascanius. Wall painting from *Stabiae* (from Zanker 1987: figure 162, with permission).

This example is an important reminder of the subversive and satirical aspects of mimesis and the necessity of approaching carefully the meaning of imitations where less contextual information is available. 'Imperfect' copies or deviance from the model, often interpreted as lack of ability on the part of the performer, might have more to do, in some cases, with an only too well informed 'mime'. No matter how detached a copy might seem to be from the original, parody is only possible when the model is widespread enough to allow variations and still be recognisable as the main reference. It was, therefore, the constant repetition of a small group of conventional representations related to Augustus in public and everyday contexts that resulted in the possibility of superimposing new meanings on the images.

Theorising mimesis

The Romans imitated Greek culture in various ways to reassert their Romanness (Wallace-Hadrill 1998). These borrowings included the concept of mimesis that is usually translated into Latin as *imitatio*. Although it is recorded from at least the fifth century BC, it rarely appears in ancient texts before Plato (fourth century BC). It has been suggested that the word stems from the root *mimos*, which referred to both a person who imitates (a 'double') and a specific genre of performance based on stereotypical characters (Gebauer and Wulf 1992: 27–30; see Jiménez 2010 for a fuller discussion).

Mimesis in Plato and Aristotle

Mimesis is an essential feature of Plato's philosophy, and his analysis remains the obligatory point of departure of any research on the subject. Mimesis is discussed most explicitly in the famous allegory of the cave and other passages of the *Republic* (books 7 and 2, 3 and 10 respectively). According to Plato, physical objects and events are just a copy or 'shadow' of their ideal and perfect forms. He offers a negative vision of mimesis because it prevents people from searching for truth through reason and philosophy, inducing people to believe in an illusion. Plato rejects for this reason artistic representations of nature such as painting, sculpture and poetry, because they are mere copies of something that is already itself a copy of the ideal world (Plato 596d–e). He therefore already makes a crucial distinction between copy and a model that is 'original', 'ideal' and most of all 'true'.

The notion of mimesis that underlies much modern discourse of colonial contexts is also influenced by the Platonic view of the concept, which suggests that mimesis is an unconscious practice and that people have the capacity of learning through mimesis or automatic and unthinking imitation, without exercising their ethical reason. Mimesis, moreover, influences not only the observer and the audience but also the imitator, who effectively becomes a double. This is the case of narrators of epic stories, considered as liars by Plato, because they sometimes use their own voice but also imitate other characters' voices and gestures: in his view, they hide their personality behind a character (Plato 393a–b). Plato also points out, however, that these narrators cannot avoid being 'polluted' by the model they are imitating. The belief that imitating other people's behaviour in the end influences the imitator's own identity is another assumption that is frequently made in colonial studies (see below).

Slightly later, Aristotle reviewed the Platonic theory of mimesis and emphasised by contrast the positive aspects of imitation considered to be a natural characteristic of men, who are the most imitative of animals and learn their first lessons by representing things (Aristotle 3.4). He effectively laid the foundations for modern readings of mimicry by contending that mimesis always involves interpretation or translation, because the mimetic act cannot produce an exact copy of the original object/subject. Artistic representations are therefore able to portray things as more or less beautiful than they are in reality (Aristotle 2.1–3). Artists may represent things as they could or should be, but mimesis must remain limited to a selection of general, typical and essential aspects that render the imitation realistic. The perfect copy would not be the most detailed, but the one that reveals a general truth and that gives more pleasure to the audience, because it allows understanding of the universal causes of things (Golden 1992: 63). Mimesis, therefore, cannot faithfully represent reality but only offer a stylised portrait, in which certain features may be highlighted by means of exaggeration. According to Davis (1999), the relationship between mimesis and reality in Aristotle may be compared to that between dancing and walking, as imitation always implies a selection of features from the experience's continuum. Mimesis thus frames reality, signalling at the same time that the things framed are simply unreal. The more real imitation may seem to be, therefore, the more illusory it has become (Davis 1999: 3). The selection of traces to be imitated by the performer, however, transforms the mime into an active agent. To some extent the poet could be considered the creator of an 'original' copy based on what we know to be probable or feasible from experience and in a creative use of tradition (Aristotle 9.6–7, 14.11).

Roman ideas about mimesis

The transformative character of imitation makes it possible to think of mimesis as more than a mere copy. Roman authors effectively recommended practising imitation as emulation, an idea clearly expressed by Seneca in his *Epistles*: 'we should follow, men say, the example of the bees, which flit about and cull the flowers that are suitable for producing honey, and then arrange and assort in their cells all that they have brought in' (Seneca 84.3).[3] A good literary imitation, according to Seneca, is meant to resemble and to differ from its model at one and the same time, in the same way a child looks like his/her parents. Gathering ideas has transformative power, which may be compared to the way in which digestion extracts nourishment from food and absorbs it for the benefit of the body, or how numerous individual voices in a choir are combined to produce a new unity. In this kind of mimesis 'it is impossible for it to be seen who is being imitated, if the copy is a true one; for a true copy stamps its own form upon all the features which it has drawn from what we may call the original' (Seneca 84.9; Potolsky 2006: 54–7).[4]

The same kind of reasoning underlies Horace's recommendation to study Greek models day and night as a means of artistic innovation (Horace 268–9). These views are thus emblematic of the importance in Graeco-Roman culture of rooting all forms of status and identity in a prestigious past repeatedly imitated, and of the encounter of Rome and Hellenism that culminated in the appropriation *and* emancipation of Greek models (Woolf 2001: 176; Whitmarsh 2001: 6; Wallace-Hadrill 2008: 213–58).

Mimesis and postcolonial theory

Imitation and identity came to the fore in modern thinking during the course of the nineteenth century. Freud (1962: 29), in his theories about the ego, claimed that selfhood and identity are not given at birth but develop from an unconscious identification with or imitation of others taken as role models. While identity was based on imitating ideal models, he also claimed that conflicting identifications could be maintained at the same time, a suggestion that is particularly relevant for studying interaction between different groups in colonial situations.

The French psychologist Lacan (2001), by contrast, insisted that children have to identify reflectively with themselves before they can imitate their parents or other role models. But even in the earliest act of constructing the ego, when a child recognises him- or herself in a mirror for the first time (the so-called 'mirror stage'), we turn to an *imago*, a 'double'. Only through this figure or character (*Gestalt*), a copy or reflection that establishes a relation between the inner world (*Innenwelt*) and the environment (*Umwelt*), do we learn who we are (Lacan 2001: 1–8). Butler (1991: 24) has more recently argued that also after the early stages of identification – self-identification and mimesis of our parents – there is no volitional subject behind the mime, as we imitate behaviour from anonymous cultural repertoires. In colonial contexts, enforced imitation of such features (a supposedly 'Roman' or 'Occidental' way of doing and consuming things, for example), will eventually produce a 'reality effect', which in turn forms the basis of the 'natural' appearance or 'truth' of repeated conventions.

It is in this sense that frequently repeated mimesis takes on a normative and disciplinary dimension that tends to reinforce dominant discourses about what is acceptable (Butler 1991: 28). In *Black Skin, White Masks*, Fanon (1952) argues how inclusion in this new reality affects the identity of the mime. He discusses instances of the gap created for the educated colonial subject rejected by a civilisation that he has nevertheless assimilated with. In these cases the identification of the colonial subjects with the colonisers in a world where they are treated as 'others' leads to the conflicting identifications already pointed out by Freud (Fanon 1952: 93, 147).

The work of the cultural theorist Bhabha is also closely connected with the psychoanalytical view of mimicking. The starting point of his famous essay 'Of mimicry and man' is precisely a fragment of 'The line and light' by Lacan (1977: 99): 'Mimicry reveals something in so far as it is distinct from what might be called an itself that is behind. The effect of mimicry is camouflage … It is not a question of harmonizing with the background, but against a mottled background, of becoming mottled – exactly like the technique of camouflage practised in human warfare.' By using the word 'mimicry' instead of 'mimesis', Bhabha expands the meaning of imitation to include the strategic aspects of mimetism. The term 'mimicry' is used in the biological sciences to refer to the act, practice or art of imitation as possessed by some animals and plants. It is the capacity to resemble a different object or species in order to hide and pass unnoticed by predators. Thus mimicry is not repression of difference, but a form of resemblance that defends the individual by means of displaying only in part, metonymically, the menacing subject (Bhabha 1994: 90), and this double vision is the cause, in turn, of the menace of mimicry for the coloniser, according to Bhabha.

The civilising mission and the surveillance process are threatened, in the area between mimicry and mockery, by the displacing gaze of imitator, when 'the observer becomes the observed and "partial" representation rearticulates the whole notion of *identity* and alienates it from essence' (Bhabha 1994: 89, original emphasis). In his view, mimicry affects both the image of the coloniser and local populations, and it is through imitation that individuals or conquered groups may become almost like their conquerors, 'but not quite' (Bhabha 1994: 86). As Bhabha (1994: 86) emphasises, the discourse of imitation revolves around ambivalence, a desire to transform 'the Other' into a recognisable individual, who is almost the same but not quite, because 'in order to be effective mimicry must continually produce its slippage, its excess, its difference'. From a colonial perspective, he argues, colonised natives had to become similar enough to the colonisers to be permissible and to have the potential to be reformed and civilised but at the same time they had to remain sufficiently different in order to justify their subordinated and exploited position in colonial society (Bhabha 1994: 88).

Original truth, materiality, copying, belonging

The *fora* of the three provincial capitals of *Hispania* are an outstanding example of 'material presence' by the metropolis in a colonial context. They show a powerful means of dissemination abroad of discourses related to the emperor and Roman ancestry through a metonymic representation of Rome in the provincial capitals. Elements carefully selected to compose this *pars pro toto* (the *forum* for Rome) were set up by the emperor or provincial governors and convey very valuable information about images considered to be worth reproducing mimetically (Romulus, Aeneas, *summi viri*) in certain cities (colonies) of conquered regions. Mimicking the *forum* of Augustus in the provinces was meant to have didactic characteristics and to influence the audience in a similar way to a theatrical play or the *Aeneid*. In this recreated scenario people could walk through, it was possible to learn not only what it was to be Roman, but also to create in the provinces a Roman past completely oblivious of anything that was not Rome (see Woolf 1996 on forgetfulness of local pasts). Nevertheless, copies of Augustus' *forum* in the three capitals of *Hispania* can be considered a stylised portrait of the original based, as we have seen, on a selection of traits considered stereotypical but not completely accurate. *Clipei* of *Jupiter Ammon* were combined in *Hispania* with *clipei* decorated with the face of Medusa and were found, in the case of *Corduba*, not in the *forum* but in the theatre. The caryatids of *Emerita* were only freely adapted from the Roman model. The transformative character of mimesis is especially evident in the copies of the capitals and statues of men wearing a toga of *Emerita's forum* reproduced with a distinctively local flavour by local artisans.

Meaning transformation is, as expected, more intense in the echoes of the Augustan *forum* found in private settings, where the dynastic line linking Anchises, Aeneas and

Ascanius could be altered to portray the image of a little girl or a grotesque representation of son, father and grandfather (Figures 3.5 and 3.7). The conscious drive to imitate Rome outside Rome includes pious imitation of role models as well as mockery of Roman heroes.

The *forum* with its statues and public monuments was not, however, the only place where provincial towns presented their self-image. Coins are a good example, since they projected an official representation that diverts from the latter in integrating through imitation local iconographies and traditions absent in the imagery of the *forum*. Rome allowed the cities of *Hispania* to mint their own currency until the reign of Claudius (mid-first century AD). The provincial coinages show a wide range of symbols and sometimes languages other than Latin that underscore the importance of official representations of local pasts in *Hispania*, at least until the middle of the first century BC.

The coins of *Abdera* in southern Spain can be taken as an example of the polluting effects of mimesis in the identity of the imitator and how apparently conflicting identifications with Punic and Roman pasts were reworked in material culture. Images from the first issues are repeated again and again; every remake, however, included new ways of transforming the original. Initially, under the republic and perhaps under Augustus as well, the bronze coins of this originally Phoenician–Punic town show a temple on the obverse and two tunas with the town's name in neo-Punic characters on the reverse (Figure 3.8.1). Subsequently, from Tiberius onwards, the obverse is occupied by the image of the emperor and the temple is transferred to the reverse, where the town's name is retained in neo-Punic characters in the pediment,

Figure 3.8 Consecutive series of coins (*asses*) from *Abdera* (Adra, Almería, Spain) (from Trillmich 2003: figures 1–4, with permission).

while the tunas are incorporated in this image by transforming them into 'columns' (Figure 3.8.2.). Eventually, the town's name was spelled out in Latin letters between the columns of the temple and the Punic legend was replaced by a star (Figures 3.8.3 and 3.8.4). Trillmich discusses similar examples from the Ebro valley in northeastern Spain, such as *Bilbilis*, *Sebobriga*, *Osca* and *Turiaso*. In the last, the characteristic local horseman was transformed into an equestrian statue of perhaps Augustus himself, while in the town of *Iltirta* a local representation of a wolf was equated in later issues with the Roman she-wolf (Trillmich 1997; 1998; 2003).

These instances show that in studying Roman material culture in the provinces we should take into account an inventive use of Roman tradition *as well as* mimesis and artistic innovation based in various perceptions of local pasts (Bendala 2002; van Dommelen and Terrenato 2007: 10; Revell 2009: 40–79). This equally applies to private contexts, where individual and family identities are also frequently rooted in imitation as emulation. In *Corduba* the re-creation of Augustus' *forum* in the heart of the town was simultaneously on display with monumental burial mounds – also copied elsewhere – that imitated in the necropolis Augustus' tomb in Rome (Figure 3.9). Again, it has been suggested that the monumental tomb of Augustus was itself in all likelihood modelled after the tomb of Alexander, which the emperor had visited

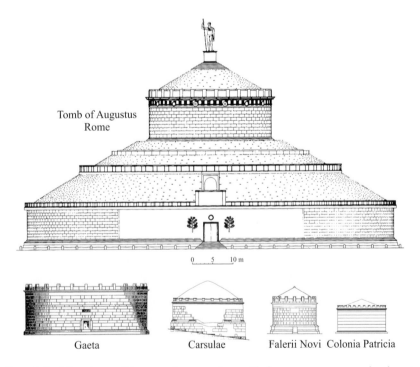

Tomb of Augustus
Rome

0   5   10 m

Gaeta   Carsulae   Falerii Novi   Colonia Patricia

Figure 3.9   Mausoleum of Augustus in comparison with funerary monuments elsewhere in Spain and Italy (after Murillo *et al.* 2002: figure 23).

after the conquest of Egypt (Arce 1988: 61). In *Corduba*, however, the cremation burials in the tomb were often deposited in urns that recalled much older Iron Age pottery (Figure 3.10). Rather than interpreting this practice as an instance of 'failed Romanisation', it may more usefully be understood as a case of mimesis of a local past 'translated' into the language of Augustan times.

If Roman colonies have been described as 'little Romes' abroad, the city of Rome itself was in turn said to be in Augustan times, not always in positive terms, a compendium of the empire. The city attracted people and products from the nearest and farthest provinces to the extent that Rome became the place where every city in the empire seemed to have established its own colony (Edwards and Woolf 2003: 4). The *Miliarium Aureum*, a reputedly golden milestone set up by Augustus in the *Forum Romanum* that marked the starting point of all roads in the Roman Empire, was a prominent physical reminder of the fact that all roads led to Rome (Plutarch 24). The Roman world was represented in Rome by a huge map in the *Porticus Vipsania* in Augustan times and a gallery of statues in the *Porticus ad Nationes* built by Augustus that personified all the conquered nations (Favro 2005: 244–5). Rome was thus a 'cosmopolis', because '[e]verywhere in the city elements of the conquered world had

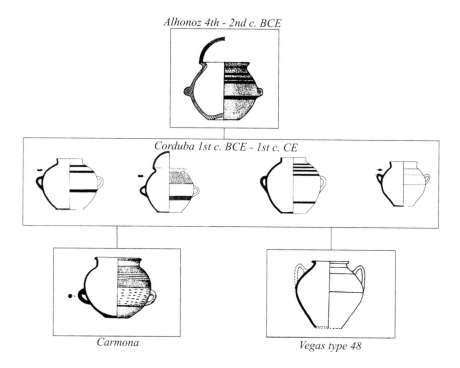

Figure 3.10 Development of one type of funerary urn from the pre-Roman into the Imperial period (after García Matamala, 2002: figure 8. No scale provided.).

been appropriated and recontextualised; the city had absorbed the world' (Edwards and Woolf 2003: 2; Moatti 1997: 444, 452). It represented a synthesis of the world and was – and is – accordingly presented by ancient and many modern authors alike as the source of everything valuable. Italy, wrote Pliny (37.201–5) is the 'second mother of the universe' (*parens mundi altera*), a myth of Roman ancestry, exemplified later by Symmachus's assertion in the fourth century AD that Rome was the mother of all peoples (Symmachus 3.11.3; Moatti 1997: 459).

Conclusion: mobility, materiality, Mediterranean identities

The creation of colonies abroad in the wake of the Roman expansion across the Mediterranean resulted in a substantial increase of movement and migration among the inhabitants of Mediterranean regions and the wider Roman Empire. Local and regional identities were no less implicated in these processes and as a result were expressed in novel ways through material culture. While several chapters in this book address the question of tracing connectivity within the diversity of Mediterranean peoples in a range of periods, the 'Romanisation' process poses the question of diversity within perceived homogeneity (Mattingly 2004: 8–9; van Dommelen and Terrenato 2007: 7). It is not only the case that connectivity might in some contexts add to differences among regions in contact, but also that apparent similarities in the material records of different regions may mask the subtleties of emulation practices and the strategic qualities of mimicry. This is perhaps particularly true for Roman colonial contexts, where discourses spread through written texts, material culture and social practices are mediated particularly in earlier times by the violence of conquest (Mattingly 2007: 91–4).

If we ignore preconceived ideas of the supremacy of a true original over the copy, it will be possible to get a better understanding of processes of mimicking during Roman times. Ancient material culture permits insight not only into commercial connections and people's mobility, but also into symbolic networks established by 'quoting' from past or distant material realities. Precisely because repeated imitation is what makes the 'original' an 'original' in the first place, transforming it into a model to be copied, it would seem beside the point to try and find out whether an imitation is accurate or not, or whether the 'real' and ultimate original source can be found. It is arguably far more relevant to understand why people looked to Rome, a provincial capital or a local town as a model at a given moment in time and how they tried to 'represent' what they saw in the *forum*, the house or the burial monument.

Repeated mimesis re-created both the image of the colonised and the coloniser. Roman identity in Imperial times was precisely constructed as a result of interaction between the metropolis and a series of subjugated provinces. When Roman writers claimed that the *urbs* had become an epitome of the empire, they were contending that the city had come to be the centre of the world or the point where the gaze of all its peripheries intersected. But in fact, by selecting and integrating foreign elements into the city, Rome was building a new identity that had no *real* correspondence with the world of the provinces. Rome became a partial copy of the empire through a selective synthesis of a series of provincial elements useful or tolerated in the metropolis.

If mimesis is unable to produce a copy of a true original, as Plato wrote, it can only create a world of shadows in a mirror, where pure ideas are always beyond reach. This world of simulacra falls apart, however, if we acknowledge the fuzzy distinction between original and copy and think of mimesis as an act of repetition and stop interpreting Roman provincial culture in relation to its success or failure in emulating Rome (Mattingly 1997: 11; van Dommelen 2001: 71). From this perspective, the Platonic opposition between a 'fake copy' and a 'true original' has lost its relevance, because any 'text' we 'read' or object we interpret as part of a discourse always implies a network of copies that do not lead back to a singular truth (Derrida 1970: 206–7; 1972; 1975; Melberg 1995: 152–3). The logical conclusion of this argument is that there is no such thing as a 'pure' Roman culture, because Rome and Italy were themselves trapped in a network of cultural references to the Hellenistic, Italic and Mediterranean worlds (Keay 2001b: 129; Wallace-Hadrill 2008: 73–143). The public spaces of late Republican and Augustan Rome offer a fine example, as they had been inspired by the public architecture of Hellenistic capitals like Pergamon and Alexandria in the eastern Mediterranean. They became archetypes themselves later on, as they were reproduced in both the western provinces and in the Greek east under Roman rule (Woolf 2001: 176).

On the one hand, there is no clearly defined set of 'truly Roman' artefacts or architecture that can be found in every Mediterranean region and province of the Roman Empire (Freeman 1993: 443–4; Terrenato 1998; Woolf 1998: 7; Keay 2001a: 113; Roth 2007: 7–8). On the other hand, imitation is always translation and interpretation, as stated by Aristotle, implying the existence of a necessary empty space between 'original' and 'copy', as between Fanon's black skin and white masks, and between the theatrical mask that 'reveals as much as it hides' (Derrida 1970: 206) and the actor behind it. Therefore, mimicking does not create an exact double, but reproduces a partial representation of a model that becomes different through repetition (Bhabha 1994: 90). The illusion, however, stems from the 'fictional pact' between the mime and the audience: mimesis is the reproduction of a difference that usually claims to be just the same as the original model.

Endnotes

1 '*quasi effigies parvae simulacraque*': translation Bispham 2006: 79. See Bispham 2006 for the legal and propagandistic implications of this paragraph in the second century AD and Bispham 2000 for a discussion of the relationships between Rome and her colonies in the republican period.

2 *CIL* X 808. 8348, *CIL* I² p. 189 n. I.

3 Translation R.M. Gummere. Loeb Classical Library. London and Cambridge, MA, 1970.

4 Translation R.M. Gummere. Loeb Classical Library. London and Cambridge, MA, 1970.

Classical authors and texts

Aristotle, *Poetics*.
Aulus Gellius, *Attic Nights*.
Horace, *The Art of Poetry*.
Ovid, *Fasti*.
Plato, *Republic*.
Pliny, *Natural History*.
Plutarch, *Lives. Galba*.
Res Gestae: *Res Gestae Divi Augusti*.
Seneca, *Epistles*.
Symmachus, *Epistles*.
Virgil, *Aeneid*.

References

Arce, J. 1988 *Funus Imperatorum. Los funerales de los emperadores romanos*. Madrid: Alianza.

Ayerbe, R., T. Barrientos and F. Palma (eds) 2009 *El foro de Augusta Emerita. Génesis y evolución de sus recintos monumentales*. Anejos del Archivo Español de Arqueología 53. Mérida: Consejo Superior de Investigaciones Científicas.

Bendala Galán, M. 2002 Perduraciones y romanización en Hispania a la luz de la arqueología funeraria: notas para una discusión. *Archivo Español de Arqueología* 75: 137–58.

Bettini, M. 1988 *Anthropology and Roman Culture: Kinship, Time, Images of the Soul*. Baltimore: Johns Hopkins University Press.

Bhabha, H.K. 1994 *The Location of Culture*. London: Routledge.

Bispham, E. 2000 Mimic? A case study in early Roman colonisation. In E. Herring and K. Lomas (eds), *The Emergence of State Identities in Italy in the First Millennium BC*, 157–86. London: Accordia Research Centre, University of London.

—— 2006 *Coloniam deducere*: how Roman was Roman colonization during the middle Republic? In G. Bradley and J.P. Wilson (eds), *Greek and Roman Colonization. Origins, Ideologies and Interactions*, 73–160. Swansea: Classical Press of Wales.

Blake, E., and A.B. Knapp 2005 *The Archaeology of Mediterranean Prehistory*. Oxford: Blackwell.

Butler, J. 1991 Imitation and gender insubordination. In D. Fuss (ed.), *Inside/Out: Lesbian Theories, Gay Theories*, 13–31. New York and London: Routledge.

Davis, M. 1999 *The Poetry of Philosophy: On Aristotle's Poetics*. South Bend, IN: St. Augustine's Press.

de la Barrera, J.L., and W. Trillmich 1996 Eine Wiederholung der Aeneas-Gruppe vom Forum Augustum samt ihrer Inschrift in Mérida (Spanien). *Mitteilungen des Deutschen Archäologischen Instituts. Römische Abteilung* 103: 119–38, plates 28–39.

de Pina-Cabral, J. 1989 The Mediterranean as a category of regional comparison: a critical view. *Current Anthropology* 30: 399–406.

—— 1992 The primary social unit in Mediterranean and Atlantic Europe. *Journal of Mediterranean Studies* 2: 25–41.

Derrida, J. 2004 The double session. In J. Derrida, *Dissemination*, 18–235. London: Continuum; Chicago: University of Chicago Press (2nd edition).

—— 1971 La mythologie blanche (la métaphore dans le texte philosophique), *Poétique* 5: 1–52.

—— 1975 Economimesis. In J. Derrida, *Mimesis – des articulations*. Paris: Aubier-Flammarion.

Dupré, X. (ed.) 2004a *Las capitales provinciales de Hispania. 1. Córdoba. Colonia Patricia Corduba.* Rome: L'Erma di Bretschneider.

—— 2004b *Las capitales provinciales de Hispania. 2. Mérida. Colonia Augusta Emerita.* Rome: L'Erma di Bretschneider.

—— 2004c *Las capitales provinciales de Hispania. 3. Tarragona. Colonia Iulia Urbs Triumphalis Tarraco.* Rome: L'Erma di Bretschneider.

Edwards, C., and G. Woolf (eds) 2003 *Rome the Cosmopolis.* Cambridge: Cambridge University Press.

Fanon, F. 1952 [1986] *Black Skin, White Masks.* London: Pluto Press.

Favro, D. 2005 Making Rome a world city. In K. Galinsky (ed.), *The Cambridge Companion to the Age of Augustus*, 234–63. Cambridge: Cambridge University Press.

Freeman, P. 1993 'Romanisation' and Roman material culture. *Journal of Roman Archaeology* 6: 438–45.

Freud, S. 1962 *The Ego and the Id.* Standard Edition of the Complete Psychological Works of Sigmund Freud 19. London: Hogarth Press and the Institute for Psycho-Analysis.

García Matamala, B. 2002 Enterramientos con urnas de tradición indígena en Corduba. In D. Vaquerizo (ed.), *Espacio y usos funerarios en el Occidente Romano*, 275–95. Córdoba: Seminario de Arqueología, Universidad de Córdoba.

Gebauer, G., and C. Wulf 1992 *Mimesis: Culture, Art, Society.* Berkeley: University of California Press.

Golden, L. 1992 *Aristotle on Tragic and Comic Mimesis*, Atlanta, GA: Scholars Press.

Harris, W.V. (ed.)

—— 2005 *Rethinking the Mediterranean.* Oxford: Oxford University Press.

Haselberger, L. 2007 *Urbem Adornare: die Stadt Rom und ihre Gestaltumwandlung unter Augustus.* Journal of Roman Archaeology Supplementary Series 64. Portsmouth, RI: Journal of Roman Archaeology.

Herzfeld, M. 1987 'As in your own house': hospitality, ethnography, and the stereotype of Mediterranean society. In D. Gilmore (ed.), *Honor and Shame and the Unity of the Mediterranean.* American Anthropological Association Special Publication 22: 75–89. Washington, DC: AAA.

Hingley, R. 2003 Recreating coherence without reinventing Romanization. In A. Merryweather and J. Prag (eds), *'Romanization'? Proceedings of a Post-graduate Colloquium (London, 15 November 2002).* Digressus Supplement 1: 111–19. Available at www.digressus.org. London: Institute of Classical Studies, University of London.

Hingley, R. 2005 *Globalizing Roman Culture*. London: Routledge.

—— 2009 Cultural diversity and unity: Empire and Rome. In S. Hales and T. Hodos (eds), *Material Culture and Social Identities in the Ancient World*, 54–75. Cambridge: Cambridge University Press.

Hitchner, R.B. 2008 Globalization avant la lettre: globalization and the history of the Roman empire. *New Global Studies* 2 (2): article 2. Available at http://www.bepress.com/ngs/vol2/iss2/art2.

Horden, P., and N. Purcell 2000 *The Corrupting Sea: A Study of Mediterranean History*. Oxford: Blackwell.

Jiménez, A. 2008a *Imagines hibridae. Una aproximación postcolonialista al estudio de las necrópolis de la Bética*. Anejos del Archivo Español de Arqueología 43. Madrid: Consejo Superior de Investigaciones Científicas.

—— 2008b A critical approach to the concept of resistance: new 'traditional' rituals and objects in funerary contexts of Roman Baetica. In C. Fenwick, M. Wiggins and D. Wythe (eds), *TRAC 2007: Proceedings of the Seventeenth Theoretical Roman Archaeology Conference (London 2007)*, 15–30. Oxford: Oxbow Books.

—— 2010 Mímēsis/mimicry: teoría arqueológica, colonialismo e imitación. In R. Graells, M. Krueger, S. Sardà, G. Sciortino (eds), *El problema de las 'imitaciones' durante la protohistoria en el Mediterráneo centro-occidental: entre el concepto y el ejemplo*. Iberia Archaeologica 14. Mainz am Rhein: von Zabern (in press).

Keay, S. 2001a Introduction. In S. Keay and N. Terrenato (eds), *Italy and the West. Comparative Issues in Romanization*, 113–16. Oxford: Oxbow Books.

—— 2001b Romanization and the Hispaniae. In S. Keay and N. Terrenato (eds), *Italy and the West. Comparative Issues in Romanization*, 117–44. Oxford: Oxbow Books.

Kellum, B. 1997 Concealing/revealing: gender and the play of meaning in the monuments of Augustan Rome. In T.N. Habinek and A. Schiesaro (eds), *The Roman Cultural Revolution*, 158–81 Cambridge: Cambridge University Press.

Lacan, J. 2001 *Écrits. A Selection*. London and New York: Routledge (2nd edition).

—— 1977 The line and the light. In J. Lacan, *The Four Fundamental Concepts of Psychoanalysis*, 91–104. London: Hogarth Press and the Institute of Psycho-Analysis.

La Rocca, E. 2001 La nuova immagine dei fori imperiali. Appunti in margine agli scavi. *Mitteilungen des Deutschen Archäologischen Instituts, Römische Abteilung* 108: 171–213.

Malitz, J. 2000 Globalisierung? Einheitlichkeit und Vielfalt des Imperium Romanum. In W. Schreiber (ed.), *Vom Imperium Romanum zum Global Village. 'Globalisierungen' im Spiegel der Geschichte*, 37–52. Neuried: Ars Una.

Mattingly, D.J. 1997 Introduction. Dialogues of power and experience in the Roman Empire. In D.J. Mattingly (ed.), *Dialogues in Roman Imperialism: Power, Discourse, and Discrepant Experience in the Roman Empire*. Journal of Roman Archaeology Supplementary Series 23: 7–24. Portsmouth, RI: Journal of Roman Archaeology.

—— 2004 Being Roman: expressing identity in a provincial setting, *Journal of Roman Archaeology* 17, 5–26.

—— 2007 *An Imperial Possession. Britain in the Roman Empire*. London: Penguin Books.

Melberg, A. 1995 *Theories of Mimesis*. Cambridge and New York: Cambridge University Press.

Moatti, C. 1997 *La razón de Roma: el nacimiento del espíritu crítico a fines de la República*. Madrid: A. Machado Libros.

Morris, I. 2005 Mediterraneanization. In I. Malkin (ed.), *Mediterranean Paradigms and Classical Antiquity*, 30–55. London: Routledge.

Murillo, J.F., J.R. Carrillo, M. Moreno, D. Ruiz and S. Vargas 2002 Los monumentos funerarios de Puerta de Gallegos. Colonia Patricia Corduba. In D. Vaquerizo (ed.), *Espacio y usos funerarios en el Occidente Romano*, 247–74. Córdoba: Seminario de Arqueología, Universidad de Córdoba.

Nogales, T. 2008 Rómulo en el Augusteum del foro colonial emeritense. In E. La Rocca, P. León and C. Parisi Presicce (eds), *Le due patrie acquisite: studi di archeologia dedicati a Walter Trillmich*, 301–12. Rome: L'Erma di Bretschneider.

Nogales, T., and J. M. Álvarez 2006 Fora Augustae Emeritae: la 'interpretatio' provincial de los patrones metropolitanos. In D. Vaquerizo and J.F. Murillo (eds), *El concepto de lo provincial en el mundo antiguo: homenaje a la profesora Pilar León Alonso*, vol. 1, 419–50. Córdoba: Servicio de Publicaciones, Universidad de Córdoba.

Potolsky, M. 2006 *Mimesis*. New York and London: Routledge.

Revell, L. 2009 *Roman Imperialism and Local Identities*. Cambridge: Cambridge University Press.

Rodríguez Mayorgas, A. 2010 Romulus, Aeneas and the cultural memory of the Roman Republic. *Athenaeum* 98: 89–109.

Rose, C.B. 2008 Forging identity in the Roman Republic: Trojan ancestry and veristic portraiture. In S. Bell and I. Lyse Hansen (eds), *Role Models in the Roman World. Identity and Assimilation*, 97–131. Ann Arbor: University of Michigan Press.

Roth, R. 2007 Roman culture between homogeneity and integration. In R. Roth and J. Keller (eds), *Roman by Integration: Dimensions of Group Identity in Material Culture and Text*. Journal of Roman Archaeology Supplementary Series 66: 7–10. Portsmouth, RI: Journal of Roman Archaeology.

Rowlands, M. 1987 Centre and periphery: a review of the concept. In M. Rowlands, M. Larsen and K. Kristiansen (eds), *Centre and Periphery in the Ancient World*, 1–11. Cambridge: Cambridge University Press.

Spannagel, M. 1999 *Exemplaria Principis: Untersuchungen zu Entstehung und Ausstattung des Augustusforums*. Heidelberg: Verlag Archäologie und Geschichte.

Sweetman, R. 2007 Roman Knossos: the nature of a globalized city. *American Journal of Archaeology* 111: 61–81.

Terrenato, N. 1998 The Romanization of Italy: global acculturation or cultural bricolage? In C. Fercey, J. Hawthorne and R. Whitcher (eds), *TRAC 1997: Proceedings of the Seventeenth Theoretical Roman Archaeology Conference (Oxford 1997)*, 20–7. Oxford: Oxbow Books.

Trillmich, W. 1992 El niño Ascanio ('Diana cazadora') de Mérida en el Museo Arqueológico Nacional. *Boletín del Museo Arqueológico Nacional* 10: 25–38.

Trillmich, W. 1996 Los tres foros de *Augusta Emerita* y el caso de *Corduba*. In P. León (ed.), *Colonia Patricia Corduba. Una reflexión arqueológica (Córdoba 1993)*, 175–95. Seville: Consejería de Cultura, Junta de Andalucía.

—— 1997 El modelo de la metrópoli. In J. Arce, S. Ensoli and E. La Rocca (eds), *Hispania romana. Desde tierra de conquista a provincia del Imperio*, 131–41. Madrid: Electa.

—— 1998 Las ciudades hispanorromanas: reflejos de la metrópoli. In M. Almagro-Gorbea and J.M. Álvarez (eds), *Hispania. El legado de Roma. En el año de Trajano*, 163–74. Zaragoza and Madrid: Ayuntamiento de Zaragoza and Dirección General de Bellas Artes y Bienes Culturales.

—— 2003 Überfremdung einheimischer Thematik durch römisch-imperiale Ikonographie in der Münzprägung hispanischer Städte. In P. Noelke (ed.), *Romanisation und Resistenz in Plastik, Architektur und Inschriften der Provinzen des Imperium Romanum. Neue Funde und Forschungen*, 619–33. Mainz am Rhein: von Zabern.

Ungaro, L. 1997 El modelo del foro de Augusto en Roma. In J. Arce, S. Ensoli and E. La Rocca (eds), *Hispania romana. Desde tierra de conquista a provincia del Imperio*, 170–5. Madrid: Electa.

—— 2008 Storia, mito, rappresentazione: il programma figurative del Foro di Augusto e l'Aula del Colosso. In E. La Rocca, P. León and C. Parisi Presicce (eds), *Le due patrie acquisite: studi di archeologia dedicati a Walter Trillmich*, 399–417. Rome: L'Erma di Bretschneider.

van Dommelen, P. 1998 *On Colonial Grounds. A Comparative Study of Colonialism and Rural Settlement in 1st Millennium B.C. West Central Sardinia*. Archaeological Studies Leiden University 2. Leiden: Faculty of Archaeology, Leiden University.

—— 2001 Cultural imaginings. Punic tradition and local identity in Roman Republican Sardinia. In S. Keay and N. Terrenato (eds), *Italy and the West. Comparative Issues in Romanization*, 68–84. Oxford: Oxbow Books.

—— 2006 Colonial matters. Material culture and postcolonial theory in colonial situations. In C. Tilley, W. Keane, S. Kuechler, M. Rowlands and P. Spyer (eds), *Handbook of Material Culture*, 104–24. London: Sage.

—— 2007 Beyond resistance: Roman power and local traditions in Punic Sardinia. In P. van Dommelen and N. Terrenato (eds), *Articulating Local Cultures. Power and Identity under the Expanding Roman Republic*. Journal of Roman Archaeology Supplementary Series 63: 55–70. Portsmouth, RI: Journal of Roman Archaeology.

van Dommelen, P., and N. Terrenato 2007 Introduction. Local cultures and the expanding Roman Republic. In P. van Dommelen and N. Terrenato (eds), *Articulating Local Cultures. Power and Identity under the Expanding Roman Republic*. Journal of Roman Archaeology Supplementary Series 63: 7–12. Portsmouth, RI: Journal of Roman Archaeology.

Vaquerizo, D. (ed.) 2001 *Funus cordubensium: costumbres funerarias en la Córdoba romana*. Córdoba: Universidad de Córdoba. Seminario de Arqueología.

Vives-Ferrándiz, J. 2006 *Negociando encuentros: situaciones coloniales e intercambios en la costa oriental de la Península Ibérica (ss. VIII–VI a. C.)*. Cuadernos de Arqueología Mediterránea 12. Barcelona: Bellaterra.

Wallace-Hadrill, A. 1998 To be Roman, go Greek: thoughts on Hellenization at Rome. In M. Austin, J. Harries and C. Smith (eds), *Modus Operandi: Essays in Honour of Geoffrey Rickman*, 69–82. London: Institute of Classical Studies, University of London.

—— 2008 *Rome's Cultural Revolution*. Cambridge: Cambridge University Press.

Whitmarsh, T. 2001 *Greek Literature and the Roman Empire. The Politics of Imitation*. Oxford: Oxford University Press.

Witcher, R. 2000 Globalisation and Roman imperialism. Perspectives on identities in Roman Italy. In E. Herring and K. Lomas (eds), *The Emergence of State Identities in Italy in the First Millennium BC*. Accordia Specialist Studies on Italy 8: 213–25. London: Accordia Research Institute.

Woolf, G. 1990 World systems analysis and the Roman Empire. *Journal of Roman Archaeology* 3: 44–58.

—— 1996 The uses of forgetfulness in Roman Gaul. In H.-J. Gehrke and A. Möller (eds), *Vergangenheit und Lebenswelt. Soziale Kommunikation, Traditionsbildung und Historisches Bewußtsein*. Scripta Oralia 90: 361–81. Tübingen: Narr.

—— 1997 Beyond Romans and natives. *World Archaeology* 28: 339–50.

—— 1998 *Becoming Roman: The Origins of Provincial Civilization in Gaul*. Cambridge: Cambridge University Press.

—— 2001 The Roman cultural revolution in Gaul. In S. Keay and N. Terrenato (eds), *Italy and the West. Comparative Issues in Romanization*, 173–86. Oxford: Oxbow Books.

Zanker, P. 1968 *Forum Augustum: das Bildprogramm*. Tübingen: Wasmuth.

—— 1987 *Augusto y el poder de las imágenes*. Madrid: Alianza.

4

FROM COLONISATION TO HABITATION

Early cultural adaptations in the Balearic Bronze Age

Damià Ramis[*]

Introduction

As research stands at present, the earliest human settlement of the Balearics forms a topic with many unresolved issues. Nonetheless, important contributions have been made in recent years, enabling us to focus more closely on the settlement process of the first prehistoric groups in a virgin archipelago, and to improve our under-standing of the cultural identity of these early colonisers. All the indicators suggest that Mallorca and Menorca were still unoccupied in the fourth millennium Cal BC, while the earliest clear evidence for human presence dates – somewhat imprecisely – to the second half of the third millennium Cal BC. Thus there is a period of uncer-tainty related to the earliest human arrival in the archipelago, which covers nearly all the third millennium Cal BC. Currently, the earliest reliable chronological and archae-ological evidence for human presence in Mallorca (and thus the Balearic archipelago) may be dated to approximately 2300–2000 Cal BC (Ramis *et al.* 2002).

The material culture of the late third/early second millennia Cal BC in the Balearics is considered the product of successive introductions during that time period. This study offers an alternative explanation, and suggests that most of the cultural elements of the Balearics' earliest prehistory were introduced roughly simultaneously in the first stage of human occupation of the archipelago. Later, the local evolution of these materials represents the development of an already indigenous culture. A very general view of the early prehistory of the Balearic Islands is provided through the analysis of the most significant elements of its materiality.

The Balearic Islands form a heterogeneous landscape composed of two clearly defined archipelagoes, the Gymnesian (Mallorca and Menorca) and Pityusan Islands (Ibiza and Formentera). This study mainly addresses Mallorcan and Menorcan

---

[*] The preliminary version of this paper was improved significantly by comments from members of the *Material Connections* project.

material evidence and, in particular, early architectonic manifestations. Cyclopean architecture (*sensu* Rosselló-Bordoy 1965) is a characteristic feature of late prehistory in the western Mediterranean islands. Different manifestations can be found in Corsica, Sardinia, Malta and the Balearics during the Bronze and Iron Ages, all with an apparently local origin. A trend among insular cultures towards a distinctive elaboration of certain traits – material and mental – has been suggested by several authors (e.g. Evans 1977; Coll 1997; Robb 2001; Knapp 2009), but the precise social and cultural developments that lay behind different cyclopean structures in the western Mediterranean remain unclear.

In the Balearics, the first manifestation of cyclopean architecture is the habitational structure known as the *naveta* (different from the burial *naveta*, which exists only in Menorca and is a later development). The *naveta* (Figure 4.1) consists of a naviform construction with a horseshoe-shaped plan (e.g. Rosselló-Bordoy 1964–5; Plantalamor 1991; Pons 1999; Salvà 2001). The walls, double-faced and constructed of large dry blocks and inner filling, are about 2 m wide. The complete length of the more monumental examples reaches about 20 m. The inner breadth of the chamber is typically about 3 m. Although the megalithic burial tradition in the archipelago dates back to the late third millennium Cal BC, the origin of cyclopean domestic architecture is currently placed around the mid-second millennium Cal BC (Lull *et al.* 1999; Calvo and Guerrero 2002; Waldren 2002; Micó 2005; 2006). Nevertheless, the recent excavation of one these structures – S'Arenalet de Son Colom – has produced

Figure 4.1 *Naveta* 3 at the Bronze Age village of S'Hospitalet Vell: excavated in 2008–9 by a team from the Museum of Manacor. This is the characteristic type of habitational structure in Mallorca and Menorca during the second half of the second millennium Cal BC.

a culturally homogenous assemblage of the late third millennium Cal BC (Ramis *et al.* 2007). Given the singularity of this site in the context of the Balearic record, a general description of the excavation is included below.

The process of colonisation

Current understanding of the mechanisms of colonisation in the Balearics is based widely on the Graves and Addison (1995) model developed for the Hawaiian Islands (e.g. Costa 2000; Guerrero 2001; Calvo *et al.* 2002; Guerrero and Calvo 2008). The process of colonisation has been divided into several phases (from discovery to definitive establishment) and, according to the time span of each, several models of colonisation have been defined. The theoretical value of this approach has been recognised but, simultaneously, it has been shown that its application to the archaeological and palaeoecological record of several case studies, beginning with the Hawaiian case itself (Tuggle and Spriggs 2000), is problematic. In the Balearic example, the scholars noted above have included the same types of archaeological evidence in different phases of the process described by Graves and Addison (1995), continuously modifying their chronology and evidence. All this demonstrates the impossibility of applying these models accurately to the present case, as Cherry (1990: 197–9) argued for similar earlier proposals related to other Mediterranean islands.

How we define the beginning of long-term settlement is the most important issue in studying an island's occupation (Anderson 1995). Generally speaking, the earliest visits to or brief occupations of an island are entirely different, unless they formed part of the settlement process. Their existence, however, has to be demonstrated rather than assumed. Of course, if an exploitation or utilisation phase (*sensu* Cherry 1990) can be defined previous to the occupation, as in Melos (Cherry and Torrence 1982) or on Cyprus (e.g. Ammerman *et al.* 2008), it would have to be taken into account. But there is no indicator for an exploitation phase in the Balearic case. The kind of archaeological evidence we have for the third millennium BC in the Balearics – e.g. settlements in different geographic areas (coast, central plains, mountains), existence of collective burials – fits well with the criteria expected of fully established communities (Cherry 1981; Vigne and Desse-Berset 1995).

In the Balearics, the third millennium BC archaeological materials show several close parallels with the mainland (e.g. Claustre *et al.* 2002; Martín *et al.* 2002), in contrast to later periods, when local evolution of different elements seems apparent. This suggests that the moment of divergence from the mainland matrix is not far from the chronologies that indicate an established human presence in the Balearics. In turn, this means that the human groups who settled in the islands were influenced by different factors from those who remained in the source region; contact between both groups diminishes and becomes reduced as a result of a more or less intense level of isolation. As a consequence, the insular groups took their own course as a characteristic local culture developed (Anderson 1995).

The relief of the Balearic archipelago is not severe; only the northern mountains of Mallorca, Serra de Tramuntana, show a steep landscape and some high altitude areas. In fact, some of the earliest archaeological deposits are at high points on these mountains, while other roughly synchronous sites are found along the coast and in the plain of Mallorca.

Other examples of a rapid human colonisation include, for example, the people of the pre-Clovis complex, who reached the southern extremes of America in about one millennium after crossing the Bering Strait (Fiedel 2000; Dixon 2001; Meltzer 2002), or the Neolithic communities who arrived from the Gulf of Genoa along the Iberian Atlantic coast within six generations (Zilhâo 2001). Another rapid process of colonisation and territorial occupation is also suggested for New Zealand, where the archaeological and paleoecological record is insufficient to establish chronological differences between the occupation of the north and south islands, or between the first coastal sites and those of the interior (e.g. McGlone *et al.* 1994; Anderson 1995). From the empirical record and from external comparisons, then, it is possible to suggest that the early stages of long-term settlement on an island like Mallorca and in an archipelago like the Balearics were relatively brief processes, and that the first arrival of human beings is not very distant in time from the present chronology established for an early human presence.

The colonisation of the Balearic Islands as part of a wider cultural process

Human expansion across the planet formed part of a very long process in which insular territories generally were some of the last to be settled (Gamble 1994). Thus, human arrival in the Balearics could be seen simply as one more step in that process. A comparative look at other Mediterranean islands, however, shows the earliest Balearic occupation to be much later than that of all the other large islands – more than five millennia later than the earliest occupied islands (Cyprus, Corsica-Sardinia) and more than three millennia in all other cases (Ramis and Alcover 2004). Although the reasons that lay behind the singularity of this very recent human settlement are imprecise, some elements for reflection can be suggested.

Navigation is recorded in the Mediterranean since the beginning of the Holocene by Mesolithic or Epipalaeolithic peoples (e.g. Simmons 1999; Galanidou and Perlès 2003; Sampson 2006; Ammerman *et al.* 2008; Knapp 2010). The Neolithic expansion across the Mediterranean basin, from at least the ninth millennium Cal BC in the east (Peltenburg *et al.* 2001) to the sixth millennium Cal BC in the west (Zilhâo 2001), involved the first human colonisation of many of its insular territories. Additionally, a maritime network dedicated to obsidian exchange in the central Mediterranean is recorded during the Neolithic (e.g. Tykot 1996). But the Balearics seem to have remained outside all such developments. By the third millennium Cal BC, however, the material evidence shows that the Balearics were involved in the dynamics of the surrounding European mainland (Rosselló-Bordoy *et al.* 1980; Lewthwaite 1985; Chapman 1990).

Biogeographic explanations (late colonisation as a result of distance from source region and/or limited surface/resources) are not entirely convincing in the attempt to understand such a late settlement. Small and isolated islands had been settled since the early Neolithic in the central Mediterranean. Moreover, the existence of a long phase of unstable human presence on Mallorca (in parallel with the human settlement of other Mediterranean islands) lacks any clear archaeological evidence in the Balearics; in any case, all the ecological indicators suggest the absence of humans before about 3000 Cal BC.

Braudel (1976: 140–2) noted that the Mediterranean basin cannot be considered historically as a homogeneous space, but rather should be divided into several cultural areas defined by specific geographic traits. The archaeological record seems largely compatible with this idea. In the western Mediterranean, there is an almost complete absence of islands lying in close proximity to the mainland coast, islands that would have impelled navigational practice or served as stepping-stones to reach other islands. In contrast the Aegean, the Tyrrhenian and the Adriatic all display a very different configuration. Navigation in those areas can be seen as a progressive strategy, with Mesolithic practices leading to the emergence of maritime networks during the Neolithic (e.g. Bass 1998; Ammerman 2010; Knapp 2010). Such a gradual process could explain the early human presence in distant and isolated islands, like the Maltese archipelago and Lampedusa from the early Neolithic.

It could also be argued that the maritime activities of the western Mediterranean communities were not favoured by their geography, and the evidence that currently exists for navigation in the region during prehistory remains extremely limited. The arrival of the domestic mouse in the western Mediterranean in the first millennium Cal BC – after its spread in the east Mediterranean from the eighth millennium Cal BC – is linked to the intensification of maritime contacts in the region (Cucchi *et al.* 2005) and fits well with a scenario of several 'isolated' regions in the Mediterranean. Another argument for the lack of interest in navigation on the northwest Mediterranean mainland during the early Holocene is the slim evidence for fishing. Additionally, the faunal remains (Ramis 2006) and isotopic data (Van Strydonck *et al.* 2002a) related to early populations in Mallorca and Menorca reveal the absence or very limited presence of marine resources in the diet.

From such considerations, it follows that the early settlement of the remote – albeit visible from mainland – Balearic archipelago may have resulted from the particular conditions of populations in the source regions. Lewthwaite (1985) and Chapman (1990) tried to explain what they considered an intensification in the human occupation of the Balearics during the third millennium Cal BC as a consequence of several phenomena in the western Mediterranean: demographic growth, colonisation of new uninhabited regions and development of maritime contacts.

The settlement structure (Fernández-Miranda 1987), the specific traits of the Mallorcan and Menorcan megaliths (Plantalamor 1976; Hoskin 1994), the presence of early tin alloys (Hoffman 1991, 1995; Rovira *et al.* 1991), the decoration on Beaker pottery (Waldren 1982; Fernández-Miranda 1984–5) and the evidence for an egalitarian society with low levels of socio-political complexity (Coll 1993), all suggest a close relationship of the early settlers with the Languedoc region of southern France and with the Iberian northeast (e.g. Lull *et al.* 2004; Alcover 2008). This pattern stands in contrast with that of southern Iberia, where the more complex societies of the Valencian Bronze and El Argar cultures were developing; there tin alloys only came later, and there was an absence of (or difference in) megalithic burials compared to the Mallorcan and Menorcan examples.

The minimum distance between the Pityusan Islands and the mainland is about 90 km, roughly the same that exists between these islands and Mallorca, which itself is about 200 km from the mainland. Mallorca can be seen from some points of northeast Iberia under adequate environmental conditions and, despite the greater distance to this island, northerly winds and currents are dominant in this area. These factors could well favour the northern origin of the early settlers and a direct crossing to Mallorca and Menorca, themselves separated by just 40 km. Following an approach based on ethnographic data (Broodbank 1989), to complete the navigation route to Mallorca by rowing would probably take at least five days. It has been proposed that an insular colonisation by a group with a Neolithic economy, formed tentatively by about 40 individuals, would require them to carry about 15–19 metric tons to reproduce a viable way of life in their destination (Broodbank and Strasser 1991). The duration of such a crossing could act as a limiting factor in reaching the islands, because of the need to feed and water the livestock as well as the people along the way (Case 1969; Broodbank 2000). But the successful transfer of the Neolithic package to remote islands like Lampedusa (Radi 1972) and Malta (Evans 1984; Robb 2001) had been achieved by the sixth millennium Cal BC. Moreover, the chronological framework shows that human arrival in the Balearics was earlier than certain technological developments recorded in the Aegean during the late third millennium Cal BC (Agouridis 1997; Broodbank 2000). Although maritime journeys using unkeeled vessels propelled by winds, currents and rowing could be long and unsafe, the late settlement of the Balearics cannot be considered simply as limited by the technological level of navigation.

The risk and complexity of this colonisation also indicate that it was not a casual event (i.e. derived simply from curiosity or adventure), but rather was likely motivated by some political and/or socio-economic pressure. The third millennium Cal BC was a time of intense cultural change in the Iberian northeast (e.g. Martín 1992; Alcalde et al. 1998; Molist et al. 2002) and in southern France (e.g. Mills 1983; Guilaine 1991). Demographic increase and socio-economic reorganisation are inferred from the archaeological record, which shows new settlement patterns, with the exploitation of previously unoccupied, marginal (i.e. highly unproductive) areas. Compared to earlier periods, the higher mobility of the population, smaller communities, an increase in the importance of caprines among herding species and settlements in high mountain sites can all be detected. Such traits fit well with those recorded in the early communities of Mallorca.

Some of the previously cited works also mention the importance of climatic change during the third millennium Cal BC as one aspect of this socio-economic reorganisation. There is growing evidence for such an event and its cultural effects in surrounding Mediterranean regions (e.g. Cullen et al. 2000; DeMenocal et al. 2000; DeMenocal 2001; Schilman et al. 2001; Fábregas et al. 2003). Nonetheless, the cultural groups from these possible source regions were increasingly involved in long-distance trade after a period of marked self-sufficiency (Delibes and Fernández-Miranda 1993; Gascó 2004). A certain acceleration of maritime contacts can be detected in the northwest Mediterranean, defined as a 'maritime interaction sphere' by Lewthwaite (1985), one in which the Balearics seem to have participated, even if marginally (Rosselló-Bordoy *et al.* 1980).

To summarise, the specific geographic traits and cultural identities in the western-most Mediterranean basin – with a low level of navigational development during the Neolithic – could be the main elements that resulted in the late human colonisation of Mallorca, and probably the whole Balearic archipelago (i.e. in the general context of the Mediterranean islands). The precise causes that motivated the movement of some human groups from the mainland during the middle Holocene (at an undetermined time within the third millennium Cal BC) are currently unknown, but it seems clear that they must be considered from the perspective of the cultural dynamics in the northwest Mediterranean at that time.

S'Arenalet de Son Colom: a new key site in the early prehistory of the Balearics

The isolated stone structure of S'Arenalet de Son Colom is located along Mallorca's northern coast at Badia (bay) d'Alcúdia. The site was excavated in October 2004, and a preliminary report has appeared (Ramis *et al.* 2007). The architectural remains were extremely eroded (Figure 4.2). The preserved part consisted of a central area with two parallel dry-stone walls about 5 m long oriented N–S. Both are about 1–1.5 m wide and were built using the cyclopean technique of a double face with vertical large

Figure 4.2 Intense erosion of the structure at S'Arenalet de Son Colom can be seen in these images. Only fragments of two parallel dry-stone walls, about 5 m long and oriented N–S, were preserved. They were built using the cyclopean technique of a double face with vertical large blocks and inner filling, with a width of 1–1.5 m and delimiting a chamber about 4 m wide.

blocks and inner filling, delimiting a chamber about 4 m wide. The two extremes of this elongated structure are not preserved, the northern one because of marine erosion, the southern one probably because of agricultural activities.

From the earliest report of these remains (Mascaró Passarius 1967), they have been considered as part of a habitational *naveta*. Nevertheless, the possible apse and entrance are lost, and the walls are not as thick and impressive as those of the classic *navetes* of the mid–late second millennium Cal BC. Yet the shape, orientation and technique of the structure at S'Arenalet de Son Colom are similar to those of the habitational *navetes* of the Balearics (e.g. Rosselló-Bordoy 1964–5; Plantalamor 1991), while similarities with other kinds of architectural structures are not apparent.

This building contained a well-stratified deposit, with a homogeneous material assemblage belonging to a single occupation horizon. Two radiocarbon determinations have been obtained from bone samples of this deposit – KIA-26215: 3670±35 BP (2190–1940 Cal BC) and KIA-26226: 3660±35 BP (2140–1930 Cal BC). Following Bronk Ramsey's (2005) calibration, both dates overlap almost completely at 2s ranges in the approximate interval of 2150–1950 Cal BC. The recorded pottery types are characteristic of the late third millennium (Figure 4.3), and include some incised Beaker fragments belonging to the two local styles defined in Mallorca (e.g. Rosselló-Bordoy 1960; Cantarellas 1972). Morphological parallels can be established with other reliable Mallorcan assemblages, like the rock shelter of Coval Simó (Coll

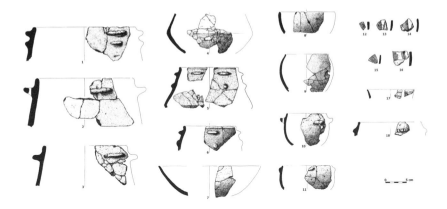

Figure 4.3   Representative pottery types from S'Arenalet de Son Colom, which are characteristic of the late third millennium Cal BC in Mallorcan assemblages. They include cylindrical or convex containers with horizontal handles (1–3), carinated or globular pots with a round base (4–6), bowls with thin rim (7–8) and small spherical or globular shapes (9–11). The decorated pottery consists of fragments of local Beaker pottery (12–17) and pieces with an engraved collar (18), which are not considered contemporary.

2001) and the lower level of the open-air site of Ca na Cotxera (Cantarellas 1972), both of which are roughly contemporary. Several fragments of smelting crucibles and small metallic items (e.g. a rivet, an awl) were also found. Their mineral composition is still undergoing analysis. Remains of chipped stone material were very scarce, as is usual in Balearic sites. Faunal remains consisted of very fragmented bones of caprine, cattle and pig, and a considerable quantity of marine and terrestrial molluscs. Analyses of environmental vegetation and its human exploitation are in progress. In summary, we can infer that this was a site where people lived and produced their food.

The attribution of the structure at S'Arenalet de Son Colom to the late third millennium BC is based on the characteristics of the deposit, a horizontal sedimentation layer between the inner faces of the wall, with no evidence of disturbance. This layer was deposited on the floor of the structure (both walls are built directly on a level of compressed sandy sediment). The two dated samples come from the deposit between the walls. Of course, this context is not representative of the time when the monument was constructed but rather during its use or abandonment. Nevertheless, a single phase of use is inferred from the stratigraphy as well as the materials excavated. The cultural homogeneity of the materials from the chamber has been emphasised. The complete pottery assemblage (the most representative of which is presented in Figure 4.3) is very uniform, and can be linked to reliable Mallorcan contexts dated to the third millennium BC. Moreover, material items that are characteristic of the mid–late second millennium, i.e. the assumed time period for this kind of monument, are completely absent at S'Arenalet de Son Colom.

Discussion

The implications of this new dating information from S'Arenalet de Son Colom are relevant for understanding the origins of early material culture in the Balearics. The cyclopean technique in domestic architecture can now be linked to the earliest well-defined phase of human occupation on the islands (Ramis *et al.* 2002). An origin for the habitational *navetes* in Mallorca in the third millennium Cal BC had been proposed earlier as the result of the excavations at the so-called 'old settlement' of Son Olesa (e.g. Waldren 1984; 1987); this dating was followed in several synthetic works (e.g. Chapman 1985; Lewthwaite 1985; Delibes and Fernández-Miranda 1993). Nevertheless the lack of vertical stratigraphy at Son Olesa has led to several reinterpretations of the sequences at that site, all of which propose different ages for the cyclopean structures: *c.* 1600 Cal BC (Lull *et al.* 1999), *c.* 1700 Cal BC (Calvo and Guerrero 2002) or *c.* 1800 Cal BC (Waldren 2002). These dates have hitherto been considered indicative of the origin of the *navetes* on the Balearics, within the context of the chronological data available from other sites (Rosselló-Bordoy 1979; Plantalamor and Van Strydonck 1997; Pons 1999; Salvà 2001).

It has been widely accepted that early Mallorcan settlers dwelt in huts built mostly of non-durable materials. Although none of these structures has ever been adequately recorded, it is possible that the putative megalithic tombs of Son Olesa (Waldren 2001) and other open-air sites with Beaker pottery but without recorded architectural remains – such as the lower level of Ca na Cotxera (Cantarellas 1972) – could be related to such huts (e.g. Calvo and Guerrero 2002). In the light of the new work at S'Arenalet de Son Colom, however, both habitat types would seem to have coexisted in Mallorca during the late third and early second millennia BC (as recorded also in Menorca for the second millennium Cal BC: Plantalamor 1991).

Some studies have emphasised the existence of technical and morphological parallels between the *navetes* and the houses of some third millennium Cal BC cultures in the French Midi, particularly the Fontbouisse group in Languedoc (Plantalamor and Rita 1984; Plantalamor 1990–1; 1991). This argument was questioned on the basis of an apparent lack of synchrony between the monuments (e.g. Fernández-Miranda 1993). Nevertheless, the new evidence presented here indicates a close temporal link between the last phase of the Fontbouisse group and the structure at S'Arenalet de Son Colom. Currently there is still a narrow gap between the end of the Fontbouisse culture – *ca.* 2200 Cal BC (e.g. Gascó 2003) – and the chronology of S'Arenalet de Son Colom. This, however, could be a by-product of insufficient sampling, an archaeological derivation of the so-called Signor–Lipps effect (Signor and Lipps 1982). Identifying southern France as a possible source region for the early settlers of the Balearics seems to agree with other features of the Balearic archaeological record, including the early presence of tin alloys, possibly as early as the Beaker tradition horizon (Hoffman 1995). In addition, most artefact types from the Balearic late third millennium BC seem to corroborate this suggestion. Another supporting argument involves the width of both the walls and the chamber at S'Arenalet de Son Colom, which accords closely with those reported from the Fontbouisse group (Gascó 1976). In turn, the walls at S'Arenalet de Son Colom contrast with those of the later Balearic *navetes*, with walls about 2–2.5 m wide and chambers about 3 m wide.

Two chronological and cultural periods are currently accepted as having occurred prior to the Talaiotic culture, which itself embraces the late second–first millennia Cal BC. The earliest culture is termed variously 'Chalcolithic', 'Early and Late Beaker' or 'Campaniform and Epicampaniform'; the name given to the following culture in recent literature is 'Naviform' (e.g. Lull *et al.* 1999; Calvo and Guerrero 2002). One of the most characteristic elements of the earliest period is the presence of incised pottery of a local Beaker tradition ('incised A'), which occurs down to about 2000 Cal BC and is then replaced by a poorer quality pottery with more restricted incised decoration ('incised B'), called 'Late Beaker' or 'Epicampaniform'. The key element for the beginning of the so-called Naviform period, as evident in the term itself, is the emergence of the habitational *naveta* as the first type of cyclopean architecture in the Balearic Islands.

The link between both periods is imprecise. For some authors, it consists of a number of changes in the habitation system, the settlement pattern, the burial rites, the pottery styles and technology. These do not seem synchronous, and even a slow transition of about two centuries would define two very different cultural realities (Lull *et al.* 1999), characterised by the disappearance of the decorated pottery styles, the introduction of collective burial ritual in natural caves, rock-cut tombs or megalithic graves and the introduction of the horseshoe-shaped habitation structures called *navetes*. These last were elaborated through the use of the cyclopean technique, which replaced more perishable constructions. Other authors emphasise the arrival of new human groups as responsible for the material changes (Pons 1999). The chronology of this event or process is also very imprecise, because of the limitations of the available radiocarbon record, with several slightly different proposals, all placing the breaking point somewhere between 1800 and 1600 Cal BC. The excavation of S'Arenalet de Son Colom, however, has revealed the synchronous presence of the two incised pottery types inside the single cyclopean building, now radiocarbon dated to the late third millennium Cal BC.

Other elements presumed to have been synchronous with the previously accepted age span of the *navetes* can now be seen as belonging to an earlier period. It was assumed that the collective inhumation ritual in megaliths, natural caves and round rock-cut tombs appeared at an imprecise moment in the first half of the second millennium Cal BC. Nevertheless, some inhumations in the rock-cut tombs with megalithic face and corridor at Biniai Nou have been dated to the late third millennium Cal BC (Plantalamor and Marquès 2001). New dates for human bones from collective burials in the natural cave of Can Martorellet (Van Strydonck *et al.* 2002b) and the rock-cut tomb of Son Mulet (Gómez and Rubinos 2005) fall in the first quarter of the second millennium Cal BC. Some of the new, reliable dates for the human remains from the natural cave of Moleta fall within the second half of the third millennium Cal BC (Ramis *et al.* 2002; Van Strydonck *et al.* 2005). Additionally, some materials recovered in the megaliths of Ca na Costa (Formentera) and Ses Roques Llises (Menorca) belong to the Beaker tradition (Fernández *et al.* 1976; Rosselló-Bordoy *et al.* 1980). All these funerary practices seem to have been established in the archipelago during the late third millennium Cal BC, and remained in use until the mid–late second millennium Cal BC.

Most of the artefactual assemblage considered to be characteristic of the mid-second millennium BC can indeed also be found in contexts from the late third millennium BC. Only incised pottery decorated in the Beaker tradition seems to disappear around 2000 Cal BC, even though its limited presence in the archipelago should be noted. This means that Beaker pottery is a very marginal material upon which to base any analysis of the early Balearic cultural sequence. It is unknown in Menorca and missing from several Mallorcan assemblages of the late third millennium BC, like those at Coval den Pep Rave (Coll 1991) or Cova des Moro (Ramis *et al.* 2005). Nevertheless most other items – perforated polished stone plaques (traditionally known as 'wrist guards'), metal awls, pyramidal and prismatic V-perforated buttons, flaked knives and characteristic undecorated pottery types – are present for several centuries after the disappearance of the local Beaker tradition pottery. Furthermore, the two incised pottery styles have been found together in the reliable archaeological contexts of the recent excavations at Coval Simó (Coll 2001) and S'Arenalet de Son Colom. This suggests their simultaneous origin and a longer duration for the late incised pottery (as well as the undecorated one) after the disappearance of the Beaker style.

The evidence gathered at S'Arenalet de Son Colom suggests that the Balearic habitational *navetes* have an origin earlier than currently accepted, dating back to the late third millennium Cal BC. This new chronological scenario lends support to previous hypotheses that associated these structures with the Fontbouisse group. This synchronism is reinforced by the clear influence exerted by the Pyrenean–Languedocian culture on Balearic materials during the late third millennium Cal BC.

Globally, the initial mobility of some human groups in certain coastal regions of the northwest Mediterranean at an uncertain point during the third millennium Cal BC can be proposed from this analysis. Nevertheless, it was immediately followed by a marked 'insularity' of the early Balearic populations, characterised by very low intensity in mobility and external contacts outside the archipelago. The material record suggests that elements of cultural continuity seem much more significant than those of possible changes during the late third and first half of the second millennia Cal BC. On the contrary, the later Bronze Age involves some important cultural modifications in this dynamic. Although settlement patterns and habitational structures remain stable, profound changes are apparent in mortuary systems, artefact typologies and a greater intensity of external contacts (e.g. Lull *et al.* 1999; 2004).

Conclusion

From a general point of view, the material presented here offers a Mediterranean example for studying the process of insular long-term settlement as argued by Anderson (1995). On the basis of the available archaeological assemblages, contacts related to the earliest settlement phase in the islands can be linked mainly to the northwest Mediterranean basin. Most cultural elements of early Balearic prehistory were introduced almost simultaneously in this first stage of human occupation in the archipelago. Although the Balearics are not oceanic islands, and a more intensive relationship with the source regions could be assumed here than in the Pacific, a linear historical trajectory can be interpreted for the late third and first half of the second millennium Cal BC. The information from S'Arenalet de Son Colom, together with the evidence gathered from other sites, emphasises the persistence of most cultural traits in the Balearics during this period. The archaeological record of the late third millennium Cal BC fits well with a *colonisation* stage, while the so-called *habitation* stage can be detected with the emergence and development of the first indigenous culture around the mid-second millennium Cal BC. It is characterised by very slow developments in the material culture, which can be interpreted as the product of very conservative behaviour by these early communities. One of the main aspects to be noted here is the increasing monumentality of the habitational structures.

Finally, although a very marked homogeneity exists in the early archaeological record of the Balearics, with a clear connectivity between the two major islands, some differences may be observed (e.g. very limited presence of megaliths in Mallorca, absence of incised Beaker pottery in Menorca, certain pottery types found only in the Menorcan record). Whether these differences are due to a founder effect, to the specific characteristics of the communities in each island or region or simply to the incomplete material record, are questions to be resolved by future research. Nonetheless, different practices may be detected in this early material record, both in habitational (round huts, cyclopean elongated structures) and funerary (megaliths, rock-cut tombs, natural caves) systems. This suggests a relatively varied development of diverse material traditions in the colonisation phase of the Balearic archipelago.

The creation of a local cultural identity involved an increasing divergence between Mallorca and Menorca. The main element that illustrates this during the second half of the second millennium Cal BC is the local development of mortuary monuments in Menorca, with the appearance of the burial (inhumation) *naveta* (Figure 4.4), probably a local development of megaliths (Plantalamor 1991; Gili *et al.* 2006).

Figure 4.4 The *naveta* at des Tudons is an example of the kind of cyclopean funerary monument built on Menorca during the late second millennium Cal BC. These *navetas*
are widely considered to be a local development from Early Bronze Age megaliths,
which occurred only on that island.

References

Agouridis, C. 1997 Sea routes and navigation in the third millennium Aegean. *Oxford Journal of Archaeology* 16: 1–24.

Alcalde, G., M. Molist, M. Saña and A. Toledo 1998 *La transició del III al II mil·lenni AC a Catalunya. Workshop (Olot, 7 de juny de 1997)*. Olot: Museu Comarcal de la Garrotxa/Universitat Autònoma de Barcelona.

Alcover, J.A. 2008 The first Mallorcans: prehistoric colonization in the western Mediterranean. *Journal of World Prehistory* 21: 19–84.

Ammerman, A.J. 2010 The first argonauts: towards the study of the earliest seafaring in the Mediterranean. In A. Anderson, J. Barrett and K. Boyle (eds), *The Global Origins and Development of Seafaring*, 81–92. Cambridge: McDonald Institute for Archaeological Research.

Ammerman, A., P. Flourentzos, R. Gabrielli, T. Higham, C. McCartney and T. Turnbull 2008 Third report on early sites on Cyprus. *Report of the Department of Antiquities, Cyprus*: 1–32.

Anderson, A. 1995 Current approaches in East Polynesian colonisation research. *Journal of the Polynesian Society* 30: 110–32.

Bass, B. 1998 Early Neolithic accounts: remote islands, maritime exploitations, and the trans-Adriatic cultural network. *Journal of Mediterranean Archaeology* 11: 165–90.

Braudel, F. 1976 *El Mediterráneo y el mundo mediterráneo en la época de Felipe II*. México: Fondo de Cultura Económica.

Bronk Ramsey, C. 2005 OxCal Program v3.10. Available at: http:/www.rlaha.oc.ac.uk/oxcal/oxcal.htm.

Broodbank, C. 1989 The longboat and society in the Cyclades in the Keros-Syros culture. *American Journal of Archaeology* 93: 319–37.

—— 2000 *An Island Archaeology of the Early Cyclades*. Cambridge: Cambridge University Press.

Broodbank, C., and T.F. Strasser 1991 Migrant farmers and the Neolithic colonisation of Crete. *Antiquity* 65: 233–45.

Calvo, M., and V.M. Guerrero 2002 *Los inicios de la metalurgia en Baleares. El Calcolítico (c. 2500–1700 cal. BC)*. Palma: El Tall.

Calvo, M., V.M. Guerrero and B. Salvà 2002 Los orígenes del poblamiento balear. Una discusión no acabada. *Complutum* 13: 159–91.

Cantarellas, C. 1972 *Cerámica incisa en Mallorca*. Palma: Caja de Ahorros y Monte de Piedad de las Baleares.

Case, H. 1969 Neolithic explanations. *Antiquity* 43: 176–86.

Chapman, R.W. 1985 The later prehistory of western Mediterranean Europe: recent advances. In F. Wendorf and A.E. Close (eds), *Advances in World Archaeology* 4: 115–87. New York: Academic Press.

Chapman, R.W. 1990 *Emerging Complexity: The Later Prehistory of South-East Spain, Iberia and the West Mediterranean*. Cambridge: Cambridge University Press.

Cherry, J.F. 1981 Pattern and process in the earliest colonisation of the Mediterranean islands. *Proceedings of the Prehistoric Society* 47: 41–68.

Cherry, J.F. 1990 The first colonisation of the Mediterranean islands: a review of recent research. *Journal of Mediterranean Archaeology* 3: 145–221.

Cherry, J.F., and R. Torrence 1982 The earliest prehistory of Melos. In C. Renfrew and M. Wagstaff (eds), *An Island Polity. The Archaeology of Exploitation in Melos*, 24–34. Cambridge: Cambridge University Press.

Claustre, F., F. Briois and N. Valdeyron 2002 Culture matérielle, économie et commerce du Néolithique Final à l'Age du Bronze sur le versant nord des Pyrénées méditerranées. In *Pirineus i veïns al 3r mil·lenni. XII Col·loqui Internacional d'Arqueologia de Puigcerdà (10–12 novembre 2000)*, 323–43. Puigcerdà: Institut d'Estudis Ceretans.

Coll, J. 1991 Seriación cultural de los materiales del coval den Pep Rave (Sóller, Mallorca). Elementos calcolíticos y talaióticos. *Trabajos de Prehistoria* 48: 75–101.

—— 1993 Aproximación a la arqueología funeraria de las culturas iniciales de la prehistoria de Mallorca. *Pyrenae* 24: 93–114.

—— 1997 Arquitectura ritual versus arquitectura doméstica en la cultura talaiótica. In *La pedra en sec. Obra, paisatge i patrimoni. Actes del IV Congrés Internacional de Construcció de Pedra en Sec (Mallorca, 1994)*, 467–82. Palma: Consell Insular de Mallorca.

—— 2001 Primeres datacions absolutes del jaciment de coval Simó. *Endins* 24: 161–8.

Costa, B. 2000 Plantejaments per a l'anàlisi del procés d'establiment humà en petits medis insulars. El cas de l'arxipèlag balear. In V.M. Guerrero, V.M. and S. Gornés (eds), *Colonización humana en ambientes insulares. Interacción con el medio y adaptación cultural*, 11–71. Palma: Universitat de les Illes Balears.

Cucchi, T., J.-D. Vigne and J.-C. Auffray 2005 First occurrence of the house mouse (*Mus musculus domesticus* Schwarz & Schwarz, 1943) in the Western Mediterranean: a zooarchaeological revision of subfossil occurrences. *Biological Journal of the Linnean Society* 84: 429–45.

Cullen, H.M., P.B. DeMenocal, S. Hemming, G. Hemming, F.H. Brown, T. Guilderson and F. Sirocko 2000 Climate change and the collapse of the Akkadian empire: Evidence from the deep sea. *Geology* 28: 379–82.

Delibes, G., and M. Fernández-Miranda 1993 *Los orígenes de la civilización. El Calcolítico en el Viejo Mundo*. Madrid: Síntesis.

DeMenocal, P.B. 2001 Cultural responses to climatic change during the Late Holocene. *Science* 292: 667–73.

DeMenocal, P.B., J. Ortiz, T. Guilderson, J. Adkins, M. Sarnthein, L. Baker and M. Yarusinsky 2000 Abrupt onset and termination of the African Humid Period: rapid climate responses to gradual insolation forcing. *Quaternary Science Reviews* 19: 347–61.

Dixon, E.J. 2001 Human colonisation of the Americas: timing, technology and process. *Quaternary Science Reviews* 20: 277–99.

Evans, J.D. 1977 Island archaeology in the Mediterranean: problems and opportunities. *World Archaeology* 9: 12–26.

—— 1984 Maltese Prehistory – a reappraisal. In W.H. Waldren, R. Chapman, J. Lewthwaite and R. Kennard (eds), *The Deya Conference of Prehistory. Early*

Settlement in the Western Mediterranean Islands and their Peripheral Areas. British Archaeological Reports International Series 229: 489–97. Oxford: British Archaeological Reports.

Fábregas, R., A. Martínez Cortizas, R. Blanco and W. Chesworth 2003 Environmental change and social dynamics in the second–third millennium BC in NW Iberia. *Journal of Archaeological Science* 30: 859–71.

Fernández, J.H., L. Plantalamor and C. Topp 1976 Excavaciones en el sepulcro megalítico de Ca Na Costa. *Mayurqa* 15: 109–38.

Fernández-Miranda, M. 1984–5 Elementos de filiación campaniforme en las Islas Baleares: valoración y significado cultural. In *Homenaje al Prof. Gratiniano Nieto*. Cuadernos de Prehistoria y Arqueología 11–12: 25–36. Madrid: Universidad Autónoma de Madrid.

—— 1987 Relaciones entre la Península Ibérica, Islas Baleares y Cerdeña durante el Bronce Medio y Final. In *La Sardegna nel Mediterráneo tra il secondo e il primo millennio a.C. Atti del II Convengo di studi 'Un millennio di relazioni fra la Sardegna e i Paesi del Mediterraneo'. Selargius-Cagliari, 27–30 novembre 1986*, 479–92. Cagliari: Amministrazione Provinciale di Cagliari.

—— 1993 Relaciones exteriores de las Islas Baleares en tiempos prehistóricos. *Cuadernos de Arqueología Marítima* 2: 137–57.

Fiedel, S.J. 2000 The peopling of the New World: present evidence, new theories, and future directions. *Journal of Archaeological Research* 8: 39–103.

Galanidou, N., and C. Perlès (eds) 2003 *The Greek Mesolithic: Problems and Perspectives*. British School at Athens Studies 10. London: British School at Athens.

Gamble, C. 1994 *Timewalkers: The Prehistory of Global Colonisation*. Cambridge, MA: Harvard University Press.

Gascó, J. 1976 *La communauté paysanne de Fontbouisse*. Toulouse: Archives d'Écologie Préhistorique.

—— 2003 Les Vautes et les données du C14 dans le sud de la France. In J. Guilaine and G. Escallon (eds), *Les Vautes (Saint-Gély-du-Fesc, Hérault) et le Néolithique final du Languedoc oriental*, 217–25. Toulouse: Archives d'Écologie Préhistorique.

—— 2004 Les composantes de l'Âge du Bronze, de la fin du Chalcolithique à l'Âge du Bronze en France méridionale. *Cypsela* 15: 39–72.

Gili, S., V. Lull, R. Micó, C. Rihuete and R. Risch 2006 An island decides: megalithic burial rites on Menorca. *Antiquity* 80: 829–42.

Gómez, J.L., and A. Rubinos 2005 Informe de la datación del material óseo procedente de dos yacimientos prehistóricos mallorquines. *Mayurqa* 30: 359–67.

Graves, M.W., and D.J. Addison 1995 The Polynesian settlement of the Hawaiian Archipelago: integrating models and methods in archaeological interpretation. *World Archaeology* 26: 380–99.

Guerrero, V.M. 2001 The Balearic Islands: Prehistoric colonisation of the furthest Mediterranean islands from the mainland. *Journal of Mediterranean Archaeology* 14: 136–58.

Guerrero, V.M., and M. Calvo 2008 Resolviendo incertidumbres. Nuevos datos sobre las primeras ocupaciones humanas de las Baleares. In M. Hernández, J.A.

Soler and J.A. López (eds), *Actas del IV Congreso del Neolítico Peninsular (Alicante, 27 al 30 noviembre 2006)*, vol. II, 331–9. Alicante: Museo Arqueológico de Alicante.

Guilaine, J. 1991 Vers une préhistoire agraire. In J. Guilaine (ed.), *Pour une archéologie agraire. À la croisée des Sciences de l'Homme et de la Nature*, 31–80. Paris: Armand Colin.

Hoffman, C.R. 1991 The metals of Son Matge, Mallorca, Spain. Technology as cultural activity and behaviour. In W.H. Waldren, J. Ensenyat and R. Kennard (eds), *IInd Deya Conference of Prehistory. Archaeological Techniques, Technology and Theory*. British Archaeological Reports International Series 574: 169–87. Oxford: British Archaeological Reports.

—— 1995 The making of material culture – the roles of metal technology in late prehistoric Iberia. In K.T. Lillios (ed.), *The Origins of Complex Societies in Late Prehistoric Iberia*. International Monographs in Prehistory, Archaeological Series 8: 20–31. Ann Arbor, MI: International Monographs in Prehistory.

Hoskin, M. 1994 La Prehistoria de las Islas Baleares. In J.A. Belmonte (ed.), *Arqueoastronomía hispánica: prácticas astronómicas en la prehistoria de la Península Ibérica y los Archipiélagos Balear y Canario*, 161–81. Madrid: Sirius.

Knapp, A.B. 2009 Monumental architecture, identity and memory. In *Proceedings of the Symposium: Bronze Age Architectural Traditions in the East Mediterranean: Diffusion and Diversity (Gasteig, Munich, 7–8 May, 2008)*, 47–59. Weilheim: Verein zur Förderung der Aufarbeitung der Hellenischen Geschichte.

—— 2010 Cyprus's earliest prehistory: seafarers, foragers and settlers. *Journal of World Prehistory* 23: 79-120.

Lewthwaite, J. 1985 Social factors and economic change in Balearic prehistory, 3000–1000 B.C. In G. Barker and C. Gamble (eds), *Beyond Domestication in Prehistoric Europe*, 205–31. London: Academic Press.

Lull, V., R. Micó, C. Rihuete and R. Risch 1999 *La Cova des Càrritx y la Cova des Mussol. Ideología y sociedad en la prehistoria de Menorca*. Barcelona: Consell Insular de Menorca.

—— 2004 Los cambios sociales en las islas Baleares a lo largo del II milenio. *Cypsela* 15: 123–48.

Martín, A. 1992 Estrategia y culturas del Neolítico Final y Calcolítico en Cataluña. In P. Utrilla (ed.), *Aragón/Litoral mediterráneo: intercambios culturales durante la prehistoria*, 389–97. Zaragoza: Institución Fernando el Católico.

Martín, A., M.A. Petit and J.L. Maya 2002 Cultura material, economia i inter-canvis durant el III mil·lenni AC a Catalunya. In *Pirineus i veïns al 3r mil·lenni. XII Col·loqui Internacional d'Arqueologia de Puigcerdà (10–12 novembre 2000)*, 295–321. Puigcerdà: Institut d'Estudis Ceretans.

Mascaró Passarius, J. 1967 *Corpus de toponimia de Mallorca*. Palma: Miramar.

McGlone, M., A.J. Anderson and R. Holdaway

—— 1994 An ecological approach to the early settlement of New Zealand. In D.G. Sutton (ed.), *Origins of the First New Zealanders*, 136–63. Auckland: Auckland University Press.

Meltzer, D.J. 2002 What do you do when no one's been there before? Thoughts of the exploration and colonisation of new lands. In N. Jablonski (ed.), *The First Americans: The Pleistocene Colonisation of the New World*, 27–58. San Francisco: University of California Press.

Micó, R. 2005 *Cronología Absoluta y Periodización de la Prehistoria de las Islas Baleares*. British Archaeological Reports International Series 1373. Oxford: British Archaeological Reports.

—— 2006 Radiocarbon dating and Balearic prehistory: reviewing the periodization of the prehistoric sequence. *Radiocarbon* 48: 421–34.

Mills, N. 1983 The Neolithic of Southern France. In C. Scarre (ed.), *Ancient France. Neolithic Societies and their Landscapes 6000–2000 BC*, 91–145. Edinburgh: Edinburgh University Press.

Molist, M., F. Burjachs and R. Piqué 2002 Paisatge, territori i hàbitat als vessants meridionals dels Pirineus, en el III mil·lenni. In *Pirineus i veïns al 3r mil·lenni. XII Col·loqui Internacional d'Arqueologia de Puigcerdà (10–12 novembre 2000)*, 179–98. Puigcerdà: Institut d'Estudis Ceretans.

Morell, C., and A. Querol 1987 Flint implements of the Son Oleza Bell Beaker settlement in the Balearic Island of Mallorca. In W.H. Waldren and R.-C. Kennard (eds), *Bell Beakers of the Western Mediterranean. Definition, Interpretation, Theory and New Site Data. The Oxford International Conference 1986*. British Archaeological Reports International Series 331: 283–306. Oxford: British Archaeological Reports.

Peltenburg, E., S. Colledge, P. Croft, A. Jackson, C. McCartney and M.A. Murray 2001 Neolithic dispersals from the Levantine corridor: a Mediterranean perspective. *Levant* 33: 35–64.

Perlès, C. 1979 Des navigateurs méditerranéens il y a 10000 ans. *La Recherche* 96: 82–3.

Plantalamor, L. 1976 Algunas consideraciones sobre los sepulcros megalíticos de Menorca. *Sautuola* 2: 157–73.

—— 1990–1 La arquitectura pretalayótica de Menorca en relación a las construcciones del Languedoc Oriental. In *Le Chalcolithique en Languedoc. Ses relations extra-régionales. Colloque International Hommage au Dr. Jean Bernal (Saint-Mathieu-de-Tréviers, Hérault, 1990)*, 307–14. Hérault: Archéologie en Languedoc.

—— 1991 *L'arquitectura prehistòrica i protohistòrica de Menorca i el seu marc cultural*. Treballs del Museu de Menorca 12. Maó: Museu de Menorca.

Plantalamor, L., and M.C. Rita 1984 Formas de población durante el segundo y primer milenio BC en Menorca. Son Mercer de Baix, transición entre la cultura pretalayótica y talayótica. In W.H. Waldren, R. Chapman, J. Lewthwaite and R. Kennard (eds), *The Deyà Conference of Prehistory. Early Settlement in the Western Mediterranean Islands and their Peripheral Areas*. British Archaeological Reports International Series 229: 797–826. Oxford: British Archaeological Reports.

Plantalamor, L., and M. Van Strydonck 1997 *La cronologia de la prehistòria de Menorca (Noves datacions de 14C)*. Treballs del Museu de Menorca 20. Maó: Museu de Menorca.

Plantalamor, L., and J. Marquès (eds) 2001 *Biniai Nou. El megalitisme mediterrani a Menorca*. Treballs del Museu de Menorca 24. Maó: Museu de Menorca.

Pons, G. 1999 *Anàlisi espacial del poblament al Pretalaiòtic final i al Talaiòtic I de Mallorca*. Palma: Consell de Mallorca.

Radi, G. 1972 Trace di un insediamento neolitico nell'isola di Lampedusa. *Atti de la Società Toscana di Scienze Naturali* 79: 197–205.

Ramis, D. 2006 Estudio faunístico de las fases iniciales de la Prehistoria de Mallorca. Unpublished PhD dissertation, Program in Prehistory, Universidad Nacional de Educación a Distancia, Madrid.

Ramis, D., and J.A. Alcover 2004 Irrupción humana y extinción faunística en las grandes islas del Mediterráneo durante el Holoceno. In *Miscelánea en Homenaje a Emiliano Aguirre. IV. Arqueología*, 390–401. Alcalá de Henares: Museo Regional de la Comunidad de Madrid.

Ramis, D., J.A. Alcover, J. Coll and M. Trias 2002 The chronology of the first settlement of the Balearic Islands. *Journal of Mediterranean Archaeology* 15: 3–24.

Ramis, D., L. Plantalamor, J. Carreras, M. Trias and G. Santandreu 2007 S'Arenalet de Son Colom (Artà) i l'origen de l'arquitectura ciclòpia a les Balears. *Bolletí de la Societat Arqueològica Lul·liana* 63: 295–312.

Ramis, D., G. Santandreu and J. Carreras 2005 Resultats preliminars de l'excavació arqueològica a la cova des Moro entre 1999 i 2002. In *III Jornades d'Estudis Locals de Manacor 2004. Espai, fet urbà i societats (21 i 22 de maig de 2004)*, 127–42. Manacor: Ajuntament de Manacor.

Risch, R. 2001 Aproximació a les plaques de pedra de les Balears: anàlisi funcional d'un exemplar procedent de la cova des Moro (Manacor). In M. Calvo, V.M. Guerrero and B. Salvà (eds), *La cova des Moro (Manacor, Mallorca). Campanyes d'excavacions arqueològiques 1995–1998*, 53–63. Palma: Consell de Mallorca.

Robb, J. 2001 Island identities: ritual, travel and the creation of difference in Neolithic Malta. *European Journal of Archaeology* 4: 175–202.

Rosselló-Bordoy, G. 1960 Cerámicas incisas de Mallorca. *Studi Sardi* 16: 300–15.

—— 1964–5 Las navetas de Mallorca. *Studi Sardi* 19: 261–314.

—— 1965 Arquitectura ciclópea mallorquina. In L. Pericot (ed.), *Arquitectura megalítica y ciclópea catalano-balear*, 133–49. Barcelona: Consejo Superior de Investigaciones Científicas.

Rosselló-Bordoy, G. 1979 *La Cultura Talayótica en Mallorca: bases para el estudio de sus fases iniciales*. Palma: Cort.

Rosselló-Bordoy, G., L. Plantalamor and A. López 1980 Excavaciones arqueológicas en Torre d'En Gaumés (Alayor, Menorca). I. La sepultura megalítica de Ses Roques Llises. *Noticiario Arqueológico Hispánico* 8: 71–138.

Rovira, S., I. Montero and S. Consuegra 1991 Metalurgia talayótica reciente: nuevas aportaciones. *Trabajos de Prehistoria* 48: 51–74.

Salvà, B. 2001 *El pretalaiòtic al llevant mallorquí (1700–1100 AC). Anàlisi territorial*. Palma: Documenta Balear.

Sampson, A. 2006 *The Cave of the Cyclops: Mesolithic and Neolithic Networks in the Northern Aegean, Greece 1: Intra-Site Analyses, Local Industries, and Regional*

Site Distribution. Institute for Aegean Prehistory, Prehistory Monographs 21. Philadelphia: Institute for Aegean Prehistory Academic Press.

Schilman, B., M. Bar-Matthews, A. Almogi-Labin and B. Luz 2001 Global climate instability reflected by Eastern Mediterranean marine records during the late Holocene. *Palaeogeography, Palaeoclimatology, Palaeoecology* 171: 157–76.

Signor, P.W., and J.H. Lipps 1982 Sampling bias, gradual extinction patterns and catastrophes in the fossil record. In R.T. Silver and P.H. Schultz (eds), *Geological Implications of Impacts of Large Asteroids and Comets on the Earth.* Geological Society of America Special Paper 190: 353–71. Boulder, CO: Geological Society of America.

Simmons, A.H. 1999 *Faunal Extinction in an Island Society: Pygmy Hippopotamus Hunters of Cyprus.* Dordrecht and Boston: Kluwer Academic/Plenum.

Tuggle, H.D., and M. Spriggs 2000 The age of the Bellows Dune site O18, O'ahu, Hawai'i, and the antiquity of Hawaiian colonisation. *Asian Perspectives* 39: 165–88.

Tykot, R.H. 1996 Obsidian procurement and distribution in the central and western Mediterranean. *Journal of Mediterranean Archaeology* 9: 39–82.

Van Strydonck, M., M. Boudin and A. Ervynck 2002a Stable isotopes (13C and 15N) and diet: animal and human bone collagen from prehistoric sites on Mallorca, Menorca and Formentera (Balearic Islands, Spain). In W.H. Waldren and J. Ensenyat (eds), *World Islands in Prehistory. International Insular Investigations. V Deià Conference of Prehistory (September 13–18, 2001).* British Archaeological Reports International Series 1095: 189–97. Oxford: British Archaeological Reports.

Van Strydonck, M., M. Boudin and A. Ervynck 2005 Humans and *Myotragus*: the issue of sample integrity in radiocarbon dating. In J.A. Alcover and P. Bover (eds), *International Symposium. Insular Vertebrate Evolution. The Palaeontological Approach (September 16–19, 2003, Mallorca).* Monografies de la Societat d'Història Natural de les Balears 12: 369–76. Palma: Societat d'Història Natural de les Balears.

Van Strydonck, M., M. Landrie, M. Boudin, P.M. Grootes, M.-J. Nadeau, R. Sparks and E. Keppens 2002b *Royal Institute Cultural Heritage Radiocarbon Dates* 18. Brussels: Institut Royal du Patrimoine Artistique.

Vigne, J.-D., and N. Desse-Berset 1995 The exploitation of animal resources in the Mediterranean Islands during the Pre-Neolithic: the example of Corsica. In A. Fischer (ed.), *Man and Sea in the Mesolithic*, 309–18. Oxford: Oxbow Books.

Waldren, W.H. 1982 *Balearic Prehistoric Ecology and Culture. The Excavation of Certain Caves, Rock Shelters and Settlements.* British Archaeological Reports International Series 149. Oxford: British Archaeological Reports.

—— 1984 Chalcolithic settlement and beaker connections in the Balearic islands. In W.H. Waldren, R. Chapman, J. Lewthwaite and R. Kennard (eds), *The Deya Conference of Prehistory. Early Settlement in the Western Mediterranean Islands and their Peripheral Areas.* British Archaeological Reports International Series 229: 911–65. Oxford: British Archaeological Reports.

—— 1987 A Balearic Beaker model. Ferrandell-Oleza, Valldemossa, Mallorca. In W.H. Waldren and R. Kennard (eds), *Bell Beakers of the Western Mediterranean. Definition, Interpretation, Theory and New Site Data. The Oxford International*

Conference 1986. British Archaeological Reports International Series 331: 207–55. Oxford: British Archaeological Reports.

Waldren, W.H. 2001 A new megalithic dolmen from the Balearic island of Mallorca: its radiocarbon dating and artefacts. *Oxford Journal of Archaeology* 20: 241–62.

—— 2002 A case history: evidence of ancient animal, water and land management, exploitation and depletion, Son Oleza Chalcolithic Old Settlement, Valldemossa, Mallorca, Baleares, Spain. In W.H. Waldren and J. Ensenyat (eds), *World Islands in Prehistory. International Insular Investigations. V Deià Conference of Prehistory (September 13–18, 2001)*. British Archaeological Reports International Series 1095: 301–11. Oxford: British Archaeological Reports.

Zilhâo, J. 2001 Radiocarbon evidence for maritime pioneer colonisation at the origins of farming in west Mediterranean Europe. *Proceedings of the National Academy of Sciences of the USA* 98: 14180–5.

5

SOCIAL IDENTITIES, MATERIALITY AND CONNECTIVITY IN EARLY BRONZE AGE CRETE

*Marina Gkiasta**

Introduction

Studying the social has been the primary goal of the human sciences, which have long approached person and society from a variety of viewpoints, all trying to understand how and why humans function, evolve and form their social reality. Each discipline has followed its own trajectory, but there has also been a continuous interchange of diverse theories and viewpoints. The achievements of the social sciences throughout the last century have naturally influenced archaeological interpretation, which has borrowed theoretical schemes from sociology, anthropology, history and geography, shifting stance according to fashionable theories (Gkiasta 2008: chapter 1). A common characteristic in most approaches is the emphasis on general models, an effort to ease our anxiety over what society is and by extension what humans are, in effect social beings. The importance of acknowledging culture-specific factors has of course been stressed, while the traditional conflict between focus on either the social or the personal has been eased (Maisonneuve 1973; Gkiastas 2008). A psycho-sociological perspective emphasises the inseparable relationship between the two: it combines notions from ethnology, sociology and psychology and has developed a relevant language and terminology – e.g. interaction, communication, role and influence instead of class, rules, values (sociological) or motives and identification (psychological).

Archaeology stands to benefit much from such a perspective. Although archaeological data admittedly do not consist of living human beings, but of material remains that represent conscious or unconscious human practices and which are even harder to decipher, a bottom-up approach that pays respect to social identities allows better insights into social constructions and embraces a potential of differentiation as well as

* This paper results from my participation in the *Material Connections* project, directed by Bernard Knapp and Peter van Dommelen, to whom I owe many thanks for encouragement and feedback. Many thanks also to my brother, Dr I. Gkiastas, for stimulating discussion and my colleagues A. Sarpaki, V. Lipa and S. Dobson for their willingness to assist in various ways.

the possibility of broader schemes of explanation. Social practices, present or past, hide human actions, interactions, beliefs, emotions – in other words a complex frame of relationships and identifications that construct the social. Because my own interest lies in raising questions and suggesting possible frameworks of interpretation that might enlighten social dynamics on prehistoric Crete, I undertake a study of the material record that goes beyond description and identification of large social schemes and seeks to uncover the fine social lines that hold the social framework together, and that operate at multiple levels, starting from the construction of personal and social identity.

This chapter considers the meaning of social identity and how it is linked to materiality and the landscape; it proceeds with an overview of the Early Bronze Age archaeological record, looking for material signatures that can reveal processes of social identity construction.

Studying identity

Many sociologists and psychologists have studied identity and the processes of its formation, stressing its emergence and development through mechanisms of social incorporation (Codol 1984; Tap 1988). Freud (1921) discussed personality as structured through a series of identifications, and Mead (1934) noted that through social interaction people see themselves from the view of the 'general other' with which they identify themselves. People evolve with society in a way that makes it impossible to separate one from the other. It is through social interactions that humans construct their dynamic identity or identities: they adopt roles, they establish their status, they experience being part of a group or differing from another group and they participate in symbolic practices that form part of their specific social world perception. Identity can thus be viewed as the node between the personal and the social. Groups are the living space of persons, whose interactions see the emergence of 'rules' or of communal prototypes (Durkheim 1895), which in turn strengthen the coherence and effective function of the group (Sherif 1936a, b).

To derive and maintain a distinct social identity is a primary goal of the person. Sociological research has shown that commitment to a distinctive social identity may override people's concern with deriving high status or positive self-esteem from their group membership (Ellemers *et al.* 1999: 2); studying social identity therefore cannot be restricted only to elite manifestations. The investigation of social identity and self-categorisation may allow better insights into which behaviours and attitudes are seen as the values and norms of the group, depending on social context. It is through self-categorisation and the adoption of a salient social identity that people redefine themselves according to membership in a shared social category and its associated prototypes (Turner 1984: 528), in a process from individual to collective behaviour.

There are two further points in addition to the individual's dependence on the group: inter-group relations, including conflict, and dynamics of change. It has been advocated that we are not born with a specific identity, but that we build our multiple identities within the specific social networks we embrace throughout our lives. Since identity depends on the image that our social environment expects from us, changing social environments will have an effect on our identity/ies, which should thus be seen as potentially changeable. Self-categorisation is a dynamic process, content dependent (Turner 1999:13), and identity is the self-prototype of belonging to or differing from a group. Social categorisation into distinct groups, however, triggers behaviour of in-group favouritism and inter-group discrimination and competition. When different groups meet and identities are called into question, people tend to emphasise their own identity in order to claim the social position with which they identify themselves. Thus, group contact tends to result in the reinforcement of group identity, as in-group bias is a common strategy to achieve positive social identity. An inter-group approach to social conflict is not new (Sherif 1967), but except for inter-group competition and the reinforcement of specific identities, contact situations among groups can also result in new identities through the constant negotiation between different prototypes, as people will tend to adjust their identities to their changing social environment.

Based on the above, I believe that in order to understand how prehistoric society was structured we need to study communities at various scales and through their various functions. In other words we need to identify groups, their social practices and interrelationships through material remains and landscape signatures. Given that multiple groups operated in prehistoric Crete, it is important to look at their relations and natural competition, and to study community identity in relation to materiality, the landscape, mode of living and developed social practices.

Materiality and social identity

Even though objects have traditionally been the focus of attention in archaeology, their meaning has been rather controversial, often equated with cultural categories. The social significance of material objects, however, lies in the conscious decisions around their production, use or elimination, in their meaning as linked to social practices and social relations. People build emotional and cognitive relationships with objects; they use them to express symbolic meanings, to signify identities, relationships and perceptions. Materiality may be understood as the expression of social identity and group behaviour through the use of specific objects and related social practices. The significance of the social biography of objects in illuminating fine webs of social networks and relationships has been formally acknowledged (Meskell 2005). Through object diasporas we can trace people's movements and encounters and approach the experience of 'meeting the other' whether in a colonial, migratory or other environment of socio-economic and ideological encounter. There are numerous opportunities for people of different backgrounds to meet, since the most influential occasions of mobility relate to everyday social actions, which support systems of subsistence, ideological position and social existence. Especially relevant to Crete and taking advantage of a rich ethnographic record, we can discern numerous mobile groups (craftsmen, shepherds, traders) and opportunities for mobility (religious festivals, subsistence factors, social competition).

Landscape identities: insularity versus connectivity

The island of Crete constitutes a unique landscape for the study of communities and social identity. The coexistence of local differentiation and a certain uniformity in cultural production and ideological expression have been quite intense historically, depending on the intensity of a landscape that at the same time promotes insularity and connectivity. Insularity operates at two levels. It is the result of Crete being an island and, indeed, quite distant from other islands and coasts, but also large enough to create and preserve its own trajectory of socio-cultural developments. Access to the island depends on winds and coastal formations, and neither are as sailing-friendly as one would expect, even today. On the local scale, it is a very mountainous island (Figures 5.1 and 5.2) with a broken landscape of at least 20 peaks over 2200 m, numerous gorges and other land-dividing features (Rackham and Moody 1996), all of which encourage regional developments and variation – in other words, a landscape conducive to the formation of quite coherent groups that feel their differentiation in relation to others. People create very strong bonds with their landscape, and even today Cretans identify themselves first on the basis of the place they come from; all other social identities (being Cretan, Greek, a professional, etc.) come afterwards. It is indeed within a specific landscape that the group adopts modes of living and material expression, forms perceptions of existence, expresses metaphysical concerns or even copes with intra- and inter-group rivalries.

Beyond its insular characteristics, however, Crete offers good opportunities for groups to connect, either by sea or through land routes and peak views. Regionalism

Figure 5.1   Crete: a mountainous island. View across Mirabello Bay. Photo by Bernard Knapp.

Figure 5.2   View of Mount Ida (2456 m a.s.l.) in the Psiloritis mountains of central Crete.

is attested in almost all classes of material and all kinds of relationships between people and the landscape; nonetheless we note a significant diversity of objects, materials and ideas moving over sea and land routes that change over time depending on social relations. This can only reflect a diversity of contacts and of reasons for contact – and of course the conscious choices behind them. The physicality of the landscape plays an important role in insularity and connectivity. The coastal areas, for example, seem to develop styles of pottery and other material categories faster than upland areas, which is a diachronic phenomenon since movement and hence cultural exchange is harder within the mountains of inland Crete. Both insularity and connectivity, however, are more often than not socially constructed. For example, isolated and defensible locations reflect conscious choices relative to historical contingencies and social needs, whereas in other cases groups occupy a much more connected physical and social landscape. As the space of the symbolic investment of society, landscape is partly observable through materiality and is an active agent in the construction, perpetuation and change of social identity. Social relations in Crete, inseparable from their physical and symbolic landscape, represent the convergence between two antithetical points, both in the present and in the past: the apparent idiosyncrasy of regional groups and their participation in larger ideological groups.

Social identities and relations in Early Bronze Age Crete

Since social identity may be represented through materiality and in the construction of social landscapes, these factors should be studied in terms of the regional diversity of social relations seen in burials, rituals and settlements, and in environmental and economic relationships. In this section, aspects of materiality are considered as evidence of social representation that reveal identities relative to regional idiosyncrasies and contact situations. Prepalatial burials constitute the greater part of material evidence that informs us about social practices. Tomb architecture, as well as patterns of offerings and rituals, attest to a characteristic declaration of regional identity, but at the same time similarities in perceptions, practices and material objects show a growing connectivity among communities and their participation in common ideological structures (Figure 5.3).

In the initial stages of the Early Bronze Age we note the coexistence of Neolithic traditions (cave burials) with new, distinct burial practices, which may be indicative of group differentiation and coherence. In eastern Crete, the large EM I–IIa cemetery of Hagia Photia (Davaras and Betancourt 2004) consists of single inhumation burials in Cycladic-type tombs (Figure 5.4). Burial customs and the large quantity of 'Cycladica' as well as 'Minoan' materials and objects from a wider area have led to intense discussions over the ethnicity of the community (Doumas 1976; Zois 1998; Day *et al.* 2000). What seems evident is that a large group of people who appear to have strong affiliations with the sea and the Cyclades but who also interact widely with the interior of the island constructed their community identity based on their mode of living and their contact with other communities, and identified themselves as a group distinct from others through their living practices (even if now observable only through their mortuary practices). Other communities in the east buried their dead in enclosures that included multiple burials over long periods of time. Group coherence is represented by the placement of bones and associated

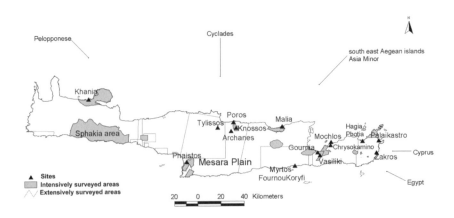

Figure 5.3 Map of Crete showing the location of study areas and sites discussed.

offerings in ossuaries, a practice that perhaps relates to the process of transition from being a member of the community to entering the realm of the ancestors. This tradition, observed typically at Palaikastro (EM IA–MM IIA), Gournia (EM II–MM), Malia (EM I IA–MM) and Zakros (MM IA – see Table 5.1 for dates and terms), together with offerings from other areas within and beyond the island, informs us about connectivity among communities at an inter- and trans-regional scale.

At Mochlos, tombs came in the form of roofed built chambers with an entrance closed by standing slabs; these are commonly known as house tombs (Soles 1992). Graves received multiple burials and a slab-paved courtyard seems to relate to communal burial practices and an attention to the monumentality of mortuary ground. Mochlos also held one of the three largest hoards of gold in the Aegean at the time (the other two are from Poliochni and Troy). Precious materials and objects reveal as much about the acquisition of wealth and the participation in networks of materials and technologies exchanged or established over great distances as they do about the participation in practices that underline intra- and inter-group social identity. Social identity, however, does not seem to relate as much to intra-group wealth differentiation and the rise of an elite (Soles 1988; 1992) as it does to a sense of a rather homogeneous social group, wherein ceremonial activity and display reflect social values supported by the group as community (Vavouranakis 2007).

The Mesara (plain) in southern Crete (Figure 5.5) represents an impressive burial landscape with *tholos* tombs (Figures 5.6 and 5.7), which was in use from the end of the Neolithic or beginning of the Early Bronze Age (e.g. Moni Odigitrias). They contain multiple burials and are thought to have fulfilled an important role as territorial markers for the respective communities (Murphy 1998; Vavouranakis 2007). Minoan *tholoi* are often reinforced through the addition of annex-rooms and paved areas where drinking and eating rituals may have been carried out; there is a spatial specification and a growing importance of mortuary rituals. Animal bones, some chopped and burned, drinking cups, pottery and other implements associated with drinking and feasting, annexes and paved areas for practices involving many people (Branigan 1991; 1993) inform us about the use of space for the living, as it is through group practices that collective memory and group identities are formed, altered or maintained (Halbwachs 1950). The social significance of mortuary rituals for the

Table 5.1 Minoan chronology (after Dickinson 1994)

Chronology		Abbreviations	
EM I:	3300–2900 BC	EM	Early Minoan
EM IIA:	2900–2550 BC	MM	Middle Minoan
EM IIB:	2550–2300 BC	LM	Late Minoan
EM III/MM IA:	2300–1900 BC	Prepalatial	EM I–MM IA
MM IB/IIA–MM IIB/IIIA:	1900–1700 BC	Palatial	MM IB–LM IB
MM IIIB:	1700–1600 BC		

Figure 5.4 Partial view of the Hagia Photia cemetery.

Figure 5.5 View of the Mesara plain in central Crete.

Figure 5.6   Remains of one of the *tholos* tombs near Platanos (EM II–MM II).

Figure 5.7   Remains of a *tholos* tomb with associated rectangular side rooms near Apesokari (EM III–MM I).

living members of the group is particularly evident in feasting and drinking practices (Hamilakis 1998; Hitchcock *et al.* 2008). After death, however, the manipulation of bones (Branigan 1987), social display through rare and precious objects and materials, the continuous rearrangement of burial space and the growing intensification of burial practices involving large numbers of people show a complex social reality where people constantly negotiate their identities. Mortuary ceremonies, whether they represented cycles of death and life in nature (Branigan 1993) or marked the passage of the dead members of the community to the world of the ancestors (Murphy 1998), reinforced group identity and functioned as an arena of in-group social identity through mechanisms of sensory experience and memory production (Hamilakis 1998).

Overall, we observe certain differences in mortuary architecture, practices and patterns of offerings that represent regional idiosyncrasies and value systems relevant to intra-group identity. Group identity seems to have been expressed through the construction of monumental mortuary landscapes, and the possible use of cemeteries at Zakros, Palaikastro and Mochlos as navigation landmarks (Vavouranakis 2007) also implies the communities' declaration of a bond with their land over great distances. Ossuaries in the burial enclosures of eastern Crete and the Mesara *tholoi*, as well as the unique case of Myrtos-Pyrgos, where hundreds of skulls have been found in two ossuaries, are closely linked with designated areas and objects of ritual ceremonies; they seem to provide testimony of the bonds that the living maintained with their ancestors and their past. The differential preference of offerings signifies contact networks as well as a certain variability in the social importance of objects among different communities. There are, however, several points where regional identities converge. For example, a common metaphysical ideology relating to fertility may be seen in the figurine-like rhyta found in Mochlos, Myrtos-Fournou Koryfi, Zakros and Malia (Zois 1998) and in cult objects such as *kernoi*; in cult rooms and annexes related to drinking and feasting; in the monumentality of burial ground and the courtyards and paved areas where many people gathered for mortuary rituals. The wide circulation of pottery and other objects of specific origin across the island and beyond shows a level of connectivity that increased throughout the Early Bronze Age, and would have supported the development of island-wide ideologies. Furthermore, the coexistence of different burial types, most characteristically in the case of Archanes, may testify to the physical coexistence of members of different regional communities, whose identities were in constant negotiation.

Mortuary evidence may be representative of both intra-group and inter-group relations. The growing monumentality of burial grounds and the intensification of mortuary rituals at the end of the prepalatial period may indicate some level of competition among communities (Hamilakis 1998) that sought to reinforce their identity as members of a specific community that bonded with and claimed a specific landscape. Furthermore, examples of amplified rituals in MM IA spread from Mochlos and Chrysolakos-Malia to Archanes and the Mesara *tholoi* (Apesokari, Kamilari, Ayia Kyriaki, Siva, etc.) and may support the argument that some kind of role specialisation was required, a role that elite groups may have used to legitimise ritual power and by extent political power (Murphy 1998). Craft production also must have played an

94

important role in social display attested in ceremonies and rituals; its appropriation by emerging elites is a likely hypothesis (Day and Wilson 2002).

Concerning the materiality of the settlement record and the possibilities it offers to explore social identities, some basic observations may give further insights into the context of social identity construction. Within the limitations of the survey record (Gkiasta 2008: 26–7), we note an increased mobility and expansion of settlement throughout the island at the beginning of the Early Bronze Age. Interpretations favour the existence of different communities settling the landscape in a somewhat dispersed pattern, both on the coast and inland, but nucleated sites also exist, especially in the east. Haggis (2002) argued that the prepalatial landscape demonstrates characteristics of integration, where contacts among communities and links to the environment were multiple and agro-pastoral activities diverse. Given that habitation was continuous in several sites from the Neolithic through prepalatial to palatial times (Knossos, Phaistos, Vasiliki, etc.), and was linked with symbolic codes (e.g. mortuary practices) and material categories that showed no abrupt changes and rather fuzzy time borders, the notion of cultural continuity on the island finds strong support.

In some cases, however, the same site exhibits a clear stratigraphic distinction between Final Neolithic and EM I (e.g. Petras: Zois 1998; Nodarou et al. 2007), while sites such as Hagia Photia, Poros-Katsambas and Nea Roumata-Chania – with a strong Cycladic character – show signs of interaction with and possibly the co-presence of people from different cultural backgrounds. The beginning and the end of the Early Bronze Age are marked by signs of defensibility that point to conflict among communities and possibly newcomers, even though the difficult recognition and interpretation of the EM III material record obscures the reconstruction of a social landscape (Watrous 1994: 717). The northern coastal areas developed bigger towns with a higher degree of connectivity (as seen in evidence of exchange within and beyond the island), while inland areas and the high mountains were inhabited by communities that may have been primarily – but not exclusively – involved in pastoralism. Published excavation data are unfortunately rather poor, but important towns have revealed building structures such as the double-walled houses in Vasiliki, Tylissos, Palaikastro, Phaistos, Mallia and Knossos, often with associated paved court-yards, which should probably be seen as the result of collective efforts covering the social needs of the entire group.

Declared difference is a characteristic indicator of distinct group identities, although the boundaries between such groups can be rather fluid in time and space. Beyond certain social practices, regional communities in Early Bronze Age Crete seem to differentiate themselves through various classes of material representation, pottery being the most important indicator for archaeologists. Ceramic regionalism is quite obvious among different wares (Cycladic-type pottery, Vasiliki ware, Mesara wares, east Cretan wares) whose production seems to have been restricted to specific centres, e.g. in the Isthmus of Ierapetra, or in southern (Mesara) or central Crete (Wilson and Day 1994; Day et al. 1997). Pottery manufacture seems to fall into traditions, seen in characteristic decorative styles such as Vasiliki ware, but also in the close relationship between shapes, techniques and fabrics. The diversity of techniques and fabrics and a quite high level of technical proficiency reveal a significant degree of specialisation in skill, resources and technologies relative to functional needs (Day *et al.* 1997). Divergent pottery styles should be seen as deliberate efforts of communities and workshops to distinguish themselves, not only in an effort to attract consumers, but perhaps also at an artistically, ideologically and socially competitive level. Ceramic data suggest groups of potters who specialise in producing specific wares and who, no doubt, identify themselves socially through their work. Throughout the Early Bronze Age, however, the rather strong regionalism in ceramic production goes hand in hand with the wide distribution of wares across the island (Wilson and Day 1994; Day *et al.* 1997), and thus we can note that potters' identities transcended the borders of their community and reached a trans-regional level.

Beyond pottery, metallurgy enjoys an important position among crafts as a material expression and evidence of social identity, particularly during the Early Bronze Age, since metal technologies may be considered the driving force behind reinforced networks of interregional contacts. That both metals and their technologies were valuable for the people of Early Bronze Age Crete is suggested by sites such as Chrysokamino, which played an important role in interregional connections; it is also indicated by the high standard of craftsmanship recognised in numerous objects (Muhly 2006). Patterns of similarities in shapes and designs, which have allowed speculations over workshops and the spread of materials and/or technologies, need meticulous study if we are to identify their significance in the construction of social identities in Early Bronze Age Crete. The presumed Cycladic source of bronze and silver (Kythnos: Stos-Gale 1998 and Sifnos: Stos-Gale 1985), as well as regional and interregional similarities and differences in metalworking, indicate the participation of Cretan people in an Aegean-wide network of exchange and the growing importance of these new materials in Crete as a means of expressing social identity.

The possibility of studying social identity in relation to metallurgy spreads from the owner of an object to the specialised producer, craftsman and trader. Seals are also a characteristic expression of Cretan art, technology and social representation at the time. They are typically found in the mortuary record, and even though it is difficult to make associations between seals and burial populations, some studies have argued for their use as symbols of status, probably during the owner's life and following that in death (Karytinos 1998; 2000). The amount of labour and technological expertise required, as well as the exotic materials used, reveal their place in society as prestige goods; they are the result of different groups' involvement in the materials' trade, production and circulation, as a symbolic representation embedded in social relations and structures. Based on the available data and current state of research, it seems reasonable to suggest that one of the reasons behind seal acquisition was the desire for social display within and among communities.

Consumption, therefore, particularly as seen in the mortuary record, shows distinct trends and informs us of multiple and diverse movements within and beyond Crete. Even though technologies and objects from elsewhere may be considered as a source of power (Nakou 1995), consumption reveals the conscious choices for contact – or not – among communities and therefore their cultural differences. For example, in the Mesara tombs, contacts with Egypt, the Levant and Syria are particularly evident (Branigan 1988: 139, 179–95). Cycladic pottery, however, is hardly present and the same holds for obsidian (Carter 1998: 72). *Pyxides* (small ceramic boxes) and figurines seem to occur as frequently in the south as in the north, while metal objects from Kythnian copper are even more frequent, and Siphnian silver is used for most silver objects. This factor shows a conscious choice of material exchange best suited for the social needs of the Mesara communities, and in some respects calls into question the view that the south formed just a peripheral zone of Cycladic trade. Even if we assume that their contact with the Cyclades took place only via communities along the northern coast of the island, other areas were certainly not unaware of Cycladic culture and social practices; most likely they chose what objects, ideas and symbols to exchange. The important point here is that people in the Mesara were not so interested in Cycladic material technology (obsidian and pottery), but rather in specific objects with a symbolic connotation such as *pyxides*, figurines and metals. Seals, daggers and exotica from lands south and southeast of Crete are also connected with the display of social identity. Thus, whereas mortuary architecture and practices hint at the display and reinforcement of community identity, offerings are filled with symbolic meaning; their production and deposition relate to social identity, representing social relations and belief systems. Evidently precious materials and sophisticated technologies had a distinct position among objects from foreign lands, even though some figurines might have been less demanding in terms of execution in comparison with elaborate pottery.

Overall, the island seems to have been inhabited by numerous communities that built strong links with their landscape relevant to their subsistence strategies and social needs. These communities had a differential level of connectivity or insularity that accordingly affected group and social identity. In cases where a higher connectivity was promoted depending on geographical, economic and social factors, groups and social identities met and were continuously involved in the construction of a dynamic social reality, with new materials, technologies and social relations contributing to the historical continuum. Although Crete has a spatial, geographical and cultural autonomy, it seems unreasonable to treat the island as a unified entity and deny its regional diversity, which is so apparent even in the present.

Mobility across the landscape: social groups, objects and ideas

The wide distribution of large quantities of pottery and the movement of other classes of material indicate complex socio-economic networks through which communities were interconnected. One way to approach social relations in prehistoric Crete is to look at the diversity of movement in the landscape, which operates at different levels; it may be the mode of living for specific communities or the result of economic relations and ideological exchanges pursued. In Crete, group connectivity operated at two levels: (1) between Cretan and non-Cretan communities and

(2) among intra-island communities that had their distinct position in the island's social arena. But who moved around the island and what kind of social identities were at work?

It is of course mobile objects that inform us about the ideas and identities that moved; however, it is important to imagine the people behind them. A most indicative example is the case of craftsmen. Craft communities have traditionally been rather closed to the outside world, transferring knowledge almost exclusively to their members and sharing a social identity intrinsically linked to their profession and its social meaning. As indicated in historical and ethnographic records, it is quite likely that craftsmen moved (Leondidis 1996), and in the case of potters it makes sense, at least regarding the production of large *pithoi*, as it is certainly much safer and easier to move clay and skill than it is to move pots. Whether potters, builders, artisans in metal, textile or stone, craftsmen have customarily travelled to sell their expertise and products. At the same time there are other people who trade and exchange materials and finished products; pots in particular were traded for their contents. In all cases, we learn what was considered important to move. There are also other groups whose mobility is not so visible in the material record, but who were nonetheless involved in transferring social codes. Whereas in some cases it is the exchange of materials and objects that triggers people's connections, the establishment and expansion of social relations may also be involved. A good example to support this suggestion is the social behaviour of pastoral communities in Crete, which are by default mobile and seek to establish rights of passage and allies through intermarriage and baptisms. Beyond artisans, traders and pastoralists, mobile communities might also consist of people who were charcoal makers, musicians, textile and basket specialists, woodsmen or ship-builders.

Regarding extra-island connectivity, from the beginning of the Early Bronze Age the spread of Cycladic objects attests to established contacts between Cretan and Cycladic people who, regardless of their ethnicity, were involved in the trade of obsidian, copper and silver ores, objects and technologies. Overseas mobility and activity seem to have been more vigorous in the north of the island, a fact that may relate to the circulation of metal and related technologies through the southern Aegean at the time. Cycladic objects have been found across Crete (Poros Katsambas, Pyrgos Cave, Mochlos, Petras). The case of Hagia Photia, however, seems unique, as many objects are definitely of Cycladic provenance and it seems that the community moved large quantities of pottery from elsewhere (Cyclades and central Crete) as well as Cycladic metals and stone objects (Day *et al.* 1998). The available evidence does not support the view that Cycladic exotica were used simply as signs of prestige by the Hagia Photia community; rather they seem to have been representative of the community's identity. The simultaneous use of material culture from distinct cultural horizons makes Hagia Photia a characteristic case of overlapping material culture. Instead of trying to explain this as a result of diffusionism, or stylistic influences in indigenous development, we could also think of the possible co-presence of people from different ethnic and cultural backgrounds, who through interaction formulated a distinctive, new group identity.

Towards the end of the prepalatial period, Crete seems to have become the centre of intense mobility in south Aegean. The MM IA material record reveals that a substantial quantity of oriental objects and Cretan pottery reached Cyprus at the same time (Watrous 1994, 1998). Based on imports and imitations, Crete's external contacts seem to have been oriented towards the southeastern Mediterranean (southeast Aegean, Cyprus, Egypt) and southwestern Aegean (Kythera, southern and eastern Peloponnesos) in antithetical terms. That is, whereas Egypt and the Orient seem to have a strong influence on Cretan materiality and ideology, the Greek islands and the Peloponnesos import and imitate Cretan shapes related to social practices and ideology, such as drinking cups and pouring vessels (Broodbank 2000: 354–5). At the same time, the apparent lack of contacts between Crete and the Cyclades is quite characteristic. This fact, combined with the different contact routes pursued by Cretan-centred and Cycladic-centred trade, as well as evidence for defensible sites at both ends at this time, may be seen as the result of competition between Cretan and Cycladic communities (Broodbank 2000: 359–61).

In general, we can observe distinctive regional identities and increasing mobility between these communities, both of which become more intense towards the end of the Early Bronze Age. In turn, the Middle Bronze Age social landscape appears to have been more uniform ideologically, but more intense and hierarchical with respect to the social relations involved. In MM IA, mortuary landscapes were reinforced and, at a time when several settlements were destroyed or abandoned, they might have been used to emphasise lineage and historical identities as well as land claims (Haggis 1999; Vavouranakis 2007). Social conflict may be viewed in the apparent – but not always evident – defensibility of settlements (Kouphota, Malia, Palaikastro, Katalymata, Myrtos-Pyrgos), and a new ritual landscape makes its appearance with the 'peak sanctuaries' (Kyriakidis 2005). The circulation of seals, which are linked with personal display, was expanded and the increased use of *pithoi* in burials seems to have been related to some sort of differentiation within the group. Perhaps Broodbank's (2000: 357) dendritic pattern concerning later palatial trade and the close associations with Egypt should be seen in the light of the growing competition among Cretan and Cycladic communities throughout the Early Bronze Age. Competition, however, should not be seen in terms of culture but rather at the level of communities, which dynamically encompass, alter and produce cultural traits through connectivity and social relations.

People move, meet, exchange materials, technologies and objects, and with them symbolic ideas and ideologies; they materialise new social landscapes that embed memory and social meaning, and they constantly negotiate their social identities. The diversity of movement, which cannot be explained by simple factors such as proximity, reflects conscious choices made to meet needs imposed by people's social reality, which in turn is constantly restructured through inter-group connectivity. Although the multiplicity of groups that interconnect for different reasons through various land and sea routes is evident, we need to do further research into such movements if we are to understand the continuous restructuring of social landscapes, whose continuum actually structures history.

Conclusion

Crete, big enough to support idiosyncratic natural and cultural developments, is characterised by its distinctive position in the middle of the southeast Mediterranean basin. It has been a place of focus and trans-regional meetings, a natural and cultural crossroads, since prehistoric times. Unique as it may be, however, no understanding of its socio-historical trajectory can be achieved unless considered within the wider interaction spheres of the region. Discrete islands are not necessarily ideal analytical units; we should instead consider them by looking at the community level and by studying intra-island diversity as well as inter-island and trans-regional relationships. In the Early Bronze Age we can see emerging regional trajectories with the formation and production of discrete styles in material expression, particularly in pottery and mortuary architecture. Communities seem to have developed distinct identities and a close bonding with their landscape (communal burials, ancestor cults, specific crafts and lifestyle). Nonetheless we can see the convergence of different groups in island-wide ideologies, for example in mortuary rituals and the use of open spaces and designated areas for large groups.

The evidence from prepalatial Crete reveals a certain degree of specialisation and may be seen as a means to define social identity within 'a continuum of technological practice and economic intensification' (Day *et al.* 1997: 275). Specialisation is usually seen as an aspect of complex societies. However, contrary to views that see social complexity as a constituent of palatial society in contrast with the simpler level of social organisation based on the household economy in the Early Bronze Age (Cherry 1983), society should not be seen as a static set of social relations corresponding to artificial chronological periods, but rather as a part of dynamic progress and change. It seems unreasonable to study prepalatial Crete only by comparing it with the obscure notion of 'social complexity' during palatial times; palatial social structure is neither an event, nor an evolution – it is simply part of a social and historical continuum. Heterogeneity and inequality are constituents of social reality, and differences between the two artificial chronological categories and their respective societies may be differences more of degree than of kind (Hamilakis 2002 :15). Minoan societies are not homogenous and cannot be understood through descriptions based on ethnic or cultural identity (Knapp 1998), or through simple evolutionary frameworks of social development. If we understood better all aspects of the prepalatial Early Bronze Age, the assumed social phenomena of the palatial periods would appear as a natural consequence.

To conclude, I believe it is important to appreciate the significance of the multiplicity of scales within which social dynamics evolved on prehistoric Crete. From very strong local identities and major social and material differences, to island-wide ideologies and identities, one thing is certain: social identity on Crete has always formed part of a dynamic negotiation among people, landscapes and diverse social contexts. Within the conceptual framework explored here, namely studying social and ideological practices, modes of living, material expressions and the role of the landscape in our search for social identity, we may come to understand prehistoric societies much better. We need to study communities at various scales and in the context of various functions; in other words we need to identify groups, their social practices and interrelationships through material remains and landscape signatures. It is extremely difficult to uncover social beliefs and symbolic codes of the past, which are reflected in rules, history and myth as the cultural and psychological investment of society (Lévi-Strauss 1950). Archaeological data are certainly not convenient for all such profound psycho-sociological explorations. We have only fragmentary data at our disposal; we lack organised and complete records of archaeological data that would promote the investigation of the above themes; and we need to find ways of correlating semantic systems with empirical data in order to formulate hypotheses. Still, we can try to approach past social identities by exploring the formation and coherence of groups of different size and kind and their dynamic changes through social interactions. We can look for people and socio-cultural prototypes for intra- and inter-group relationships of various kinds (based on age, sex, economy, group coherence, beliefs, symbolic practices, ideology). We should be examining how material culture was used to express, maintain or alter social identities, and we should be considering the meaning of people's specific choices in using objects and technologies, the evidence for times of intense socio-cultural encounters and their implications in social construction.

A social archaeology dictates a change of focus from the intense 'hyper-specialisation' that characterises the discipline, especially in Aegean and southeast Mediterranean archaeologies (Cherry 2004), and the need to ask new questions of our material based on a better understanding of social construction. It is important to study objects in social terms and to trace their distributions, in order to explore patterns of technologies, social practices and belief systems that will illuminate contact situations and their role in the construction of social (religious, political, economic, etc.) realities. People are no doubt active social agents and not passive representatives of a specific social reality; as a consequence, investigating the rich and diverse social landscape of a given time rather than ascribing it predefined attributes should certainly provide much better insight into past societies.

References

Branigan, K. 1987 Ritual interference with human bones in the Mesara tholoi. In R. Laffineur (ed.), *Thanatos: Les Coutumes Funéraires en Egée de l'Age du Bronze. Actes du Colloque de Liège, 21–23 Avril 1986.* Aegaeum 1: 43–50. Liège: Université de Liège.

—— 1988 *Pre-Palatial. The Foundations of Palatial Crete. A Survey of Crete in the Early Bronze Age.* Amsterdam: Adolf M. Hakkert.

—— 1991 Funerary ritual and social cohesion in Early Bronze Age Crete. *Journal of Mediterranean Studies* 1: 183–92.

—— 1993 *Dancing with Death: Life and Death in Southern Crete c. 3000–2000 BC.* Amsterdam: Adolf M. Hakkert.

Broodbank, C. 2000 *An Island Archaeology of the Early Cyclades.* Cambridge: Cambridge University Press.

Carter, T. 1998 Reverberations of the international spirit: thoughts upon 'Cycladic' in the Mesara. In K. Branigan (ed.), *Cemetery and Society in the Aegean Bronze Age*. Sheffield Studies in Aegean Archaeology 1: 59–77. Sheffield: Sheffield Academic Press.

Cherry, J.F. 1983 Evolution, revolution and the origins of complex society in Minoan Crete. In O. Krzyszkowska and L. Nixon (eds), *Minoan Society: Proceedings of the Cambridge Colloquium 1981*, 23–32. Bristol: Bristol Classical Press.

—— 2004 Cyprus, the Mediterranean, and survey: current issues and future trends. In M. Iakovou (ed.), *Archaeological Field Survey in Cyprus: Past History, Future Potentials*. British School at Athens Studies 11: 23–35. London: The British School at Athens.

Codol, J.P. 1984 Social differentiation and non-differentiation. In H. Tajfel (ed.), *The Social Dimension: European Developments in Social Psychology*, vol. 1, 314–37. Cambridge: Cambridge University Press.

Davaras, C., and Ph. Betancourt 2004 *The Hagia Photia Cemetery* I: *The Tomb Groups and Architecture*. Prehistory Monographs 14. Philadelphia: INSTAP Academic Press.

Day, P.M., and D.E. Wilson 2002 Landscapes of memory, craft and power in pre-palatial and proto-palatial Knossos. In Y. Hamilakis (ed.), *Labyrinth Revisited: Rethinking 'Minoan' Archaeology*, 143–66. Oxford: Oxbow Books.

Day, P.M., D.E. Wilson and E. Kiriatzi 1997 Reassessing specialization in prepalatial Cretan ceramic production. In R. Laffineur, and Ph. P. Betancourt (eds), *TEXNH: Craftsmen, Craftswomen and Craftsmanship in the Aegean Bronze Age: Proceedings of the 6th International Aegean Conference, 18–21 April 1996*. Aegaeum 16: 275–89. Liège: Université de Liège.

—— 1998 Pots, labels and people: burying ethnicity in the cemetery at Aghia Photia, Siteias. In K. Branigan (ed.), *Cemetery and Society in the Aegean Bronze Age*. Sheffield Studies in Aegean Archaeology 1: 133–49. Sheffield: Sheffield Academic Press.

Day, P.M., D.E. Wilson, E. Kyriatzi and L. Joyner 2000 Η κεραμική από το ΠΜ Ι νεκροταφείο στην Αγία Φωτιά Σητείας: Τοπική ή εισηγμένη; *Πεπραγμένα Η' Διεθνούς Κρητολογικού Συνεδρίου*, vol. Α1, 341–53. Heraklion: Εταιρεία Κρητικών Ιστορικών Μελετών.

Dickinson, O. 1994 *The Aegean Bronze Age*. Cambridge: Cambridge University Press.

Doumas, C. 1976 Προϊστορικοί Κυκλαδίτες στην Κρήτη. *Αρχαιολογικά Ανάλεκτα εξ Αθηνών* 9: 69–80.

Durkheim, E. 1895 *Règles de la Méthode Sociologique*. Paris: Presses Universitaires de France.

Ellemers, N., R. Spears and B. Doosje 1999 Introduction. In N. Ellemers, R. Spears and B. Doosje (eds), *Social Identity*, 1–5. Oxford: Blackwell.

Freud, S. 1921 [1994] *Group Psychology and the Analysis of the Ego* (Greek translation K. Trikerioti). Athens: Epikouros.

Gkiasta, M. 2008 *The Historiography of Landscape Research in Crete*. Archaeological Studies Leiden University 16. Leiden: Leiden University Press.

Gkiastas, I. 2008 Για μια κλινική του κοινωνικού δεσμού. *Διάλογος Ψυχανάλυσης και Κοινωνικού δεσμού*: Επιστημονικό Συνέδριο, *Αθήνα 11–12 Απριλίου 2008*. Athens: Εταιρεία Σπουδών Σχολών Μωραΐτη.

Haggis, D. 1999 Staple finance, peak sanctuaries, and economic complexity in late prepalatial Crete. In A. Chaniotis (ed.), *From Minoan Farmers to Roman Traders: Sidelights on the Economy of Ancient Crete*, 53–85. Stuttgart: Franz Steiner Verlag.

2002 Integration and complexity in the late prepalatial period. In Y. Hamilakis (ed.), *Labyrinth Revisited: Rethinking 'Minoan' Archaeology*, 121–42. Oxford: Oxbow Books.

Halbwachs, M. 1950 *La Mémoire Collective*. Paris: Presses Universitaires de France.

Hamilakis, Y. 1998 Eating the dead: mortuary feasting and the politics of memory in Aegean Bronze Age societies. In K. Branigan (ed.), *Cemetery and Society in the Aegean Bronze Age*. Sheffield Studies in Aegean Archaeology 1: 115–32. Sheffield: Sheffield Academic Press.

—— 2002 What future for the 'Minoan' past? Re-thinking Minoan archaeology. In Y. Hamilakis (ed.), *Labyrinth Revisited: Rethinking 'Minoan' Archaeology*, 2–28. Oxford: Oxbow Books.

Hitchcock, L.A., R. Laffineur and J. Crowley (eds.) 2008 *DAIS. The Aegean Feast. Proceedings of the 12th International Aegean Conference, University of Melbourne, Centre for Classics and Archaeology, 25–29 March 2008*. Aegaeum 29.Liège, Austin, Texas: Université de Liège, University of Texas at Austin.

Karytinos, A. 1998 Sealstones in cemeteries: a display of social status? In K. Branigan, (ed.), *Cemetery and Society in the Aegean Bronze Age*. Sheffield Studies in Aegean Archaeology 1: 78–86. Sheffield: Sheffield Academic Press.

—— 2000 The stylistic development of seals from Archanes-Phourni throughout the prepalatial period – style and social meaning. In W. Müller (ed.), *Minoisch-mykenische Glyptik: Stil, Ikonographie, Funktion*. Corpus der Minoischen und Mykenischen Siegel Beiheft 6: 123–34. Berlin: Mann.

Knapp, A.B. 1998 Mediterranean Bronze Age trade: distance, power and place. In E.H. Cline and D. Harris-Cline (eds), *The Aegean and the Orient in the Second Millennium: Proceedings of the 50th Anniversary Symposium, Cincinnati, 18–20 April 1997*. Aegaeum 18: 193–207. Liège: Université de Liège; Austin: University of Texas at Austin.

Kyriakidis, E. 2005 *Ritual in the Bronze Age Aegean. The Minoan Peak Sanctuaries*. London: Duckworth.

Leondidis, A. 1996 Αγγειοπλαστικά κέντρα και περιοδεύοντες τεχνίτες. Η περίπτωση των Μαργαριτών Μυλοποτάμου Ρεθύμνης. *Κεραμικά εργαστήρια στην Κρήτη από την Αρχαιότητα ως Σήμερα: Πρακτικά ημερίδας, Μαργαρίτες 30 Σεπτεμβρίου 1995*, 71–7. Rethimnon: Ιστορική Λαογραφική Εταιρεία Ρεθύμνης.

Lévi-Strauss, C. 1950 [2004] Introduction à l'œuvre de Marcel Mauss. In M. Mauss, *Sociology and Anthropology* (Greek translation Th. Paradellis), 11–61. Athens: Ekdoseis tou eikostou protou.

Maisonneuve, J. 1973 [2001] *Introduction à la Psychosociologie* (Greek translation N. Christakis). Athens: Typothito-Y. Dardanos Press.

Mead, G.H. 1934 *Mind, Self and Society*. Chicago: University of Chicago Press.

Meskell, L. (ed.) 2005 *Archaeologies of Materiality*. Blackwell: Oxford.

Muhly, J.D. 2006 Chrysokamino in the history of early metallurgy. In Ph. Betancourt (ed.), *The Chrysokamino Metallurgy Workshop and its Territory*. Hesperia Supplement 36: 155–77. Princeton: American School of Classical Studies at Athens.

Murphy, J. 1998 Ideology, rites, and rituals: a view of prepalatial Minoan tholoi. In K. Branigan (ed.) *Cemetery and Society in the Aegean Bronze Age*. Sheffield Studies in Aegean Archaeology 1: 27–40. Sheffield: Sheffield Academic Press.

Nakou, G. 1995 The cutting edge: a new look at early Aegean metallurgy. *Journal of Mediterranean Archaeology* 8.2: 1–32.

Nodarou, E., I. Iliopoulos and Y. Papadatos From the Neolithic to the Early Bronze Age: provenance and technology of early ceramics from Sitia, east Crete. Poster. EGU General Assembly 2007. *Geophysical Research Abstracts* 9. Available at: http://www.cosis.net/abstracts/EGU2007/11428/EGU2007-J-11428.pdf.

Rackham, O., and J. Moody *The Making of the Cretan Landscape*. Manchester: University of Manchester Press.

Sherif, M. 1936a Influence du groupe sur la formation des normes et des attitudes. In A. Levy (ed.), *Psychologie Sociale: Textes Fondamentaux Anglais et Américains*, vol. 2, 222–40. Paris: Dunod.

—— 1936b *The Psychology of Social Norms*. New York: Harper.

—— 1967 *Group Conflict and Co-operation: Their Social Psychology*. London: Routledge and Kegan Paul.

Soles, J. 1988 Social ranking in prepalatial cemeteries. In E.B. French and K.A. Wardle (eds), *Problems in Greek Prehistory*, 49–61. Bristol: Bristol Classical Press.

—— 1992 *The Prepalatial Cemeteries at Mochlos and Gournia and the House Tombs of Bronze Age Crete*. Hesperia Supplement 24. Princeton: American School of Classical Studies at Athens.

Stos-Gale, Z. 1985 Lead and silver sources for Bronze Age Crete. Πεπραγμένα Ε' Διεθνούς Κρητολογικού Συνεδρίου, vol. A1, 365–72. Heraklion: Εταιρεία Κρητικών Ιστορικών Μελετών.

—— 1998 The role of Kythnos and other Cycladic islands in the origins of Early Minoan metallurgy. In L.G. Mendoni and A. Mazarakis Ainian (eds), *Kea-Kythnos: History and Archaeology: Proceedings of the International Symposium Kea-Kythnos, 22–25 June 1994*. Meletimata 27: 717–35. Paris: Diffusion de Boccard; Athens: Research Centre for Greek and Roman Antiquity, National Hellenic Research Foundation.

Tap, P. 1988 *La Société Pygmalion? Intégration Sociale et Réalisation de la Personne*. Paris: Dunod.

Turner, J.C. 1984 Social identification and psychological group formation. In H. Tajfel (ed.), *The Social Dimension: European Developments in Social Psychology* 2: 518–38. Cambridge: Cambridge University Press; Paris and Éditions de la Maison des Sciences de l'Homme.

—— 1999 Some current issues in research on social identity and self-categorization theories. In N. Ellemers, R. Spears and B. Doosje (eds), *Social Identity*, 6–34. Oxford: Blackwell.

Vavouranakis, G. 2007 *Funerary Landscapes East of Lasithi, Crete, in the Bronze Age*. British Archaeological Reports International Series 1016. Oxford: Archaeopress.

Watrous, L.V. 1994 Crete from earliest prehistory through the protopalatial period. *American Journal of Archaeology* 98: 695–753.

—— 1998 Egypt and Crete in the early Middle Bronze Age: a case of trade and cultural diffusion. In E.H. Cline and D. Harris-Cline (eds), *The Aegean and the Orient in the Second Millennium: Proceedings of the 50th Anniversary Symposium, Cincinnati, 18–20 April 1997*. Aegaeum 18: 19–28. Liège: Université de Liège.

Wilson, D.E., and P.M. Day 1994 Ceramic regionalism in prepalatial central Crete: the Mesara imports at EM I to EM IIA Knossos: The 1907–08 south front tests. *Annual of the British School at Athens* 89: 1–87

Zois, A. 1998 ΚΡΗΤΗ: Η Πρώιμη Εποχή του Χαλκού. Athens: Απόδεξις.

6

FOREIGN MATERIALS, ISLANDER MOBILITY AND ELITE IDENTITY IN LATE BRONZE AGE SARDINIA

*Anthony Russell**

Introduction

The Late Bronze Age in Sardinia (*c.* 1300–900 BC) is characterised by an elaboration of some Nuragic tower settlements, which themselves indicate differing levels of territorial, economic and administrative control. This period also saw an increase in the amount of foreign material entering the island. This has led some archaeologists to propose a connection between foreign contact and the development of complex society (e.g. Rowland 2001: 65; Giardino 1995: 294). In such interpretations, various changes are attributed to Aegean presence and activities in the central Mediterranean. These changes include population growth, surplus production, intensified metallurgical activity, increased trade and the creation of site hierarchies (Blake 2008: 25). Others have suggested that the attempt to connect any sort of cultural development to 'the effects of external trade contacts or other influences … [is] easily challenged on archaeological grounds' (Webster 1996: 108). One key problem with postulating island-wide changes as the result of extra-insular contacts is the lack of centralised political authority (Knapp 1990: 143), although this lack would also prevent any kind of blanket response to contact, such as a collective strategy of social insularity.

This link between foreign contact and complex social development is rooted in *ex Oriente lux* frameworks, wherein presumably less complex or 'backward' societies are taught to live a more civilised, urban lifestyle by superior, complex societies originating in the Aegean and eastern Mediterranean (Chapman 1985: 115; Dyson and Rowland 2007: 54). While few scholars would postulate a settled foreign presence in Sardinia before the first millennium BC, this idea of active, advanced, eastern traders still influences models of interaction with Nuragic peoples, who are largely portrayed

* I would like to thank Dr Richard Jones (University of Glasgow) and Professor Lucia Vagnetti (Istituto di studi sulle Civiltà dell'Egeo e del Vicino Oriente, Rome) for sharing not only their thoughts on Aegean-looking pottery in Italy, but also some previously unpublished information.

as passive, stationary recipients of higher culture. Interpretations that insist upon an Aegean presence in Sardinia are based on outdated colonialist models which posit some ill-defined 'thalasso-phobia' for indigenous populations (Leighton 1999: 208) and do not allow mobility or agency for islanders and island societies.

Whereas in traditional interpretations an Aegean object demands an Aegean presence, here I argue that when certain material forms become popular, such as Late Helladic (LH) III pottery, their spread may only be indicative of an original, symbolic homeland. An object's diaspora involves the movement of styles, technologies and practices, in conjunction with the development of local tastes (Harding 1984: 229). In such a spread, the identities of manufacturers, transporters and traders stand distinct from each other.

In order to assess the capacity of foreign, in this case eastern Mediterranean, contacts to promote and entrench the social elites of Sardinian society, this study first examines the distribution of eastern materials to see if there is any spatial relationship between the findspots of such objects and the location of the most 'complex' Nuragic towers. This scenario presupposes that the most entrenched, politically powerful elites were those who lived in complexes that required the greatest wealth and labour input to construct and maintain. Such a distributional analysis will show that there is no clear relationship between what we presume to be the most powerful elites in Sardinian society and their level of contact with the eastern Mediterranean world. Rather, their wealth and territorial control seem to be rooted in local phenomena, such as agricultural potential, diversified landscapes and access to labour.

Should we dismiss any and all influence of eastern materials upon Sardinian Late Bronze Age society? Although such materials represent but a small fraction of the total material assemblage at Nuragic sites, certainly they are widespread enough for us to assume that these objects, and the contacts represented by them, were not circumscribed. By looking at such material in context, from a local and consumption-based perspective, it is possible to infer material influences upon social practices that, while they may have had limited impact from a geographic (or diachronic) standpoint, nonetheless suggest the negotiation of elite status within their specific, local context. In the case study provided – investigating the consumption of Aegean-looking pottery at *nuraghe* Antigori – it is argued that while the assumption of an Aegean presence may be ill-founded, LH III pottery did influence ceramic production, at least for awhile, and it may have influenced elite practice as well, at least with respect to this site and its immediate hinterland during the Late Bronze Age.

Following a brief outline of the varying types of Nuragic settlements, based on Webster's three-class system (Webster 1996: 111–17; see Figure 6.1, B–D) and an assessment of some of the social and structure implications of this apparent hierarchy of sites, I provide a review of the evidence for foreign contacts, and the distributional relationship this material has to the more complex *nuraghi*. I then consider the ways in which developing elites in Sardinia may have used traditional Nuragic features in order to legitimise and promote their identity before comparing the Nuragic situation with that in Late Bronze Age Sicily, and the foreign materials found there. Finally, a close look at the materiality of 'Aegean-style' pottery at *nuraghe* Antigori shows that it is necessary to look even farther afield, at the Italian peninsula, in order to reconstruct the specific material connection represented by these wares, and the patterns of mobility engendered therein.

Nuragic typology

Most of the *nuraghi* on Sardinia were originally constructed as single megalithic towers during the local Middle Bronze Age, *c.* 1800–1300 BC (Webster 1996: 111 – see Figure 6.1, B). In the Late Bronze Age these single-towered sites still represented over 70 per cent of all Nuragic settlements, and are evenly distributed throughout the island. Most include a scattering of more modest circular buildings, generally termed huts, where the majority of the population in such settlements would have lived.

In the traditional interpretation of the development of *nuraghi*, some single-towered sites began to be elaborated from early in the Late Bronze Age, with the main tower now lying in the middle of one to four subsidiary towers, all joined by encasing walls, and having upper galleries and courtyards (Figure 6.1, C). Such sites also had surrounding huts, which lay outside the tower-complex, and which were typically more numerous than those found around single-towered *nuraghi*. These multi-towered sites are also found evenly spread around the island, and comprise

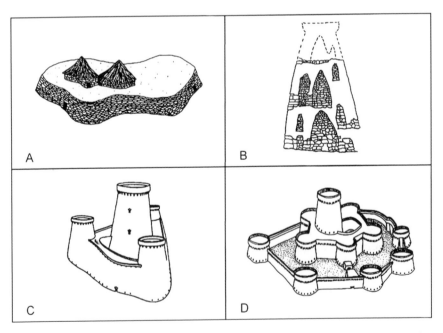

Figure 6.1 *Nuraghe* typology. A: protonuraghe; B: single tower; C: multi-tower; D: complex multi-tower (A, B, D after Webster 1996: figures 22b, 31, 44; C after Lilliu 1988: figure 194).

about 28 per cent of all *nuraghi* (Webster 1996: 113). Finally, towards the end of the Late Bronze Age, there was a further elaboration of a select number of Nuragic sites, where the multi-towered 'core' was augmented by another surrounding wall, within which more structures are found, including a circular building often referred to as the meeting hut, or civico-ritual building (Blake 1997: 152) (Figure 6.1, D). There were also several extra-mural huts. This, the most elaborate type of Nuragic site, is not evenly distributed over the island: there are only 14 known examples, which tend to lie in the south and west (Webster 1996: 117).

A more recent interpretation of the typology of *nuraghi* towers, however, posits that many of the more complex sites were originally planned as such, and did not develop out of single-towered cores. This new model accuses the traditional interpretation of being too evolutionary in its progression, and based on a closer analysis of the stratigraphy of certain class III sites such as Arrubiu, the idea of originally planned complex structures has been gaining support (Cossu 2003: 28). For the purposes of this study, which seeks to find a connection between the more complex *nuraghi* and the presence of exotica, whether these sites developed from simpler *nuraghi* or were designed as multi-towered edifices from the start is not pertinent. The ability of extra-insular contacts to contribute to the wealth of the elite who built the most complex *nuraghi*, whether from scratch or out of an existing structure, is the relevant issue.

These three *nuraghi* classes are believed to have had varying levels of administrative and territorial control: the single towers controlling their immediate locales and not much else; the multi-towered complexes exercising some hinterland control; and the most elaborate controlling other, lesser Nuragic settlements within a region of about 200 sq km. Webster (1996: 130–1) envisions a two-level hierarchy of sites in the north, where (with the exception of Palmavera) there are only class I and II *nuraghi*, and a three-level hierarchy in the south, where all three classes are represented. For the sake of this study the validity of this three-class Nuragic typology, or the differing authority levels proposed, need only be accepted in general terms. These distinctions are nonetheless useful because they both illustrate the elaboration of *nuraghi* during the Late Bronze Age and indicate a developing elite identity, where monumental architecture served 'to negotiate the relationships between dominant and consenting groups in class-structured societies' (Kolb 2005: 156).

In order to assess any potential contribution that certain extra-insular contacts had on the social development of the most sophisticated *nuraghi*, what follows is a review of the principal material evidence for contacts between Sardinia and the eastern Mediterranean. Following that I provide a distributional analysis of the findspots of these eastern materials vs. the location of the most complex class III sites.

Foreign goods and complex *nuraghi*

Although the construction of *nuraghi* themselves was originally thought to indicate a familiarity with building practices in the Aegean, this idea has largely been dismissed. Instead, scholars tend to see local prototypes leading to the development of the corbel-vaulted *nuraghi* (Cavanagh and Laxton 1987: 45) (Figure 6.1, A). In fact, the Sardinian practice of megalithic construction has been argued to fit better within the central and western Mediterranean sphere of dry-stone architecture, including Corsican *torre*, Balearic *talayots* and Iberian *motillas* (Kolb 2005: 171). Aside from this hypothetical architectural evidence, there is clear evidence of foreign materials discovered in Nuragic contexts, usually interpreted as indications of trading links (see Figure 6.2).

For example, Aegean (and occasionally Cypriot) pottery has been found in Nuragic settlements. While is true that most stratified samples are found in Webster's class II and III sites, this may reflect an excavation bias towards more elaborate settlements (Webster 1996: 142). There are other problems, however, with the ceramic evidence: there is not much of it, both in terms of the number of sites involved and the total number of sherds found. Of the 14 class III sites, only three have yielded Aegean pottery (Antigori, Arrubiu and Su Nuraxi-Barumini) and, based on limited physico-chemical analyses, not all of this pottery is imported (Jones and Day 1987). In terms of quantity, only Antigori has produced an amount significant enough to suggest anything more than sporadic, indirect contact (Webster 1996: 140).

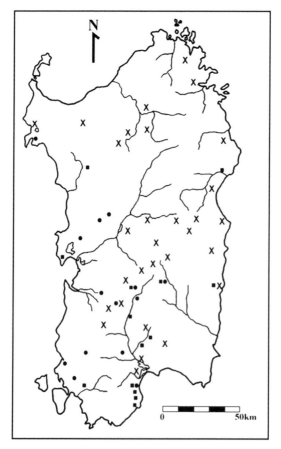

Figure 6.2
Distribution map of foreign materials vs. class III *nuraghi*. ■ = class III *nuraghi*;
● = Aegean pottery findspot; X = oxhide ingot findspot.

The other class of object commonly associated with eastern contact is the oxhide-shaped copper ingot. The provenance of these ingots has been hotly debated (e.g. Gale and Stos-Gale 1987; Knapp 2000), with some claiming an indisputable Cypriot origin, and others believing that lead isotope analysis as a provenance technique must be carefully qualified, particularly in an environment where ore sources may have been mixed, and metal artefacts themselves heavily recycled. An eastern 'association' could be indicated by the few examples that have Cypro-Minoan-looking markings on them (Kassianidou 2005: 333). For the sake of this study, the original source of the copper in these oxhide ingots is less significant than the recognition that some knowledge of eastern Mediterranean practices, through direct or indirect contacts, is indicated by the presence of such ingots. If such contacts were mediated, it is not clear through whom: there are only two examples on Sicily, one on Lipari, and none on the mainland (Vianello 2005: 92).

There are 34 sites on Sardinia that have produced samples of oxhide ingots, almost all of them fragmentary (Lo Schiavo 2005) (Figure 6.2). In terms of distribution, there is no spatial relationship between these ingots and class III *nuraghi*. No class III sites have yielded fragments of these ingots, and only two sites, the Nuragic village near Monte Zara (Monastir) and *nuraghe* Nastasi (Tertenia), have produced both Aegean pottery and oxhide ingot fragments together (Lo Schiavo 2005: 326; Vianello 2005: 162).

Some Sardinian metallurgical tools are thought to have been influenced by Cypriot or Levantine implements, based on their similar morphology and their dissimilarity to tools used in Anatolia, Greece or Italy (Lo Schiavo *et al.* 1985: 22–8). Again, though, the distribution bears no relationship to the location of the complex *nuraghi*, instead showing a decided bias towards the north of the island. A few other metal objects that may indicate some eastern influence in their manufacture, such as Cypriot-looking tripod stands (Lo Schiavo 1985a: 8–9), or Syro-Palestinian style bronze figurines (Lo Schiavo *et al.* 1985: 52–5), have been found in Sardinia, but never at a class III *nuraghe*. A seated female figurine, thought to be of Cypriot or Levantine derivation, was found in the sacred well sanctuary of Santa Cristina (Lo Schiavo *et al.* 1985: 55), which may have fallen under some kind of administrative control of the nearby class III site of Lugherras-Paulilatino (4 km to the north). The dating of this figurine, however, is uncertain (eleventh–eighth centuries BC) and its deposition may post-date by many years the development of Lugherras into a complex site.

There may be a loose correlation between the development of class III *nuraghi* and the location of copper ore deposits. This is not to say that wherever a good source of copper ore is known, there is a corresponding complex *nuraghe* nearby; rather wherever we find one of the 14 class III sites, there is often an ore source nearby, or at least one accessible via a river valley. There is also a relationship, however, between the quality of soils and the placement of these sites, with only two lying in areas considered to have less than 'good' quality soils (Webster 1996: 35). Certainly sites of this size would require decent agricultural yields to sustain their larger populations. They are also usually found in areas where there is a greater density of smaller settlements, from which elites may have drawn their labour needs (Webster 1996: 129, 131). Even if metal ores represented a significant part of the wealth of class III Nuragic elites, this does not necessarily mean that wealth derived primarily via extra-insular exchange with eastern Mediterranean traders, and there is no detectable centralisation of the metals industry, or a corresponding site hierarchy relating to it, as could be argued for other Mediterranean islands like Cyprus (Knapp 2008: 138–9).

Aside from the aforementioned Aegean pottery found at three class III sites, the only objects of possible eastern origin found in these sites are a faience rosette (of uncertain origin) and some amber and quartz beads (of possible Aegean origin), all discovered at Antigori (Vianello 2005: 158). If we want to understand better why certain *nuraghi* developed into complex, fortress-like sites, with wealthy elite residents, it is necessary to look beyond contacts with the east, or control of access to eastern materials.

Internal strategies for developing elite status

Nuragic elites would have legitimised their social standing through a process of negotiation over what their status entailed. While controlling foreign contacts might have had some ideological value towards this goal, Sardinian elites also appropriated certain traditional symbols and material practices of Nuragic society, some of which were less restricted previously. The most obvious restriction is the act of living in the *nuraghe* itself. However one characterises Late Bronze Age Sardinian society (e.g. 'chiefdom', 'proto-urban'), it is clear that those living in the towers would have exercised more social influence than those living in huts outside the walls. The authority represented by the tower is illustrated by a new material feature of the Late Bronze Age, i.e. the miniature models of the *nuraghi*, which have been found in central positions in the civico-ritual buildings at certain class III sites (e.g. Palmavera, Barumini) (Moravetti 1995: 31–2; van Dommelen 1998: 78). While it is uncertain what specific function these models served, they were effective reminders of status for any activities taking place within these structures. Another appropriation involved restricting burials in the so-called giants' tombs to the tower-dwelling elite. This restriction is inferred by the Late Bronze Age increase in population, which outpaced the ability of the relatively few giants' tombs to function as community-wide burials, as they are believed to have done in the Early and Middle Bronze Ages (Webster 1996: 143–4). Giants' tombs constructed in the Late Bronze Age also seem to show a closer spatial relationship to the Nuragic complex, and they adopt some of its architectural features (Blake 1999: 47–8).

While extra-insular contacts may have enabled Sardinian elites to appropriate and restrict foreign exotica as one method of differentiation, it seems unlikely that such contacts represented the prime mover in the development of a more rigidly hierarchical society. A brief comparison with Sicily should illustrate why other mechanisms of change must be sought. Sicily's Late Bronze Age reveals abundant evidence for contact with the eastern Mediterranean (Vianello 2005: 207), and some archaeologists have even postulated possible Mycenaean residents (e.g. Bietti Sestieri 1988: 24). While certain scholars have argued that Sicily saw an increased level of social stratification during this period, followed by a return to a more egalitarian society in the eleventh century BC (e.g. Leighton 1999: 188), the evidence for this ranked Middle–Late Bronze Age Sicilian society is not particularly pronounced, and when considered alongside Nuragic Sardinia, Sicily does not appear to be noticeably stratified at all. So, even with greater eastern contact, there seems to be much less elite distinction. One might argue that the presence of metal ores on Sardinia allowed for the greater accumulation of wealth by Nuragic elites, with foreign contacts contributing to this wealth. The distribution of exotica around the island, however, does not indicate that elites living in more complex *nuraghi* were privy to more extensive foreign contacts than those from single-towered sites, nor were they were engaged in metallurgical activities on a larger scale than the smaller settlements (Webster 1996: 137).

Based on the contrasting developments between Sicily and Sardinia, is it more appropriate to suggest that insularity contributed to the development of Sardinia's unique stratified society? Or does this interpretation retreat too far the other way, insisting upon the cultural closure of Sardinia in its social evolution? 'Did the world beyond an island's shores represent a source of anxiety ... or a welcome fund of innovation and exciting novelties?' (Cherry 2004: 235). The lack of centralised political authority on the island may work against any model of sweeping changes brought about by external contact, but this lack of unity would equally confound frameworks that stress insularity as a key factor, particularly if we define such isolation as an 'agreed social strategy' designed to produce a 'distinctive island identity' (Knapp 2008: 19).

Limited influences: *Nuraghe* Antigori and Aegean-looking pottery

A crucial problem ... [is] the use of painted Mycenaean wares to assess the diffusion of 'Mycenaean culture' ... [These] can only serve as indicators of exchange activity and say nothing about the permanent presence of 'Mycenaeans' (Harding 1984: 229).

Since the distribution patterns of foreign materials do not indicate any relationship between contact with foreigners and the development of complex *nuraghi*, it may be more fruitful to look for less sweeping influences at key points of contact, to see if any changes in material practice are evident. It has been argued in the past that eastern merchants may only have actually visited a select number of ports in Italy and Sicily, and the same may be true for Sardinia (Knapp 1990: 143). The obvious place to look is *nuraghe* Antigori (see Figure 6.3).

Antigori is located in the south of Sardinia, along the west coast of the Gulf of Cagliari, and was occupied between the fourteenth and eighth centuries BC (Ugas 2005: 39). It represents a convenient part of the island for traders coming from the east and south, and has produced the only significant quantity of Aegean-looking pottery in Sardinia. Stratigraphic excavations at Antigori point to contacts over a prolonged period (Ferrarese Ceruti 1979; 1985; Ferrarese Ceruti and Assorgia 1982),

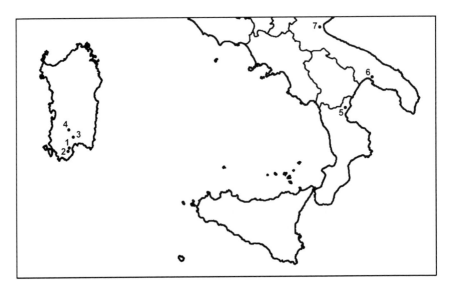

Figure 6.3   Map of the central Mediterranean showing location of main sites mentioned in the text. 1: *nuraghe* Antigori; 2: *nuraghe* Domu'e S'Orku; 3: Monte Zara (Monastir); 4: *nuraghe* Corti Beccia (Sanluri); 5: Broglio di Trebisacce; 6: Scoglio del Tonno; 7: Coppa Nevigata.

and at least a selection of its pottery has undergone physico-chemical analyses (Jones and Day 1987). Antigori falls within Webster's class III, as it involves multiple towers, but is unusual in also incorporating the natural crags of the hill on which it sits for defensive purposes. Compared to other class III structures Antigori is not well preserved, and a look at its plan (Figure 6.4) shows only an indication of some of the towers, a few other ill-defined areas and many blank spaces.

Two features of the pottery analyses stand out: (1) the prevalence of open shapes over closed, indicating dining, drinking and serving vessels (Jones *et al.* 2005: 542) and (2) the provenance findings which show that the majority of Aegean-style painted pottery examined was of local manufacture (Ferrarese Ceruti *et al.* 1987: 36). The presence of these imports and imitations, found within the nuragic complex (mostly within room 'a' on the plan), would seem to indicate the import of high-status painted pottery, not necessarily based on its contents (Blake 2008: 17), followed by the commission of similar wares locally, possibly as a result of the rather infrequent arrival of eastern traders or eastern goods.

Those who have studied Antigori closely tend to favour the notion that the Aegean pottery found there is the result of 'Mycenaean' sailors coming to the island, and even living among the local population (e.g., Ferrarese Ceruti and Assorgia 1982: 170), similar to the scenario presented by others to explain Aegean-style pottery in southern

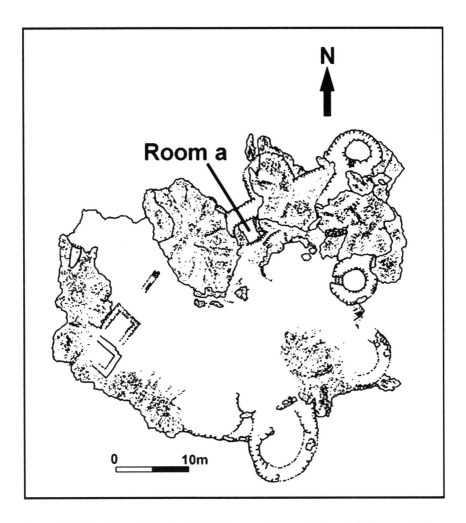

Figure 6.4 Plan of *nuraghe* Antigori (after Ferrarese Ceruti and Assorgia 1982: plate LIX).

Italy (e.g. Jones *et al.* 2005: 543). On the mainland, however, the amount of data, and the nature of the evidence, allows a plausible construction of interactive models that posit an Aegean presence there, which may have involved itinerant, highly skilled potters. This is not the case at Antigori, where the amount of data is significantly less, and the nature of its (re)production is distinct. A closer look at the similarities, and key differences, in the materiality of Aegean wares at Antigori vs. southern Italy indicates some level of mobility and interaction between those two regions, and makes much less likely an interpretation involving direct Aegean presence on the island of Sardinia.

Table 6.1 Features of the consumption of Aegean-type pottery, southern Italy vs. that at
nuraghe Antigori

Category	Southern Italy	Nuraghe Antigori
Aegean imports	Quantity: 1,000+ Percentage: < 5% of total pottery	Quantity: *ca.* 200 Percentage: ?, very small amount
Locally made Aegean-looking pottery	Wheel-made, levigated buff clay, painted Dramatic increase in production during LHBIII/C phase Credited to 'itinerant potters' or local Italic peoples trained by Aegeans	Made on 'very slow wheel', matte paint Represents the majority of painted pottery Credited to Mycenaean residents by some, but here argued as a Sardinian product
Grey ware	*Ceramica grigia:* local *impasto* shapes made on a wheel, with clay selection/preparation, high-firing kiln similar to Aegean practice	*Ceramica grigio-ardesia:* foreign to Nuragic pottery shapes (Trojan? Italian?), made by hand, high firing temperatures
Dolia/pithoi	Mainly locally made examples, buff levigated clay, high fired, with some wheel shaping Raised-band decoration	Only two examples, both imported Cretan 'herring-bone' decoration and Cypriot wavy-band
Provenience analysis of imports	Peloponnese Central Crete Rhodes Central Greece Sardinia? (from Scoglio del Tonno)	Peloponnese Central Crete Western Crete Southern Cyprus –
Motifs	Curved lines with dotted border (Scoglio del Tonno) Spirals (very common) Diamond with cross-hatched interior (Scoglio del Tonno)	Curved lines with dotted border – Spirals Diamond with cross-hatched interior (locally made example)
Shapes	Predominantly table wares	Predominantly table wares

A broad look at the patterns of consumption of these wares shows some remarkable similarities between Antigori and the mainland (Table 6.1). Although sherd counts tend to be somewhat higher in Italy than on Sardinia (perhaps because of its geographic proximity to the Aegean), in both areas the percentage of these Aegean-looking sherds in relation to the full pottery assemblage is low. For Italy, it is never more than 5 per cent, and usually much lower (Vagnetti 1999: 141). At Antigori no total count has been published, yet it seems likely that its approximately 200 sherds represent a similarly low percentage (Ferrarese Ceruti and Assorgia 1982: 170; Ferrarese Ceruti 1986). This would appear to include locally made Aegean-style ware, not just imports. The presence of locally made imitations of Aegean pottery is another point of similarity between the two areas, and has been confirmed by provenance analyses

(Jones *et al.* 2005). In fact, such imitations are more plentiful than actual imports at Antigori (Ferrarese Ceruti *et al.* 1987: 36), and they increase dramatically in southern Italy during the LH IIIB/C phase, which is the same phase represented stylistically by the Antigori sherds (Jones *et al.* 2005: 541). Furthermore, in both southern Italy and at Antigori the practice of making grey-ware pottery (called *ceramica grigia* on the mainland and *ceramica grigio-ardesia* – 'slate grey' – on Sardinia) begins in the Late Bronze Age; this pottery is always found in association with Aegean pottery (Ferrarese Ceruti *et al.* 1987: 36; Borgna and Càssola Guida 2005: 497).

There are also some common, albeit broad, provenance results for both areas, including clay sources from central Crete and the Peloponnese. In terms of pottery shapes, southern Italy has a similar proportion of open vs. closed vessels to Antigori (Jones *et al.* 2005: 542), and both regions stand distinct from Sicily (Blake 2008: 17). The grey-ware shapes are more difficult to compare from profile pictures, although Giardino (1995: 45) has noted some rough correspondences between the profiles of the grey-ware sherds from Antigori and those of both impasto and *ceramica grigia* at Broglio di Trebisacce. Ferrarese Ceruti (1985: 606) has also pointed out the dissimilarity between *ceramica grigio-ardesia* shapes and those of traditional Nuragic ware. With regard to painted motifs, some similarities between the mainland and Antigori can be detected (Figure 6.5). These include: concentric curved lines bordered with dots (Taylour 1958: plate 15; Ferrarese Ceruti 1985: 608, M4); spirals (a very common motif wherever Aegean-looking pottery is made); and diamond shapes with cross-hatched interiors (Taylour 1958: plate 13; Ferrarese Ceruti 1985: 607, M2).

Along with these similarities, there are also significant differences in the materiality of Aegean-looking pottery and its derivatives between Antigori and the mainland. There is a serious discrepancy between the way that both locally made Aegean pottery and grey wares are produced. In southern Italy, the production method is very similar to that of the Aegean itself, with the preparation of well-levigated buff clay, decoration using lustrous paint, high firing temperatures and, perhaps most significantly, evidence of manufacture on the wheel (Vagnetti 1999: 143). On Sardinia, Aegean imitations were also fired at a high temperature, but were decorated in matte paint (Ferrarese Ceruti and Assorgia 1982: 173–4), and were fashioned either by hand or on a very slow wheel (R. Jones, pers. comm.). Similarly, the grey wares in Italy, shaped to resemble the handmade *impasto* pottery that was traditional to the area, were prepared with well-levigated clay, formed on the wheel and fired in such a way as to produce the grey finish. There are conflicting reports as to whether the Sardinian slate-grey pots were handmade or wheelmade. Giardino (1995: 44) posited that they betray clear signs of having been turned, while Smith (1987: 99) claimed they were handmade. It is possible that they were made using the same slow wheel as potters used to fashion the local Aegean-looking pottery. In either case, while these pots were made with better levigated clay and were more evenly fired than contemporary Nuragic pottery (Ferrarese Ceruti 1979), they diverge significantly in their method of production from southern Italian grey ware (L. Vagnetti, pers. comm.), in much the same way that the local Aegean-looking pottery at Antigori differs from that made on the mainland.

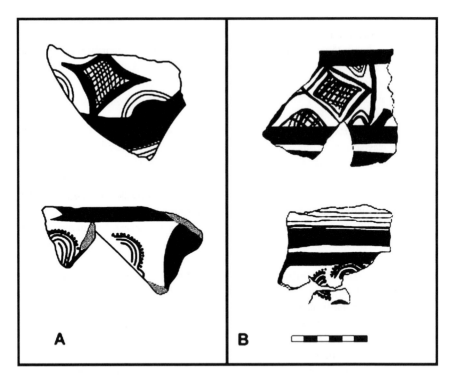

Figure 6.5   Similar motifs on pots from Scoglio del Tonno (A) and Antigori (B) (after Taylour 1958: plates 13, 15; and Ferrarese Ceruti and Assorgia 1982: plates LXIII, LXV).

A final point of distinction between the two areas involves the presence of large storage vessels (*pithoi* or *dolia*). Here there seems to be significant differences in practice, with locally made examples well known on the mainland, but only two examples, both of imported vessels, at Antigori. In terms of decoration, raised bands and later grooved bands are found on the Italian examples (Vagnetti 1999: 147), while one of the imports in Sardinia has a Cretan-style herringbone pattern, and the other a Cypriot-style wavy band (Ferrarese Ceruti *et al.* 1987: 16, 18). Provenance analysis has confirmed these assignments (Jones and Day 1987: 262–3).

Discussion: contact – how and with whom?

It is clear that the way in which Aegean-looking pottery was imported and produced at Antigori and southern Italy involves both similarities and key differences. The similarities indicate a shared experience, argued here to be contact between the islanders of Sardinia and the Italian mainlanders, while the differences indicate an important contrast in the contact situation between these areas. These differences are best explained as indications of the direct presence and interaction of Aegean traders or craftsmen in south Italy, but only indirect contact between Aegeans and Sardinians at Antigori, mediated through mainland Italian societies. In other words, the difference in the local reproduction of Aegean-looking wares at Antigori can be explained as the result of the imperfect (or at least partial) transfer of Aegean know-how to Sardinian potters, who perhaps only had final products and some technological hearsay with which to work.

This contact between mainlanders and Sardinians could have taken place at Antigori, with mainland sailors bringing both the imports, and perhaps imperfect knowledge of how to produce them, to the island. Alternatively, the imported pottery may have been acquired by Sardinian merchants sailing in the central Mediterranean. Such wares are certainly well represented in Sicily, the Aeolian Islands and southern Italy. As locally made imitations of Aegean pottery are not well known in Sicily (Jones *et al.* 2005: 543), and only a single sherd of grey ware has been found in Lipari (Vianello 2005: 128), contact with the mainland seems the best fit. Furthermore, from a chronological perspective the consumption of Aegean pottery in Sardinia seems largely to postdate the presence of such wares in Sicily or Lipari (Blake 2008: 7).

Sardinian merchants also could have brought home information on the types of dining or drinking practices associated with such wares, and imparted this knowledge to the elites of Antigori. That the elites found such practices worthwhile would seem to be indicated by the commissioning of local copies. This practice could have involved the introduction of wine drinking to Sardinia, although there is little evidence at present concerning the adoption of Mediterranean polyculture to Sardinia in the Late Bronze Age (Lo Schiavo 1985b: 257–8). Furthermore, as Blake (2008: 15) has observed, the assumption that eastern Mediterranean societies introduced the trappings of civilised life (such as the practice of wine drinking) to the central Mediterranean and elsewhere has been overused, and these explanations repeat themselves when it comes to the colonial movements of the eighth century BC (i.e. Greeks and Phoenicians). Of course, it is often the case that such ideas originate from interpretations of these later colonial movements, read back and recycled in the Late Bronze Age.

Room 'a' at Antigori, where the bulk of the Aegean pottery was found, is a small confined space. Ferrarese Ceruti (1980: 392), basing her opinion not only on the pottery but also on a small lead object that she called a votive axe (which she later clarified was not from this room – Ferrarese Ceruti and Assorgia 1982: 170), claimed that this space should be considered a foreign shrine, one which Mycenaean traders would have used during their visits to the site. Another, perhaps more plausible reconstruction suggests that room 'a' is simply a rubbish area, where discarded Aegean pottery was deposited (Lilliu 1988: 401). This supposition seems to be corroborated by the fact that only two of the four walls of room 'a' are finished, while the east and west wall are formed from the natural rock (Ferrarese Ceruti and Assorgia 1982: 167–8). If so, then any reconstruction of the actual practices pursued with these

Aegean pots, and where specifically such practices took place, remains uncertain. At present, the most we can say is that the preponderance of open shapes, especially mixing bowls and cups, may indicate drinking and dining practices. Whether these were foreign dining practices or simply Nuragic ones that made use of foreign materials cannot be ascertained.

The idiosyncratic way in which Aegean wares were imitated at Antigori may be due to the conservatism of pottery practices there, or the lack of necessary information about the production sequence. Even skilled potters who practise competently in handmade traditions are not automatically equipped to adopt wheel-making techniques (Loney 2007: 199), particularly in a situation where only a finished product is known. Investigating the adoption of wheel-making techniques on the Italian mainland, Loney (2007: 202) stresses that the conservative nature of pottery production in southern Italy, where direct contact with Aegean craftsmen may be interpreted, meant that the wheel was only adopted 'disjointedly'. On Sardinia, where there is little evidence for the presence of Aegean merchants or craftsmen, conservatism was also compounded by technological ignorance, leading to a 'negative transfer' of skills (Loney 2007: 183), which resulted in the less exact imitations of the Aegean wares that were produced at Antigori.

If both the Aegean imports, and a vague knowledge of how to produce them, came to Sardinia via the Italian peninsula, then the possibility must also exist that some presumed imports at Antigori and other Nuragic sites might actually be Italian imitations. Some evidence for this may be seen in the common provenance noted between pottery found at Antigori and that at Scoglio del Tonno (Jones 1986: 208). The chemical signatures of five suspected imports at the latter site, which contained relatively high levels of iron and nickel, were not readily comparable to known clay sources in the Aegean or around Scoglio itself. They may have been manufactured on Sardinia, as some examples at Antigori also showed high iron and nickel content (Jones 1986: 212–13, table 2). Given how closely Aegean wares were imitated on the mainland, and conversely how far they departed from Aegean production techniques at Antigori, however, it would surely be unusual for the inhabitants of Scoglio del Tonno to desire the inferior Sardinian copies. Instead, both the Sardinian and Italian pottery with these chemical signatures may have been produced on the mainland, using an unknown clay source. Jones (1986: 208) does acknowledge that if these samples were made in Sardinia, their clay source has not yet been established.

Interestingly, when the import of Aegean pottery comes to an end at Antigori, the practice of making local copies also ends, although grey ware production persists (Ferrarese Ceruti et al. 1987: 35). To some this may indicate that an Aegean presence at Sardinia, in the form of traders or itinerant potters, had ceased. Ferrarese Ceruti and Assorgia (1982: 171) stressed a link between Mycenaean contact at Antigori and their desire for access to metal ores, citing convenient routes from the *nuraghe* to metal-bearing regions (e.g. Sulcis-Iglesiente). While a valid hypothesis, there is no evidence for the production or transhipment of metals at the site itself, so any intensive involvement in metals exchange networks by the elite at Antigori remains unproven. Lilliu (1988: 401) makes reference to ingots found 'nearby' in Capoterra and Assemini, but at approximately 9 and 20 km distance respectively, such connections seem at best conjectural.

The end of Aegean pottery consumption at Antigori, however, should stress the value of such wares to local elites: when the imports no longer arrived, such material lost its exotic association for successive generations of Antigori elites, and they were probably disinclined to have it copied any longer. It may be possible to see Antigori as a failed entrepôt for Aegean pottery, one whose elite attempted unsuccessfully to promote such materials (and associated practices) to other elite groups in the region. There is some, admittedly slight supporting evidence for such an idea. The site with the second largest stratigraphic cache of Aegean ware is the nearby (class II) site of *nuraghe* Domu 'e S'Orku, where six sherds were recovered (Webster 1996: 140). Of these, one has been interpreted as being of local manufacture, with a similar fabric to three locally made sherds at Antigori (Jones and Day 1987: 260). Some grey-ware pottery was also recovered there (Webster 1996: 110). In addition, a survey of the *Nora/Pula* region just to the south of Sarroch has produced two other Aegean sherds, found on the surface near *nuraghe* Is Baccus. One of these sherds is considered to be a local imitation (Botto *et al.* 2000: 262). Similarly, at an increasingly greater distance from Antigori, two other sites, Monte Zara (Monastir) and *nuraghe* Corti Beccia (Sanluri) have produced Aegean-looking sherds that have been tentatively classified as local (Vianello 2005: 134; Ugas 1982: 41, no. 82). It would be interesting if petrographic analysis of these sherds also indicated a clay source similar to or in common with those found at Antigori.

If scholars are to maintain that *nuraghe* Antigori had direct contact with Aegean sailors travelling west, then the issue of why Aegean imports are not generally found during the LH IIIC period (twelfth century BC) at intervening places like Sicily and Lipari must be addressed. While a route along Sicily's southern coast may take the Aeolian Islands out of the picture geographically, surely Sicily itself would have represented a convenient stopping point for any Aegean merchants on the way to Sardinia? The most plausible explanation is that there were no Aegean ships voyaging to Sardinia in the twelfth century BC, and that any Aegean materials found on the island at that time reflect the mobility and activity of societies in Sardinia and south Italy: the latter represents the one region in the central Mediterranean that had clear connections with the eastern Mediterranean throughout the Late Bronze Age.

As the Late Bronze Age progressed, certain Nuragic complexes became more fortified (Trump 1992: 199), suggesting that an elite class was becoming more entrenched, wealthier and able to exert administrative control over larger territories. In such an environment – also seen on the mainland at sites such as Coppa Nevigata, where a defensive wall was constructed in the Late Bronze Age (Loney 2007: 200) – one may expect to find increased craft specialisation, as elites began to consume more labour-intensive materials, both local and imported, to promote ideologically their privileged positions within their communities. Along with this increased fortification and (localised) centralisation, as illustrated by Webster's three-level settlement hierarchy, there may be a certain amount of technical experimentation (Loney 2007: 200), such as the attempt to produce Aegean-style pottery and *ceramica grigia* locally at Antigori.

Conclusion

Based on the distribution patterns of exotica and foreign-influenced materials, it is difficult to discern any relationship between contacts with the eastern Mediterranean and the development of complex Nuragic sites on Sardinia. More apparent is the appropriation of elements of traditional island culture by elites to justify or entrench their status, and perhaps to facilitate their control over resources such as metal ores, decent agricultural land and labour. Sardinia did not exist in a cultural bubble in the Late Bronze Age, however, as the scattered presence of foreign material testifies, nor would there have been any adopted policy to isolate themselves, given the lack of island-wide political centralisation. In such an environment the responses to contact would necessarily be diverse, as would be the values placed on foreign materials. Thus at Antigori there appears to be an active engagement of locals with foreign pottery, unparalleled elsewhere in Sardinia.

Sardinian involvement in international exchange networks also needs to include the possibility of mobile Sardinian merchants sailing within the central Mediterranean, absorbing foreign materials and practices at other points of contact. There is no reason to assume that the level of maritime activity and the technologies involved were inadequate in Nuragic society (Harding 1984: 258), particularly for voyages within the Tyrrhenian Sea. The patterns of consuming Aegean-looking pottery at Antigori would seem to indicate Sardinian familiarity with Italian mainland practices; they heavily favour a model of interaction between those two regions rather than an assumption that Aegean traders or craftsmen arrived to deal with or manipulate passive, receptive and stationary islanders. Even the differences in practice, such as contrasting production methods seen in the reproduction of Aegean imitations and *ceramica grigia*, are not necessarily an obstacle in interpreting material connections between *nuraghe* Antigori and southern Italy. These differences simply indicate differing identities of the local producers themselves – Sardinian potters at Antigori and Italian (or itinerant Aegean) potters on the mainland. Indeed, it would be unusual for material practices to be identical between these regions.

There is one factor which tells against interpreting a material connection between Antigori and southern Italy: the lack of Late Bronze Age Nuragic finds on the mainland. Why would there be an emulation of certain mainland practices at Antigori, and an importation of Aegean goods (here argued to have been mediated through southern Italy), but nothing detectable archaeologically travelling in the opposite direction? It seems too convenient to assume that, in return for Aegean products, Sardinians provided mainland societies with materials that do not survive (e.g. livestock, slaves, agricultural produce). The most obvious material that southern Italians may have sought is copper ore, which, given the possible mixing of ores during secondary smelting, may not be traceable to a Sardinian source. Furthermore, the hyper-specialisation and extreme regionalisation of Mediterranean archaeology as a practice (Cherry 2004: 236) may have militated against Nuragic materials being detected in the first place, as few mainland archaeologists have more than a passing familiarity with such products. The fact that both earlier (e.g. Early or Middle Bronze

Age obsidian – Blake 1999: 40) and later (e.g. Iron Age miniature bronze boats and other bronzes – Lo Schiavo 2000: 155) Sardinian products have been found on the mainland would make it unusual for there to have been *no* communication between the two regions in the Late Bronze Age. It is only during the period of apparent Aegean involvement in both places that such a connection has been missing, or neglected.

Instead of looking for island-wide changes that result from external contacts, concentrating on the specific sites or areas where foreign materials are found may help to illustrate changes in material practices within a more limited area, such as the manufacture of local Aegean-style pottery at Antigori. Furthermore, broadening the definition of foreign contact to include areas other than the Aegean or Cyprus will give a more accurate representation of the full spectrum of extra-insular contacts, and of potential material practices and influences. These methods could shed light on other material connections, such as between Palmavera (Sassari) and the western Mediterranean sphere, or Sa Sedda 'e Sos Carros (Nuoro) and central Italy.

References

Bietti Sestieri, A.M. 1988 The 'Mycenaean connection' and its impact on the central Mediterranean societies. *Dialoghi di Archeologia* 6: 23–51.

Blake, E. 1997 Strategic symbolism: miniature nuraghi of Sardinia. *Journal of Mediterranean Archaeology* 10: 151–64.

—— 1999 Identity-mapping the Sardinian Bronze Age. *European Journal of Archaeology* 2: 35–55.

—— 2008 The Mycenaeans in Italy: a minimalist position. *Papers of the British School at Rome* 76: 1–34.

Borgna, E., and P. Càssola Guida 2005 Some observations on the nature and modes of exchange between Italy and the Aegean in the Late Mycenaean period. In R. Laffineur and E. Greco (eds), *Emporia: Aegeans in the Central and Eastern Mediterranean. Proceedings of the 10th International Aegean Conference, Athens, Italian School of Archaeology, 14–18 April 2004*. Aegaeum 25: 497–505. Liège: Université de Liège.

Botto, M., S. Melis and M. Rendeli 2000 Nora e il suo territorio. In C. Tronchetti (ed.), *Ricerche su Nora I (Anni 1990–1998)*, 255–84. Cagliari: Soprintendenza Archeologica per le Provincie di Cagliari e Oristano.

Cavanagh, W.G., and R.R. Laxton 1987 Notes on the building techniques in Mycenaean Greece and Nuragic Sardinia. In M.S. Balmuth (ed.), *Nuragic Sardinia and the Mycenaean World*. Studies in Sardinian Archaeology 3. British Archaeological Reports International Series 387: 39–55. Oxford: British Archaeological Reports.

Chapman, R.W. 1985 The later prehistory of western Mediterranean Europe: recent advances. *Advances in World Archaeology* 4: 115–87.

Cherry, J.F. 2004 Mediterranean island prehistory: what's different and what's new? In S.M. Fitzpatrick (ed.), *Voyages of Discovery: The Archaeology of Islands*, 233–48. Westport: Praeger.

Cossu, T. 2003 L'età del Bronzo Medio: i primi nuraghi e l'occupazione dell'altopiano di Pran'e Muru. In T. Cossu, F. Campus, V. Leonelli, M. Perra and M. Sanges (eds), *La vita nel nuraghe Arrubiu*. Arrubiu 3: 15–31. Orroli: Comune di Orroli.

Dyson, S.L., and R.J. Rowland Jr 2007 *Archaeology and History in Sardinia from the Stone Age to the Middle Ages: Shepherds, Sailors, and Conquerors*. Philadelphia: University of Pennsylvania Museum of Archaeology and Anthropology.

Ferrarese Ceruti, M.L. 1979 Ceramica micenea in Sardegna (nota preliminare). *Rivista di Scienze Preistoriche* 34: 242–52.

—— 1980 Micenei in Sardegna! *Rendiconti della Accademia Nazionale dei Lincei* 8.35: 391–3.

—— 1985 Documenti micenei nella Sardegna meridionale. In E. Atzeni, F. Barreca, M.L. Ferrarese Ceruti, E. Contu, G. Lilliu, F. Lo Schiavo, F. Nicosia and E. Equini Schneider (eds), *Ichnussa. La Sardegna dalle Origini all'Età Classica*. Antica Madre. Collana di Studi sull'Italia Antica: 605–12. Milan: Garzanti, Scheiwiller.

—— 1986 I vani c, p, q, del complesso nuragico di Antigori. In M. Marazzi, S. Tusa and L. Vagnetti (eds.), *Traffici Micenei nel Mediterraneo. Problemi Storici e Documentazione Archeologica, Atti del Convegno di Palermo, 11-12 Maggio e 3–6 Dicembre 1984*, 183–8. Taranto: Istituto per la Storia e l'Archeologia della Magna Grecia.

Ferrarese Ceruti, M.L., and R. Assorgia 1982 Il complesso nuragico di Antigori (Sarroch, Cagliari). In L. Vagnetti (ed.), *Magna Grecia e Mondo Miceneo. Nuovi Documenti. XXII Convegno di Studi Sulla Magna Grecia, Taranto, 7–11 Ottobre 1982*, 167–76. Taranto: Istituto per la Storia e l'Archeologia della Magna Grecia.

Ferrarese Ceruti, M.L., L. Vagnetti and F. Lo Schiavo 1987 Minoici, Micenei e Ciprioti in Sardegna nella seconda metà del II millennio a.C. In M.S. Balmuth (ed.), *Nuragic Sardinia and the Mycenaean World*. Studies in Sardinian Archaeology 3. British Archaeological Reports International Series 387: 7–37. Oxford: British Archaeological Reports.

Gale, N.H., and Z.A. Stos-Gale 1987 Oxhide ingots from Sardinia, Crete, and Cyprus. New scientific evidence. In M.S. Balmuth (ed.), *Nuragic Sardinia and the Mycenaean World*. Studies in Sardinian Archaeology 3. British Archaeological Reports International Series 387: 135–78. Oxford: British Archaeological Reports.

Giardino, C. 1995 *Il Mediterraneo Occidentale fra XIV ed VII Secolo a.C: Cerchie Minerarie e Metallurgiche. The West Mediterranean between the 14th and 8th Centuries B.C.: Mining and Metallurgical Spheres*. British Archaeological Reports International Series 612. Oxford: Tempus Reparatum.

Harding, A.F. 1984 *The Mycenaeans and Europe*. London: Academic Press.

Jones, R.E. 1986 Chemical analysis of Aegean-type Late Bronze Age pottery found in Italy. In M. Marazzi, S. Tusa and L. Vagnetti (eds), *Traffici Micenei nel Mediterraneo. Problemi Storici e Documentazione Archeologica, Atti del Convegno di Palermo, Maggio–Dicembre 1984*, 205–14. Taranto: Istituto per la Storia e l'Archeologia della Magna Grecia.

Jones, R.E., and P.M. Day 1987 Late Bronze Age Aegean and Cypriot-type pottery on Sardinia: identification of imports and local imitations by physico-chemical analysis. In M.S. Balmuth (ed.), *Nuragic Sardinia and the Mycenaean World*. Studies in Sardinian Archaeology 3. British Archaeological Reports, International Series 387: 257–70. Oxford: British Archaeological Reports.

Jones, R.E., S.T. Levi and M. Bettelli 2005 Mycenaean pottery in the central Mediterranean: imports, imitations and derivatives. In R. Laffineur and E. Greco (eds), *Emporia: Aegeans in the Central and Eastern Mediterranean. Proceedings of the 10th International Aegean Conference, Athens, Italian School of Archaeology, 14–18 April 2004*. Aegaeum 25: 539–45. Liège: Université de Liège.

Kassianidou, V. 2005 Cypriot copper in Sardinia. Yet another case of bringing coals to Newcastle? In F. Lo Schiavo, A. Giumlia-Mair, U. Sanna and R. Valera (eds), *Archaeometallurgy in Sardinia from the Origins to the Beginning of the Early Iron Age*. Monographies Instrumentum 30: 333–42. Montagnac: Éditions Monique Mergoil.

Knapp, A.B. 1990 Ethnicity, entrepreneurship, and exchange: Mediterranean inter-island relations in the Late Bronze Age. *Annual of the British School at Athens* 85: 115–53.

—— 2000 Archaeology, science-based archaeology and the Mediterranean Bronze Age metals trade. *European Journal of Archaeology* 3: 31–56.

—— 2008 *Prehistoric and Protohistoric Cyprus. Identity, Insularity, and Connectivity.* Oxford: Oxford University Press.

Kolb, M.J. 2005 The genesis of monuments among the Mediterranean islands. In E. Blake and A.B. Knapp (eds), *The Archaeology of Mediterranean Prehistory*, 156–79. Oxford: Blackwell Publishing.

Leighton, R. 1999 *Sicily before History: An Archaeological Survey from the Palaeolithic to the Iron Age*. Cornell: Cornell University Press.

Lilliu, G. 1988 *La Civiltà dei Sardi dal Paleolitico all'Età dei Nuraghi*. Turin: Nuova ERI.

Lo Schiavo, F. 1985a *Nuragic Sardinia in its Mediterranean Setting: Some Recent Advances*. Department of Archaeology Occasional Paper 12. Edinburgh: University of Edinburgh.

—— 1985b Economia e società nell'età dei nuraghi. In E. Atzeni, F. Barreca, M.L. Ferrarese Ceruti, E. Contu, G. Lilliu, F. Lo Schiavo, F. Nicosia and E. Equini Schneider (eds), *Ichnussa. La Sardegna dalle Origini all'Età Classica*. Antica Madre. Collana di Studi sull'Italia Antica, 255–347. Milan: Garzanti, Scheiwiller.

—— 2000 Sea and Sardinia: Nuragic bronze boats. In D. Ridgeway, F.R. Serra Ridgeway, M. Pearce, E. Herring, R.D. Whitehouse and J.B. Wilkins (eds), *Ancient Italy in its Mediterranean Setting. Studies in Honour of Ellen Macnamara*. Accordia Specialist Studies on the Mediterranean 4: 141–59. London: Accordia Research Institute.

—— 2005 The oxhide ingots of Sardinia: updated catalogue. In F. Lo Schiavo, A. Giumlia-Mair, U. Sanna and R. Valera (eds), *Archaeometallurgy in Sardinia from the Origins to the Beginning of the Early Iron Age*. Monographies Instrumentum 30: 317–31. Montagnac: Éditions Monique Mergoil.

Lo Schiavo, F., L. Vagnetti and E. Macnamara 1985 Late Cypriot imports to Italy and their influence on local bronzework. *Papers of the British School at Rome* 53: 1–71.

Loney, H.L. 2007 Prehistoric Italian pottery production: motor memory, motor development and technological transfer. *Journal of Mediterranean Archaeology* 20: 183–207.

Moravetti, A. 1995 Complesso nuragico di Palmavera (Alghero, Sassari). In A. Moravetti and C. Tozzi (eds), *Guide Archeologiche Preistoria e Protostoria in Italia* 2: *Sardegna*, 26–37. Forlì: A.B.A.C.O. Edizioni.

Rowland, R.J., Jr 2001 *The Periphery in the Center: Sardinia in the Ancient and Medieval Worlds*. British Archaeological Reports, International Series 970. Oxford: Archaeopress.

Smith, T.R. 1987 *Mycenaean Trade and Interaction in the West Central Mediterranean 1600–1000 B.C.* British Archaeological Reports International Series 371. Oxford: British Archaeological Reports.

Taylour, W. 1958 *Mycenaean Pottery in Italy and Adjacent Areas*. Cambridge: Cambridge University Press.

Trump, D.H. 1992 Militarism in Nuragic Sardinia. In R.H. Tykot and T.K. Andrews (eds), *Sardinia in the Mediterranean: A Footprint in the Sea*. Monographs in Mediterranean Archaeology 3: 198–202. Sheffield: Sheffield Academic Press.

Ugas, G. 1982 Corti Beccia. Il nuraghe e i reperti. In M.C. Paderi and O. Putzolu (eds), *Ricerche Archeologiche nel Territorio di Sanluri. Mostra Grafica e Fotografica, Sanluri, Palazzo Civico, 16–26 Giugno 1982*, 39–44. Sanluri: Comune di Sanluri.

—— 2005 *L'Alba dei Nuraghi*. Cagliari: Fabula.

Vagnetti, L. 1999 Mycenaean pottery in the Central Mediterranean: imports and local production in their context. In J.P. Crielaard, V. Stissi and G.J. van Wijngaarden (eds), *The Complex Past of Pottery: Production, Circulation and Consumption of Mycenaean and Greek Pottery (16th–Early 5th Centuries BC). Proceedings of the ARCHON International Conference held in Amsterdam, 8–9 November 1996*, 137–61. Amsterdam: J.C. Gieben.

van Dommelen, P. 1998 *On Colonial Grounds: A Comparative Study of Colonialism and Rural Settlement in First Millennium BC Western Sardinia*. Archaeological Studies Leiden University 2. Leiden: Faculty of Archaeology, University of Leiden.

Vianello, A. 2005 *Late Bronze Age Mycenaean and Italic Products in the West Mediterranean: A Social and Economic Analysis*. British Archaeological Reports, International Series 1439. Oxford: Archaeopress.

Webster, G.S. 1996 *A Prehistory of Sardinia 2300–500 BC*. Monographs in Mediterranean Archaeology 5. Sheffield: Sheffield Academic Press.

7

NEGOTIATING ISLAND INTERACTIONS

Cyprus, the Aegean and the Levant in the Late Bronze to Early Iron Ages

Sarah Janes

Introduction

This chapter takes as its subject the island of Cyprus from the end of the Late Bronze Age to the Early Iron Age (1100–700 BC), a period of great upheaval, transition and increased mobility following the collapse of the large, regional palatial societies across the Mediterranean. Building on previous research, this study considers issues of insularity, connectivity and identity, focusing on the multiple internal and external interactions and encounters on the island at that time. Through the examination of the complex yet extensive extant mortuary remains, I explore the materiality of social and cultural interaction on the island, considering how people of diverse cultures and backgrounds interacted on the island through multiple connections – including maritime interactions, migrations, colonial encounters and intra-island contact. I then discuss how these interactions combined to contribute to the emergence of small, local, hybridised polities involving native Cypriots and incoming people from the Aegean and Levant.

Island connections

Cyprus has long been seen as a 'crossroads' of multiple, complex interactions, acting as a stepping-stone between east and west. Accordingly, the island has played a central role in studies of trade and exchange – long-distance and local, entrepreneurial and centralised – and of the movement and transfer of ideas, material culture and traditions across the Mediterranean. It is unsurprising, therefore, that Cyprus was deeply affected by the upheavals at the end of the thirteenth century BC, when the major states of the Late Bronze Age Mediterranean, including Mycenaean palatial systems and Levantine centres such as Ras Ibn Hani and Ugarit, seem to have undergone a major social and economic collapse (Iacovou 1998: 334–5; 1999b: 4–5; 2001:

86; 2006a: 33–5; Karageorghis 1987: 117; 1992: 81; Rupp 1987: 147), leaving the Mediterranean effectively free from outside interference by other states from the twelfth to the eighth centuries BC (Iacovou 1999a: 141–2; 2002: 84; 2005b: 21; 2006a: 33–4; Mazar 1994: 39). The impact of these Mediterranean-wide upheavals on Cyprus is reflected in the archaeological record by a series of abandonments and destructions at several Late Bronze Age sites across the island. The disruption to the island, however, was relatively short-lived, and old urban and state structures seem to have been replaced rather soon by the emergence of a new socio-political landscape – the Archaic city-kingdoms (Iacovou 1999a: 145–6; 2005b: 20–1).

Despite the upheavals of the thirteenth century BC, the complex cultural mix that constituted Late Bronze Age Cyprus continued to diversify throughout the Iron Age, facilitated by increased Mediterranean-wide mobility and movements. New and established connections, both within and beyond the island, significantly impacted on its socio-political trajectory. The emerging social, political and cultural land-scapes of the Cypriot Iron Age, however, have traditionally been explained in terms of external stimuli alone, with a particular focus on the influence of both displaced Aegean peoples and incoming Phoenicians on Cypriot culture and society during the eleventh to ninth centuries BC. This one-dimensional approach simplifies the mechanics of social and cultural interaction and underplays the complexity of the island's socio-political development. The dynamic changes underway on the island in the Early Iron Age were the result of multiple social and spatial dynamics, including internal island interactions and cross-island connections. This chapter seeks to develop a more holistic approach, examining the materiality of all complex social and cultural encounters on the island at that time – both within it and beyond it – exploring how these connectivities impacted on the renegotiation of social and political identities.

The simplification of Late Bronze Age to Early Iron Age socio-political and cultural development

Traditional interpretations of the Late Bronze to Early Iron Age social and polit-ical trajectory rely heavily on the perceived 'ethnicity' embedded in material culture and in the social and political practices that appeared on the island at the begin-ning of the Iron Age. The perceived Aegean colonisation of the island, the so-called 'colonisation narrative' (Knapp 2008: 249–58; Leriou 2002), argues for two waves of Aegean migration to the island. The first wave supposedly occurred in LC IIC (around 1200 BC) following the collapse of Mycenaean palatial society, causing wide-spread unrest across the island but remaining somewhat invisible archaeologically (following Leriou 2002: 170; cf. Jung 2009). The second wave supposedly occurred in the Protogeometric (PG) period (otherwise LC IIIB), when Aegean material culture and practices become apparent on the island – new mortuary locations, tomb architecture, Mycenaean-inspired pottery and other artefacts, and the Greek language (Iacovou 1998: 334–5; 1999a: 148–52; 2001: 89–90; 2003: 81–3; 2005a: 127; 2006a; 2006b; Karageorghis 1994: 6; Leriou 2002: 170–1). From this point on the ethnically dominant element on Cyprus in the Iron Age is argued to be Aegean

Table 7.1 Dates and abbreviations

Period	Abbreviation	Date
Late Bronze Age	LBA	~1200–1100 BC
Protogeometric (traditional LCIIIB)	PG	1100–1050 BC
Cypro-Geometric I	CGI	1050–950 BC
Cypro-Geometric II	CGII	950–850 BC
Cypro-Geometric III	CGIII	850–700 BC
Cypro-Archaic I	CA	700–475 BC
Cypro-Classical	CC	400–325 BC

in origin, with a new political system based on Greek kingship (Gjerstad 1926; 1948; Iacovou 1998: 339; Karageorghis 2002: 36; Rupp 1998: 209; Snodgrass 1988: 12).

The cause of such major changes to the social and political trajectory of the island has also been delegated to the Phoenicians, and again is corroborated mainly through the presence of 'Phoenician' material culture: certain temples in Kition dedicated to the Semitic deities Astarte and Melqart (Coldstream 1985: 51–3; Iacovou 1999a: 153; 1999b: 16; Karageorghis 1982: 123; Yon: 1999: 20), architecture, glyptic and statuary (Reyes 1994: 128–31); tombs and burial practices, in particular the association of the Phoenicians with cremation burials at Salamis and Amathus from the eleventh century onwards (Agelarakis *et al.* 1998; Bikai 1989: 209; Calvet 1980; Christou 1998); and pottery (Bikai 1983; 1989: 204; Karageorghis 1983), in particular Cypriot imitations of the small Phoenician globular jug (Black-on-Red ware) in the Cypro-Geometric II period (CG II) (Coldstream 1985: 52–3; Iacovou 2004; 2005a: 131; Schreiber 2003). Traditional interpretations maintain that Phoenician settlers arrived in the ninth century BC, colonizing Kition as a trading outpost, although more recent interpretations have brought the date of this colonisation forward to the eleventh to tenth centuries BC (e.g. Bikai 1987; 1989: 204). Accordingly, the Phoenicians have been credited with providing the economic stimulus for secondary state formation (Rupp 1987; 1998) and their arrival is said to have been followed by a period of cultural and economic expansion across the island.

This focus on ethnicity has led to oversimplified interpretations of the complex multiple internal and external contact situations on the island during the Late Bronze to Early Iron Age. The meaning of ethnicity seems at time confused, and its value to archaeological research as an analytical concept has been called into question. Ethnicity has long been used to support the construction and fulfilment of political and nationalistic agendas, and the manipulation and misinterpretation of archaeological and historical data for the creation, authentication and maintenance of political viewpoints is often a feature of archaeological research (Banks 1996: 2; Jones 1997). Academically, it is significant that its meaning varies not just between academic disciplines but also within them (Knapp 2001: 32).

Moreover, as a dynamic concept, ethnicity operates 'in a mythological arena of feelings and beliefs' (Banks 1996: 3) through a collection of intangible 'shared ideologies' such as kinship, self-esteem and primordial bonds, and is grounded in a shared history, genealogy, territory, language and material culture (Banks 1996: 3, 5; Hall 1997: 2; Jenkins 1997: 9; Knapp 2001: 31; Knapp and Antoniadou 1998: 21). As with all identities, ethnicities fluctuate in response to social or political stimuli and are constantly being redefined to maintain distinction between the 'self' and the 'other' (Knapp 2001: 32–3, 38). To a certain extent cultural and material practices reflect some of the underlying bonds of ethnicity, but it is generally accepted that these are simply 'indicia', and are not fully reflective of an ethnic identity (Jones 1997: 12; Knapp 2001: 32–4; Sherratt 1992). These indicia may allow us to draw limited conclusions about ethnicity in pre- or protohistoric periods. Yet if we accept that ethnic identity is in essence a matter of personal perception, that in part 'ethnic groups constructed themselves discursively' (Hall 1998: 267), and that ethnicity can only partially be represented by material culture – concealed in symbols and codes that are only truly understood within the culture within which they operated – then ethnicity in the prehistoric mortuary record is largely intangible.

Leading scholars in Cypriot archaeology now agree that the archaeological record of the Cypro-Geometric (CG) period is ill-equipped to deal with attempts to establish distinct ethnicities in the Early Iron Age, instead advocating a focus on the processes of socio-political and cultural change and on the ways that the Early Iron Age horizon was formed (Iacovou 2005a; 2006a, 2006b). Moreover, the major impact on Early Iron Age Cypriot material and social practices assigned by these traditional approaches to Aegean peoples or Phoenicians reflects a top-down, colonialist approach to cultural interactions. This widely criticised approach (e.g. Knapp 2008: 53–5) emphasises the 'simple replacement of a less complex society's material and symbolic resources by those of a more complex ("donor") society' (Knapp 2008: 53). Instead, socio-political development on Early Iron Age Cyprus should be understood in terms of the manifold cultural interactions that occurred at that time. These involved a mixture of different groups across the Mediterranean, both east and west, as well as complex internal developments that resulted in the dynamic hybridisation of social and cultural practices and the creation of new social and cultural traditions. The burial record of Late Bronze to Early Iron Age Cyprus can be understood within these complex interactions and socio-political negotiations.

Unravelling complex identities in the mortuary record

Identity is an elaborate, multifaceted and dynamic social construct. The creation and maintenance of identities, both personal and group, are the means by which people differentiate between themselves and others through perceived feelings of belonging, a means of positioning themselves within a wider world context (Diaz-Andreu and Lucy 2005: 2; Knapp 2008: 31–3; Knapp and Antoniadou 1998: 21). Throughout our lives we possess many fluid, dynamic and fluctuating identities that are subjective and 'lodged in contingency' (Knapp 2008: 32); together these make up one's social identity (Keswani 1989: 10). Specific to each individual, social identities involve a complex combination – e.g. family, kinship group, community, religious group or tribe, as well as personal identities, including one's gender, biological sex, age and occupation (Keswani 1989: 10; Knapp 2001: 40). In contact situations, people meet and mix and, along with their material culture, become transformed; the material remains of these dynamic cultural interactions can often be identified in the mortuary record.

Mortuary data are the material remains of both simple and complex thoughts and actions (O'Shea 1984: 24; Steel 1995: 199; Webb 1992: 87). The extant mortuary remains of a given society cannot easily be understood when detached from the rituals that formed their original context (Hallote 2002: 108; Keswani 2004: 9). The data we study are far removed from their original contexts and constitute only the remnants of the ritual observances of death that have, by chance, survived in the mortuary context. Thus the mortuary record represents only a certain percentage and cross-section of society, the nature of which can be hard to discern (Dickinson 2006: 176; Keswani 2004: 22; Parker Pearson 1999: 5), and our interpretations are further influenced by the disparate nature of the extant mortuary data.

As Morris (1992: 14–15) says, however, 'not knowing everything that originally happened does not mean we are powerless', and as the material remains of rituals performed in a specific arena of social contact, mortuary data are ideal for examining the changes underway in the social landscape. These data can, therefore, provide insights into inter- and extra-island contacts involving Cyprus in the Late Bronze and Early Iron Ages. Indeed, mortuary behaviour and burial practices reveal more about the living than the dead (Bloch-Smith 2002: 121; Chapman 1977: 21–2; Manning 1998: 40; Parker Pearson 1999: 3–4). The rites and rituals surrounding death are associated with change, and the living use death and burial as a tool for social regeneration and the 're-negotiation of social hierarchies' (Keswani 2004: 1; Manning 1998: 40). What we witness in the material record are the remains of attempts to represent social reality, or rather re-present it, in a manner that conforms to the needs of the living (Cavanagh and Mee 1998: 122; Hallote 2002: 105–8; Keswani 2004: 1; Murphy 1998: 32; Van Gennep 1960; Voutsaki 1998: 44).

Significantly, mortuary behaviour alters in response to 'changes in the social and political environment' (Karageorghis 2001: 53; Keswani 1989: 20; 2004: 9; Knapp 2001: 33). As an occasion to display or promote oneself, or to transfer rights and positions in society, mortuary behaviour – a significant social activity – offers an opportunity to enact physically and symbolically the renegotiation of personal and social identities to create or maintain socio-political control (Keswani 2004: 1; Murphy 1998: 32, 36–8; Voutsaki 1998: 41). In the context of the multiple social and spatial dynamics of the Late Bronze to Early Iron Age on Cyprus, careful examination of the complex material remains of the mortuary record provides the ideal way to explore the complexities of social interaction, to examine the ways in which different groups renegotiated their identities in the light of multiple and diverse cultural contacts.

My previous research involved the analysis of an unprecedentedly large body of mortuary data from the island, dating from the Late Bronze to Cypro-Archaic (CA) period, and provided a new approach and a fresh perspective to data which have long been hampered by the association of outdated, inaccurate interpretations as discussed above (Janes 2008). The following section examines three aspects of mortuary behaviour – tomb architecture and extramural burial areas at Palaepaphos, and child pithos burials at Salamis. It also explores the complex internal and external connections at Salamis. These examples illustrate how the multiple, diverse cultural interactions on Cyprus in the Early Iron Age were negotiated through the hybridisation of materials and practices; they also highlight how truly complex and nuanced island connections were at that time.

Complex burial practices

The introduction of 'Mycenaean' square-chamber and long-dromos tombs found in many burial areas during the Cypro-Geometric period has played a major role in the longevity of the colonisation narrative (Iacovou 1999b: 7–8; 2001: 89–90). This specific tomb type is widely considered to be a direct import from the Aegean and has been used in many cases – for example at Salamis (Yon 1971: 7), Palaepaphos (Karageorghis 1983: 5–6; Raptou 2002: 116), Lapethos (Gjerstad *et al.* 1934) and Gastria *Alaas* (Karageorghis 1975) – to indicate discrete groups of Mycenaean settlers on Cyprus (for the sites, see Figure 7.1). It is necessary, however, to question the Mycenaean origin of this tomb type (cf. Iacovou 2005a: 131). Chamber and dromos tombs already had a long tradition on Cyprus before the start of the Iron Age (Karageorghis 1970b: 223). Indeed, such tombs were in use on the island

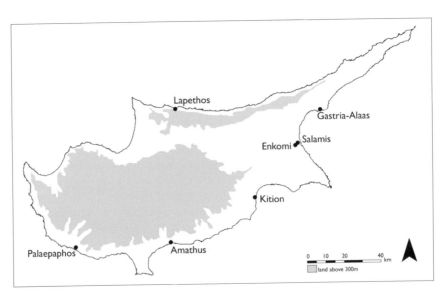

Figure 7.1 Map of Cyprus detailing all sites mentioned in the text.

from as early as the Bronze Age and remained in use right up to the Roman period (Karageorghis 1970b: 223; see Figure 7.2).

Tomb type and extramural burial areas

Similarly, the anomalous Amathusian tomb type – the shaft and dromos – has been understood as an ethnic marker, in this case that of indigenous Cypriots living at Amathus in the Early Iron Age (Coldstream 1985: 50; Gjerstad 1948: 432). It has been used to corroborate the notion that Amathus was settled by a 'non-Greek' monarchy (e.g. Iacovou 2003: 84). Characterising this burial architecture as an entirely 'Cypriot' innovation is erroneous, and the development of this tomb type has a multitude of possible interpretations, from economic restriction, to the promotion of social hierarchy (Given 1998: 23; Gjerstad et al. 1934: 140–1; Karageorghis and Iacovou 1990: 76).

Significantly, the use of the 'Mycenaean' dromos and chamber tomb architecture coincided with the shift, across the whole island, in the location of most burial grounds, from intra- to extramural. At Palaepaphos, the Early Iron Age burial areas of Skales, Plakes, Xerolimni and Lakkos tou Skarnou (Figure 7.3) were all located in highly visible areas at a considerable distance from the Late Bronze Age tombs, in particular Mantissa, Kaminia, Asproyi, Laonas and Evreti, which were located in and around the main habitation area (Maier and Wartburg 1985: 146–8).

One widely accepted explanation for this switch to extramural burial areas is that the abandonment of Late Bronze Age tombs and the construction of new ones reflected the displacement of communities and/or the arrival of a new group with no ties to the established population. At Palaepaphos, this has been attributed to the

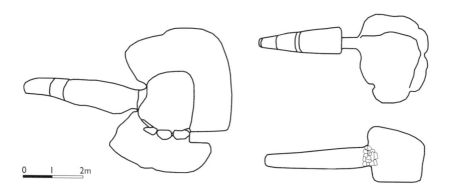

0 | 2m

Figure 7.2   Overview of tomb types: *left*: a Late Cypriot tomb from Milia (after Åström 1972b: 45, figure 25); *top right*: a Middle Cypriot III tomb from Ayios Iakovos (after Åström 1972a: 9, figure 1); *bottom right*: 'Mycenaean-style' tomb from Palaepaphos *Skales* (after Karageorghis 1983: figure 35).

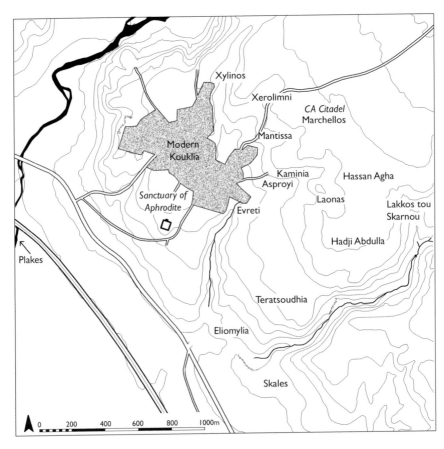

Figure 7.3   Map of the Palaepaphos area, detailing the Late Bronze Age and Cypriot Geometric sites discussed in the text (after Bezzola 2004: map 1).

second wave of migration from the Aegean at the end of the Late Bronze Age. Such an interpretation, in conjunction with the perceived Mycenaean tomb architecture, implies the arrival of a 'dominant' foreign culture that significantly impacted on the traditions of the local community, and makes no allowance for any internal impetus for such a change. An analysis of the burial record of the Late Bronze Age tombs at Palaepaphos and those of Early Iron Age Palaepaphos *Skales*, however, reveals clear continuity in tomb assemblages between the Late Bronze and Early Iron Age as well as continued prosperity. The burials at Skales, therefore, do not represent a distinct new group or population (Janes 2008: 145–6, 148, 151).

Periods of relative social and political stability are usually reflected through patterns in mortuary practices and in gradually shifting symbolic and material markers of identity. Sudden changes in ritual, however, tend to be physical expressions of competition, display and hierarchy (Manning 1998: 40), indicating moments of instability as groups or individuals feel pressured to define themselves symbolically and mark themselves off from neighbours and possible rivals. The tombs at Palaepaphos show very gradual changes and developments across the twelfth century BC transition, with the introduction of a few new architectural elements and the shift to extra-mural cemeteries. Beyond these developments, the next 400 years exhibit a series of gently fluctuating changes in the portrayal of identities and deposition of materials – a gradual shift in the socio-political landscapes, from elite competition for power and control in the Late Bronze Age to the single group/individual ruling line of the Cypro-Archaic Palaepaphian city-kingdoms. The mortuary remains do not indicate a sudden change in population or the arrival of a dominant foreign contingent (Janes 2008: 157–8).

Moreover, the tombs at Skales illustrate clearly the use of the chamber and dromos tomb in response to internal island developments propelled by the unrest of the twelfth century BC. Late Bronze Age society at Palaepaphos, as at many sites across the island, centred on elite groups competing for control of resources and vying for pre-eminence within the community. These elite groups are highly visible in the mortuary record at Palaepaphos through the use of large, deep tombs designed to contain multiple individuals over many generations; they are positioned in restricted access areas within the town itself (Janes 2008: 143–5, 157–8). The very deliberate positioning of the tombs was part of negotiating social boundaries through the use of physical ones (Fisher 2007: 289; Keswani 2004: 87). The funerals themselves would have been restricted to members of other elite or high status families; thus these intramural tombs performed the function of creating and maintaining inter-familial competition and emphasising the rights of the ancestral line (Fisher 2007: 288; Keswani 2004: 158–9).

In contrast, the highly prosperous extramural burials of the Early Iron Age were deliberately placed in high-visibility areas and made use of tomb architecture that was both clearly visible on the landscape and suited to small family or kinship burials (on average one to three individuals per tomb; Janes 2008: 130). In response to the unrest of the twelfth century BC, the Palaepaphians strengthened their community identity through the visible promotion of their wealth, collective identity and community bonds (Janes 2008: 149).

In summary, there is no direct evidence that the new tomb architecture was not simply an adaptation of local traditions for new social or political requirements (Karageorghis 1975: 25; Leriou 2007: 574–6) – in this case in response to the new social order and the need to promote a collective community identity in the face of general unrest across the island. It is, however, not implausible that certain cultural traditions or aspects of material culture of new groups or foreign contacts provided the inspiration for the changes evident at Palaepaphos, such as the tomb type. The use of this architectural form might illustrate the hybridisation of burial practices during the Early Iron Age. The inspiration for such change thus would have been stimulated by cultural contacts from beyond the island, used to address a specific need of the

Early Iron Age Palaepaphian community, namely the need to establish the community boundaries of the town with the island context.

Child pithos burials

The variety of child pithos burials at Salamis exemplifies the hybridisation of mortuary practices that resulted from increased internal and external connectivities across Cyprus at the start of the Iron Age. The earliest child pithos burials were discovered within the early settlement – under the basilica of Campanopetra, under later Archaic buildings inside the eleventh century BC wall and slightly outside the wall in the same area. These intramural pithos burials all contained newborn babies or prenates and all but one dates to the end of the tenth or beginning of the ninth century BC (Calvet 1980). The single burial dating to the eighth century BC may indicate that this intramural practice continued throughout the Cypro-Archaic (CA) and Cypro-Classical (CC) periods, although it remains archaeologically invisible as a result of a lack of extant settlement evidence. The jars and bodies are now highly fragmentary, but the jars were all Phoenician imports, modified to allow the small bodies to be placed inside. These burials illustrate that babies or prenates were buried in a different manner from older children and adults; the main burial areas from the eleventh century BC onwards were all extramural. It has been argued that the use of Phoenician pithoi, and the spatial differentiation based on age, represent Phoenician influences on burial traditions from this early period (Calvet 1980), or perhaps the presence of Phoenician settlers.

During the Cypro-Geometric (CG) period, burials at Salamis played a significant role in competitive, elite group competition for power. At the end of the CG, however, there was a strategic shift in burial areas from just outside the walls of the city to a plateau to the west (Figure 7.4). This shift was enforced by the new, pre-eminent ruling group in an attempt to consolidate their power through the active rewriting of the social history of the area, ensuring burial traditions associated with other ancestries and previous ruling groups were 'actively forgotten, renegotiated, and rewritten' (Manning 1998: 53, discussing a similar situation in the Late Bronze Age in the Maroni Valley; Janes 2008: 308–9, 317). A large number of burials were made in the area of Cellarka (Figure 7.5) in the CA–CC periods. These tombs belonged to family/kinship groups who emphasised and maintained their position in the community and their relationship to the ruling lineage line through their position on the burial plateau in relation to the lineage line burials at the Royal Tombs (Janes 2008: 317–19, and see Figure 7.4).

Burial practices in the Cellarka tombs strictly adhered to tradition. For example, the pottery assemblages remained homogeneous across the periods, each tomb was reused many times and the area continued to be built in even when space was limited, resulting in haphazardly placed, oddly shaped and awkwardly oriented constructions (Janes 2008: 317–18, and see Figure 7.5). Furthermore, markers and boundary walls were placed above the tombs, and there is evidence of offering pyres and rituals that marked the family/kinship space at the time of closure. This devotion to tradition in

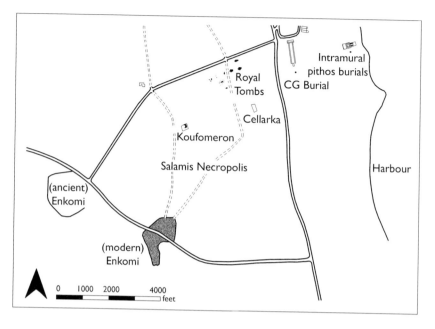

Figure 7.4 Map of the Salamis area, showing the main burial areas (after Karageorghis 1978: 2).

mortuary practice highlights just how important family/kinship associations really were. The living adopted mortuary practices to re-emphasise their family/kinship associations and maintain their position within the wider social hierarchy.

Infant amphora inhumations, similar to those inside the walls of the town, were found across the site, buried in pits in dromoi within the boundary walls of at least twelve tombs (Karageorghis 1970a). The number of these burials is very low, certainly too few to conclude that all infants were interred in this manner in the CA and CC periods. Rather, it is likely that the distinctive practice of burying young infants in Phoenician pithoi was adopted by family/kinship groups as symbolic markers associated with the final sealing of the tomb, linked to the creation of family/kinship space using boundary walls, markers and pyres.

Funerary rites and rituals are situated directly within the temporal and spatial context of the society within which they operate (Barrett 1988: 30), and goods placed in tombs act as symbols and markers that can only truly be understood within the specific community in which they were deposited (Hall 1997). Moreover, even within the given community, the symbolism associated with burial practices may be interpreted in different ways by different people (Cavanagh and Mee 1998: 105; Morris 1992: 15). It is a challenge, therefore, to understand the meaning behind the use of this distinct practice in such different contexts. The material remains were almost

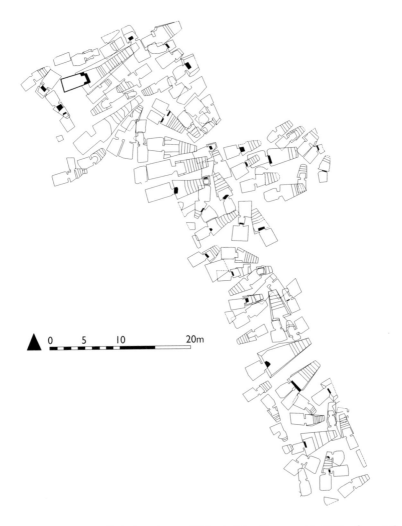

Figure 7.5 The Cellarka burial area of Salamis (after Karageorghis 1970a: figure 16).

identical, but the symbolism and significance behind the deposition of infants in Phoenician jars in the various contexts were entirely different. By the eighth century BC the practice that had begun as intramural burials in the early town had been adopted and adapted to suit the specific needs of the CA and CC community burying their dead at Cellarka – the promotion of family/kinship identity.

A further example of hybridisation of mortuary practices at Cellarka is the use of boundary walls and markers, a practice attested in other areas throughout the Mediterranean, e.g. at Naxos in the Greek Geometric period (Lambrinoudakis 1988:

246), as well as other areas of Cyprus where they were in use from as early as LC II, for example Enkomi *Ayios Jakovos* Tomb 11 (Karageorghis 1970a: 225). The Cellarka pyres, however, were used in a different way from other Mediterranean examples in that they were used only once, and the role they played was very specific to the requirements of the Salaminian population buried at Cellarka, i.e. for sealing the tomb and for emulating powerful family/kinship associations.

Complex regional interactions: the case of Salamis

Salamis' geographical position on the east coast of Cyprus was instrumental in the role it played in Near Eastern and Egyptian spheres of interaction. Complex overseas relations ensured a combination of influences at Salamis that were clearly reflected in mortuary practices, often through indirect transmission as opposed to direct contact (Reyes 1994: 67). This mixture of influences was diverse and is reflected from the start of the CG period in pottery vessels, materials, iconography, other artefacts and burial practices from the Aegean, the Near East, Phoenicia and Egypt. Wooden furniture inlaid with ivory reflects Assyrian, Syrian and Phoenician influences, while bronze bowls, ivories and terracotta candelabra are all part of the Assyrian repertoire, as seen at Nimrud (Mallowan 1978; Reyes 1994: 63). The Cypriot imitations found in the burials at Salamis, however, merely took inspiration from these foreign forms; they were not exact copies. The ivories and inlaid furniture, for example, were often decorated with nonsensical hieroglyphics; their value lay in the associations inspired by the object, not in the faithful representation of an original form and meaning.

Another eastern tradition seen at Salamis is the sacrifice of horses, which occurs in all the burials at the Royal Tombs. This seems to be an imitation of rituals from elite Assyrian burials, but there are also precedents in tombs throughout the old world: at Marathon, Nauplia and Argos in Greece, Osmankayasi and Gordion in Anatolia, south Russia, eastern Europe, China, Sudan and Egypt (Karageorghis 1965; 1967: 117). These horse sacrifices are thought to have served as symbols of extreme power and wealth (Carstens 2005; Karageorghis 1965; Reyes 1994: 63). Jewellery, for example diadems and mouthpieces, with eastern iconography such as lions and sphinxes is found across the island in a multitude of burial contexts. Scarabs, seals and amulets represent a distinct Egyptian influence, as does the presence of alabaster bottles and paintings in the style of Egyptian sarcophagi on the roof of Tomb 80 at the site of Koufomeron on the Salamis burial plateau (Karageorghis 1973: 123–7; Figure 7.4). Finally, both Aegean pottery and burial practices were included in the Salaminian burial repertoire, including cremation and offering pyres (discussed above).

The adoption and adaptation of foreign elements in mortuary practices at Salamis had two main purposes. First and most important was the maintenance and control of internal island dynamics and local competition. Salamis was a prosperous and wealthy city from the moment of its foundation in the eleventh century BC. The main impetus for the move from Enkomi to Salamis was the natural harbour around which the town developed and flourished throughout the CG period. Evidence for increasing wealth during the CG includes the move from rock-cut to monumental rock-built tombs in a very short space of time (Iacovou 2005b: 26–7), and the vast increase in disposable wealth deposited in mortuary contexts (Janes 2008: 307–8). This wealth became firmly established in the hands of a small number of individuals from the ruling lineage towards the end of the CG III period. The Royal Tombs constructed in CG III stand as testament to this, as powerful visual statements of control and legitimised entitlement created by those at the 'apex of a stratified social hierarchy' (Rupp 1988: 124). The very aim of the tombs was to be as visual as possible to as many people as possible, both during and after the funeral itself, imparting different messages to different individuals and groups (Janes 2008: 308–9). Their consistent orientation towards the town and the sea during the CG III period was by no means accidental. The strategic positioning of these tombs indicates the messages were clearly aimed at locals, other islanders and foreigners.

The ruling lineage was concerned with the indirect contacts they maintained with the Assyrian empire. Traditionally, the use of eastern motifs, iconography and burial practices has been regarded as representative of the Assyrian relationship with Cyprus at the beginning of the Archaic period, and the question of Assyrian domination of Cyprus at that time has been examined extensively (Knapp 2008: 345–7). The assumption has been that increased external connectivities made the most significant impact on the town's development. The mortuary evidence, however, does not support this notion. The Assyrian element was just one of many operating in and around the island at that time; the close proximity of Salamis to the Levantine mainland, and extensive interaction with traders, merchants and overseas representatives, ensured that the ruling elite remained aware of Assyrian developments. It is this factor that we see reflected in the bold statements of power and control in mortuary behaviour from the end of the CG period onwards. The mortuary behaviour of the Salaminian ruling line thus reflected a reaction to both internal and external situations of which they were very much in control. The wealth deposited in the Royal Tombs emphasised the ability of the Salaminian rulers to equal the disposable wealth of their powerful neighbours (Karageorghis 1969: 14) as the new, 'state-controlled market' emerged in the Near East (Iacovou 2005b: 27; 2006b: 317–18; Rupp 1998: 111). Indeed, the burials at Salamis asserted the power and importance of the town to other political entities operating in the same trading spheres at that time, both internal and external, 'an assertion of ... pride, dignity and equality' (Karageorghis 1969: 14–16; Rupp 1988: 112).

Conclusion

The cultural relations of Cyprus in the Late Bronze to Early Iron Age were diverse, and internal connections were as significant as external connectivities in the development of the island's socio-political and cultural landscapes. The placement of the tombs around Palaepaphos, for example, illustrates the concern of the town with projecting its community identity to neighbours and foreigners alike. The burials of the ruling lineage line at Salamis at the end of the CG and the CA periods, however, clearly show more concern over the control of internal affairs than that of external connections. Each site across the island experienced its own unique combination of internal and external connections that shaped, and are reflected in, the material culture of mortuary practices across Cyprus during the Late Bronze to Early Iron Age.

Similar practices that appear across the island had a wide variety of social and cultural meanings, such as the child pithos burials in the CG and CA–CC periods at Salamis. Another clear example is the practice of horse sacrifice at Salamis, which emphasised the power of the ruling lineage to their eastern neighbours whilst also enabling these elites to consolidate their power within the ongoing intensive internal competition for control of the area. In contrast, however, the new political and social systems that emerged in the CA period at Palaepaphos developed gradually and relatively unchallenged, either from within the island or from beyond. The mortuary evidence is testament to this, revealing the inclusion of new elements of conspicuous display, such as larger tombs and two single horse burials in the CA tombs at Eliomylia; yet the reserved nature of these burials suggests nothing more than the desire to emulate the conspicuous displays of the powerful city-kingdom of Salamis (Janes 2008: 156–7), another intra-island connection.

The mechanics of cultural contact are complex and nuanced, involving both internal and external stimuli. When the restrictions imposed by traditional interpretations of Iron Age socio-political and cultural development are removed, and when the discussion moves away from the ethnicity of cultural traits and material culture, we can begin to reassess our understanding of the processes of interaction. The focus must remain on the nature of cultural encounters and the renegotiation of identities, established through careful study of the materiality of multiple encounters and interactions as reflected in everyday practices.

References

Agelarakis, A.P., A. Kanta and N. Stampolidis 1998 The osseous record in the western necropolis of Amathus: an archeo-anthropological investigation. In V. Karageorghis and N. Stampolidis (eds), *Eastern Mediterranean. Cyprus–Dodecanese–Crete 16th–6th centuries BC. Proceedings of the International Symposium, Rethymnon, Crete, May 1997*, 217–32. Athens: University of Crete and the Leventis Foundation.

Åström, P. 1972a *The Swedish Cyprus Expedition* IV: 1B. *The Middle Cypriote Bronze Age*. Lund: Swedish Cyprus Expedition.

—— 1972b *The Swedish Cyprus Expedition* IV: 1C. *The Late Cypriote Bronze Age: Architecture and Pottery*. Lund: Swedish Cyprus Expedition.

Banks, I. 1996 Archaeology, nationalism and ethnicity. In J.A. Atkinson, I. Banks and J. O'Sullivan (eds), *Nationalism and Archaeology*, 1–11. Glasgow: Cruithne Press.

Barrett, J.C. 1988 The living, the dead and the ancestors: Neolithic and Early Bronze Age mortuary practices. In J.C. Barrett and A. I. Kinnes (eds), *The Archaeology of Context in the Neolithic and the Bronze Age; Recent Trends*, 30–42. Sheffield: Department of Archaeology, University of Sheffield.

Bezzola, S. 2004 *Lucerne fittili dagli scavi di Palaepaphos (Cipro)*. Alt-Paphos 5. Mainz am Rhein: Verlag Phillip von Zabern.

Bikai, P. 1983 The imports from the east. In V. Karageorghis, *Palaepaphos-Skales: An Iron Age Cemetery in Cyprus*. Alt-Paphos 3: 396–406. Constanz: Universitätsverlag.

—— 1987 Trade networks in the Early Iron Age: the Phoenicians at Palaepaphos. In D.W. Rupp (ed.), *Western Cyprus: Connections*. Studies in Mediterranean Archaeology 77: 125–8. Göteborg: Paul Åströms Förlag.

—— 1989 Cyprus and the Phoenicians. *Biblical Archaeologist* 52: 203–9.

—— 1992 Cyprus and Phoenicia: literary evidence for the Early Iron Age. In G.C. Ioannides (ed.), *Studies in Honour of Vassos Karageorghis*, 241–8. Nicosia: Society of Cypriot Studies.

Bloch-Smith, E. 2002 Life in Judah from the perspective of the dead. *Near Eastern Archaeology* 65: 120–30.

Calvet, Y. 1980 Sur certains rites funéraires à Salamine de Chypre. In M. Yon (ed.), *Salamine de Chypre, Histoire et Archéologie: état des recherches*. Colloques Internationaux du Centre National de la Recherche Scientifique 578: 115–20. Paris: Éditions du Centre National de la Recherche Scientifique.

Carstens, A.M. 2005 To bury a ruler: the meaning of the horse in aristocratic burials. In V. Karageorghis, H. Matthäus and S. Rogge (eds), *Cyprus: Religion and Society from the Late Bronze Age to the end of the Archaic Period. Proceedings of an International Symposium on Cypriote Archaeology, Erlangen, 23–24 July 2004*, 57–76. Möhesse: Leventis Foundation; Institute for Classical Archaeology, University of Erlangen-Nuremberg; Institute for Interdisciplinary Cypriot Studies, University of Münster.

Cavanagh, W., and C. Mee 1998 *A Private Place: Death in Prehistoric Greece*. Studies in Mediterranean Archaeology 125. Jonsered: Paul Åströms Förlag.

Chapman, R.W. 1977 Burial practices: areas of mutual interest. In M. Spriggs (ed.), *Archaeology and Anthropology: Areas of Mutual Interest*. British Archaeological Reports, International Series 19: 19–33. Oxford: British Archaeological Reports.

Christou, D. 1998 Cremations in the western necropolis of Amathus. In V. Karageorghis and N. Stampolidis (eds), *Proceedings of the International Symposium: Eastern Mediterranean. Cyprus–Dodecanese–Crete 16th–6th centuries B.C.*, 207–15. Athens: University of Crete and the Leventis Foundation.

Coldstream, J.N. 1985 Archaeology in Cyprus, 1960–1985: the Geometric and Archaic periods. In V. Karageorghis (ed.), *Archaeology in Cyprus, 1960–1985*, 125–41. Nicosia: Leventis Foundation.

Diaz-Andreu, M., and S. Lucy 2005 Introduction. In M. Diaz-Andreu, S. Lucy, S. Babić and D.N. Edwards (eds), *The Archaeology of Identity: Approaches to Gender, Age, Status, Ethnicity and Religion*, 1–12. London: Routledge.

Dickinson, O. 2006 *The Aegean from the Bronze Age to the Iron Age*. London and New York: Routledge.

Fisher, K.D. 2007 Building Power: Monumental Architecture, Place and Social Interaction in Late Bronze Age Cyprus. Unpublished PhD dissertation, Department of Anthropology, University of Toronto.

Given, M. 1998 Inventing the Eteocypriots: imperialist archaeology and the manipulation of ethnic identity. *Journal of Mediterranean Archaeology* 11: 3–29.

Gjerstad, E. 1926 *Studies on Prehistoric Cyprus.* Uppsala: Uppsala Universitets Arsskrift.

—— 1948 *The Swedish Cyprus Expedition* IV: 2. *The Cypro-Geometric, Cypro-Archaic and Cypro-Classical Periods.* Stockholm: Swedish Cyprus Expedition.

Gjerstad, E., J. Lindos, E. Sjoqvist and A. Westholm 1934 *Swedish Cyprus Expedition* I, II. *Finds and Results of the Excavations in Cyprus 1927–1931.* Stockholm: Swedish Cyprus Expedition.

Hall, J.M. 1997 *Ethnic Identity in Greek Hellenism.* Cambridge: Cambridge University Press.

—— 1998 Review feature – ethnic identity in Greek antiquity. *Cambridge Archaeological Journal* 8: 265–83.

Hallote, R.S. 2002 Real and ideal identities in Middle Bronze Age tombs. *Near Eastern Archaeology* 65: 105–11.

Hodder, I. 1982 *Symbols in Action.* Cambridge: Cambridge University Press.

Iacovou, M. 1998 Philistia and Cyprus in the 11th century BC: from a similar prehistory to a diverse protohistory. In S. Gitin, A. Mazar and E. Stern (eds), *Mediterranean Peoples in Transition: Thirteenth to Eleventh Centuries BCE,* 332–44. Jerusalem: Israel Exploration Society.

—— 1999a Excerpta Cypria Geometrica: materials for a history of Geometric Cyprus. In M. Iacovou and D. Michaelides (eds), *Cyprus: The Historicity of the Geometric Horizon,* 141–66. Nicosia: Archaeological Research Unit, University of Cyprus; Bank of Cyprus Cultural Foundation; Ministry of Education and Culture.

—— 1999b The Greek exodus to Cyprus: the antiquity of Hellenism. *Mediterranean Historical Review* 14 (2): 1–28.

—— 2001 Cyprus from Alashiya to Iatnana. In S. Böhm and K.V. von Eickstedt (eds), *ITHAKH: Festschrift für Jörg Schäfer zum 75. Geburtstag am 25 April 2001,* 85–92. Würzburg: Ergon Verlag.

—— 2002 From ten to naught: formation, consolidation and abolition of Cyprus' Iron Age polities. *Cahier du Centre d'Études Chypriotes* 32: 73–87.

—— 2003 The Late Bronze Age origins of Cypriot Hellenism and the establishment of the Iron Age kingdoms. In S. Hadjisavvas (ed.), *From Ishtar to Aphrodite: 3200 Years of Cypriot Hellenism. Treasures from the Museums of Cyprus,* 79–85. New York: Onassis Public Benefit Foundation.

—— 2004 Phoenicia and Cyprus in the first millennium B.C.: two distinct cultures in search of their distinct archaeologies. *Bulletin of the American Schools of Oriental Research* 336: 61–6.

—— 2005a Cyprus at the dawn of the first millennium BCE: cultural homogenisation versus the tyranny of ethnic identification. In J. Clarke (ed.), *Archaeological Perspectives on the Transmission and Transformation of Culture in the Eastern Mediterranean.* Levant Supplementary Series 2: 125–34. Oxford: Council for British Research in the Levant and Oxbow Books.

—— 2005b The Early Iron Age urban forms of Cyprus. In R. Osborne and B. Cunliffe (eds), *Mediterranean Urbanization 800–600 BC,* 17–43. Oxford: Oxford University Press.

Iacovou, M. 2006a 'Greeks', 'Phoenicians' and 'Eteocypriots': ethnic identities in the Cypriote kingdoms. In J. Chrysostomides and C. Dendrinos (eds), *'Sweet Land ...': Lectures on the History and Culture of Cyprus*, 27–59. Camberley, Surrey: Porphyrogenitus.

—— 2006b From the Mycenaean *qa-si-re-u* to the Cypriote *pa-si-le-wo-se*: the *basileus* in the kingdoms of Cyprus. In S. Deger-Jalotzy and I.S. Lemos (eds), *Ancient Greece: From the Mycenaean Palaces to the Age of Homer*. Edinburgh Leventis Studies 3: 315–35. Edinburgh: Edinburgh University Press.

Janes, S.M. 2008 The Cypro-Geometric Horizon, a View from Below: Identity and Social Change in the Mortuary Record. Unpublished PhD dissertation, Department of Archaeology, University of Glasgow.

Jenkins, R. 1997 *Rethinking Ethnicity: Arguments and Explorations*. London: Sage.

Jones, S. 1997 *The Archaeology of Ethnicity. Constructing Identities in the Past and Present*. London and New York: Routledge.

Jung, R. 2009 Pirates of the Aegean: Italy–the east Aegean–Cyprus at the end of the second millennium BC. In V. Karageorghis and O. Kouka (eds), *Cyprus and the East Aegean: Intercultural Contacts from 3000 to 500 BC*, 72–93. Nicosia: Leventis Foundation.

Karageorghis, V. 1965 Horse burials on the island of Cyprus. *Archaeology* 18: 282–9.

—— 1967 Nouvelles tombes de guerriers à Palaepaphos. *Bulletin de Correspondance Hellénique* 91: 202–47.

—— 1969 *Salamis in Cyprus. Homeric, Hellenistic and Roman*. London: Thames and Hudson.

—— 1970a *Excavations in the Necropolis of Salamis* II. Nicosia: Department of Antiquities.

—— 1970b Chronique des fouilles et découvertes archéologiques à Chypre en 1969. *Bulletin de Correspondance Hellénique* 94: 191–300.

—— 1973 *Excavations in the Necropolis of Salamis* III. Nicosia: Department of Antiquities.

—— 1975 *Alaas: A Protogeometric Necropolis in Cyprus*. Nicosia: Department of Antiquities.

—— 1978 *Excavations in the Necropolis at Salamis* VI. Nicosia: Department of Antiquities.

—— 1982 *Cyprus. From the Stone Age to the Romans*. London: Thames and Hudson.

—— 1983 *Palaepaphos-Skales: An Iron Age Cemetery in Cyprus*. Alt-Paphos 3. Constanz: Universitätsverlag.

—— 1987 Western Cyprus at the close of the Bronze Age. In D.W. Rupp (ed.), *Western Cyprus: Connections*. Studies in Mediterranean Archaeology 77: 115–24. Göteborg: Paul Åströms Förlag.

—— 1992 The crisis years: Cyprus. In W.A. Ward and M.S. Joukowsky (eds), *The Crisis Years. The 12th Century BC from beyond the Danube to the Tigris*, 79–86. Dubuque, IA: Kendall/Hunt.

Karageorghis, V. 1994 The prehistory of an ethnogenesis. In V. Karageorghis (ed.), *Cyprus in the 11th Century BC*, 1–10. Nicosia: Leventis Foundation.

—— 2001 Some innovations in the burial customs of Cyprus (12th–7th centuries B.C.). *Eulimene* 2: 53–65.

—— 2002 Hellenism beyond Greece: Cyprus. In I.A. Todd, D. Komini-Dialeti and D. Hatzivassiliou (eds), *Greek Archaeology without Frontiers*, 31–43. Athens: National Hellenic Research Foundation and Leventis Foundation.

Karageorghis, V., and M. Iacovou 1990 Amathus Tomb 521: A Cypro-Geometric I group. *Report of the Department of Antiquities, Cyprus*, 75–100.

Keswani, P. 1989 Mortuary Ritual and Social Hierarchy in Bronze Age Cyprus. Unpublished PhD dissertation, Department of Anthropology, University of Michigan.

2004 *Mortuary Ritual and Society in Bronze Age Cyprus*. Monographs in Mediterranean Archaeology 9. London: Equinox.

Knapp, A.B. 2001 Archaeology and ethnicity: a dangerous liaison. *Archaeologia Cypria* 4: 29–46.

—— 2008 *Prehistoric and Protohistoric Cyprus. Identity, Insularity, and Connectivity.* Oxford: Oxford University Press.

Knapp, A.B., and S. Antoniadou 1998 Archaeology, politics and the cultural heritage of Cyprus. In L. Meskell (ed.), *Archaeology under Fire. Nationalism, Politics and Heritage in the Eastern Mediterranean and Middle East*, 13–43. London and New York: Routledge.

Lambrinoudakis, V.K. 1988 Veneration of ancestors in Geometric Naxos. In R. Hägg, N. Marinatos and G.C. Nordquist (eds), *Early Greek Cult Practice. Proceedings of the Fifth International Symposium at the Swedish Institute at Athens, 26–29 June, 1986*, 235–46. Stockholm: Paul Åströms Förlag.

Leriou, N. 2002 The Mycenaean colonisation of Cyprus under the magnifying glass: emblematic indicia versus defining criteria at Palaepaphos. In G. Muskett, A. Koltsida and M. Georgiadis (eds), *SOMA 2001: Symposium on Mediterranean Archaeology*. British Archaeological Reports: International Series 1040: 169–77. Oxford: Archaeopress.

—— 2007 Locating identities in the eastern Mediterranean during the Late Bronze Age–Early Iron Age: the case of 'hellenised' Cyprus. In S. Antoniadou and A. Pace (eds), *Mediterranean Crossroads*, 563–91. Athens: Pierides Foundation.

Maier, F.G., and M.-L. von Wartburg 1985 Reconstructing history from the earth, *c.* 2800 B.C.–1600 A.D.: excavating at Palaepaphos, 1966–1984. In V. Karageorghis (ed.), *Archaeology in Cyprus 1960–1985*, 142–72. Nicosia: Leventis Foundation.

Mallowan, M. 1978 *The Nimrud Ivories*. London: British Museum Publications.

Manning, S. 1998 Changing pasts and socio-political cognition in Late Bronze Age Cyprus. *World Archaeology* 30: 39–58

Mazar, A. 1994 The 11th century B.C. in the land of Israel. In V. Karageorghis (ed.), *Cyprus in the 11th Century B.C.*, 39–57. Nicosia: Leventis Foundation.

Morris, I. 1992 *Death-Ritual and Social Structure in Classical Antiquity*. Cambridge: Cambridge University Press.

Murphy, J.M. 1998 Ideologies, rites and rituals: a view of prepalatial Minoan tholoi. In K. Branigan (ed.), *Cemetery and Society in the Aegean Bronze Age*, 27–40. Sheffield: Sheffield Academic Press.

O'Shea, J.M. 1984 *Mortuary Variability. An Archaeological Investigation.* Studies in Archaeology. Orlando, FL, and London: Academic Press.

Parker Pearson, M. 1999 *The Archaeology of Death and Burial.* Stroud: Sutton.

Raptou, E. 2002 Nouveaux témoignages sur Palaepaphos à l'époque Géométrique. *Cahier du Centre d'Études Chypriotes* 32: 115–33.

Reyes, A.T. 1994 *Archaic Cyprus: A Study of the Textual and Archaeological Evidence.* Oxford: Clarendon Press.

Rupp, D.W. 1987 Vive le roi: the emergence of the state in Iron Age Cyprus. In D.W. Rupp (ed.), *Western Cyprus: Connections.* Studies in Mediterranean Archaeology 77: 147–68. Göteborg: Paul Åströms Förlag.

—— 1988 The Royal Tombs at Salamis, Cyprus: ideological messages of power and authority. *Journal of Mediterranean Archaeology* 1: 111–39.

—— 1998 The seven kings of the Land of Ia', a district on Ia-ad-na-na: Achaean bluebloods, Cypriot parvenus, or both? In K.J. Hartswick and M. Sturgeon (eds), *Stephanos: Studies in Honor of Brunilde Sismondo Ridgway,* 209–22. Philadelphia: University Museum, University of Pennsylvania.

Schreiber, N. 2003 *The Cypro-Phoenician Pottery of the Iron Age.* Leiden: Brill.

Sherratt, E.S. 1992 Immigration and archaeology: some indirect reflections. In P. Åström (ed.), *Acta Cypria* 2. Studies in Mediterranean Archaeology and Literature Pocket-book 117: 316–47. Jonsered: Paul Åströms Förlag.

Snodgrass, A. 1988 *Cyprus and Early Greek History.* Fourth Annual Lecture, Bank of Cyprus, Cultural Foundation. Nicosia: Bank of Cyprus Cultural Foundation.

Steel, L. 1995 Differential burial practices in Cyprus at the beginning of the Iron Age. In S. Campbell and A. Green (eds), *The Archaeology of Death in the Ancient Near East.* Oxbow Monograph 51: 199–204. Oxford: Oxbow Books.

Van Gennep, A. 1960 *The Rites of Passage.* Chicago: University of Chicago Press.

Voutsaki, S. 1998 Mortuary evidence, symbolic meanings and social change: a comparison between Messenia and the Argolid in the Mycenaean period. In K. Branigan (ed.), *Cemetery and Society in the Aegean Bronze Age.* Sheffield Studies in Aegean Archaeology 1: 41–58. Sheffield: Sheffield Academic Press.

Webb, J.M. 1992 Funerary ideology in Bronze Age Cyprus – toward the recognition and analysis of Cypriote ritual data. In G.C. Ioannides (ed.), *Studies in Honour of Vassos Karageorghis,* 87–99. Nicosia: Society of Cypriot Studies.

Yon, M. 1971 *Salamine de Chypre* II: *La Tombe T.I du XIe s. av. J.C.* Paris: De Boccard.

—— 1999 Salamis and Kition in the 11th–9th century BC: cultural homogeneity or divergence? In M. Iacovou and D Michaelides (eds), *Cyprus: The Historicity of the Geometric Horizon,* 17–33. Nicosia: Archaeological Research Unit, University of Cyprus; Bank of Cyprus Cultural Foundation; Ministry of Education and Culture.

8

ENTANGLED IDENTITIES ON IRON AGE SARDINIA?

Jeremy Hayne

Introduction

Iron Age Sardinia is often defined by its Phoenician or Carthaginian settlements, or at best its interactions with foreign colonists, while the native populations are largely ignored (Bernardini 2007). In fact, throughout its history, Sardinia has usually been seen as an island that submits to change rather than being proactive; as such it fits in well with generally conceived ideas of islands as isolated and 'insular' (Broodbank 2000; Rainbird 2007; Waldren 2002). But although it was largely autonomous in the Bronze Age with its indigenous culture organised around local chiefdoms and based on a network of 'cantons' (Russell, this volume), from the thirteenth century BC onwards Sardinia became part of the connectivity networks that characterised the changes from the Bronze to Iron Age in the Mediterranean. From the ninth century BC onwards, its central position in the western Mediterranean meant that it was ideally placed for interaction with the increasing number of people from overseas; these renewed and intensified contacts led Sardinians to develop a greater awareness of their different identities within the island. By taking the examples of a few north Sardinian sites, this study examines how differences in local identities emerged in the Iron Age and how such differences were represented in the material record. I argue that the islanders' relationship with their landscape, their mobility and their connectivity were important factors in transforming their identities throughout the first millennium BC.

Traditionally, discussions of prehistoric Sardinian identities have been framed around the divide between local and indigenous Sardinians and incoming foreign settlers. This colonial focus has tended to force us to see Sardinia in dualist terms (them and the 'other'), but if instead we concentrate on the materiality of the indigenous populations, we can unlock information that usually remains hidden from such colonialist perspectives (van Dommelen 2006: 115–16). I focus on northern Sardinia, a part of the island often ignored during the Iron Age because it was never colonised. Rather it was a contact zone where interaction between locals and foreigners was more sporadic and equal (Alexander 1998) and would have shaped local culture in a variety of ways. By highlighting the types of contact between indigenous communities and foreign peoples, and by emphasising local geography and landscape as well as the material culture of the inhabitants, I examine the differences between local identities as defined in the Introduction to this volume (p. 2–4). To see identity as transitory (Introduction, p. 2) helps us to bridge the gap between what has traditionally been seen as the *Nuragic culture* of the Bronze Age and the *Sardinians* of the classical period and later. The broad questions I ask are: (1) how long did the Nuragic culture continue in the north; (2) can we see an increasing regionalisation as Bronze Age culture was transformed; and (3) what does the evidence of contact tell us about Sardinian society or societies during this period?

Connectivity

As an island community, the Sardinians' relationships with overseas peoples form part of this book's central themes of mobility and contact. These two themes and the issue of the island's place in the wider community can be subsumed under the heading of connectivity (Horden and Purcell 2000: 123–32). These issues have been discussed in recent years with the understanding that connectivity or isolation involves active decisions by communities to regulate their identity through contact, so that they determine on their own terms how cross-cultural interactions take place (Broodbank 2000: 20–1). Whether or not the Iron Age inhabitants of northern Sardinia moved by sea, relationships between identity and connectivity revolve around both inter- and intra-island contacts in the first millennium BC: between contact with external peoples as well as with the Phoenician and Punic inhabitants of southern Sardinia. Because of the variety of interactions, we cannot see Sardinian identities being formed solely in reaction to foreign colonisation. In order to look at associations between identity and connectivity between indigenous and external communities, I have selected two areas of the north that have dense and continuous occupation throughout the Iron Age but that are also well placed for contacts with overseas peoples (Figure 8.1). I suggest that the relations with foreigners and with the rest of Sardinia led to regional developments in the Nuragic culture.

These two areas comprise the Nurra region in northwest Sardinia and the central eastern region of Dorgali and Barbagia (Figure 8.1). The former is a mostly flat fertile promontory that served as a stopping-off place for navigators and traders between Spain and continental Italy; the latter is more mountainous but with access possible along the wide gulf of Orosei and the Cedrino and Posada rivers. The long time span of contact, from the late second millennium BC down to Roman times, is attested in the Nurra region by a Syrian/Phoenician bronze statuettes from Flumenelongu and Olmeda (Gras and Tore 1981), the Roman villa at Sant'Imbenia and Roman baths at Olmeda (Caputa 2000; Gras and Tore 1981). In the central east and the area around the gulf of Orosei contacts with foreigners are attested from the thirteenth century BC by Mycenaean pottery (Ceruti 1985; Re 1995) as well as by Cypriot-style cauldrons from Cala Gonone and Sa Sedda 'e Sos Carros (Lo Schiavo 2006; Lo Schiavo *et al.* 1985).

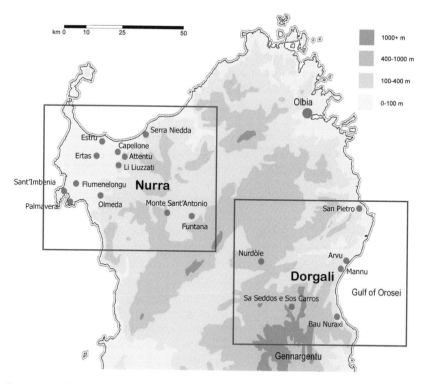

Figure 8.1 The two areas of northern Sardinia under discussion.

Identities

Group identity is reinforced through material culture and during the Bronze Age Sardinian identity was closely entwined with the construction and presence of the most characteristic buildings of the island, the *nuraghi* (Blake 1998; 1999: 39–40; Lucy 2005: 96). But since these monuments ceased to be built from around the turn of the first millennium BC, it becomes increasingly difficult to identify the indigenous communities with the *nuraghi* themselves. If we no longer see the inhabitants of Sardinia as 'Nuragic' the problem remains of how to understand who the people were that lived in Sardinia during this period and how their identities were marked in the material record they left behind. At the end of the period under consideration here, the Roman literary sources tend to define Sardinian society in colonial urban terms, which has no meaning for Nuragic society, as it was clearly non-urban (Diaz-Andreu 1998: 202–7; Mastino *et al.* 2005: 205–16). A colonial perspective also emphasises those parts of Sardinia that were directly affected by the arrival of settlers from the eighth century BC onwards, at the expense of other regions that in turn are usually seen in opposition to the invaders. If, however, 'it is in the meeting of internal and external definition that identity, whether social or personal, is created' (Jenkins 1994: 199, commenting on Barth 1969; see also Knapp 2007; 2008), we must also be aware that this identity refers to a myriad of relationships marked in subtle ways, not just with reference to one dualistic set (Lucy 2005: 96–7). This is especially true in northern Sardinia, where we find a 'long-term, gradual and non-directed process of interaction' (Alexander 1998: 485; Dietler 1998; Thomas 1991), and where evidence of a specific colonial presence is lacking until the 'Romanisation' of Sardinia after the second century BC. In fact what is more important are the continuing changes throughout the Final Bronze and Iron Ages, which were part of a longer reassessment of Sardinian society possibly influenced by contact with Cypriot, Phoenician and even Euboean traders in the west Mediterranean from the thirteenth century BC onwards (Tronchetti and van Dommelen 2005).

Evidence of identities being directly formed through relationships with foreign presences is likely to be slight and difficult to find in the material record. Because of the inherent problems of identifying local communities as either Nuragic or colonial, scholars have often found it easier to reinforce differences than to acknowledge continuity in the Iron Age, often assuming a gap between the Bronze Age culture and the arrival of the Romans and emphasising the 'reuse' of *nuraghi*. I suggest that the very difficulty of seeing what was happening in northern Sardinia is the result of society's transformation in this period. By recognising that identity is transitory, we need not look for distinctive and separate cultures but rather ones that change over time under the influence of a variety of factors, such as contact with other people. Throughout the Final Bronze and Iron Ages, the material expression of this change is seen in many ways, including the construction and development of sanctuary sites, well temples and the organisation of villages, distinctive pottery in the form of askoid jugs with geometric and circular decorations and bronze models of humans, animals and objects. The ritual centres with their associated objects in bronze or clay are important foci of identity; indeed I believe we should view developments in pottery styles and decorations as expressions of social identity rather than as mere chronological markers, which is usually the case.

Material culture

An example of how identity may be traced through material culture is offered by the bronze figurines of Iron Age Sardinia. These statuettes represent perhaps the most distinctive material aspect of the evolving Sardinian culture and as ritual objects often associated with sanctuaries constitute significant markers of identity (Knapp 2007: 40–3). Although they have been found throughout the island, many are associated with the well sanctuaries of the uplands in the central eastern part of the island (Lilliu 2003: 636–7). Debate rages over their dates but it is now mostly agreed that they were manufactured over a broad period of time from the Final Bronze Age to the mid-sixth century BC (Bernardini 2002; Tronchetti 1997; Tronchetti and van Dommelen 2005). The uniqueness of these so-called *bronzetti* (made using the lost-wax process so no two are identical) and the detail lavished on their dress (Figure 8.2) suggest that, compared to the Bronze Age communities, Iron Age Sardinians were increasingly aware of their individuality and status.

While these figurines show types rather than actual individuals (Knapp and van Dommelen 2008: 18), the fact that they demonstrate a distinctive interest in embodying identities in society at a time when indigenous communities were more intensively in contact with overseas regions fits in nicely with the notion that identity is formed at the intersections between inside and outside (Knapp and van Dommelen 2008: 18; Lilliu 2003: 890; Tronchetti 1997). The agency of the Sardinians is displayed in the choices they made in selecting various poses, including stylised forms of 'greeting', offerings and displays of martial and physical prowess, many of which

Figure 8.2 Nuragic archer from Teti (drawn by Angela Demontis and reproduced by kind permission of the author: Demontis 2005: 115).

seem to carry ritual connotations, and that may be associated with the increased importance of sanctuary sites in this period. Whatever they mean, these figurines reflect a complex and articulated society and as such are a far cry from the traditional notions of isolated and backwards island communities (Knapp 2007: 47; McKechnie 2002; Talalay 2005).

These statuettes not only constitute a new mode of representation but also a new way of processing bronze, a technique possibly introduced to Sardinia through contact with Phoenician or Cypriot traders (Lo Schiavo *et al.* 2005: 289; Webster 1996: 198). These new metallurgical skills confirm an increasingly complex society at the start of the Iron Age, because they imply a division of labour with specialist workshops and specific expertise, evidence of which can be found within the large cultic centres, such as in the northeast at Sa Sedda 'e Sos Carros (Lo Schiavo *et al.* 2005 223–5) and Nurdòle (Fadda 1991; 1992).

A second class of objects that indicates changes in local identities are the so-called askoid jugs. These distinctive containers that served as containers for specific liquids are found in a variety of contexts (both ritual and habitation) from the end of the Bronze Age onwards; in the Iron Age, however, both the manufacturing process and style of these vessels underwent significant changes that may be related to contacts with foreign communities. The discovery of substantial numbers of precisely these vessels outside Sardinia, therefore, provides further evidence of the importance of the island at a time when international relations were on the rise (Botto 2007b: 19; Campus and Leonelli 2006: 392; Cygielman and Pagnini 2002; Køllund 1995; Pes and Fiori 1997; Rovina 2002).

The statuettes and pottery provide examples of a new materiality reflecting changes in both Sardinian society and the ways Sardinians were displaying their diverse identities. Stylistic and technological choices in the production of material culture are deeply linked to social and cultural changes in society (Dietler and Herbich 1998: 246). These are in turn related to a central theoretical point of my argument, namely Bourdieu's notion of *habitus* (Bourdieu 1977), where a disposition to act in a certain way both orders and is receptive to changes in the way people act in their society. As these changes in dispositions are more marked in areas where people from different cultural backgrounds met and interacted (Tronchetti and van Dommelen 2005: 193), it is not surprising to find evidence of changes to material culture in the contact zones of north Sardinia. Because identity is especially marked by the material culture of symbolic objects (here *bronzetti* and askoid jugs) (Lucy 2005: 96), it is likely that changes in local identities will be most evident at sanctuary sites.

Iron Age society in northern Sardinia

A broad-brush chronology of the period divides the first millennium BC between the indigenous cultures of the Iron Age and the Phoenician or Carthaginian colonies. This distinction is felt more keenly in the north, as the absence of Phoenician colonies from this region means that the Iron Age continues for longer, while in the south the Iron Age is seen as coterminous with Phoenician colonisation. Throughout the island, indigenous Nuragic periodisation is linked to style, and the Iron Age chronology in particular is based on the distinction between geometric and orientalising pottery (Contu 1995: 67; 2006).

The chronology of Iron Age Sardinia, both in the north and elsewhere on the island, is based on evidence from excavated sites in the southern and central regions, like Su Nuraxi, Santu Brai, Sant' Anastasia, Santa Vittoria and Villanovaforru (Campus and Leonelli 2006; Lilliu 1955; Ugas 1986; Zucca and Lilliu 2005). The distinction between the Nuragic Bronze and Iron Age tends to be based on generic stylistic arguments such as the geometric and orientalising designs used on specific pottery types like askoid or piriform vases (Bernardini 1992; Lilliu 1982; 2003; Ugas *et al.* 2000: 400). These pottery types are widely used as chronological markers for the Iron Age, while everyday types of pottery like storage jars and domestic containers are typically dated to the Bronze Age, even if found in stratigraphic relationships with imported items of clearly later date (Marras and Melis 2006: 89; Rowland 1992). Because Nuragic pottery shapes are highly conservative and because the same forms often remained in use over very long periods, in some cases until the medieval period, domestic pottery remains chronologically largely undiagnostic. This stylistic approach to pottery has resulted in many misinterpretations of the evidence.

Northwest Sardinia

The Nurra and surrounding area in northwest Sardinia were densely populated in prehistory (Caputa 2000; Lilliu 2003: 569). Settlements are situated mainly in the uplands of the interior while nearer the coast concentrations may be found around the river mouths and sheltered bays, as for instance at Sant'Imbenia, Palmavera, and Flumenelongu (Figure 8.1). Contact with Olmeda in the interior depended on minor streams such as the Riu Barca and Riu Serra. From the north coast, the Riu Mannu leads to the Nuragic sites of Estru, Ertas, Capellone, Li Luzzani and Attentu, all of which show continuity of occupation throughout the first millennium BC (Caputa 2000; Lo Schiavo 1978).

Changes in Iron Age society are marked by pottery and bronzes found in this northwestern area, as only some of the Nuragic sites remained in use. Important examples are the sanctuaries of Serra Niedda and Monte Sant'Antonio and the villages of Funtana and Sant'Imbenia.

Serra Niedda-Sorso is a so-called 'sacred well' sanctuary on the north coast near modern Porto Torres (Rovina 1990; 2002). Finds from the well include bronze and stone models of *nuraghi*, pottery and *fibulae* that demonstrate connections with the rest of the Nurra region, the island as a whole and the wider Mediterranean over a long period of time from the thirteenth century BC down to Imperial Roman times. The miniature *nuraghi* in bronze and stone have been shown to be the focus of changing identities in the Iron Age (Blake 1998), while the unusual anthropomorphic statuettes imply changes in material culture in this coastal region, with possible influences from the eastern Mediterranean. Among the figurines, the 'Shepherd King' – a man with a spear and leading a goat or ram – is quite unlike the general iconography of Nuragic bronzes.

Further south, Monte Sant'Antonio-Siligo is a very large sanctuary site; standing at some 600 metres a.s.l. it holds a strategic position overlooking the surrounding countryside (Lo Schiavo 1990; Sanna 1992). To the northeast it overlooks the Marghine valley through which now sweeps the main north–south motorway of Sardinia. To the southeast it looks down the valley that leads to modern Thiesi and to the Monte Ruju sanctuary beyond (11 km as the crow flies). That this sanctuary was in use throughout the Iron Age is attested by Punic and Roman pottery, while a long period of contact with the rest of the Mediterranean is demonstrated by twelfth-century BC Cretan *fibulae* and an Etruscan amphora of eighth-century BC date. As it is situated relatively close to an area of Punic presence that includes sites with both Nuragic and Punic features (like Monte Ruju and Sa Tanca 'e Sa Mura: Madau 1991, 1997b, c), it seems likely that Monte Sant'Antonio may have served as a meeting place for different cultures throughout the Bronze and Iron Ages.

A site near Monte Sant'Antonio that has provided much evidence not just for the continuation of Nuragic culture but for changes, too, is Funtana near modern Ittireddu (Campus and Leonelli 2002; Galli 1983; 1985). This is an inland *nuraghe* and village, with evidence for metalworking and smelting from both the nearby hill of Monte Zuighe and the *nuraghe* itself (Galli 1983; Lo Schiavo *et al.* 2005: 320). Etruscan and Punic amphorae dating from the seventh to fourth centuries BC, along with a bronze hoard in a uniquely styled vase, demonstrate the importance of metallurgical activity as well as contacts with foreign traders at this site.

Ceramic evidence from Funtana demonstrates changes to Sardinian society in the Iron Age. For example, carinated bowls from Funtana and Palmavera on the northeast coast seem to have been made by the same people and are thus important pointers to the mobility and greater consolidation of indigenous communities throughout this zone in the Final Bronze and Iron Ages (Campus and Leonelli 2002: 505). The resemblance in decoration and shape of askoid jugs of this period, found both in northern Sardinia (Funtana, Monte Cau, Serra Niedda or Palmavera) and abroad (Tekkè in Crete, Carthage, Mozia and Huelva – Campus and Leonelli 2000: 398, 413; Lo Schiavo 2005; González de Canales *et al.* 2006), implies a consolidation of the material culture of northern Sardinian as well as expansion into overseas markets. The standardisation of material culture may reflect the desire for the consumption of these articles or their contents by a wider community, both regionally and internationally, that led to changes in the identity of Nuragic communities during the Iron Age.

Sant'Imbenia

One of the most important Iron Age sites in the north is the village built behind the coastal *nuraghe* of Sant'Imbenia on the large and sheltered bay of Porte Conte (Bafico 1986; 1998; Bafico and Oggiano 1997; Oggiano 2000). The Iron Age contexts of Sant'Imbenia comprise various round and rectangular buildings that open onto small courtyards (Figure 8.3). These buildings have various functions, such as storage, habitation or gatherings; in this regard the building plan conforms to those of other Iron Age Nuragic villages, for example at Serra Orrios or Barumini.

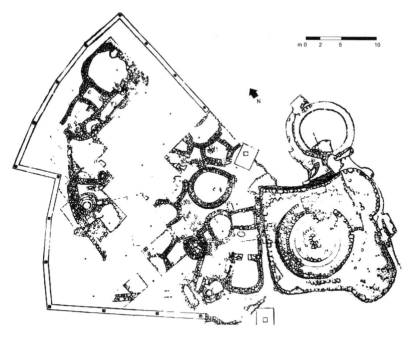

Figure 8.3   Plan of Sant'Imbenia (reproduced by permission of the Ministero per i Beni e le Attività Culturali, Soprintendenza per i Beni Archeologici della Sardegna; reproduction or duplication strictly forbidden).

The location of the site is one of the main reasons for its importance through the Bronze and Iron Ages. Probably acting as a gateway to the mineral and agricultural resources of the Nurra plain, Sant'Imbenia had an important role to play from very early times. Material evidence has provided confirmation of early contact with Greek or Phoenician traders in the form of Euboean *skyphoi* (two-handled deep wine-cups) and Phoenician red slip pottery found in the centre of the village (Bafico *et al.* 1997).

Sant'Imbenia provides clear examples of changes in *habitus* that are technological rather than stylistic. While the askoid jug and containers of Funtana and the bronzes of Serra Niedda, point to specific incidences, reflecting minimal contact with foreigners more intensive contacts with Phoenician traders stimulated local inhabitants to experiment with new materialities in the form of Phoenician pottery shapes and the possible use of turntables (Figure 8.4). The close relationship between this change in technology and trade is detected in the fact that one of these 'Sant'Imbenia amphorae' contained locally produced copper 'bun' ingots also found at other Nuragic sites, including nearby Flumenelongu and Funtana.

Control of materials and power is fundamental to groups of people who want to maintain economic control; the use of the Phoenician amphora shape implies that

155

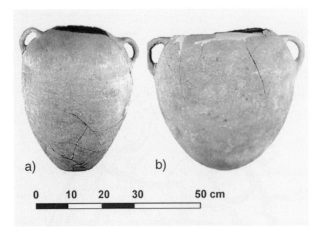

Figure 8.4   Amphorae from Sant'Imbenia: (a) Phoenician transport amphora, (b) Nuragic 'Sant'Imbenia' amphora (from Bernardini *et al.* 1997: 46, reproduced by permission of the Ministero per i Beni e le Attività Culturali, Soprintendenza per i Beni Archeologici della Sardegna; reproduction or duplication strictly forbidden).

local inhabitants wished to manage imports and exports with Phoenician (and other) traders by adapting to an international market. Recent analysis of the so-called ZitA-type Phoenician amphorae at the Decumanus Maximus site in Carthage suggests that at least some of these may be identified as 'Sant'Imbenia types' and the excavator has calculated that they make up 38 per cent of the transport amphorae in the late eighth and early seventh centuries BC, the period when Sant'Imbenia was active (Docter 2006; Docter *et al.* 1997).

Together with the Phoenician finds at Sant'Imbenia, the material evidence demonstrates close links between northern Sardinia and the wider western Mediterranean in this early period (Figures 8.4 and 8.5). Similar amphorae have been found in Huelva and Málaga in Spain, which strengthen the hypothesis of northern Sardinia's connectivity during the Iron Age. Although the 20 or so 'Sant'Imbenia amphorae' found at the site demonstrate changes in manufacture, they do not imply a transformation of social life. Although various imported drinking vessels were also found at Sant'Imbenia, they were not encountered in the kinds of contexts that might have been expected (Figure 8.5). The Euboean bird and semicircle *skyphoi* wine-cups, for example, were found in the so-called 'storage hut' along with the transport amphora, while a Phoenician amphora was found in a habitation hut. This suggests that instead of appropriating a foreign drinking culture, the local inhabitants selected only certain aspects of the Phoenician and/or Greek way of life that referred more specifically to economic rather than social factors (Rendeli 2005; Oggiano 2000). The situation at

Figure 8.5   Greek and indigenous pottery from Sant'Imbenia (reproduced by permission of the Ministero per i Beni e le Attività Culturali, Soprintendenza per i Beni Archeologici della Sardegna; reproduction or duplication strictly forbidden).

Sant'Imbenia overall has more in common with those of the mixed coastal communities of Pithekoussai (central Italy) and Huelva (Spain) (Botto 2007b; González de Canales *et al.* 2006) than with the inland indigenous sites of Funtana and Monte Sant'Antonio. This factor suggests that the inhabitants of Sant'Imbenia were more attuned to Spain and the western Mediterranean than to the Nuragic hinterland of northern Sardinia.

The site of Sant'Imbenia thus provides evidence for changes in social practice during the first millennium BC, with increased contact between indigenous communities, Phoenicians and Greeks. The evidence implies changes in only certain areas of society and suggests that indigenous culture was not heavily impacted by the foreign arrivals. Overall, the archaeological record suggests that the local communities deliberately chose only those aspects of foreign culture that appealed to them.

Central east Sardinia

Quite different relationships may be observed when we look at the eastern coast of Sardinia. The Dorgali and the Barbagia regions are less accessible from both the interior and the sea than the Nurra region, and this factor has affected the materiality and identity of the people living there. On one side the land dips sharply to the

Mediterranean, while on the other the region is protected by the highlands of the Gennargentu mountain range. The number of Nuragic sites along the coast, however, as at San Pietro-Torpè, Golunie-Cala Ossalla, Arvu, Mannu and La Favorita-Cala Gonone (Figure 8.6), demonstrate relationships with the sea that are different from the northwest. Access inland is possible through the valleys of the Posada and Cedrino rivers which are overlooked by numerous *nuraghi*, or over the passes of the Buca di Irghiria and Sutta Terra across the mountains that divide the sea from Dorgali. From there, communications further inland went along the Isalle river to Nuoro and Nurdòle or down the Cedrino to the villages of Serra Orrios, Tiscali and the sanctuary of Sa Sedda 'e Sos Carros, all of which continued in use throughout the Iron Age (Manunza 1995: 177). Further inland, the upland areas are characterised by the large sacred sites or well sanctuaries of Teti, Su Romanzesu, Gremanu, Su Tempiesu, S'Arcu 'e Forras and Noddule, all of which fulfilled region-wide functions similar to Sant'Antonio in the island's northwest (Figure 8.6).

On the basis of archaeological evidence, this east central area can therefore be divided into three zones: the coast, the inland lowlands and the highlands, each with different materialities and identities. The coastal sites, for example, show stronger, albeit sporadic, contact with the Italian mainland. Near the Posada estuary, the *nuraghi* of San Pietro and Pizzinno have provided evidence of interaction with Etruscan communities in the form of a bronze mirror and Villanovan

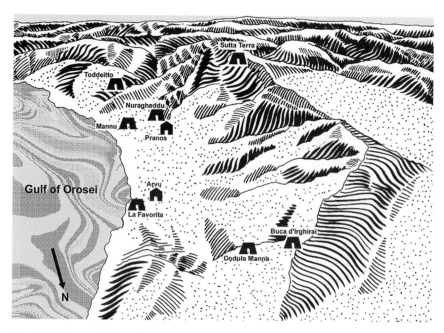

Figure 8.6 View of the Cala Gonone area with the main prehistoric settlements marked (drawing by Valeriano Scassa).

fibulae (Figure 8.7). Similar items were found in Posada itself (Fadda 2006a), while an (unpublished) crucible found at San Pietro suggests that it played a role in metal-working and trade, as was the case at Funtana.

Finds of Greek and Etruscan pottery from Posada and Siniscola and pieces of an Etruscan bossed rimmed basin from Bau Nuraxi-Triei show continuing contacts during the first millennium BC (Bernardini *et al.* 1999: 98–9; Sanciu 2006; Sanges 2002). In the Punic and Roman period the villages of Mannu and Arvu were both

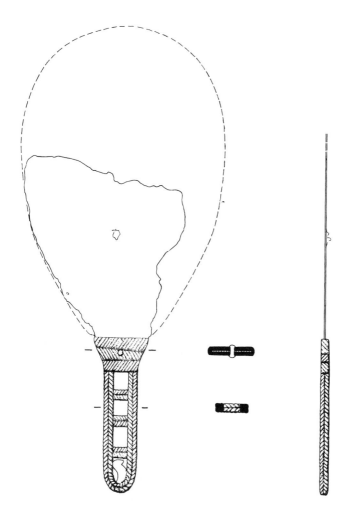

Figure 8.7   Bronze mirror from San Pietro – Torpè (from Lo Schiavo 1976b: figure 14, reproduced by permission of the Ministero per i Beni e le Attività Culturali, Soprintendenza per i Beni Archeologici della Sardegna; reproduction or duplication strictly forbidden).

159

transformed through foreign influences, as is most evident from the construction of rectangular houses of Punic and Roman style that replaced the traditional round(ed) houses (Figure 8.8) (Barreca 1988; Fadda 1980). The unusual and well-finished Nuragic pottery found at Mannu and an unusual clay figurine of possible Punic manufacture at San Pietro also point to changes in local practice and perhaps to the local inhabitants' *habitus* (Fadda 1980: 201–2).

Sa Sedda 'e Sos Carros and Nurdòle

Connectivity between local and overseas communities is more strongly demonstrated at the larger inland sites of the inner valleys and uplands of eastern Sardinia. At Sa Sedda 'e Sos Carros and Nurdòle, the material culture points more distinctly to changes in local identity during the Iron Age. Both sites have a sacred function which appears to be linked to metalworking; evidence of forging bronze and large quantities of this metal have been found (Fadda 1991: 110–14). As in the northwest, trade in metal seems to have been one of the principal reasons for foreign contacts. The control that local communities had over the mineral resources, together with their skills in metal working, no doubt stimulated trade throughout the later Bronze and Iron Ages. The proto-urban sites with their elaborate architecture and rich material culture contrasted markedly with the more domestic, small-scale villages along the Cedrino, Posada and Flumineddu rivers, even though the latter were no doubt

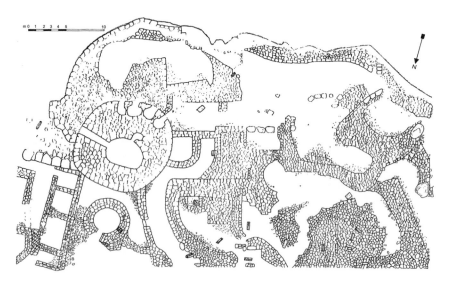

Figure 8.8 Plan of the *nuraghe* and associated village of *Mannu* (from Fadda 1980: figure 60, reproduced by permission of the Ministero per i Beni e le Attività Culturali, Soprintendenza per i Beni Archeologici della Sardegna; reproduction or duplication strictly forbidden).

instrumental for the former to maintain their coastal and overseas contacts. Sa Sedda 'e Sos Carros offers a good example of these large Nuragic centres, as it is situated deep in the Lanaittu valley and was accessible along the Cedrino and Oche river valleys (Fadda 2006b; Lo Schiavo 1976a; 1998; Salis 2006; Sanges and Lo Schiavo 1997). The material evidence displays changes in style and shape that may well have come from long exposure to continental contacts. The increasingly finely made askoid jugs, bronze *fibulae* that find close relationships with those of continental Italy and an unusually fine bronze bull-headed askoid jug are all technological and stylistic pointers to a wider Mediterranean context (Lo Schiavo 1976a, 2006; Sanges and Lo Schiavo 1997).

While Sa Sedda 'e Sos Carros is sheltered in the Lanaittu valley, Nurdòle lies in an upland plain with access to the sea and the wider Mediterranean along the Riu Isalle and Cedrino rivers. This large four-towered *nuraghe* was transformed in the Iron Age from a defensive to a sacred centre by blocking off the central tower and constructing a lustral basin. In this respect it is similar to other Nuragic sites such as nearby Noddule (Lilliu 2003: 556). Large geometrically carved blocks of stone at the top of the structure dominated the landscape, while the rich material evidence – numerous bronzes including figurines, pottery, scarabs, ornaments and glass – demonstrate its importance throughout much of the first millennium BC (Fadda 1991; Madau 1997a; 2002). In addition to indigenous material, there are Greek, Phoenician, Punic and Etruscan pottery and other artefacts indicating that the site was in use from the early Iron Age down to the fourth century BC. A good example is the small Etruscan bronze lion found here (Figure 8.9). The fact that it was found, along with much of the other material, in the vicinity of the lustral basin implies that it had a ritual use. As at Bau Nuraxi and Sant'Imbenia, the imported material was decontextualised, or rather recontextualised, by the indigenous community.

Examples of this process include the presence of Etruscan *bucchero* pottery and a Greek *skyphos* (two-handled deep wine-cup) which, as at Sant'Imbenia, have been interpreted as implying the emergence of a symposium culture in Sardinia. As demonstrated by other contexts at the interface between the classical and prehistoric worlds in France or Sicily, however, the appropriation of material culture is never an even or straightforward process (Dietler 1998; Hodos 2000). It varies from region to region, and material selected and consumed by the local community reflects its own choice of what was seen as valuable or important.

Entangled identities

As already mentioned, bronze figurines formed an important part of the materiality of late Nuragic society, but among the many animals represented, such as sheep, oxen and pigs, the lion is unknown. The lion figurine from Nurdòle therefore seems to be an import and has been identified as almost certainly an appliqué from an Etruscan bronze mixing bowl (Botto 2007a; Madau 1997a). Rather than supposing that this object demonstrates the appropriation of foreign customs in the form of a symposium culture (Botto 2007a: 106–7), it is perhaps more likely that it represents an extension

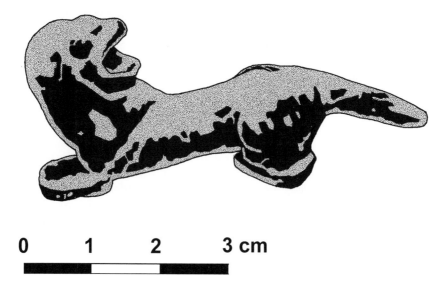

Figure 8.9 Bronze lion appliqué from Nurdòle (drawing by Valeriano Scassa).

of the local habitus of placing bronzes in sacred wells. The latter was a well-established practice, evident at Serra Niedda, Monte Sant'Antonio and La Purissima-Alghero; the Nurdòle lion thus suggests that foreign material could also be accepted occasionally as part of indigenous ritual practice. Rather than seeing these objects as evidence of appropriating a foreign practice, therefore, I would argue that they demonstrate how late Nuragic life continued along its well-established lines without being static, and that it took into account and accepted foreign practice into its own habitus. These foreign objects were therefore recontextualised by the indigenous communities as their connectivity and mobility led to modifications of the traditional lifestyle as a result of the increasing contact with other Mediterranean communities. The evidence of pottery and bronzes in Sa Sedda 'e Sos Carros and Sant'Imbenia can be read the same way.

Conclusions

Material connections between the Iron Age communities of northern Sardinian and their Mediterranean neighbours are difficult to discern in the archaeological record, partly because of nationalist and colonial perspectives that have obscured the Iron Age and partly because of the lack of solid archaeological data for the period. Seeing material culture as a reflection of evolving Sardinian identities, however, may help us to understand the gradual and partial changes that occurred across the island during the first millennium BC. Whether mediated by foreign traders or not, the Iron Age was a time when contact between local and foreign communities was on the increase and where the islanders' relationship with the sea and the people who crossed it was changing. Interactions between different communities over time led to changes in material culture, especially in zones of major contact as is evident at both settlement and sanctuary sites.

As the bronze and stone models at many sites show, early Iron Age Nuragic identities were transformed in the course of the first millennium BC. In the northwest, in areas where contact with foreigners was more intensive (as at Sant'Imbenia), we see transformations in local practices with transport amphorae being produced in the eighth and seventh centuries BC in order to gain or maintain control over trade circuits. The material culture of people with less overseas contact, as at Funtana and Serra Niedda, shows by contrast a longer continuation of traditional Nuragic identities. On the central east coast, contact with foreigners seems to have been more sporadic, and relationships with seafarers were accordingly different. The upland sanctuary sites, already important in the Final Bronze Age, maintained their Nuragic traditions and may be seen as centres of local activity and evolving local traditions. At these sites, local material culture was gradually transformed as interactions with foreigners did not result in the sharp contrasts between traditional and new types of material culture evident in colonial situations. At Nurdòle, in the high and deep hinterland of Sardinia, such developments were no doubt linked to the control of resources, and late Nuragic traditions continued until at least the fourth century BC. This is demonstrated, for example, by the sacred well at nearby Noddule, which was restructured in typical Nuragic style as late as the third or second century BC.

Because of the subjective nature of the value attached to exchanges and material culture, each site should be considered on an individual basis. In northern Sardinia, however, we can identify greater interaction between the different communities in the northwest, while on the central east coast indigenous monopolies held out for longer. During the Iron Age the desire to sustain control of resources and to enter into contact with foreigners involved a gradual change in the islanders' *habitus*. Identities, closely linked to the islanders' control of cross cultural relationships (Broodbank 2000: 21), were altered over this long period in subtle ways. By examining these from a local rather than a colonial perspective, we gain a more nuanced understanding of these developments and processes in northern Sardinia during this still poorly understood period.

References

Alexander, R.T. 1998 Afterward: towards an archaeological theory of culture contact. In J.G. Cusick (ed.), *Studies in Culture Contact. Interactions, Culture Change and Archaeology*, 476–95. Carbondale: South Illinois University.

Bafico, S. 1986 Materiale d'importazione dal villaggio nuragico di Sant'Imbenia. In G. Ugas and G. Lai (eds), *Società e Cultura in sardegna nei periodi Orientalizzante ed arcaico (Fine VIII sec. a.C.–480 a.C.). Rapporti tra Sardegna, Fenici, Etruschi e Greci. Atti del 1. Convegno di studi 'Un millennio di relazioni fra la Sardegna e i paesi del Mediterraneo': Selargius-Cagliari, 29–30 novembre 1985, 1. dicembre 1985,* 91–3. Cagliari: Stef.

—— 1998 *Nuraghe e villaggio Sant'Imbenia Algero.* Il Triangolo della Nurra. Viterbo: BetaGamma.

Bafico, S., and I. Oggiano 1997 Alghero (Sassari). Località Sant'Imbenia. Villaggio nuragico. Il contesto indigeno. Scavi 1994 e 1995. La ceramica fenicia. *Bollettino di Archeologia* 43–5: 136–41.

Bafico, S., I. Oggiano, D. Ridgway and G. Garbini 1997 Fenici e indigini a Sant'Imbenia (Alghero). In P. Bernardini, R. D'Oriano and P.G. Spanu (eds), *Phoinikes B Shrdn: I fenici in Sardegna. Nuove acquisizioni,* 45–53. Oristano: La Memoria Storica.

Barreca, F. 1988 *La civiltà fenicio-punica in Sardegna.* Sardegna Archeologica. Studi e Monumenti. Sassari: Carlo Delfino.

Barth, F. (ed.) 1969 *Ethnic Groups and Boundaries: The Social Organization of Culture Difference.* London: George Allen & Unwin.

Bernardini, P. 1992 La facies orientalizzante in Sardegna: problemi di individuazione e di metodologia. In R. Tykot and T. Andrews (eds), *Sardinia in the Mediterranean Sea: A Footprint in the Sea.* Monographs in Mediterranean Archaeology 3: 396–409. Sheffield: Sheffield Academic Press.

—— 2002 I bronzi sardi di Cavalupo di Vulci e i rapporti tra la Sardegna e l'area Tirrenica nei secoli IX–VI a.C. Una rilettura. In O. Paoletti and P.L. Tamagno (eds), *Etruria e Sardegna centro-settentrionale tra l'età del bronzo finale e l'arcaismo: Atti del XXI convegno di Studi Etruschi ed Italici Sassari–Alghero–Oristano–Torralba,* 421–31. Pisa and Rome: Istituti Editoriali e Poligrafici Internazionali.

—— 2007 Nuragici, Sardi e Fenici tra storia (antica) e ideologia (moderna). *Sardinia, Corsica et Baleares Antiquae* 5: 11–30.

Bernardini, P., R. D'Oriano and P.G. Spanu (eds) 1997 *Phoinikes B Shrdn. I Fenici in Sardegna.* Oristano: La Memoria Storica.

Bernardini, P., P.G. Spanu and R. Zucca (eds) 1999 Μάχη. *La battaglia del Mare Sardonio. Catalogo della mostra, Oristano, Antiquarium Arborense, ottobre 1998–ottobre 1999.* Oristano: La Memoria Storica.

Blake, E. 1998 Sardinia's nuraghi: four millennia of becoming. *World Archaeology* 30: 59–71.

—— 1999 Identity-mapping in the Sardinian Bronze Age. *European Journal of Archaeology* 2: 35–55.

Botto, M. 2007a I rapporti fra la Sardegna e le coste medio-Tirreniche della penisola Italiana: la prima metà del 1 millennio a.C. In G.M. Della Fina (ed.), *Etruschi, Greci, Fenici e Cartaginesi nel Mediterraneo centrale. Atti del XIV Convegno Internazionale di Studi sulla Storia e l'Archeologia dell'Etruria.* Annali della Fondazione per il Museo 'Claudio Faina' 14: 75–136. Rome: Edizioni Quasar.

—— 2007b Da Sulky a Huelva: considerazioni sui commerci fenici nel Mediterraneo antico. *Annali di Archeologia e Storia Antica. Istituto Universitario Orientale. Dipartimento di Studi del Mondo Classico e del Mediterraneo Antico* 11–12: 9–27.

Bourdieu, P. 1977 *Outline of a Theory of Practice*. Cambridge: Cambridge University Press.

Broodbank, C. 2000 *An Island Archaeology of the Early Cyclades*. Cambridge: Cambridge University Press.

Campus, F., and V. Leonelli 2000 *La tipologia della ceramica nuragica: il materiale edito*. Viterbo: BetaGamma.

—— 2002 Considerazioni sui materiali ceramici dell'età del Bronzo Finale – primo Ferro nella Sardegna settentrionale: il nuraghe Funtana di Ittiriddu. In O. Paoletti and P.L. Tamagno (eds), *Etruria e Sardegna centro-settentrionale tra l'età del bronzo finale e l'arcaismo. Atti del XXI convegno di Studi Etruschi ed Italici Sassari–Alghero–Oristano–Torralba*, 491–510. Rome: Istituti Editoriali e Poligrafici Internazionali.

—— 2006 La Sardegna nel Mediterraneo fra l'età del Bronzo e l'età del Ferro. Proposta per una distinzione in fasi. In *Studi di Protostoria in onore di Renato Peroni*, 372–92. Florence: All'Insegna del Giglio.

Caputa, G. 2000 *I nuraghi della Nurra*. Sassari: Imago Media Editrice.

Ceruti, M.L.F. 1985 La Sardegna e il mondo miceneo. In A. Antona and F. Lo Schiavo (eds), *Archaeologia della Sardegna preistorica e protostorica*, 427–36. Nuoro: Poliedro.

Contu, E. 1995 Stratigrafia ed altri elementi di cronologia della Sardegna preistorica e protostorica. In M.S. Balmuth and R.H. Tykot (eds), *Sardinia and Aegean Chronology. Towards the Resolution of Relative and Absolute Dating in the Mediterranean*, 63–76. Oxford: Oxbow Books.

—— 2006 *La Sardegna preistorica e nuragica*. Sassari: Carlo Delfino.

Cygielman, M., and L. Pagnini 2002 Presenze sarde a Vetulonia: alcune considerazioni. In O. Paoletti and P.L. Tamagno (eds), *Etruria e Sardegna centro-settentrionale tra l'età del bronzo finale e l'arcaismo. Atti del XXI convegno di Studi Etruschi ed Italici Sassari–Alghero–Oristano–Torralba*, 388–410. Rome: Istituti Editoriali e Poligrafici Internazionali.

Demontis, A. 2005 *Il popolo di bronzo: abiti, armi e attrezzatura dei bronzetti Sardi in 100 schede ilustrate*. Cagliari: Condaghes.

Diaz-Andreu, M. 1998 Ethnicity and Iberians: the archaeological crossroads between perception and material culture. *European Journal of Archaeology* 1: 199–218.

Dietler, M. 1998 Consumption, agency, and cultural entanglement: theoretical implications of a Mediterranean colonial encounter. In J.G. Cusick (ed.), *Studies in Culture Contact. Interactions, Culture Change and Archaeology*. Centre for Archaeological Investigations Occasional Paper 25: 288–315. Carbondale: South Illinois University.

Dietler, M., and I. Herbich 1998 *Habitus*, techniques, style: an integrated approach to the social understanding of material culture and boundaries. In M. Stark (ed.), *The Archaeology of Social Boundaries*, 232–63. Washington, DC: Smithsonian Institution Press.

Docter, R.F. 2006 Transportamphoren. Archaische Transportamphoren. In H.G. Niemeyer (ed.), *Karthago: Die Ergebnisse der Hamburger Grabung unter dem Decumanus Maximus*, 616–62. Mainz: Philipp von Zabern.

Docter, R.F., M.B. Annis, L. Jacobs and G.H.J.M. Blessing 1997 Early central Italian transport amphorae from Carthage: preliminary results. *Rivista di Studi Fenici* 25: 15–58.

Fadda, M.A. 1980 Nuraghe Mannu. In *Dorgali: documenti archeologici*, 199–205. Sassari: Chiarella.

—— 1991 Nurdòle. Un tempio nuragico in Barbagia. Punto d'incontro nel Mediterraneo. *Rivista di Studi Fenici* 19: 107–19.

—— 1992 Ricerca e tesaurizzazione delle offerte negli edifici culturali della Sardegna nuragica: nota preliminare. In N. Christie (ed.), *Settlement and Economy in Italy 1500 BC–AD 1500: Papers of the Fifth Conference of Italian Archaeology*. Oxbow Monographs 41: 111–22. Oxford: Oxbow Books.

—— 2006a *Il Museo Archaeologico Nazionale di Nuoro*. Sardegna Archaeologica Guide e Itinerari 17. Sassari: Carlo Delfino.

—— 2006b Oliena (Nuoro). Il complesso nuragico Sa Sedda 'e Sos Carros di Oliena. Le nuove scoperte. Riflessioni sull'architettura religiosa del periodo nuragico. *Sardinia, Corsica et Baleares Antiqvae* 4: 77–88.

Galli, F. 1983 *Archeologia del territorio: il comune di Ittireddu (Sassari)*. Quaderni della Soprintendenza ai Beni Archeologici per le Provincie di Sassari e Nuoro. Sassari: Chiarella.

—— 1985 Nota preliminare alla III e IV campagna di scavo al Nuraghe Funtana (Ittireddu-Sassari). *Nuovo Bullettino Archeologico Sardo* 2: 87–108.

González de Canales, F., L. Serrano and J. Llompart 2006 The pre-colonial Phoenician emporium of Huelva ca 900–770 BC. *BABesch* 81: 13–29.

Gras, M., and G. Tore 1981 *Bronzetti dalla Nurra*. Dessi: Ministero per i Beni Culturali e Ambientali and Soprintendenza ai Beni Archeologicai per le Province di Sassari e Nuoro.

Hodos, T. 2000 Wine wares in protohistoric eastern Sicily. In C. Smith and J. Serrati (eds), *Sicily from Aeneas to Augustus: New Approaches to Archaeology and History*, 41–54. Edinburgh: Edinburgh University Press.

Horden, P., and N. Purcell 2000 *The Corrupting Sea: A Study of Mediterranean History*. Oxford: Blackwell.

Jenkins, R. 1994 Rethinking ethnicity: identity, categorization and power. *Ethnic and Racial Studies* 17: 198–223.

Knapp, A.B. 2007 Insularity and island identity in the prehistoric Mediterranean. In S. Antoniadou and A. Pace (eds), *Mediterranean Crossroads*, 37–62. Athens: Pierides Foundation.

—— 2008 *Prehistoric and Protohistoric Cyprus: Identity, Insularity and Connectivity*. Oxford: Oxford University Press.

Knapp, A.B., and P. van Dommelen 2008 Past practices: rethinking individuals and agents in archaeology. *Cambridge Archaeological Journal* 18: 15–34.

Køllund, M. 1995 Sardinian pottery from Carthage. In M.S. Balmuth and R.H. Tykot (eds), *Sardinia and Aegean Chronology. Towards the Resolution of Relative and Absolute Dating in the Mediterranean*, 355–8. Oxford: Oxbow Books.

Lilliu, G. 1955 Il Nuraghe di Barumini e la stratigrafia nuragica. *Studi Sardi* 12–13 (1): 90–469.

—— 1982 *La civiltà nuragica*. Sardegna Archaeologica. Studi e Monumenti 1. Sassari: Carlo Delfino.

—— 2003 *La civiltà dei Sardi: dal paleolitico all'età dei nuraghi*. Nuoro: Il Maestrale.

Lo Schiavo, F. 1976a Fonderia nuragica in loc. 'Sa Sedda 'E Sos Carros' (Oliena Nuoro). In R. Caprara, F. Lo Schiavo, A. Moravatti and F. Nicosia (eds), *Nuove testimonianze archeologiche della Sardegna centro-settentrionale. Sassari – Museo Nazionale 'G.A. Sanna'. 18 luglio–24 ottobre 1976*, 69–78. Sassari: Dessì.

—— 1976b Nuraghe 'S.Pietro' (Torpè, Nuoro). In R. Caprara, F. Lo Schiavo, A. Moravatti and F. Nicosia (eds), *Nuove testimonianze archeologiche della Sardegna centro-settentrionale. Sassari – Museo Nazionale 'G.A. Sanna'. 18 luglio–24 ottobre 1976*, 51–61. Sassari: Dessì.

—— 1978 Le fibule della Sardegna. *Studi Etruschi* 46: 25–46.

—— 1990 Santuario nuragico sul Monte S. Antonio di Siligo (SS). *Nuovo Bullettino Archeologico Sardo* 3 (1986): 27–36.

—— 1998 Oliena. Loc. Sa Sedda 'e Sos Carros. In E. Anati and G. Tanda (eds), *I Sardi: la Sardegna dal paleolitico all'età romana. Guida per schede dei siti archeologici Sardi*, 223–5. Milan: Jaca Book.

—— 2005 Le brochette askoidi nuragiche nel Mediterraneo all'alba della storia. *Sicilia Archeologica* 38 (103): 101–16.

—— 2006 I recipienti metallici della Sardegna Nuragica. In *Studi di protostoria in onore di Renato Peroni*, 269–87. Florence: All'Insegna del Giglio.

Lo Schiavo, F., S. de Montis and F. Villani 1990 *Archeologia e territorio*. Nuoro: Regione Autonomia della Sardegna and Ilisso.

Lo Schiavo, F., A. Giumlia-Mair, R. Valera and U. Sanna (eds) 2005 *Archaeometallurgy in Sardinia from the Origins to the Beginning of the Early Iron Age*. Montagnac: Éditions Monique Mergoil.

Lo Schiavo, F., E. MacNamara and L. Vagnetti 1985 Late Cypriot imports to Italy and their influence on local bronzework. *Papers of the British School at Rome* 53: 1–71.

Lucy, S. 2005 Ethnic and cultural identities. In M. Diaz-Andreu, S. Lucy, S. Babić and D.N. Edwards (eds), *The Archaeology of Identity: Approaches to Gender, Age, Status, Ethnicity and Religion*, 86–109. London: Routledge.

Madau, M. 1991 Importazioni dal Nuorese e centralità delle aree interne. Nota preliminare. *Rivista di Studi Fenici* 19: 121–31.

—— 1997a Fenici e indigeni a Nurdòle di Orani. In P. Bernardini, R. D'Oriano and P.G. Spanu (eds), *Phoinikes B Shrdn: I fenici in Sardegna. Nuove acquisizioni*, 71–5. Oristano: La Memoria Storica.

—— 1997b Populazione rurali tra Carthagine e Roma: Sa Tanca 'e Sa Mura a Monteleone Roccadoria. In P. Bernardini, R. D'Oriano and P.G. Spanu (eds), *Phoinikes B Shrdn: I fenici in Sardegna. Nuove acquisizioni*, 143–5. Oristano: La Memoria Storica.

Madau, M. 1997c Populazioni rurali tra Cartagine e Roma: Monte Ruju a Thiesi. In P. Bernardini, R. D'Oriano and P.G. Spanu (eds), *Phoinikes B Shrdn: I fenici in Sardegna. Nuove acquisizioni*, 159–63. Oristano: La Memoria Storica.

—— 2002 Il complesso nuragico di Nurdòle (Orani-NU) e le relazioni con il mondo mediterraneo nella prima età del ferro. In O. Paoletti and L. Tamagno Perna (eds), *Etruria e Sardegna centro-occidentale tra l'età del bronzo finale e l'arcaismo. Atti del XXI convegno di Studi Etruschi ed Italici Sassari–Alghero–Oristano–Torralba*, 335–40. Pisa and Rome: Istituti Editoriali e Poligrafici Internazionali.

Manunza, M.R. 1995 *Dorgali: monumenti antichi. Ministero del Beni Culturali, Soprintendenza Archeologica per le Province di Sassari e Nuoro*. Oristano: S'Alvure.

Marras, M., and P. Melis 2006 Lo scavo della Tomba VIII della necropoli ipogeica di Sa Figu. Il problema delle 'domus a prospetto architettonico'. In S. Castia (ed.), *Sardegna Nuragica: analisi e interpretazione di nuovi contesti e produzioni*, 83–127. Sassari: Mediando.

Mastino, A., P.G. Spanu and R. Zucca 2005 *Mare Sardum: merci, mercati e scambi marittimi della Sardegna antica*. Rome: Carocci.

McKechnie, R. 2002 Islands of indifference. In W. Waldren and K. Ensenyat (eds), *World Islands in Prehistory: International Insular Investigations. Proceedings of the V Deia International Conference of Prehistory*, 127–34. Oxford: Archaeopress.

Oggiano, I. 2000 La ceramica fenicia di Sant'Imbenia (Alghero – SS). In P. Bartoloni and L. Campanella (eds), *La ceramica fenicia di Sardegna. Dati, problematiche, confronti. Atti del I Congresso Internazionale Sulcitano, S. Antioco, 19–21 settembre 1997*. Collezione di Studi Fenici 40: 235–58. Rome: Consiglio Nazionale delle Ricerche.

Pes, G., and F. Fiori 1997 Uri (Sassari). Il complesso nuragico-romano di Santa Caterina. Il materiale ceramico. *Bollettino di Archeologia* 43–5: 158–61.

Rainbird, P. 2007 *The Archaeology of Islands*. Topics in Contemporary Archaeology. Cambridge: Cambridge University Press.

Re, L. 1995 A catalog of Aegean finds in Sardinia. In M.S. Balmuth and R.H. Tykot (eds), *Sardinia and Aegean Chronology. Towards the Resolution of Relative and Absolute Dating in the Mediterranean*, 287–90. Oxford: Oxbow Books.

Rendeli, M. 2005 La Sardegna e gli Eubei. In P. Bernardini and R. Zucca (eds), *Il Mediterraneo di Herakles. Studi e ricerche*. Collana del Dipartimento di Storia dell'Università di Sassari: 91–124. Rome: Carocci.

Rovina, D. 1990 Il santuario nuragico di Serra Niedda (Sorso). *Nuovo Bullettino Archeologico Sardo* 3 (1986): 37–47.

—— 2002 *Il santuario nuragico di Serra Niedda e Sorso (SS)*. Viterbo: BetaGamma.

Rowland, R.J. 1992 When did the Nuragic period in Sardinia end? In *Sardinia Antiqua: studi in onore di Piero Meloni in occasione del suo settantesimo compleanno*, 165–75. Cagliari: Edizioni della Torre.

Salis, G. 2006 Nuovi scavi nel villaggio nuragico di Sa Sedda 'e Sos Carros (Oliena, Nuoro). *Sardinia, Corsica et Baleares Antiqvae* 4: 89–108.

Sanciu, A. 2006 La Baronia in età fenicio punica. *Civiltà del Mare* 1: 49–52.

Sanges, M. 2002 Materiali di provenienza tirrenica e nuragici di prima età del Ferro dal Nuorese. In O. Paoletti and P.L. Tamagno (eds), *Etruria e Sardegna centro-settentrionale tra l'età del bronzo finale e l'arcaismo. Atti del XXI convegno di Studi Etruschi ed Italici Sassari–Alghero–Oristano–Torralba*, 481–90. Pisa and Rome: Istituti Editoriali e Poligrafici Internazionali.

Sanges, M., and F. Lo Schiavo 1997 Oliena (Nuoro). Località Sa Sedda 'e Sos Carros. *Bollettino di Archeologia* 43–5: 223–6.

Sanna, A. 1992 Siligo (Sassari). Località Monte Sant'Antonio. Campagne di scavo 1990 e 1991. Relazione preliminare: lo scavo e i monumenti. *Bollettino di Archeologia* 13–15: 197–9.

Talalay, L. 2005 The gendered sea: iconography, gender, and Mediterranean prehistory. In A.B. Knapp and E. Blake (eds), *The Archaeology of Mediterranean Prehistory*, 130–55. Oxford: Blackwell.

Thomas, N. 1991 *Entangled Objects: Exchange, Material Culture, and Colonialism in the Pacific*. Cambridge, MA: Harvard University Press.

Tronchetti, C. 1997 I bronzetti 'nuragici': ideologia, iconografia, cronologia. *Annali di Archeologia e Storia Antica* 4: 9–34.

Tronchetti, C., and P. van Dommelen 2005 Entangled objects and hybrid practices: colonial contacts and elite connections at Monte Prama, Sardinia. *Journal of Mediterranean Archaeology* 182: 183–209.

Ugas, G. 1986 La produzione materiale nuragica. Note sull'apporto etrusco e greco. In G. Ugas and G. Lai (eds), *Società e cultura in Sardegna nei periodi orientalizzante e arcaico. Rapporti tra Sardegna, Fenici, Etruschi e Greci (Atti del 1 convegno di studi 'Un millennio di relazioni fra la Sardegna e i paesi del Mediterraneo', Selargius-Cagliari, 29–30 novembre, 1 dicembre 1985)*. 1o Convegno di Studi di Selargius, Dicembre 1985: 41–53. Cagliari: Stef.

Ugas, G., C. Luglie and S. Sebis 2000 La Sardegna: la ceramica. In D. Cocco Genick (ed.), *L'età del bronzo recente in Italia. Atti del Congresso Nazionale di Lido di Camaiore, 26–29 ottobre 2000*, 39–410. Viareggio: M. Baroni.

van Dommelen, P. 2006 Colonial matters: material culture and postcolonial theory in colonial situations. In C. Tilley, W. Keane, S. Küchler, M. Rowlands and P. Spyer (eds), *Handbook of Material Culture*, 104–24. London: Sage.

Waldren, J. 2002 Conceptions of the Mediterranean: islands of the mind. In W. Waldren and K. Ensenyat (eds), *World Islands in Prehistory: International Insular Investigations. Proceedings of the V Deia International Conference of Prehistory*, 1–6. Oxford: Archaeopress.

Webster, G.S. 1996 *A Prehistory of Sardinia 2300–500 BC*. Sheffield: Sheffield Academic Press.

Zucca, R., and G. Lilliu 2005 *Su Nuraxi di Barumini*. Sardegna Archeologica. Sassari: Carlo Delfino.

9

IRON, CONNECTIVITY AND LOCAL IDENTITIES IN THE IRON AGE TO CLASSICAL MEDITERRANEAN

Maria Kostoglou*

Introduction: the Late Bronze Age setting of iron technology. High connectivity and high visibility

Late Bronze Age studies have to some extent overemphasised culture contact across the Mediterranean, especially with respect to long-distance trade and the search for copper and tin taking place under centralised palatial control and driven by the market for prestige goods. In this international, cosmopolitan world between 1600 and 1200 BC, travelling craftsmen and ingenious entrepreneurs acted as free agents transmitting ideas and skills, thus echoing Childe's (1958: 169) idea that smiths, the first European specialists, 'were not tied to any one patron ... or society'. For Childe this mobility was responsible for the distinctive character of European Bronze Age metallurgy. Iron objects made of meteoric iron as well as smelted iron are found in many contexts and places from Mesopotamia to Syria, Anatolia, Egypt and Greece. Iron objects also appear in inventories and other Late Bronze Age texts and, despite debates over their meaning, they are quite informative about the trade and use of iron. These texts rarely refer to the manufacture or production of iron, with the exception of the letter of the Hittite king Hattusili around 1250 BC, which indirectly refers to smelting (for a summary see Pleiner 1969; Muhly 1980). In all cases, iron in the Late Bronze Age seems to be exotic, prestigious and the metal of choice for rituals; a politically centralised system facilitated and supported access to raw materials, technology and specialised workshops (Sherratt and Sherratt 2002).

* Special thanks are due to all participants of the *Material Connections* workshop for stimulating discussions; to Ann Bennett, Jaime Vives-Ferrándiz and Carme Rovira-Hortala for providing me with comparative material and to Dina Kalintzi and Tzeni Tsatsopoulou of the 19th Ephoreia of Prehistoric and Classical Antiquities of Greece for access to material; to Pierre Lemonnier and Mike Rowlands for inspiration; to Peter van Dommelen for inspiring and helping my newly started research interest in west Mediterranean iron; and to Bernard Knapp for sharing his Mediterranean with us.

Most scholars accept that the stimulus for the beginning of iron in the Mediterranean 'ultimately came from Mesopotamia through Syria, Cyprus and Anatolia' (Muhly 1980: 27). This view was first challenged by Snodgrass, who suggested that Mediterranean economies switched to iron in response to the shortage of copper (Snodgrass 1971); he later developed a three-phase model to explain the temporal and spatial distribution of iron (Snodgrass 1980) that was challenged by Morris with his 'deposition versus circulation' model (Morris 1989). The copper shortage hypothesis has found favour with some scholars (Sherratt 1994), while others have challenged some of the archaeological and scientific evidence for the circulation of copper in the Mediterranean (Knapp 2000), and the impact of copper technology on the discovery of iron (Piggott 1996). Nevertheless, all these scholars agree that (a) there are regional differences in the deposition of iron finds in Greece; (b) iron objects were mainly accessible to and used by elites in the early phases and became widely available with the formation of the city-states in the eighth century BC; and (c) only a few objects of copper/bronze and even fewer of iron are available at present to support these proposals. The last observation drove Morris to the extreme conclusion that the Iron Age of Greece was iron-free (Morris 1989).

This chapter addresses the key themes of this book (materiality, mobility and identity) with respect to iron technology, and offers a new, theoretically based methodology for understanding its role in Mediterranean socio-cultural developments. In order to achieve that goal, this paper is organised in three parts: the first presents the Iron Age setting and research problems posed by the materiality of iron in connection with the mobility of people and cultures over long distances; the second introduces a holistic methodology and looks at the context of iron production versus the context of iron consumption in the light of material culture practices (technological choices and *habitus*) and archaeological science; the third applies this methodology to an archaeological case study from northern Greece and demonstrates how iron may be connected to local indigenous identities, as opposed to colonial identities.

The Iron Age: low connectivity, high visibility

This brief and by no means comprehensive outline of the Bronze Age phases of iron metallurgy serves as an introduction to one of the major research problems in the study of iron and its socio-cultural impact on Mediterranean people after the end of the Bronze Age. Despite the absence of technological studies, in all major works the association of iron technology with major socio-cultural changes – such as population decrease, discontinuity in settlement patterns and change in burial customs or war practices – is never questioned (Davis 1935; Pleiner 1969; Snodgrass 1971; 1980; Morris 1992; on the renewed interest in the beginnings of iron metallurgy in Greece, see Snodgrass 2006; Muhly 2006).

If Late Bronze Age trade and exchange networks were responsible for socio-cultural changes, in the Iron Age large migrations or colonisations are considered the most influential factor (Figure 9.1). In this model, taken from Pleiner (1980), the accepted route of influence is from the Levantine coast to Cyprus, then to Crete and the Aegean, mainland Greece, and thence to the central and west Mediterranean.

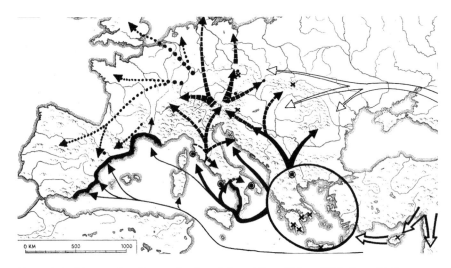

Figure 9.1 The transfer of iron technology (adapted from Pleiner 1980: figure 11.2).

This model places Greece in a circle (Figure 9.1), betraying Pleiner's diffusionist perspective and referring to the important role this region played in the transfer of new technologies from the perceived core areas to the peripheries of the ancient world. The explanatory validity of the centre/periphery model has long being criticised – by post-colonial archaeologists (Hingley 1996; Champion 1989; Rowlands 1987; Stein 2002) and anthropologists of consumption (Dietler 1998; Appadurai 1986; Bourdieu 1977) – for its economic (supply and demand) and cultural (population displacement) determinism, and for its inadequacy in accommodating local developments. On the one hand, in this model colonies organised in cities or other urban centres were thus regarded as foci of civilisation (Andersen-Damgaard *et al.* 1997; Aufrecht 1997). On the other hand, the countryside frequently inhabited by the indigenous population was regarded as primitive and uncivilised. In this context no innovation or high achievement such as the discovery of iron technology can be seen an indigenous accomplishment. Be that as it may, any long-term study of contact zones outside the 'cores' should acknowledge the fact that these regions are constant peripheries of changing cores, which makes these peripheries more interesting in studying social phenomena at the local or regional scale.

In the ever-changing world of the first-millennium BC Mediterranean, the object that exemplifies connectivity between different groups in northern Europe over a long distance network is the iron ingot. The typological distribution of European ingots (Figure 9.2a) also indicates regional patterns of use/distribution and perhaps production, with the ironsmith playing an important and often ritualistic role in European Iron Age society (for a recent review see Giles 2007).

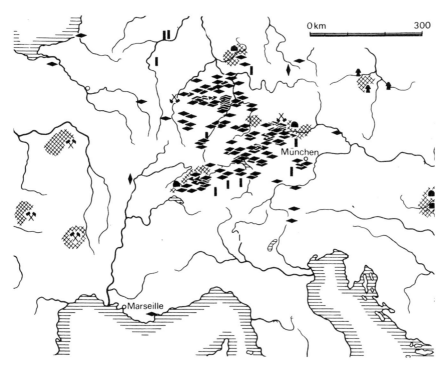

Figure 9.2a   Typology and distribution of iron ingots in northwest Europe during the Iron Age (adapted from Pleiner 1980: figure 11.1).

Figure 9.2b   Iron ingot from Messemvria-Zone in northern Greece, sixth century BC (from Kostoglou 2008a: figure 14b).

In contrast to Europe, iron ingots are completely absent from Iron Age and classical contexts in the Mediterranean. Only three ingots have been found: one from Delphi (eighth century BC); one from the sanctuary of Apollo in Kommos, Crete (seventh century BC – Risberg 1994: 188); and one from the sixth-century BC sanctuary of Apollo in Messemvria-Zone (Figure 9.2b). All three are votives; they date to different centuries, but only the Messemvria-Zone ingot has been analysed and seems to be of local production (Kostoglou 2003; 2008a: 37–40, 63–4). Based on the archaeological and analytical evidence and on research related to the value of iron based on spits (Haarer 2001), I have suggested that spits were the ingots of metallic iron with different degrees of carburisation, and thus different qualities of steel (Kostoglou 2003).

The absence of well-known iron production centres in the Mediterranean world is striking. Pleiner (1980) indicated that out of the 500 known analysed iron objects from Europe, only six originated in southern Europe (meaning Greece, Italy and Spain). The earliest smelting slag is recorded in Varvaroftsa (Macedonia) and dates to *c.* 1200 BC (Pleiner 1980: 378–9). Textual references to Hittite supremacy in smelting iron before 1000 BC still lack archaeological evidence; this is also a reoccurring problem in other areas. For example, a recently published study of iron from Anatolia points out that 'the quantity of metal recovered from early Iron Age excavations in eastern Anatolia and Armenia is not great' (McConchie 2004: 112); this would seem to support a recurring pattern of 'predominately low-carbon, inhomogeneous iron' with bronze continuing to dominate the record (McConchie 2004: 113). There is even less archaeological evidence for iron production in the western Mediterranean. Some of the earliest smelting slag is found in Ischia (Pithekoussai), Italy, from strata dated to the ninth to eighth centuries BC; an early analysis of the ore indicated a provenance from the island of Elba (Klein 1972). This in itself is a rare piece of evidence of ores being transported before Roman times (Kostoglou 2008a: 31). In Spain, the earliest known iron metallurgical activity has been recorded at the settlement of La Fonteta (Alicante): iron slag, furnace fragments and peculiar square tuyères with two holes were found in Phoenician layers dating to the first half of the eighth century BC (Renzi and Rovira 2007). Most metallurgical activity in both Italy and Spain, however, dates to a time after the sixth century BC, when iron weapons and implements appear more frequently, with some exceptional finds such as the group of 150 almost identical axes from an archaic Greek shipwreck off the north coast of Mallorca (Nieto and Santos 2008: fig. 232).

Given the inadequacy of the existing models and the growing record of archaeological finds and scientific analyses, a new framework is needed in order to assess the role of iron in some of the most complex early societies in the Mediterranean. Moreover, we need to consider questions such as: what were the mechanisms behind the transmission of iron technology? What social, economic and cultural networks facilitated this, and how can regional variations be explained? What sort of meanings and identities did iron objects hold in local cultural contexts? And how we can associate the study of local phenomena with the changes noted at the larger scale of the Mediterranean?

A new methodology

Most studies of cultural contact in the ancient Greek and Mediterranean worlds base their results on the study of pottery, architecture, coinage and other art forms. Indeed studies of the classical world and its material representations traditionally have excluded the study of metallurgy (unless related to statues or jewellery). Historically, the domination of textual and art-historical studies has created a classical world where local identities are lost or consumed by the dominant colonial ones, in this case what is perceived as Greek. I propose instead to consider some elements of continuity and the maintenance of local indigenous identities – invisible in some forms of material – that can be traced in the study of technological processes; to do so, I engage with the study of iron technology.

Nevertheless, understanding the role of material in the complex interplay between social systems, cultural practices and individual or group actions is complicated and demands an interpretative framework that cannot be found in traditional studies of the discipline. One such framework is Bourdieu's (1977) practice theory. According to practice theory, people within a specific community or class have a shared *habitus* that facilitates the understanding and coordination of action amongst peers. In that respect, culture is a 'doing' rather than a 'being' and looking at objects in this context one could argue that every single object, e.g. a pot or a spear, is a 'unit of culture'. These units, however, take on different and perhaps multiple meanings during their use-life, from production, to distribution, to use and final deposition. Unlocking these meanings demands an approach that takes into account the particularities of each context, and in the case of iron technology such an approach should differentiate the study of the context of production from the context of use, because the cultural meanings of technology cannot be fully appreciated before technology is understood on its own terms.

This approach also takes into account the fact that these phenomena are neither constantly intense nor visible in material culture. My methodology engages archaeological and scientific techniques applied to the study of ancient metallurgy as well as anthropological approaches to technologies that attribute an active social role to materials (e.g. Lemonnier 1986; 1992; 1993; Herbert 1993; Dobres and Robb 2000).

Understanding the context of production involves, first, the study of technological processes. One way to do that is by looking at the sequence of technological acts involved at every step in transforming the raw material to the usable product. This series of steps is captured by the concept of the *chaîne opératoire* as originally defined by Leroi-Gouhan (1943; Lemonnier 1993). At each step there is a series of choices in terms of the following factors: (1) energy such as ores, fuel, labour; (2) furnace types; (3) smelting and smithing techniques; (4) tools; (5) products and by-products. In an attempt to elucidate the cultural significance of technological choice, which constitutes the technology under study, the archaeologist must ask why one choice was made instead of another. (S)he also has to consider alternative choices available to the people practising this technology at any given time. Technological choices can be influenced by a number of factors associated both with the physical properties of the materials involved and the cultural context in which these materials are embedded in terms of the social, economic and ideological background of the people involved. In Bourdieu's terms they form a *habitus*. Since archaeologists rarely can identify individual acts within a technological framework, we accept that *habitus* is related to the technology that a given group of people or a given society practises and shares at a specific period of time, or over a longer time span. The discussion of iron production, from smelting to manufacturing techniques, should be understood in this context.

Moving away from the context of production to the context of use, a focus on the process of consumption may provide a particularly useful path for tracing indigenous agency and connectivity between local and colonial populations. The anthropology of consumption (Appadurai 1986) shows that demand is never an automatic response to the availability of goods, especially not in colonial situations. Indigenous people show selective preferences and choices. In an archaeological context, Dietler (1997; 1998) demonstrated this in his study of Greek imports to southern France. He showed that the archaeological study of consumption involves: (a) the consumption context and patterns of association with imported goods; (b) the relative quantitative representation of imported goods; and (c) their spatial distribution (Dietler 1998: 300–1). Analyses of ethnographic parallels for the social role of the material have demonstrated that this should take place within specific temporal and spatial dimensions (Schiffer and Miller 1999).

Consumption patterns and the use context of metal objects, however, cannot be fully understood without the context of production, since it is very difficult to separate local from imported goods without provenance studies. The study of iron objects is further complicated by the complete lack of any meaningful stylistic categories, thus making comparisons and all observations based on external morphological characteristics rather misleading. Iron objects are characterised by conservative styles, uses and practices that are resistant to change in the long term. This conservatism in style, use and practice is illustrated by the so-called Type II sword, spears and sickles found in the Mediterranean (Figure 9.3). The sword, also known as a 'fish tail' or Naue II, is a type developed in bronze during the Late Bronze Age and is widely distributed from north Europe to the Mediterranean (Catling 1961; Snodgrass 1967; Kilian-Dirlmeier 1993; Molloy 2005). The type continues to be manufactured in iron throughout the Iron Age with good examples dated to the ninth century BC and perhaps even earlier in the Lefkandi cemeteries (Popham *et al.* 1980: plates 245–6; Figure 9.3b). The latest examples are found in Vergina (Andronikos 1978) and date to the sixth century BC, extending the life span of this type to more than six centuries. The Lefkandi swords have not been analysed and the iron's state of preservation may not allow this. Analyses of the Vergina samples (Photos 1987), however, have demonstrated a lack of consistency in the carburisation process, indicating that the quality of the sword's cutting edge might be less important than its form and that steel application techniques were not widely mastered even in the sixth century BC. A similar phenomenon is noted in the styles of spearheads and spear butts, found mainly in burial contexts with swords and remaining unchanged from the Late Bronze Age to the Iron Age and Classical times.

Longevity and lack of innovation are noted not only in the form and design of iron objects but also in the socio-cultural practices associated with them. One example is the long-lasting practice of the ritual sacrifice of an object, usually a weapon. Figure 9.4 shows an iron sword bent around a ninth century BC Geometric amphora. The

Figure 9.3a *Left*: Bronze Age type II (fish-tail) swords from Huelva (Museo Arqueológico Nacional, Madrid, Spain: adapted from Hernández Pérez 2001: 102).
Figure 9.3b *Right*: Iron Age type II (fish-tail) swords from Lefkandi (adapted from Popham *et al.* 1980: plate 245).

practice is well known from the Bronze Age and in a variety of cultures from Europe and the Mediterranean (for the southern Netherlands, see Fontijn 2005; 2008; for Britain, Needham 1988; for Italy, Salzani 1998: 69). Although this tradition has long drawn scholarly attention, there is one detail that has consistently been overlooked. Indeed it is one that only a specialist of iron technology could note: bending an iron sword or similar object in such a manner requires a smith with specialised knowledge of heating iron.

Bennett (2009), having analysed a number of bent spears from ancient Thailand to prove that point, showed that the area around the bend was heat treated in order to make the spear softer and more malleable (Figure 9.5). I would argue that these ritually killed weapons provide rare but direct evidence for the prominent position of smiths in ancient Greek society and their special status in the performance of communal events such as rituals. The powerful association of iron with ritual practices and magic transformations (Herbert 1993; Rowlands 1971) is also evident in two examples from Classical times known to have survived until the second century AD.

The first is the case of simple rings with an iron disk on top, which are referred to by several classical authors as '*samothracia ferrea*' and suggested to have been worn

Figure 9.4
Geometric amphora with a sword bent around the neck used for burial (ninth century BC; image courtesy Archaeological Museum of Piraeus, Greece).

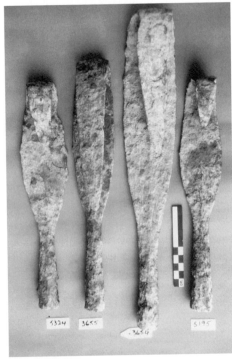

Figure 9.5
Bent spears, first millennium BC Thailand (photograph courtesy Dr A. Bennett, Analyzeart, Switzerland).

by members of an otherwise unspecified cult (Pleiner 1969: 24). All this indicates that iron was the metal of choice for these rings. The second case concerns small iron sickles found in ritual deposits of the temple of Artemis Orthia in Sparta (Dawkins 1929) and in tombs on Delos. On the basis of Classical texts, Romaios (1929) associated these finds with the cult of Artemis Orthia and suggested that they were given as trophies to youths participating in this cult. However out of date Romaios' study may be, the previously noted anthropological studies of iron in pre-industrial societies resonate in a meaningful manner with the associations between the metal (iron), the object (ring, sickle) and rituals marking key transformations in life.

These long-lived, conservative styles and practices reflect deep, established cultural memories. The predominance of specific designs such as the sword, the spear, the dagger or the sickle can be attributed to the widespread iconography of such objects. This iconography can be traced from the *stelae* and pottery of the Late Bronze Age to various types of Greek and Phoenician pottery, figurines, metal mirrors and any other object with a surface decorated with mythological scenes. The cultural significance of these depictions of objects as well as the objects themselves were remembered and reinforced through myths, songs, poems and dramatised stories eulogising powerful daemons that 'represent a unique mythological response to the historical and social force of metallurgy and its relationship to medicine, magic, political power and poetic performance' (Blakely 2006: 7; Herbert 1993). Iron objects like spears, swords and sickles thus become vessels of culture and as such play a role in ceremonial and communal events, contribute to generalised biographies and negotiate relationships in communal cultural identities (Gosden and Marshall 1999).

In order to understand iron in its own terms, we nevertheless need to consider smelting techniques for the production of wrought iron and the application of steelmaking techniques for the production of edged tools and weapons. This chapter suggests that it is not style but rather the study of manufacturing techniques – considered to be culturally embedded in society and one of the markers and makers of identity – that is more significant for understanding local patterns of iron consumption. The following sections present an example of this methodology and argue that there are two conceptual levels of material and cultural connections at play: the first level is more explicit inasmuch as it relates more to form and to what form conveys (objects as symbols and ideas). This meaning is more ephemeral and easily manipulated according to context. As Gosselain (2000: 193) has commented:

> decoration belongs to a category of manufacturing stages that are both particularly visible and technically malleable, and likely to reflect wider and more superficial categories of social boundaries. Fashioning, on the other hand, constitutes a very stable element of pottery traditions and is expected to reflect the most rooted and enduring aspects of a potter's identity … [it] is likely to remain stable throughout a potter's lifetime, and it should reflect those most rooted and enduring aspects of social identity, such as kinship, language, gender, and class subdivisions.

The second part of this quotation clearly identifies the second level as more intrinsic, since it refers to objects as memories of long-term production processes that are culturally embedded in a group's shared *habitus*. This level of meaning, namely iron technology as a set of shared practices, dispositions, and technological traditions, is more difficult to transmit.

In light of this approach, all traditional accounts presented in the first part of this paper examine iron but take no account of its materiality; nor do they offer an explanation beyond diffusion for the regional differences in the archaeological record (Rowlands 1971). The approach advocated here urges the researcher to consider that the intrinsic nature of technological acts could be responsible for the regional variation and experimentation within the same physical properties of iron. Once these variations and technological traditions are established, their meanings within those groups of people who share them might appear understandable; moreover, 'we can certainly postulate that one of the roles of technical systems is to mark difference' (Lemonnier 1986: 173). In the case of iron, this would mean that differing traditions concerning the production, use and disposal of objects within distinctive groups mark difference, and attribute a local identity characteristic of the specific group. This local identity might not be visible in the same cultural or physical dimensions as ethnic identity, as Hall for example claimed (1995; 1997), but it would be visible in the *habitus* of any social group that shares the same technology and/or use of objects. The last part of this paper presents a brief, time- and place-specific case study to exemplify the proposed methodology.

Case study: iron, connectivity and local identities in fifth century BC northern Greece

As mentioned in the Introduction to this volume, traditional scholarship involving Greek colonialism has been inadequate in exploring the complex ways of cultural contact. In Aegean Thrace (roughly northeast Greece), Iron Age settlements have been found mainly in the upland and highland zones. The information provided on these sites in the existing literature (Triantafyllos 1972; 1994; Tsimpidis-Pentazos 1971) appears to be incomplete, as none of the indigenous sites has been excavated systematically. Nevertheless the record indicates that they are about 100 in number, and that most of them are dated to the early Iron Age, according to the pottery found *in situ* (Triantafyllos 1994). Greek colonists from Athens, Corinth, Thassos, Samothrace, Paros and Asia Minor had occupied the coastline since the eighth century BC. The materiality of the colonial population and settlements, although of diverse origin, is Greek, along the lines Cherry (1987: 155) noted: 'city states with a known autonomous territorial unit, self-governing, issuing their own coinage, having a spoken language and written script, practicing the same religious, political or military structure'.

The Thracian tribes came in contact with Greek culture through the Mycenaeans and later through the colonisation of the coast (eighth and sixth centuries BC). The same literature argues that the materiality of the Iron Age population is visible only in the Iron Age and that the urban/colonial centres consequently forced the acculturation or even assimilation of the indigenous populations. In this scenario, during Classical times the Greek colonies and the indigenous settlements of the upland and highland zones formed a network of small rural subsistence economies, either complementary or competitive. Indigenous settlements practised economies based on agriculture, pastoralism, mining and smelting. Control over territories, natural resources and/or people were frequent causes of war, as documented by epigraphic and textual evidence (Kostoglou 2008a: 24–30).

I studied and compared the archaeological record of two of these colonies that have been excavated extensively over the last 40 years, and are known to have been in intensive contact during the fifth century BC. This was a period of high connectivity, i.e. intense cultural contact between the Greek colonies on the Thracian coastline, the Balkan hinterland and Aegean networks. These long-distance contacts are visible in all prominent forms of the material culture: both Avdera and Messemvria-Zone are laid out according to the so-called Hippodamian grid system; pottery and coinage indicate trade with Athens, Corinth, the Aegean Islands, the coast of Asia Minor and, in the case of Avdera, with southern Anatolia, Egypt, Mesopotamia and Syria (Triantafyllos 1984; Tsatsopoulou 1984). The only subgroup of material culture that challenges directly the intensity of contacts and the assumed freedom of accessing materials and knowledge is the technology of iron.

Messemvria-Zone

Messemvria-Zone is a 'commercial colony' (*emporion*) that was founded in the seventh century BC by the inhabitants of the island of Samothrace. Situated on the Thracian coast at the southern end of the Zonaia Mountains, it lies in close proximity to at least three different sources of iron ores. Its archaeological finds cover mainly the sixth to fourth centuries BC (Tsatsopoulou 1997), and evidence for the earliest phase of the town comes from excavations in the sanctuary of Apollo (Tsatsopoulou 1988; 1989). Several buildings, with the temple of Apollo in the north (Figure 9.6, no. 3), are organised around an open paved area. This complex occupies a total area of 35 × 45 sq. m.

Most finds were discovered both inside and outside the temple of Apollo. They include many marble and clay architectural members, fragments of marble inscriptions, parts of archaic statues (*kouroi*) and many pottery sherds; all are dated to the sixth to fifth centuries BC. The pottery is made up of Attic black-glazed and black-figured vases, mainly table-drinking wares (*skyphoi, pinakia, kylixes*) and local handmade pottery known as Thracian (Figure 9.7). Half of the 6,000 pottery fragments discovered in the temple and its vicinity bear incised inscriptions with the name of the god Apollo written in a local idiom resembling the Aeolian dialect; in this dialect, *p* is spelled with a *v* and one third of inscriptions are written in archaic manner, from right to left (Tsatsopoulou 1989). Overall the material culture appears to be a mixture of Greek and local elements with the best examples found in the cemetery (Kostoglou 2008a: 35–42; 2008b).

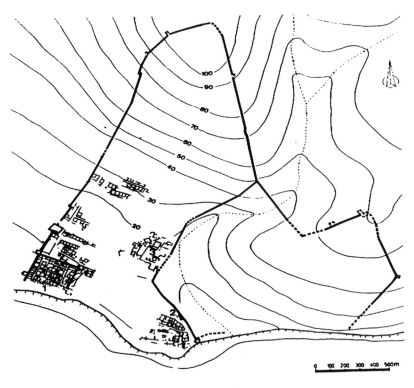

Figure 9.6 Topographic map of Messemvria-Zone (Archaeological Museum of Komotini, Greece).

Figure 9.7 Hand-made pottery labelled as "Thracian" from Messemvria-Zone (Archaeological Museum of Komotini, Greece).

Excavations in Messemvria-Zone have yielded iron finds in almost all contexts (from the temple, the settlement and the cemetery) as well as abundant slag and other industrial waste. Analysis of the industrial waste points to the existence of a very distinctive technological tradition of smelting iron characterised by the use of manganese ferrous ores, the source of which lies less than 10 km from the settlement. This source seems to have been chosen deliberately, since two other sources of good quality ores, like magnetite sands and haematite, are also located in close proximity. Based on this observations and on the analytical results of both smelting and smithing slag, as well as of slag inclusions found as residual elements in the artefacts, I concluded that a number of the iron objects found at the site, mostly swords and knives but also the ingot in Figure 9.2b, were made locally (Kostoglou 2008a: 57–66). The study of the manufacturing techniques of edged tools and weapons also demonstrated a clear preference for the heat treatment of high-carbon steel that takes a specialised smith to master (Kostoglou 2008a: 75–6).

Avdera

The site is said to have been founded first by Klazomenai (*c.* 650 BC). The excavation uncovered part of the archaic wall in the north of the city, an archaic temple of Demeter and some burials (Koukouli-Chryssanthaki 1988). The temple of Demeter was in use from the end of the sixth to the end of the fourth century BC, when the Hellenistic cemetery of the town was created (Figure 9.8). The first small colony became a city-state during Classical times and had all the typical characteristics like town walls (over 5 m high), acropolis, theatre, temples for the town's gods and heroes, two harbours, political autonomy and independent coinage. Imported pottery from Athens, Corinth and the Ionian coast, silver coins of Avdera found as far distant as Egypt and Syria, and finds from the urban cemetery indicate that the town flourished during the Archaic-Classical era (Koukouli-Chryssanthaki 1988; Isaac 1986: 73–123; Boardman 1980). The town walls cover an area of 10 acres and include areas without buildings in the east, presumably for cultivation or for herding animals (Koukouli-Chryssanthaki 1988: 41). If this is compared with the double walls of Messemvria-Zone (Figure 9.6), one could conclude that the land used for agro-pastoral activities was fortified. This evidence suggests that the *chora* territory of these two colonies was limited, a very important factor for discussing the impact of the Greek colonies on the hinterland and the so-called Hellenisation process.

Iron slag and iron finds are absent from the areas associated with the seventh and sixth centuries BC, indicating that iron was not produced locally and that most of the iron was imported in finished or semi-finished forms. The first iron artefacts are found in the settlement and cemetery of the classical colony. Iron artefacts of the fifth to fourth centuries BC include axes, wedges and spits. The first evidence for smelting and smithing iron in the site, however, belongs to the Roman period. The reason for this may be that both ores and fuel deposits were located outside the territory of Avdera's city-state. Ores and fuel nonetheless could be transported (as was the case in Ischia), and Avdera definitely belonged to a network that would have facilitated such

Figure 9.8   Topographic map of ancient Avdera (Archaeological Museum of Avdera, Greece).

transport. The analysis of manufacturing techniques of edged objects has moreover demonstrated (1) that the edges of most artefacts are made of soft, mainly ferritic iron; (2) that carburisation is inconsistently applied; and (3) that when it is, it comes in the form of welded sheets of metal with different carbon content. The technology of fifth-century BC Avdera is overall completely different from that of Messemvria-Zone, despite the high connectivity of these settlements with both one another and the outside world.

In the case of these two colonies, the application of the new methodology, based not on style but on contexts of production and consumption and on the study of technology as *habitus*, has brought to light two distinctive technologies of iron. Despite substantial formal similarities among objects such as spears, arrows and knives, smelting and manufacturing techniques suggest different local preferences and what are probably local cultural identities of distinctive groups. The materiality of iron thus becomes both a 'maker' and a 'marker' of difference in times of high connectivity; in the case of Messemvria-Zone the techniques and a long-lasting expertise in iron making were developed within the cultural milieu of the indigenous rather than colonial identity of the site.

Conclusion

The results of this study suggest that the methodological framework outlined can be successful for more general studies of cultural contact and materiality. In this model, material attributes such as form, style and decoration become secondary or 'temporary' characteristics of identity in Gosselain's terms; they can be transferred or changed more easily than the techniques. In his view, techniques are an intrinsic and thus more permanent feature of identity, and understanding the materiality of any technology therefore becomes crucial for exploring its socio-cultural meanings, transfer, regional variations and interregional exchanges in the multicultural world of the first millennium BC Mediterranean (Gosselain 2000: 191–3).

In the presentation of the northern Greek case studies, I have argued that local technological traditions are characterised by preferences for and choices of raw materials and techniques, which can be observed archaeologically and analytically. These preferences – or dispositions – are indicative of a shared *habitus* and signify a local identity that could be recognised by people sharing the same culture, attributes and hidden meanings, but these also tend to go unnoticed by traditional archaeological approaches. Careful consideration of the ways that iron and steel technologies operated in the pre-industrial world, along with archaeological case studies from contact zones between Greek colonists and indigenous people, demonstrate the serious need to reconsider diffusion as the driving force behind the transfer of technological knowledge in iron metallurgy – even in times of high connectivity between cultures. It also underscores the need to expand our attention to all categories of archaeological material, in particular beyond aesthetic criteria and to develop new approaches that will help us to understand these phenomena. Territorial expansion and contact between different cultures did not and do not equate to technological transmission, as objects travel and can be exchanged, modified, transferred, inherited or given as gifts. Technological processes and choices, however, are culturally embedded and in that sense intrinsic: this is what makes them both markers and makers of difference.

References

Andersen-Damgaard H.W.H., S. Houby-Nielsen and A. Rathje (eds) 1997 *Urbanisation in the Mediterranean in the 9th to 6th Centuries BC.* Acta Hyperborea 7. Copenhagen: Museum Tusculanum Press.

Andronikos, M. 1978 *The Royal Tombs at Vergina.* Athens: Ekdotiki Athinon.

Appadurai, A. 1986 Introduction: commodities and the politics of value. In A. Appadurai (ed.), *The Social Life of Things. Commodities in Cultural Perspective*, 3–63. Cambridge: Cambridge University Press.

Aufrecht, W.E. (ed.) 1997 *Urbanism in Antiquity from Mesopotamia to Crete*. Sheffield: Sheffield Academic Press.

Bennett, A. 2009 Late 1st millennium BC tools and weapons from a burial site in east central Thailand. Unpublished paper presented at World of Iron conference, London, 16–21 February 2009.

Blakely, S. 2006 *Myth, Ritual and Metallurgy in Ancient Greece and Recent Africa*. Cambridge: Cambridge University Press.

Boardman, J. 1980 *The Greeks Overseas: Their Early Colonies and Trade*. London: Thames and Hudson.

Bourdieu, P. 1977 *Outline of a Theory of Practice*. Cambridge: Cambridge University Press.

Catling, H. 1961 A new bronze sword from Cyprus. *Antiquity 35*: 115–22.

Champion, T.C. (ed.) 1989 *Centre and Periphery: Comparative Studies in Archaeology*. Cambridge: Cambridge University Press.

Cherry, J.F. 1987 Power in space: archaeological and geographical studies of the state. In J.M. Wagstaff (ed.), *Power in Space*, 146–72. Oxford: Basil Blackwell.

Childe, V.G. 1958 *The Prehistory of European Society*. London: Harmondsworth.

Davis, O. 1935 *Roman Mines in Europe*. Oxford: Clarendon Press.

Dawkins, R.M. 1929 *The Sanctuary of Artemis Orthia at Sparta*. London: Macmillan.

Dietler, M. 1997 The Iron Age in Mediterranean France: colonial encounters, entanglements, and transformations. *Journal of World Prehistory* 11: 269–357.

—— 1998 Consumption, agency, and cultural entanglement: theoretical implications of a Mediterranean colonial encounter. In J.G. Cusick (ed.), *Studies in Culture Contact Interaction, Culture Change and Archaeology*. Center for Archaeological Investigations Occasional Paper 25, 288–311. Carbondale: Southern Illinois University.

Dobres, M.A., and J. Robb (eds) 2000 *Agency in Archaeology*. London: Routledge.

Fontijn, D.R. 2005 Giving up weapons. In M. Parker Pearson and I.J.N. Thorpe (eds), *Warfare, Violence and Slavery in Prehistory, Proceeding of a Prehistoric Society Conference at Sheffield University*. British Archaeological Reports International Series 1374: 145–54. Oxford: Archaeopress.

—— 2008 Everything in its right place? On selective deposition, landscape and the construction of identities in later prehistory. In A. Jones (ed.), *Prehistoric Europe: Theory and Practice*, 86–106. Oxford: Blackwell.

Giles, M. 2007 Making metal and forging relations: ironworking in the British Iron Age. *Oxford Journal of Archaeology* 26: 395–413.

Gosden, C., and Y. Marshall 1999 The cultural biography of objects. *World Archaeology* 31: 169–78.

Gosselain, O.P. 2000 Materializing identities: an African perspective. *Journal of Archaeological Method and Theory* 7: 187–217.

Haarer, P. 2001 Obelloi and Iron in Archaic Greece. Unpublished PhD thesis, Department of Archaeology, University of Oxford.

Hall, J.M. 1995 Approaches to ethnicity in the Early Iron Age Greece. In N. Spencer (ed.), *Time, Tradition and Society in Greek Archaeology*, 6–17. London: Routledge.

Hall, J.M. 1997 *Ethnic Identity in Greek Antiquity*. Cambridge: Cambridge University Press.

Herbert, E. 1993 *Iron, Gender, and Power: Rituals of Transformation in African Societies*. Bloomington, IN: Indiana University Press.

Hernández Pérez, M. (ed.) 2001 *Y acumularon tesoros. Mil años de historia en nuestras tierras. Catálogo de la Exposición de la Caja de Ahorros del Mediterráneo, Valencia, Murcia, Castellón, Alicante, Barcelona*. Valencia: Conseil General de Consorci de Museus de la Comunitat Valenciana.

Hingley, R. 1996 The 'legacy' of Rome: the rise, decline and fall of the theory of Romanisation. In J. Webster and N. Cooper (eds), *Roman Imperialism: Post-Colonial Perspectives*. Leicester Archaeology Monographs 3: 35–48. Leicester: Leicester University Press.

Isaac, B.H. 1986 *The Greek Settlements in Thrace until the Macedonian Conquest*. Leiden: Brill.

Kilian-Dirlmeier, I. 1993 *Die Schwerter in Griechenland*. Prähistorische Bronzefunde. Stuttgart: Franz Steiner.

Klein, J. 1972 A Greek metalworking quarter: eighth-century excavations on Ischia. *Expedition* 14 (2): 34–9.

Knapp, A.B. 2000 Archaeology, science-based archaeology and the Mediterranean Bronze Age metals trade. *European Journal of Archaeology* 3: 31–55.

Kostoglou, M. 2003 Iron and steel currency bars in ancient Greece. *Journal of Mediterranean Archaeology and Archaeometry* 3: 63–8.

—— 2008a *Iron and Steel in Ancient Greece: Artefacts, Technology and Social Change in Aegean Thrace from Classical to Roman Times*. British Archaeological Reports International Series 1883. Oxford: John and Erica Hedges.

—— 2008b Toward an integrated approach to the study of ancient Greek technology. In Y. Fakorelis, N. Zacharias and K. Polikreti (eds), *Proceedings of the 4th International Symposium of the Hellenic Society for Archaeometry*. British Archaeological Reports International Series 1746: 456–68. Oxford: John and Erica Hedges.

Koukouli-Chryssanthaki, Ch. 1988 Οι ανασκαφικές έρευνες στα αρχαία Άβδηρα. Στο *'Η Ιστορική, Αρχαιολογική και Λαογραφική Έρευνα για τη Θράκη'*, 39–74. Thessaloniki: Ινστιτούτο Μελετών της Χερσονήσου του Αίμου.

Lemonnier, P. 1986 The study of material culture today: toward an anthropology of technical systems. *Journal of Anthropological Archaeology* 5: 147–86.

Lemonnier, P. (ed.) 1992 *Elements for an Anthropology of Technology*. Anthropological Papers 88. Ann Arbor, MI: Museum of Anthropology, University of Michigan.

—— 1993 *Technological Choices: Transformation in Material Cultures since the Neolithic*. London: Routledge.

Leroi-Gourhan, A. 1943 *L'homme et la matière*. Paris: Albin Michel.

McConchie, M. 2004 *Archaeology at the North-East Anatolian Frontier V: Iron Technology and Iron-Making Communities of the First Millennium BC*. Ancient Near Eastern Studies Supplement 13. Leuven: Peters.

Molloy, B.P.C. 2005 The adoption of the Naue II sword in the Aegean. In C. Briault, J. Green, A. Kaldelis and A. Stellatou (eds), *SOMA 2003: Symposium on*

Mediterranean Archaeology. British Archaeological Reports International Series 1391: 115–17. Oxford: Archaeopress.

Morris, I. 1989 Circulation, deposition and the formation of the Greek Iron Age. *Man* 24: 502–19

—— 1992 The early polis as city and state, in R.A. Wallace-Hadrill (ed.), *City and Country in the Ancient World*, 25–58. London: Routledge.

Muhly, J.D. 1980 The Bronze Age setting. In T.A. Wertime and J.D. Muhly (eds), *The Coming of the Age of Iron*, 25–67. New Haven: Yale University Press.

—— 2006 Texts and technology: the beginnings of iron metallurgy in the eastern Mediterranean. In T.P. Tassios and C. Polyvou (eds), *Ancient Greek Technology: Proceedings of the 2nd International Conference on Ancient Greek Technology (Oct. 2005)*, 19–31. Athens: Technical Chamber of Greece.

Needham, S.P. 1988 Selective deposition in the British Early Bronze Age. *World Archaeology* 20: 229–48.

Nieto, X., and M. Santos 2008 *El vaixell grec arcaic de Cala Sant Vicenç*. Monografies del CASC 7. Girona: CASC.

Photos, E. 1987 Early Extractive Metallurgy in North Greece: A Unified Approach to Regional Archaeometallurgy. Unpublished PhD thesis, Institute of Archaeology, University College London.

Pigott, V.C. 1996 The study of ancient metallurgical technology: a review. *Asian Perspectives* 35: 89–97.

Pleiner, R. 1969 *Iron Working in Ancient Greece*. Prague: National Technical Museum.

—— 1980 Early iron metallurgy in Europe. In T.A. Wertime and J.D. Muhly (eds), *The Coming of the Age of Iron*, 375–416. New Haven: Yale University Press.

Popham, M.R., L.H. Sackett and P.G. Themelis 1980 *Lefkandi* I: *The Iron Age*. British School at Athens Supplementary Volume 11. London: Thames and Hudson.

Renzi, M., and S. Rovira 2007 Escorias metalúrgicas del yacimiento fenicio de La Fonteta (Alicante). Estudio preliminar. In J. Molera, J. Farjas, P. Roura and T. Pradell (eds), *Avances en Arqueometría 2005. Actas del VI Congreso Ibérico de Arqueometría, Universitat de Girona del 16 al 19 de noviembre de 2005*, 163–71, available at http://copernic.udg.es/arqueometria/TOT/Arqueometria2005.pdf. Girona: Universitat de Girona.

Risberg, Ch. 1994 Evidence of metal working in early Greek sanctuaries. In C. Gillis, Ch. Risberg and B. Sjöberg (eds), *Trade and Production in Premonetary Greece: Production and the Craftsman. Proceedings of the 4th and 5th International Workshops, Athens 1994 and 1995*, 185–96. Jonsered: Paul Åströms Förlag.

Romaios, K.A. 1929 The findings of Stavropoulos in Delos. *Archaeologiko Deltio* 1929: 210–23.

Rowlands, M. 1971 The archaeological interpretation of metalworking. *World Archaeology* 3: 210–24.

1987 Centre and periphery: a review of a concept. In M. Rowlands (ed.), *Centre and Periphery in the Ancient World*, 1–11. Cambridge: Cambridge University Press.

Salzani, L. 1998 Nuovi dati sul ripostiglio della Pila del Brancon. *Quaderni di Archeologia del Veneto* 14: 66–71.

Schiffer, M.B., and A.R. Miller 1999 *The Material Life of Human Beings*. London: Routledge.

Sherratt, A., and S. Sherratt. 2002 Technological change in the east Mediterranean Bronze Age: capital, resource and marketing. In A.J. Shortland (ed.), *The Social Context of Technological Change, Egypt and the Near East, 1650–1550 BC*, 15–38. Oxford: Oxbow Books.

Sherrat, S. 1994 Commerce, iron and ideology: metallurgical innovation in the 12th–11th centuries BC in Cyprus. In V. Karageorghis (ed.), *Cyprus in the 11th Century BC*, 59–107. Nicosia: A.G. Leventis Foundation.

Snodgrass, A. 1967 *Arms and Armour of the Greeks*. London: Thames and Hudson.

—— 1971 *The Dark Age of Greece*. Cambridge: Cambridge University Press.

—— 1980 Iron and early metallurgy in the Mediterranean. In T.A. Wertime and J.D. Muhly (eds), *The Coming of the Age of Iron*, 335–74. New Haven: Yale University Press.

—— 2006 The coming of the Iron Age in Greece: Europe's earliest bronze-iron transition. In A. Snodgrass (ed.), *Archaeology and the Emergence of Greece: Collected Papers on Early Greece and Related Topics (1965–2002)*, 126–43. Edinburgh: Edinburgh University Press.

Stein, G. 2002 From passive periphery to active agents: emerging perspectives in the archaeology of interregional interaction. *American Anthropologist* 104: 903–16.

Triantafyllos, D. 1972 Locating antiquities. *Archaeological Reports* 27: 536–47.

—— 1984 Avdera. *Archaeology* 13: 27–34.

—— 1994 Αρχαία Θράκη. Στον τόμο *Θράκη*: 35–97. Thessaloniki: Γενική Γραμματεία Ανατολικής Μακεδονίας και Θράκης.

Tsatsopoulou, T. 1984 Aegean Messemvria. *Archaeology* 13: 59–64.

—— 1988 Μεσσημβρία-Ζώνη, Ημερολόγια Ανασκαφής. 19η Εφορεία Προϊστορικών και Κλασικών Αρχαιοτήτων Θράκης (unpublished excavation diaries for the years 1988–96 kept in Komotini).

—— 1989 Μεσσημβρία-Ζώνη, Ημερολόγια Ανασκαφής. 19η Εφορεία Προϊστορικών και Κλασικών Αρχαιοτήτων Θράκης (unpublished excavation diaries for the years 1988–96 kept in Komotini).

—— 1997 The excavation at Mesemvria-Zone during the last decade. In *The Archaeological Work in Macedonia and Thrace*. Thessaloniki: Kyriakidis Press.

Tsimpidis-Pentazos, E. 1971 Αρχαιολογικές Έρευνες στη Θράκη. *Πρακτικά της εν Αθήναις Αρχαιολογικής Εταιρείας*: 86–118.

10

MOBILITY, MATERIALITY AND IDENTITIES IN IRON AGE EAST IBERIA

On the appropriation of material culture and the question of judgement

*Jaime Vives-Ferrándiz**

Introduction: appropriating the topic

During the eighth and seventh centuries BC, communities of Phoenician origin arrived on the coast of Alicante (Spain) to create new settlements and to establish themselves in several indigenous sites. Very soon afterwards, indigenous groups moved to live in the new settlements as well. Like many other historical cases of contact and co-presence, these processes resulted in new social relations, the restructuring of existing identities and the appearance of new ones.

This chapter builds on aspects considered in other publications but broadens the perspective in relation to the volume's themes of mobility, materiality and identity. I begin by examining the phenomenon of the appropriation of material culture in situations of contact and co-presence associated with Phoenician trade in eastern Iberia. More specifically, I explore first how objects were used and perceived in the cemetery of Les Moreres (Crevillent, Alicante, Spain) and then move on to link these instances of usage to social changes in the domestic realm. I also touch on the material dimensions of identities in the broad social contexts of mobility, contact, conflict, co-presence and hybridisation. Throughout this chapter, I bring out the key idea, as outlined in the Introduction to this volume, that actions and perceptions were all inscribed in material culture.

* I would like to thank Bernard Knapp and Peter van Dommelen for their helpful comments in developing this research. I am also thankful to the members of the *Material Connections* group for contributing to improving previous versions of this paper presented in Malta and Glasgow. I also thank Alfredo González Prats for permission to publish material from his excavations.

Items, people and appropriation

Appropriation has an important material dimension in relation to the use of things when they change hands and contexts. Broadly speaking, appropriation is recognised partly in connection to the polysemic nature of material culture and partly in connection to perspectives derived from agency theory. The term refers to the incorporation of new material culture into a context in which the new items change function and/or meaning in relation to other contexts (Dietler 2007).

This definition is admittedly rather a generic and vague one, because every aspect of material culture can be appropriated in principle: even ideas may be appropriated. Appropriation should not be seen as a thing in itself but rather as a process embedded in an array of social practices. It may account for ways of understanding the meanings of actions and the role of objects as culturally contingent constructions, in addition to representing stressed values, symbolic communications and webs of social relations and power. It involves wider aspects such as continuity or transformation and poses the question whether other people's values were adopted or not.

In this study, I am particularly interested in the ways in which goods are appropriated, offer meaningful insights into practices of consumption and are embedded in the materiality of daily social networks. This situation also fits into other historical cases of contact, co-presence, hybridisation and change (e.g. Lightfoot 2005: 181–209). People ascribe value to things in motion from their own perspectives and in relation to patterns of consumption that they consider to be 'appropriate' (see for instance Douglas and Isherwood 1979; Appadurai 1986: 31; Dietler 1998: 300; 2007; Tilley 2006: 63; Miller 2006: 347). Instances of appropriation may thus emerge from practices related to social maintenance and reproduction, power relationships and the construction of identities. As Knapp and van Dommelen have pointed out in the Introduction to this volume (p. 6), 'the process of constructing a new world, literally and mentally, holds the key to understanding mobility and the ensuing engagements that result in the restructuring of existing identities and the reformulation of new, hybrid identities'.

The value that people attach to things and to ways of doing should be examined on a case-by-case basis. I am therefore using the concept of culture as a historical social process, in accordance with Bourdieu's (1980: 92) theory of practice and his notion of *habitus*. The performative aspects of culture are topics of interest from an archaeological perspective because of their material dimensions; this is especially germane to this volume, because practice and materiality inform each other. A material culture perspective, which considers the 'embodied realities of being in the world' (Meskell 2005: 4) may thus shed new light on these situations by stressing the dialectic between people and things, like the many objects that people become linked to in the course of their lives (Hoskins 2006: 81).

On the basic assumption that the movement of people and objects must be understood as cultural processes in a maze of social, economic and symbolic relations (Thomas 1994: 2; Meskell 2005), I begin this study by considering the key themes of mobility, materiality and identity in my case study of southeast Iberia. I then explore how new items became appropriated in one particular cemetery and consider to what extent objects played a role in facilitating contacts between social groups or in creating distance between them. The materiality of contact and co-presence is meaningful in the elucidation of individual and group values when new objects are adopted and existing ones maintained in concrete practices. This materiality can be linked to other changes in the domestic sphere. The questions at stake are manifold: which traits are taken up and which are not? Was there any conscious desire to connect to the other's view of the world? And finally, to what extent can the notion of judgement be applied to such phenomena? The main question in the background is how we may conceptualise the relationship between changes in material culture and those of practice.

On location: background of historical developments

The area of study is situated in the lower basins of the Segura and Vinalopó rivers. The most striking geomorphological feature of the area is a wetland of a coastal lagoons and marshes that was formed from the middle Pleistocene onwards. The Late Bronze Age sites did not occupy the shores of these marshes but are found inland, in areas like the mountains of Crevillent (Peña Negra, Caramoro II and El Bosch), and the basin of the Segura river (Los Saladares: Figure 10.1).

The Late Bronze Age

The most interesting aspect of this situation is the intense participation of these communities in long-distance exchange networks. Metallurgical activities and the exploitation of mining resources in the area – most likely within 18–20 km (Moratalla 2003: 164) – seem to be related to such networks. For instance, around 400 fragments of clay and stone casts to produce swords, spears, needles and axes in bronze were discovered in a single house at Peña Negra that can be dated to the eighth century BC (González Prats 1992). Most of these objects were actually currency bars. The situation in Peña Negra is matched by that in the nearby settlement of El Bosch, where dwellings are found scattered over a wide area and many stone casts, used to produce swords and axes dating to the eighth century BC, have been recorded (Trelis 1995: 185; Trelis et al. 2004: 320). This evidence indicates that specialised activities became increasingly concentrated in particular sites and especially in what we might call 'empowered houses', as some groups among the local communities gained control of the exchange networks as a means to increase their power.

Indeed, the region saw a highly dynamic process with many sites newly founded or abandoned during the ninth and seventh centuries BC, which constitutes further proof of changing power relations in the area (see Vives-Ferrándiz 2005: 180; 2008). As these developments seem to intensify around the time of the Phoenician arrival, it seems unlikely that such phenomena were unconnected.

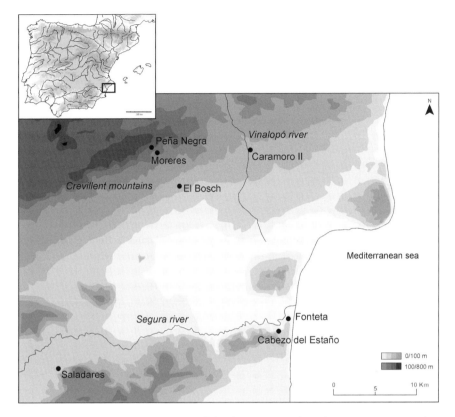

Figure 10.1   Study area in the context of the Iberian Peninsula and main sites mentioned in the text.

Phoenician identities, Phoenician mobility and local implications

Phoenician mobility stands out as one of the most widely ranging movements of goods and people in ancient Iberia, as Phoenician material culture and settlements have been identified all along the southern Mediterranean and nearby Atlantic coasts of the Iberian Peninsula (Aubet 2001; Arruda 1999–2000; López Pardo 2002). The maritime Mediterranean dimension of this encounter therefore warrants particular attention.

The so-called Phoenician trade diaspora is basically a movement of people from Tyre in modern Lebanon (Aubet 2001), which aimed at establishing trading posts in a network of settlements from the shores of the Levantine coast and Cyprus in the eastern Mediterranean to the Atlantic Ocean in what is nowadays Portugal and Morocco. Having emerged in the ninth century BC, by the seventh century a dense network of settlements was in existence, which included, for instance, the southern

193

coast of Spain. There remained, however, substantial differences between these areas, because the Phoenicians were not one single homogeneous community.

'Phoenician' is an elusive term of Greek origin recorded in archaic Greek texts; it refers mainly to people living along the Levantine coast and to merchants frequenting the Aegean region. The Phoenicians themselves used or were referred to by the Semitic term *Kinahhi/Kinahni*. Archaeologists and historians nevertheless conventionally refer to the people of the Levantine coast as Phoenicians. Some scholars have even insisted on the unity of the Phoenicians on the basis of an alleged ethnic reality that they saw documented by geography, language, culture and historical development, regardless of differences across space and time (Moscati 1993: 79). Even the eclectic nature of craftwork – such as ivories, jewellery and figurines that betray a range of local features – is brandished as an argument to stress Phoenician cultural coherence (Moscati 1988: 246).

From the very beginning, however, the outposts showed several cultural features that differed from Levantine material culture. A most telling example of this variability is the production of pottery, which was typologically and technologically diversified not only when compared to the Levantine region but also within the western and central Mediterranean.

It is evident from the heterogeneity of their materiality that the newcomers engaged in a variety of economic activities, from trade to production and consumption, and that their settlements were different from one area to another (Gómez Bellard 2003; López Castro 2006: 82). These differences cannot be understood without taking into account the motivations and perceptions of local people who had become involved in Phoenician mobility. Many oriental merchants and workshops were indeed initially established in settlements under a local authority, as for example in Kommos, Samaria, Huelva and Peña Negra (see below). In these cases, as in most histories of mobility, the heterogeneity of the contact situations in terms of the various modes of co-presence may be addressed through the materiality of the people of different cultural backgrounds involved in these contexts.

Analysing these issues from the particular perspective of the Iberian east coast forces us to assess local socio-economic developments prior to the arrival of the Phoenicians and to bear in mind the different modes of being-in-the-world in indigenous contexts (Gosden 1999: 129). The earliest Phoenician presence in eastern Iberia dates to the second half of the eighth century BC. This date accords with the chronology established by finds from the sites of La Fonteta (Guardamar del Segura, Alicante: González Prats 1998; Rouillard *et al.* 2007), Peña Negra (González Prats 1983) and Saladares (Orihuela, Alicante: Arteaga 1982), and the cemetery of Les Moreres (González Prats 2002: 376) (see Figure 10.1). Houses built with different techniques and layouts, objects produced with new technologies as well as several Phoenician inscriptions suggest that people of foreign origin – allegedly western Phoenician – settled in La Fonteta by 700 BC (Rouillard *et al.* 2007: 433). Peña Negra and Saladares had been occupied since the Late Bronze Age and the presence of the first imports, like small ivory objects such as bracelets, necklaces and beads, as well as some Phoenician-style domestic pottery, denote contacts with the new outpost on the coast.

The location of La Fonteta in an isolated area on the coast gives us an impression of the aims and the constraints the first settlers would have faced. In the first place, the location of a small strip of land between the open sea and the lagoon, surrounded by marshland, is a peripheral place, well away from the indigenous settlements that were situated in the hills farther inland. In the second place, from a Phoenician point of view, the propinquity to the sea would have facilitated connections with Mediterranean overseas networks.

La Fonteta was probably the last staging post on the Iberian coast before reaching the island of Ibiza for anyone sailing from the south of Spain to the north. From being a no man's land this area soon became a place for exchanges and production from about 700 BC onwards. In the first half of the following century it developed into an important port with new commercial facilities, storerooms, workshops and other productive spaces that changed the layout of the settlement. The fact that metallurgical activities have been recorded from the earliest levels of La Fonteta (González Prats 2005: 54) is important in this respect, because they suggest that the Phoenicians actively sought to become involved in local networks in the same way that trade diasporas attempt to cope with existing exchange networks (Aubet 2005: 118; Ruiz-Gálvez 2005: 252).

With this setting in mind, I turn to the indigenous contexts further inland, where I examine the cemetery of Les Moreres in order to gauge the practices of the people that had begun to use the new objects-in-motion. I then move on to compare contemporary domestic contexts in order to consider the broader situation in terms of mobility, materiality and identity.

The cemetery of Les Moreres

Les Moreres is a cemetery located around 200 m away from the settlement of Peña Negra. Thus far, it is the only excavated burial area in the Crevillent mountains, where the settlement is located. For this reason, it provides the best reference point to evaluate mortuary practices between the mid-ninth and seventh centuries BC. I follow the publication by González Prats (2002) for the description of the data but introduce different points of view when required. Up to 152 tombs have been identified, 17 of which yielded no human remains because of poor preservation. The funerary ritual consisted of cremating the corpse and the subsequent deposition of the remains, once washed, into a pit. A number of burials included a ceramic urn (99 tombs), sometimes covered by a lid or plate, while 36 tombs were directly deposited on the soil without any urn (Figures 10.2 and 10.3).

The nearby settlement of Peña Negra (González Prats 1983) has helped to provide good chronological information for the finds. The cemetery was in use from the mid-ninth century BC to the end of the seventh century BC. The excavator has also proposed two different phases of use, one between 900 and 750 BC and the other from around 750–625 BC (González Prats 2002: 263), but these are suspiciously similar to the phases distinguished at Peña Negra (PN I, 850–700 BC; and PN II, 700–550 BC). Tombs and associated grave goods have been assigned to one of these

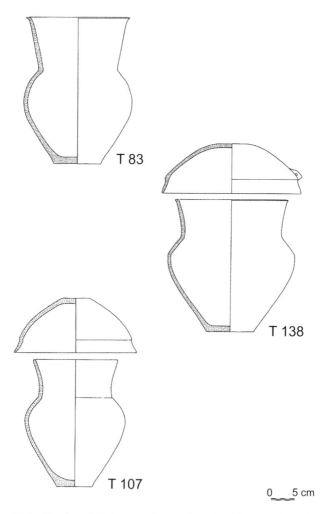

Figure 10.2 Hand-modelled urns and covers from Les Moreres (adapted from González Prats 2002: figures 126, 144 and 167).

phases on the basis of an artificial classification which may be useful for analytical objectives but which is problematic for understanding the cemetery as a space where ongoing actions were performed during more than two centuries. I therefore use the two phases only as analytical tools to present the data and adopt a more nuanced approach to the depositions.

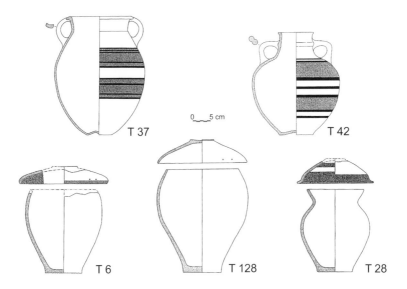

Figure 10.3   Wheel-made urns and covers from Les Moreres (adapted from González Prats 2002: figures 58, 75, 84, 90 and 160).

Tombs, rituals and objects

In addition to the burials themselves, 19 stone structures have been recorded (Figure 10.4). Constructed in order to cover the deposited remains and to demarcate burials, these structures are approximately circular in layout but vary in type and size. They have been classified as *simple, medium-complex* and *complex* structures, depending on their size, which varies from 0.4 to 1.7 m in diameter. There does not appear to be any direct relationship or association between these structures and the number of burials per tomb, associated grave goods, or in terms of gender or age. Moreover, there is no relationship between these structures and the chronology of the tombs. It is nonetheless interesting to note that more urns were used without associated stone constructions during the last phase of the cemetery, regardless of whether the urns were hand-modelled or wheel-made.

In two cases the stone structures are related to more than one tomb; these may have served for family burials. In one case, a woman with a newborn and an adult man were buried together. In the other, five people were buried together in four tombs: an adult man, another young man, a woman with an infant and a newborn. These two sets of tombs are dated to the first phase of use.

Three larger, circular constructions have been labelled as burial mounds, even though there does not seem to have been any earth mound on top of them. They

197

Figure 10.4   Stone structures as markers on top of tombs (González Prats 2002: CD with catalogue of pictures).

measure respectively 3.4, 5.0 and 7.5 m in diameter, although the last one has many problems of interpretation because the remains were poorly documented. All these structures can be dated among the earliest constructions in the cemetery and they may have contained more than one individual. Unfortunately it is difficult to be sure, because of problems with conserving the objects and because of earlier looting activities (González Prats 2002: 233).

Regarding the number of individuals deposited per tomb, there are 107 burials containing 1 individual, while 10 are double burials and 3 are triple. In the first phase, there are 24 individual, 4 double and 3 triple burials, whereas in the second phase, there are 40 individual burials and 4 double ones. These data show not only that triple burials disappeared but also that there is an increase of individual interments through time.

All age groups are represented and there is no difference between the two phases, as 26 adults, 10 infants and 5 newborns have been assigned to the early phase. The second phase provides similar figures with 28 adults, 13 infants and 7 newborns. The distribution of the deceased in terms of age suggests that mortality was common among newborns (up to 6 months) and infants (between 6 months and 7 years old) and among young adults (between 20 and 35 years of age), especially women, which perhaps highlights the risks of giving birth (Gómez Bellard 2002: 463).

Less than a third of the tombs contain grave goods and there is no clear pattern of or association between the deposition of any particular object in terms of phases, gender or age – only rings may be related to infants during both phases. Only items linked to the decoration of the body and personal ornaments are introduced in tombs during the earlier phase, such as necklaces of stone, copper and bronze beads, silver pendants and beads, copper and bronze bracelets and rings and ivory bracelets (Figure 10.6). In the later phase, bronze *fibulae* – again an element related to ornament and dress – and iron objects (two small knives in two different tombs) were introduced (Figure 10.5).

An interesting mixture: the introduction of new objects in funerary rituals

The earliest tombs contained hand-modelled urns and covers alongside simple bronze, copper and ivory bracelets and beads as grave goods. By the time of the Phoenicians' arrival a handful of cremations (9 out of 85) using wheel-made urns and covers had been introduced (see Figure 10.3, above): some of these objects are imports from southern Spain, while others are likely to be locally produced. These pottery vessels are well known in Phoenician domestic repertoires across the western Mediterranean and along the Atlantic shores; they were occasionally used as urns in some cemeteries, as for instance at Can Partit and Puig des Molins on the nearby island of Ibiza (Gómez Bellard *et al.* 1990).

These ceramics served as tableware and food containers. They are usually decorated with several bi-chrome (black and red) painted bands. Their painted decoration contrasts sharply with the absolute absence of decorations on the hand-modelled urns in the cemetery, even if hand-modelled painted bowls were quite common in the settlement of Peña Negra.

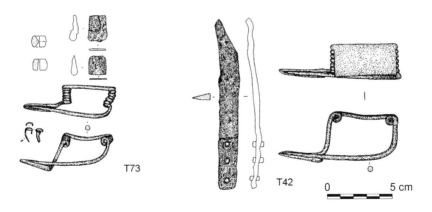

Figure 10.5 Small iron knives and bronze *fibulae* (adapted from González Prats 2002: figures 92 and 118).

None of these burials is accompanied by a structure of stone masonry, as they are single urns deposited into single pits dug in the earth. Interestingly, there seems to be a link between the new type of urn and gender, as these pots are primarily associated with adult males (in six cases; the other two were infants). The two oldest (male) adults in the cemetery were both interred in wheel-made urns. No specific grave goods, however, can be associated with these pottery vessels. Ten further tombs combine wheel-made and hand-modelled urns. This indicates that tombs with wheel-made pottery did not entirely replace those using hand-modelled ones and that they coexisted until the cemetery was abandoned by the end of the seventh century BC.

There were also other, new grave goods. These include three iron fragments – one small blade (tomb 73) and two small knives (tombs 42 and 126). In Iberia, the appearance of iron objects has traditionally been related to Phoenician trade in the eighth century BC but recent finds push this date back into the ninth century, when small iron bracelets and knives were exchanged along the Mediterranean and Atlantic shores of Iberia (Rafel *et al.* 2008: 265). Among the other new objects are two *fibulae* (brooches) that were deposited in the same tombs as the iron objects (tombs 42 and 73: Figure 10.5). Beyond the arrival date of these objects, I would point out that access to iron objects was certainly limited to very few people and the same must have applied to other materials like a new type of *fibula*.

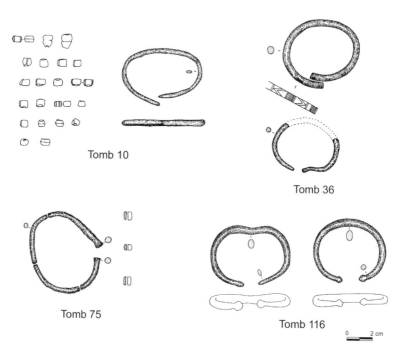

Tomb 10

Tomb 36

Tomb 75

Tomb 116

0   2 cm

Figure 10.6   Selected grave goods (adapted from González Prats 2002: figures 62, 83, 121 and 151).

In short, this cremation cemetery was continuously in use over more than two centuries. Spatial analysis does not show any special cluster in terms of burials, including urn typologies or grave goods, and all age ranges are represented in the cemetery. From a broader perspective, however, there are two major developments over time: larger structures and family burials disappear and individual tombs gradually became dominant. Newly introduced items were not associated with any particular gender or age, as only wheel-made urns were reliably associated with adult male burials.

The use of material culture: from ethnicity as a thing to identity as a process

How can we interpret these changes in material culture? To what extent were material culture and the identity of the people using it perceived as significant? Are these changes just a matter of choice? Traditionally it has been suggested that the introduction of new objects in Les Moreres meant the adoption of Phoenician rituals by indigenous communities; alternatively, it has been suggested that Phoenicians and their descendants lived in nearby Peña Negra and that they were buried in Les Moreres (González Prats 2002: 387).

This approach is problematic, because it assumes that there is such a thing as Phoenician ritual. The archaeological record in the western Mediterranean shows that Phoenician funerary rituals varied substantially from one place to another, as is demonstrated by the cremation burials in Can Partit (Ibiza: Fernández and Costa 2004) and the rich inhumation burials from southern Spain, like Trayamar in Málaga (Schubart and Niemeyer 1976). No less problematic is the way in which this interpretation employs an ethnic perspective when looking at the past, as it equates pots and people in a straightforward manner and assumes that differences in material culture are best explained in terms of different ethnic groups. As many scholars have argued, however, ethnicity is not a 'thing' somehow attached to people or objects but is rather incorporated in the processes involving differentiation and identity creation (Gosden 1999: 190; Knapp 2007). As a 'transitory and even unstable relation of difference' (Knapp and van Dommelen, this volume: p. 4), objects were used in such an array of ways that to reduce them to a single list of actions by one group of people is far too simplistic.

In what follows, I offer an alternative interpretation of the introduction of new objects into the Les Moreres cemetery, one that is not ethnically driven but based on the notion of appropriating material culture and the social perception of objects. The introduction of innovations in the cemetery denotes cultural change and informs us about the processes of creating identities as embedded in the tension between tradition and change. These two levels of analysis are not necessarily conflicting, I would argue, so let us look at them.

Funerary rituals and the practice of memory

My first point concerns the observation that people continued to perform the same rituals in the cemetery. This is in itself not surprising. But I would like to follow this up and argue that the various urn and cover types do not necessarily denote changes in funerary customs. The bottom line is that the funerary site of Les Moreres was continuously used over several generations by people creating memories and remembering themselves. Sharing a place with one's ancestors signals a willingness to belong to a community, even if its members came from different places. In my view, this cemetery must have been used by one and the same social group, even if some people preferred different types of urns.

Such an interpretation suggests that Les Moreres presents a case of appropriating new materials that changed function from one context to another, as wheel-made containers and tableware were adopted for use as cinerary urns and their covers. Taking a long-term perspective on materiality, I would stress the fact that the practice of burying has not changed at all. Precisely because burial practices remained largely unchanged despite the use of new types of urns and covers, the implication is that the introduction of wheel-made pottery did not modify funerary ritual practices. On the contrary, it appears that as long as new objects recalled existing ones, they were accepted and seen as appropriate for use in the community's practices and funerary rituals.

Unlike the above-mentioned interpretations that single out ethnicity as the only relevant variable, I suggest that this process of appropriation did not imply major structural variations. In my view, it is the shared and continued use of the same burial ground that is fundamental for understanding what was going on at Les Moreres. Because shared origins are one of the most powerful ways to express a sense of community, regardless of whether these origins are real or imagined (Bradley 2002: 17), a community that continued to perform the same funerary rituals effectively confirmed its relationship with the past and its ancestors through these practices. Social memory was stressed in such practices, as tombs of the second phase are closely associated spatially with the earliest cremations deposited in hand-modelled urns.

The funerary practices were ambivalent. As the community employed the same burial ground and followed the same ritual practices (urns and covers in pits), the people using this cemetery as a place of remembering were heirs to Late Bronze Age groups. In Bourdieu's terms this means that the *doxa* or naturalised, unselfconscious and discursively mute set of structures that guide practice was not contested and that 'ideological strategies' may have been implemented to symbolise group values, shared origins and/or a sense of group through burial practices that we would label 'conservative' or 'traditional' (Bourdieu 1994: 129).

In brief, I suggest that using the same space and maintaining established mortuary practices are ways of constructing memory by re-enacting past practices. This does not mean, however, that changes of material culture do not matter, because actions and things are always meaningful in funerary rituals and usually highly codified. It is in fact possible to discern minor variations in the selection of urns, in the structure associated with the tomb or in the ornaments that were deposited with the bodies.

Some community members apparently introduced new objects like the wheel-made urns and covers and personal objects like iron knives and *fibulae* from the beginning of the seventh century BC onwards, if not before, and these variations show that practices were not automatically or routinely reproduced, and that changes did occur. This observation leads me to my second point, which is to connect materiality, taste and social networks of interaction in order to explore how things changed in the same way identities did.

Materiality, taste and local networks of interaction

This section treats other material dimensions of the burial practices. These complement those just discussed and lead us to a fuller and more complex view of the ways in which identities were expressed, how material culture was used and how these changes might have been embodied and embedded in daily social networks.

We have seen that the introduction of wheel-made urns and covers is the most striking feature of the new tombs. As noted above, their introduction marked cultural change and thus, strictly speaking, modified Late Bronze Age customs and practices. But other changes regarding the burial practices should not be neglected:

- The new tombs usually do not include grave goods but in those cases where they do, the objects are innovative as well, e.g. the *fibulae* and small iron knives.
- There is an increase in the number of individual burials.
- Circular structures, associated with the earliest tombs, tend to disappear during the seventh century BC.

There can be no doubt that these changes express different identities. But what is it precisely that they express? Why did these changes occur? How does the idea of 'taste' fit in with these developments and how could it broaden our understanding of the community and its members? Patterns of consumption are embedded in materiality (Miller 2006: 347) as well as taste, which is 'something difficult to define, but easy to recognise in practice, forming a vital part of social life' (Gosden 1999: 164).

It is this aspect of life that I would stress. If judgements about taste derive from people's *habitus* (*sensu* Bourdieu), the innovations observed in Les Moreres may be explained in relation to people's reliance on daily interaction. Taste and judgement as obvious preferences are defined by Bourdieu (1979: 59) as the practical affirmation of difference that tunes into the materiality of social life and into contemporary perception of identity as an 'unstable relation of difference' (Knapp and van Dommelen, this volume: p. 4).

Mobility and identity-making in the landscape

For a broader understanding I will consider the burial practices of Les Moreres in their regional context by connecting them to the settlement of Peña Negra and other sites in the Vinalopó and Segura valleys. The Phoenician presence in this area brought a new framework of social relations that involved indigenous communities and Phoenician newcomers alike, despite their own cultural and social heterogeneity. Material connections between these settlements suggest not only that trade took place between them but also that people of different origins lived together in these settlements. The key issue is the identification of practices of different origins and cultural backgrounds (van Dommelen 2006: 139).

The early phase of La Fonteta offers clear evidence of such links with indigenous settlements, as hand-modelled cooking pots and bowls from the earliest levels (eighth century BC) can be related typologically to pottery from nearby indigenous settlements like Peña Negra and Saladares. Equally interesting is the fact that connections were not unidirectional: Phoenician-type pottery has also been found in indigenous settlements from the eighth century BC onwards. A Phoenician inscription on a locally produced plate from Peña Negra (Figure 10.7) even suggests that Phoenician-speaking (or at least -writing) people also lived in indigenous sites. Such mobility may also be detected in individual households, as is suggested by the materiality of 'foodways': as I have argued elsewhere, pots, plates and bowls in Peña Negra were actively transformed around the same time as cooking practices and social relations changed (Vives-Ferrándiz 2008).

In short, the intensity of contacts between indigenous and Phoenician groups is crucial, as it is only in situations of close interaction that hybrid practices may be forged. I stressed above that this scenario was shaped by both indigenous people and foreign inhabitants. Moreover, La Fonteta has in fact been labelled as an *emporion*, where indigenous and Phoenicians lived side-by-side (Rouillard *et al.* 2007: 433), while Peña Negra has also been described as a site where both groups lived together (González Prats 1983: 272).

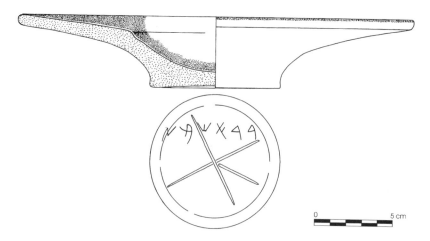

Figure 10.7   Phoenician inscription from Peña Negra (after González Prats 1986: figure 6).

These settlement contexts of daily interaction must be compared and contrasted with the conservative pattern of the continuously used cemetery. Rather than working out whether particular tombs might have belonged to Phoenician or indigenous inhabitants, I am much more interested in the interpretative potential offered by the evident contrast between change and continuity. This was generated by the tension between, on the one hand, the attachment to traditional memories, and on the other hand the innovations of formal variations that enabled new ways of doing in a traditional setting.

This allows us to assess how materiality interferes with the construction of distinctive identities and how embodied social values were attached to objects. Materiality thus enables us to distinguish group and individual practices, even within the same cemetery. I think that the few tombs where new objects were introduced may be interpreted as the 'materialisation' of people's involvement in different networks and webs of interaction within the local context. This context is the one where the arrival of people with wider Mediterranean connections opened up and boosted economic developments for some people and expanded existing trading relations to maintain and strengthen their power. Marks, seals and signs on amphorae in Peña Negra and other settlements in the Vinalopó valley suggest that there was an interest in controlling exchange networks (Vives-Ferrándiz 2005: 188). My point is that people who were already engaged in these networks may have changed their judgement of what was a proper vessel for containing ashes at a burial. In terms of materiality, this pot was not always just a pot and it was certainly not the same one for those who chose to use a new one.

We may take these connections and subjectivities even further, as materiality informs us how objects contributed to the construction of differences through the training of bodily manners. As long as people were connected to these networks, their senses and perceptions might have been modified as a result. In the foregoing, I have introduced the ideas that new 'foodways' changed people's perceptions and judgements and that the new pottery types used in burials are thus likely to be related to these landscapes of perception. Body practices offer another example, as the *fibulae*, first introduced around the time of the Phoenician arrival, attest to new ways of dressing and again different preferences and tastes. All these changes underscore the significance of connections during people's lives, as they affected their judgement, perception and conception of the body. Because the new objects are almost invariably associated with adult male individuals, we might suggest that perceptions and judgements themselves became increasingly gendered.

The oblivion of social memory

The cemetery of Les Moreres went out of use around the end of the seventh century BC, two or three generations before the settlement at Peña Negra was abandoned (González Prats 1983). How might we explain this chronological difference? As long as Les Moreres is the only cemetery associated with Peña Negra, it may be argued *ex silentio* that the archaeological record is partial, and that other, as yet unidentified, burial grounds are likely to have existed alongside the one at Les Moreres (González Prats 2002: 376).

As it is, we only have the particular materiality of this cemetery. The social memory created and maintained by the practices realised in the cemetery was forgotten, never recalled. It is tempting to link this forgetting to the competition for resources and contacts that I have referred to above. At Peña Negra, major changes affected houses and the settlement itself by the end of the seventh century BC; these include new buildings on large terraced areas and new houses with complex internal divisions. Along with increased use of the fast potter's wheel, these developments clearly point to social change. It should not come as a surprise that the place for burial changed around the same time: Les Moreres was no longer used, because cemeteries elsewhere show that new ideologies emphasised other expressions of identities, notably the introduction of iron weapons and other warrior items as grave goods.

Summing up

Culture is often used to explain the processes by which an array of materialities such as those found in the archaeological record articulate differences. Contemporary social theory emphasises that creating and maintaining these differences lie at the heart of expressing one's identity. This expression is therefore best understood in terms of processes rather than finished and static attributes.

In this chapter, I have explored a specific dimension of the materiality of contacts between Phoenician and indigenous communities in eastern Iberia. I have shown how material culture was mobilised and how through their activities in the cemetery people created similarities but also differences between the ways in which group and individual identities were expressed. These expressions worked at two distinct but not necessarily conflicting levels of meaning:

1 Group values were maintained and repeated during two centuries. People adhered to tradition and continued to do things as they learned from the past, formal experience and their families. Social memory was thus constructed and maintained.

2 Other innovations did not alter structural practice – memory and the sense of group, place and origin – and this illustrates the rich and complex dimensions of identities. These conscious choices, and their material traces, may be understood as means of communication and thus as relating to the *habitus*, judgements and connectivities of this area.

To conclude, I would draw attention to what I term the material constitution of social groups, which is based on the notion that the material culture of consumption (Miller 2006: 349) – eating, drinking, clothing, burial – affects users and their being-in-the-world. As such, this paper may be seen as a study of the ways in which the materiality of daily life contributes to the creation, maintenance and alteration of people's identities.

References

Appadurai, A. 1986 Introduction: commodities and the politics of value. In A. Appadurai (ed.), *The Social Life of Things. Commodities in Cultural Perspective*, 3–63. Cambridge: Cambridge University Press.

Arruda, A. M. 1999–2000 *Los fenicios en Portugal. Fenicios y mundo indígena en el centro y sur de Portugal (siglos VIII–VI a.C.)*. Cuadernos de Arqueología Mediterránea 5–6: Barcelona: Laboratorio de Arqueología, Universidad Pompeu Fabra.

Arteaga, O. 1982 Los Saladares 80. Nuevas directrices para el estudio del horizonte protoibérico en el levante meridional y sudeste de la Península Ibérica. *Huelva Arqueológica* 6: 131–83.

Aubet, M.E. 2001 *The Phoenicians and the West: Politics, Colonies and Trade*. Cambridge and New York: Cambridge University Press (2nd edition).

—— 2005 El 'orientalizante': un fenómeno de contacto entre sociedades desiguales. In S. Celestino and J. Jiménez (eds), *El periodo orientalizante*. Anejos de Archivo Español de Arqueología 35: 117–28. Madrid: CSIC.

Bourdieu, P. 1979 *La distinction. Critique sociale du jugement*. Paris: Éditions de Minuit.

—— 1980 *Le sens pratique*. Paris: Éditions de Minuit.

—— 1994 *Raisons pratiques. Sur la théorie de l'action*. Paris: Le Seuil.

Bradley, R. 2002 *The Past in Prehistoric Societies*. London: Routledge.

Dietler, M. 1998 Consumption, agency, and cultural entanglement: theoretical implications of a Mediterranean colonial encounter. In J.G. Cusick (ed.), *Studies in Culture Contact: Interaction, Culture Change and Archaeology*. Center for Archaeological Investigations Occasional Paper 25: 288–315. Carbondale: Southern Illinois University.

—— 2007 Culinary encounters: food, identity, and colonialism. In K. Twiss (ed.), *The Archaeology of Food and Identity*: 218–42. Carbondale: Southern Illinois University.

Douglas, M., and B. Isherwood 1979 *The World of Goods*. London: Allen Lane.

Fernández, J.H., and B. Costa 2004 Mundo funerario y sociedad en la Eivissa arcaica. Una aproximación al análisis de los enterramientos de cremación en la necrópolis del Puig des Molins. In A. González Prats (ed.), *El mundo funerario, Actas del III Seminario Internacional sobre Temas Fenicios*, 315–408. Alicante: Direcció General d'Ensenyament and Instituto de Cultura 'Juan Gil-Albert'.

Gómez Bellard, C. 2003 *Ecohistoria del paisaje agrario. La agricultura fenicio-púnica en el Mediterráneo*. Valencia: Universitat de València.

Gómez Bellard, C., B. Costa, F. Gómez Bellard, R. Gurrea, E. Grau and R. Martínez 1990 *La colonización fenicia en la isla de Ibiza*. Excavaciones Arqueológicas en España 157. Madrid: Ministerio de Cultura.

Gómez Bellard, F. 2002 Apéndice I. Estudio antropológico de las cremaciones. In A. González Prats, *La necrópolis de cremación de Les Moreres (Crevillente, Alicante, España) (s. IX–VII AC)*, 461–75. Alicante: Universidad de Alicante.

González Prats, A. 1983 *Estudio arqueológico del poblamiento antiguo de la Sierra de Crevillente*. Alicante: Universidad de Alicante.

González Prats, A. 1986 Las importaciones y la presencia fenicia en la Sierra de Crevillente (Alicante). In G. del Olmo and M. E. Aubet (eds), *Los fenicios en la Península Ibérica*, 279–302. Sabadell: AUSA.

—— 1992 Una vivienda metalúrgica en la Peña Negra (Crevillente, Alicante). Aportación al conocimiento del Bronce Atlántico en la Península Ibérica. *Trabajos de Prehistoria* 49: 243–57.

—— 1998 La Fonteta. El asentamiento fenicio de la desembocadura del río Segura (Guardamar, Alicante, España). Resultados de las excavaciones de 1996–97. *Rivista di Studi Fenici* 26: 191–228.

—— 2002 *La necrópolis de cremación de Les Moreres (Crevillente, Alicante, España) (s. IX–VII AC)*. Alicante: Universidad de Alicante.

—— 2005 Balanç de vint-i-cinc anys d'investigació sobre la influència i presència fenícia a la província d'Alacant. *Fonaments* 12: 41–64.

Gosden, C. 1999 *Anthropology and Archaeology. A Changing Relationship*. London: Routledge.

Hoskins, J. 2006 Agency, biography and objects. In C. Tilley, W. Keane, S. Küchler, M. Rowlands and P. Spyer (eds), *Handbook of Material Culture*, 74–84. London: Sage.

Knapp, A.B. 2007 Insularity and island identity in the prehistoric Mediterranean. In S. Antoniadou and A. Pace (eds), *Mediterranean Crossroads*, 37–62. Athens: Pierides Foundation.

Lightfoot, K.G. 2005 *Indians, Missionaries, and Merchants. The Legacy of Colonial Encounters on the California Frontiers*. Berkeley: University of California Press.

López Castro, J.L. 2006 Colonials, merchants and alabaster vases: the western Phoenician aristocracy. *Antiquity* 80 (307): 74–88.

López Pardo, F. 2002 Los fenicios en la costa atlántica africana: Balance y proyectos. In B. Costa and J. H. Fernández (eds), *La Colonización fenicia de Occidente: Estado de la investigación en los inicios del siglo XXI*. XVI Jornadas de Arqueología fenicio-Púnica. Treballs del Museu Arqueològic d'Eivissa i Formentera 50: 19–48. Eivissa: Museu Arqueològic d'Eivissa i Formentera.

Meskell, L. 2005 *Archaeologies of Materiality*. Malden, MA: Blackwell Publishing.

Miller, D. 2006 Consumption. In C. Tilley, W. Keane, S. Küchler, M. Rowlands and P. Spyer (eds), *Handbook of Material Culture*, 341–54. London: Sage.

Moscati, S. 1988 Artigianato e arte. In S. Moscati (ed.), *I Fenici*, 244–47. Milano: Bompiani.

—— 1993 *Nuovi studi sull'identità fenicia*. Memorie della Accademia Nazionale dei Lincei, classe di scienze morali, storiche e filologiche 9.4.1. Rome: Accademia Nazionale dei Lincei.

Moratalla, J. 2003 Organización del territorio y modelos de poblamiento en la Contestania ibérica. Unpublished PhD dissertation, Universidad de Alicante.

Rafel, N., J. Vives-Ferrándiz, X.L. Armada and R. Graells 2008 Las comunidades de la Edad del Bronce entre el Empordà y el Segura: espacio y tiempo de los intercambios. In S. Celestino, N. Rafel and X.L. Armada (eds), *Contacto cultural entre el Mediterráneo y el Atlántico (siglos XII–VIII ane). La precolonización a debate*, 239–71. Rome: CSIC and EEHAR.

Rouillard, P., E. Gailledrat and F. Sala Sellés 2007 *L'établissement protohistorique de La Fonteta (fin VIIIe–fin VIe siècle av. J.-C.)*. Collection de la Casa de Velázquez 96: Madrid: Casa de Velázquez.

Ruiz-Gálvez, M. 2005 *Der fliegende Mittlemeermann*. Piratas y héroes en los albores de la Edad del Hierro. In S. Celestino and J. Jiménez (eds), *El periodo orientalizante*. Anejos de Archivo Español de Arqueología 35: 251–75. Madrid: CSIC.

Schubart, H. and H.G. Niemeyer 1976 *Trayamar: los hipogeos fenicios y el asentamiento en la desembocadura del río Algarrobo*. Excavaciones Arqueológicas en España 90. Madrid: Ministerio de Educación y Ciencia.

Thomas, N. 1994 *Colonialism's Culture. Anthropology, Travel and Government*. Cambridge: Polity Press.

Tilley, C. 2006 Objectification. In C. Tilley, W. Keane, S. Küchler, M. Rowlands and P. Spyer (eds), *Handbook of Material Culture*, 60–73. London: Sage.

Trelis, J. 1995 Aportaciones al conocimiento de la metalurgia del Bronce Final en el sureste peninsular: el conjunto de moldes de El Bosch (Crevillente-Alicante). *Actas del XXIII Congreso Nacional de Arqueología*, 185–90. Elche: Ajuntament d'Elx.

Trelis, J., F.A. Molina, M.A. Esquembre and J.R. Ortega 2004 El Bronce Tardío e inicios del Bronce Final en el Botx (Crevillente, Alicante): nuevos hallazgos procedentes de excavaciones de salvamento. In L. Hernández Alcaraz and M.S. Hernández Pérez (eds), *La Edad del Bronce en tierras valencianas y zonas limítrofes*, 319–23. Alicante: Ayuntamiento de Villena and Instituto de Cultura 'Juan Gil-Albert'.

van Dommelen, P. 2006 The Orientalizing phenomenon: hybridity and material culture in the western Mediterranean. In C. Riva and N. Vella (eds), *Debating Orientalization. Multidisciplinary Approaches to Change in the Ancient Mediterranean*. Monographs in Mediterranean Archaeology 10: London: Equinox.

Vives-Ferrándiz, J. 2005 *Negociando encuentros. Situaciones coloniales e intercambios en la costa oriental de la península Ibérica (ss. VIII–VI a.C.)*. Cuadernos de Arqueología Mediterránea 12. Barcelona: Laboratori d'Arqueologia de la Universitat Pompeu Fabra.

——— 2008 Negotiating colonial encounters: hybrid practices and consumption in eastern Iberia (8th–6th centuries BC). *Journal of Mediterranean Archaeology* 21: 241–72.

11

TRADING SETTLEMENTS AND THE MATERIALITY OF WINE CONSUMPTION IN THE NORTH TYRRHENIAN SEA REGION

*Corinna Riva**

Introduction: approaching material connections in the north Tyrrhenian Sea region

The sixth and fifth centuries BC were a time of heightened mobility in the northern Tyrrhenian Sea region, visible in the wide circulation of objects across the region and the establishment of trading settlements in coastal areas from southern Etruria to southern France. Current studies have been concerned either with the challenging task of linking these objects to specific ethnic carriers and consumers (e.g. Gori and Bettini 2006), or with understanding the 'colonial' relationships between Greek and Etruscan traders and the indigenous communities of southern France (Dietler 1996; 1997; 2005; 2006). This chapter aims to complement these studies and move beyond their concerns by exploring the material dimension of cultural encounters and the consumption practices – mostly related to wine drinking – through which people constructed or altered their identities and negotiated cultural boundaries during the encounter. In line with studies on materiality in anthropology and archaeology (Miller 2005; 2006; Meskell 2004; 2006), I focus on the role of objects in establishing or indeed subverting the ways in which individuals related to themselves and to one another in situations of intense mobility. In doing so, I downplay the polarising labels of 'colonial' and 'indigenous' that have been widely used to understand

* I would like to thank Bernard Knapp and Peter van Dommelen for inviting me to participate in the *Material Connections* project, and all the project members, especially Jaime Vives-Ferrándiz, for providing much criticism and food for thought both at the EAA conference in Malta (September 2008) and at the Glasgow workshop (March 2009). Robin Osborne read an earlier version of the text and offered some important feedback. I also wish to thank him for inviting me to present an earlier version to the Oxford meeting of the European Network for Greek History, where participants gave comments and helped me sharpen my ideas. Any mistakes lie solely with me. Finally, I would like to thank Silvia Bosi and Luciano De Camillis for the illustrations.

cultural relations in the region. It is my aim instead to explore the nature of cultural interaction *tout court* and the ways in which the changing circumstances of trading activities deeply affected and transformed the latter.

A key aspect of the changing circumstances and the materiality of mobility in the region is the establishment of coastal trading settlements across the northern Tyrrhenian Sea and *emporia* in southern Etruria: while these settlements are comparable with respect to their function, it is important to underline the often overlooked and profound differences between them. The term *emporion*, in particular, requires explanation. Although it is useful to employ Polanyi's (1963) definition of the Greek word *emporia* as ports of trade, the nature of Etruscan *emporia* is distinctly different from that of the Greek ones. Gras (1993: 107, 109) has already noted the importance of the local context when attempting to define a specific type of *emporion* across the Mediterranean, although he also calls the indigenous coastal trading settlements of southern France *emporia*. In reality, however, the latter are primarily independent indigenous settlements that were established for purposes of trade and that accommodated non-indigenous traders as a result. Southern Etruscan *emporia*, on the other hand, were characterised by a distinct political and economic relationship with the large inland centres that controlled them; their short-lived existence was clearly influenced by this relationship and control. While they largely consisted of sanctuaries and industrial, harbour and commercial installations, Etruscan *emporia* were not indigenous, foreign or colonial settlements: they were multi-cultural, cosmopolitan and socially diverse spaces, as attested by the offerings at the sanctuaries. Both these *emporia* and the coastal settlements of southern France reflect a crucial phase of transition between highly localised patterns of exchange and broader regional patterns that led to the entanglement of objects and the identities of those implicated in the exchange. Because of this entanglement, this paper argues that we need to examine a wide sphere of interaction, considering Phocean–Etruscan relations within Etruria in order to understand the movement of objects and people in the changing context of southern France (Figure 11.1).

The incidence of Etruscan, Massaliote and other Greek wine drinking vessels and amphorae on Iron Age sites of Provence, Languedoc and Roussillon in southern France during the sixth and fifth centuries BC is incontestable evidence of a flourishing wine trade in the northern Tyrrhenian Sea region. The archaeological evidence available from French coastal sites and sunken ship cargoes indicates that indigenous communities imported wine from southern Etruria from the early part of the sixth century BC, while a few sites show the presence of Etruscan amphorae as early as the end of the seventh century BC (Dietler 2005: 43). After the beginning of the sixth century BC, other types of wine amphorae, such as Chian, Attic, SOS, named after the 'SOS' pattern on their neck, and the so-called Ionian amphorae occur on some coastal sites. From the second quarter of the sixth century, wine amphorae and pottery vessels from elsewhere also reached indigenous sites on the coast and in the hinterland. These included pottery such as the so-called Pseudo-Ionian and Grey-Monochrome ware produced in the Phocean Greek settlement of Massalia as well as by indigenous workshops (Dietler 2005: 70–101). Imported from overseas were

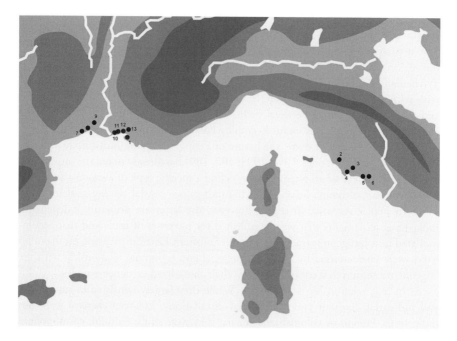

Figure 11.1   Map of the northern Tyrrhenian Sea showing sites discussed in southern France (Provence) and central Italy (Etruria). Key to sites: (1) *Massalia*; (2) *Vulci*; (3) *Tarquinia*; (4) Gravisca; (5) Pyrgi; (6) *Caere*; (7) Lattes; (8) Tonnerre I; (9) La Liquière; (10) Saint-Blaise; (11) Saint-Pierre-Les-Martigues; (12) L'Arquet; (13) Tamaris.

Ionian cups (Villard and Vallet 1955), Attic Black Figure and Black Gloss ware, as well as small numbers of Punic amphorae (Dietler 2005). That the majority of these Greek ceramic imports at indigenous sites were wine-drinking or pouring vessels, namely cups and *oinochoai*, contrasts greatly with the much wider variety of imported pottery shapes at Marseilles, and clearly demonstrates the central role of wine consumption in cultural contact and interaction in the region (Dietler 2005: 50, 56). Much attention has been devoted to the understanding of these imports and of the ways in which their acquisition and consumption in indigenous societies affected and transformed these societies, especially following the establishment of Massalia east of the Rhone river valley around 600 BC. Besides the vast amount of mainly Francophone scholarship, Dietler has published widely on the reception of these imports and the relationship between indigenous societies and the 'colonial' agents, which he identifies as Etruscan traders and Greek settlers in Massalia (Dietler 1990; 1995; 1996; 1997; 2005). Notwithstanding the problematic concept of 'colonial agent' that I question below, Dietler's work remains highly significant and influential as it represents a step away from earlier, arguably colonialist studies that focused on the impact of Etruscan traders and Greek settlers, disregarding the role of indigenous societies in culture contact or highlighting these societies' drive to emulate Greek customs (Dietler 1990: 356–8; 1995: 65; 1997: 277, 296–7; Shefton 1994; 1995).

Etruscan and Greek imports in southern France and the Battle of the Sardinian Sea

The earliest imports to southern France are isolated finds, dated to the seventh century BC. They consist of Etruscan and Greek-type objects, some unprovenanced metal *fibulae*, bronze basins deposited in *tumulus* burials, and wheel-made levigated pottery vessels from cemeteries in the Hérault and Aude districts in Languedoc (Janin 2006: 95–7). While the bronze basins were presumably Etruscan products, it is debatable whether the pottery was a Greek product or was instead manufactured in Etruria and imported from there. Their archaeological context and provenance suggest that these objects reached southern France as personal gifts among indigenous communities and are therefore evidence of sporadic contacts with the outside world.

Around 600 BC or a little earlier, when Phocean Greeks settled at the mouth of the Rhone valley, increasing numbers of Etruscan and other Greek-style pottery imports appear throughout the region. These included Etruscan products in particular, such as amphorae and *bucchero kantharoi* (high-handled drinking cups) but only rarely pouring vessels like *bucchero oinochoai* (wine jugs) and *olpai* (particular types of *oino-choai* with an elongated profile). These Etruscan imports became common at sites across the region, including Massalia, until roughly the mid-sixth century BC, but their numbers dropped markedly after that, especially in Provence and eastern Languedoc. This decline coincides with the rise of non-Etruscan, wine-related pottery, namely amphorae, drinking cups and other vessels imported from Massalia and other Greek regions. Traditionally, scholars have considered the Battle of the Sardinian Sea around 540 BC as one of the causes for the decline of Etruscan wine trade in the northern Tyrrhenian region. Close analysis of percentages of Etruscan amphora sherds on single sites in the Lower Rhone basin after this date, however, shows a heterogeneous distri- bution pattern of amphora types in this area, and Etruscan amphorae continue to occur in the region well into the fifth century BC (Dietler 2005: 46–7). The inscribed lead plaque from Pech-Maho in the Aude district not far from Emporion and dated to the mid-fifth century BC provides another, well-known reminder of the contin- uing commercial relations between Etruria and the southern French coast. The two inscriptions on the plaque, one Etruscan and one Greek, attest to trade transactions; the later Greek inscription mentions the inhabitants of Emporion/Ampurias, while the earlier Etruscan one, partly erased by the later inscription, mentions a toponym that may refer to Massalia (Ampolo and Caruso 1990–1).

Most scholars have generally relied on Herodotus' (1.166–7) account of the conflict of 540 BC between a Carthaginian and Etruscan alliance and the Phoceans who had settled on the east coast of Corsica at Alalia. However, a more recent reading of this historical account vis-à-vis the archaeological evidence suggests persuasively that the battle was triggered by Carthaginian and Etruscan fears of a Phocean influence in the north Tyrrhenian region, particularly over Phoenician settlements in Sardinia after the establishment of Phocean Alalia (Bernardini 2001). According to Herodotus, the conflict had great repercussions and ended with the victory of the Phoceans: the Phoceans abandoned Alalia, reached *Rhegium* and eventually settled in *Elea* (Velia) on the Campanian coast. Other scholars, particularly Gras (2000), have interpreted Herodotus' story in terms of a Phocean–Massaliot victory, proposing that the Phoceans who took part in the battle may have accepted the help and intervention of Massaliot Phoceans.

The established view is that the Etruscans, on the other hand, extended their trading influence over Corsica, and established a colony at Alalia/Aleria (Cristofani 1995: 133–4; Camporeale 2006). Whether we can speak of a 'colony' as Diodorus does (V.13. 3–5), however, is highly debatable. Evidence from the Aleria cemetery, which includes the regular planning of chamber tombs with corridors and the occurrence of Etruscan objects and inscriptions in tombs, suggests that some Etruscans may have resided there (Jehasse and Jehasse 1973; 1979; 2001). Significant doubts also exist whether Alalia was entirely abandoned by the Phoceans, and it has been suggested that a 'Tyrrheno-Corsican symbiosis' might have developed on the island (Jehasse and Jehasse 1979: 340; 2001: 90–3; Bernardini 2001: 152, n. 38; cf. Bats 1998: 623–4). In any event, after the mid-sixth century BC, the economic interests of some Etruscan cities, particularly *Caere*, may have shifted southwards (Cristofani 1996: 59–81; Colonna 2000b; Camporeale 2006: 18). Nonetheless, the aftermath of the battle did not stop the arrival of east Greek artisans and imports in southern Etruria. On the contrary, we see the thriving activities of east Greek craftsmen in such examples as the production of the so-called Caeretan *hydriae* (water jars) (Martelli 1981; Hemelrijk 1984: 160–1) and the Campana *dinoi* (large deep bowls), the architectural terracottas of Athena and Herakles (Lulof 2005), the Pontic vases at Vulci (Hannestad 1974; 1976; Hemelrijk 1984: 188–90) and the execution of some wall paintings in chamber tombs at Tarquinia (Cristofani 1976). The substantial occurrence of Ionian–Massaliote amphorae at the Vigna Parrocchiale site at *Caere* further indicates continuity of contacts (Cristofani 1996: fig. 5; Boss 1993). The presence of east Greeks is particularly visible at the Etruscan *emporia* (Slaska 1982; Boldrini 1994; Colonna 2004), and any change in the material culture that relates to this presence is likely to be partly the result of changing economic and political relations of those Etruscan cities that controlled the *emporia*, and the ultimate shift of economic interests from the *emporion* to the city (Torelli 1982: 321; 2004: 127; Cristofani 1996: 57, 78–81).

In reality, a succinct picture of Etruscan and Greek imports does little justice to the diversity and complexity of the archaeological evidence of sixth-century BC southern coastal France. Dietler (1997: 336; 2005) has rightly stressed the highly localised response to foreign imports: from Roussillon to eastern Provence, a multitude of people and communities acquired imported goods in diverse contexts (Figure 11.1). The indigenous settlements nearest Massalia – such as Saint-Blaise, Tamaris (Duval 1998; Dietler 2005: 242), L'Arquet (Lagrand 1986; Dietler 2005: 242) and

Saint-Pierre-Les-Martigues (Lagrand 1986) – undoubtedly felt the impact of the encounter with foreign traders and new settlers more strongly than other communities (Duval 2006).

Saint-Blaise, for example, one of the best-known and -excavated sites of the Lower Rhone basin, was clearly a flourishing indigenous trading settlement, as demonstrated by the large number and variety of imports (Arcelin 1971; Bouloumié 1976; 1979; 1979–83; 1992; Sourisseau 2003; Dietler 2005: 198). The abundance of Etruscan material and the early occurrence of Etruscan *graffiti* have prompted the suggestion that it may have been an Etruscan trading post (Bouloumié 1982; 1991). However, the dominance of local pottery finds among the excavated assemblages and recent studies that have compared the earliest imports at Saint-Blaise and Massalia prompt caution: the *graffiti* may simply indicate the mobility of Etruscan merchants who resided at Saint-Blaise (Dietler 2005: 198; Sourisseau 2003: 65).

This situation contrasts markedly with that noted in eastern Languedoc, where Etruscan and Greek material was much less abundant, even if the region was no less well connected in the earlier part of the sixth century BC and possibly earlier (Bats 1998: 625–6). Etruscan imports, for example, reached the indigenous communities of Tonnerre I and La Liquière in the Hérault before 600 BC (Py 1985; Py *et al.* 1984; Dietler 2005: 205–6, 217; Dedet and Py 2006: 123, 128–35; Bats 1998: 614–16; 2006: 82–4). Later, around the end of the sixth century BC, when *bucchero* ware and Etruscan amphorae progressively disappeared from archaeological contexts, they still reached Lattes/*Lattara*, an indigenous trading post in the Hérault that had been established around 525 BC. This and other new evidence from Lattes suggest that the site served as a landing post for Etruscan traders (Py 1988; 1995; Landes 2003; Dietler 2005: 213; Dedet and Py 2006: 138–40; Py *et al.* 2006).

Trading settlements and wine consumption

The framework for understanding these imports and the changing relations between indigenous communities and Etruscan, Massaliote or other Greek traders has largely been based on two factors: (1) the dichotomy between these communities and the 'colonial' agents, and (2) the active role of these communities in the process of a 'creative indigenisation of an alien food', namely wine (Dietler 1990; 2006: 234). While wine importation and consumption stimulated the structuring of the indigenous political economy, Dietler has argued that it did not affect the identity or cultural set-up of the local communities (Dietler 2005: 158–9, 174; 2006: 234). Significantly, one explicit aim of Dietler's work has been to dismiss the observation, now widely recognised as Hellenocentric, that indigenous communities emulated Greek sympotic or other foreign customs. He has demonstrated instead that these communities actively chose to consume certain objects and beverages, and manipulated them for their own ends and within their own highly localised feasting traditions (Dietler 1990; 1996; 1997; 2005: 174–8). While highlighting the active role of these communities, this perspective nevertheless polarises colonial and indigenous, and in doing so overlooks the nature of cultural interaction among the 'colonial' agents themselves and the ways in which this interaction impinged on their trading contacts with indigenous communities. In order to shift attention towards these important aspects, I will review two key points.

The first is the very attribution of 'colonial' status to Etruscan and Greek traders (on colonialism in antiquity and for the definition of 'colonial', see van Dommelen 1997; Osborne 2006: 155–6, citing Given 2004). It can neither be sustained nor indeed demonstrated that Etruscan traders entertained colonial relations with their trading partners, least of all with northern Tyrrhenian communities. A recent study on Etruscan settlements in the Po plain has questioned the notion of Etruscan 'colonial' and expansionist ambitions outside Etruria from the sixth century BC onwards; this is but one example of a growing scepticism towards the long-established notion of Etruscan 'colonialism' largely derived from ancient textual sources. Moreover, sustaining the dichotomy between indigenous and 'colonial' agents runs the risk of neglecting the variety of economic and political relations that each Etruscan city and its traders enjoyed with their foreign partners. This factor indubitably affected the dynamics of contacts and cultural interaction in the north Tyrrhenian region. Studies on the provenance of Etruscan amphorae, which mainly originated from *Caere* and Vulci, for example, have enabled us to understand these cities' internal socio-economic changes vis-à-vis their involvement in Tyrrhenian trade (overview in Morel 2006: 36–7).

Upon the establishment of Massalia, Phocean relationships with both their indigenous neighbours in southern France and their Etruscan partners were of a commercial nature and some Etruscan traders may have settled in Massalia, for instance at the site of the rue de la Cathédrale (Gantés 1999: 372; 2002; Gran-Aymerich 2006: 215) or in nearby indigenous settlements like Lattes or Sainte-Blaise (Py 1995).

Only in the aftermath of the Battle of the Sardinian Sea can we plausibly speak of Massalia as a colonial settlement (Bats 1992: 269), and even then we must be cautious about using 'colonial', a loaded political and ideological term that may not apply to Massalia, at least not in the sixth century BC (Dietler 2005: 180). After 540 BC, when specific zones of trading and political influence were established, Massalia became a *polis* controlling an agricultural hinterland (Bats 1998: 628). Not until the following century and later, however, did the city extend its own commercial influence further west by establishing a network of colonial settlements (Bats 1992: 273–5). This distinction between trade interaction of the first phase and colonial relations of later phases is fundamental, because it tones down the polarisation between colonial and indigenous partners. This is the second key point I would like to revisit.

Undoubtedly the differences between these partners were very real. I would argue, however, that those differences have been overstressed, thus overshadowing the profound transformations in the nature of trade and hence cultural interaction in the whole of the Tyrrhenian Sea region between the end of the seventh and the beginning of the sixth centuries BC. The extent to which these transformations affected indigenous communities and Etruscan traders equally has also been obscured, and hence the ways in which imports were acquired in local contexts. The relationships that were established between these supposed 'colonial agents' and the indigenous

References

Agostiniani, L. 1982 *Le iscrizioni parlanti dell'Italia antica.* Florence: Leo S. Olschki Editore.

Ampolo, C. 1976–7 Demarato. Osservazioni sulla mobilità sociale arcaica. *Dialoghi di Archeologia* 9–10: 333–45.

Ampolo, C., and T. Caruso 1990–1 I greci e gli altri nel mediterraneo occidentale. Le iscrizioni greca ed etrusca di Pech-Maho: circolazione di beni, di uomini di Istituti. *OPUS* 9–10: 29–48.

Appadurai, A. 1986 Introduction: commodities and the politics of value. In A. Appadurai (ed.), *The Social Life of Things: Commodities in Cultural Perspective*, 3–63. Cambridge: Cambridge University Press.

Arcelin, P. 1971 *La céramique indigène modelée de Saint-Blaise (Saint-Mitre-les-Remparts, Bouches-du-Rhône), niveaux protohistoriques VII et VI.* Paris and Aix-en-Provence: Ophrys.

Baglione, M.P. 1990 Considerazioni sui santuari di Pyrgi e di Veio-Portonaccio. *Scienze dell'Antichità* 3–4 (1989–90): 651–67.

Bagnasco Gianni, G. 1996 *Oggetti iscritti di epoca Orientalizzante in Etruria.* Florence: Leo S. Olschki Editore.

—— 2006 Caratterizzazione e diffusione delle ceramiche depurate tra Etruria e Francia meridionale. In S. Gori and M.C. Bettini (eds), *Gli Etruschi da Genova ad Ampurias. Atti del XXIV Convegno di Studi Etruschi ed Italici, Marseille, Lattes, 26 settembre–1 ottobre 2002*: 221–31. Pisa: Istituti Editoriali e Poligrafici Internazionali.

Bats, M. 1992 Marseille, les colonies massaliètes et les relais indigènes dans le trafic le long du littoral méditerranéen gaulois (VIe–Ier s. av. J.-C.). In M. Bats, G. Bertucchi, G. Conges and H. Treziny (eds), *Marseille Grecque et la Gaule. Actes du Colloque International d'Histoire et d'Archéologie et du Ve Congrès Archéologique de Gaule Méridionale, Marseille, 18–23 novembre 1990.* Aix-en-Provence, Université de Provence, Etudes Massaliètes 3: 264–76. Lattes: A.D.A.M. Éditions.

—— 1998 Marseille archaïque. Étrusques et Phocéens en Méditerranée nord-occidentale. *Mélanges de l'École Française de Rome: Antiquité* 110 (2): 609–33.

—— 2006 Systèmes chronologiques et mobiliers étrusques du midi de le Gaule au premier âge du fer (v. 600–480): les rythmes de l'archéologie et de l'histoire. In S. Gori and M.C. Bettini (eds), *Gli Etruschi da Genova ad Ampurias. Atti del XXIV Convegno di Studi Etruschi ed Italici, Marseille, Lattes, 26 settembre–1 ottobre 2002*, 81–92. Pisa: Istituti Editoriali e Poligrafici Internazionali.

Bellelli, V. 2004 Maestranze greche a Caere: il caso delle terrecotte architettoniche. In G.M. Della Fina (ed.), *I Greci in Etruria. Atti dell'XI Convegno Internazionale di Studi sulla Storia e l'Archeologia dell'Etruria.* Annali Fondazione Faina 11: 95–109. Rome: Quasar.

Bernardini, P. 2001 La battaglia del mare sardo: una rilettura. *Rivista di Studi Fenici* 29 (2): 135–58.

Boldrini, S. 1994 *Le ceramiche ioniche. Gravisca. Scavi nel Santuario Greco 4.* Bari: Edipuglia.

Boss, M. 1993 Die Transportamphoren. In M. Cristofani (ed.), *Lo scarico arcaico della Vigna Parrocchiale, Parte III*, 319–49. Rome: Consiglio Nazionale delle Ricerche.

Botto, M., and J. Vives-Ferrándiz 2006 Importazioni etrusche tra le Baleari e la penisola iberica (VIII–prima metà del V sec. A.C.). In G. M. Della Fina (ed.), *Gli Etruschi e il Mediterraneo. Commerci e politica. Atti dell'XIII Convegno Internazionale di Studi sulla Storia e l'Archeologia dell'Etruria*. Annali Fondazione Faina 13: 117–96. Rome: Quasar.

Bouloumié, B. 1976 Les amphores étrusques de Saint-Blaise (fouilles H. Rolland). *Revue Archéologique de Narbonnaise* 9: 23–43.

—— 1979 Essai de classification du bucchero trouvé à Saint-Blaise (fouilles H. Rolland). In *Le bucchero nero étrusque et sa diffusion en Gaule Méridionale. Actes de la Table-ronde d'Aix-en-Provence (21–23 mai 1975) organisée par le Centre National de la Recherche Scientifique et l'Institut d'Archéologie Méditerranéenne, Bruxelles*. Collection Latomus 160: 111–23. Bruxelles: Latomus.

—— 1979–83 La céramique étrusco-corinthienne de Saint-Blaise. *Hommage à N. Lamboglia II*, Bordighera. *Revue d'Études Ligures* 44 (1978): 51–62.

—— 1982 Saint-Blaise et Marseille au VIe siècle avant J.-C.: l'hypothèse étrusque. *Latomus* 41: 74–91.

—— 1991 Saint-Blaise: comptoir étrusque et ville massaliète. *Ο Λύχνος* 46: 53–57.

—— 1992 *Saint-Blaise (Fouilles H. Rolland). L'habitat protohistorique. Les céramiques grecques*. Aix-en-Provence: Université de Provence, Service des Publications.

Bourdieu, P. 1977 *Outline of a Theory of Practice*. Cambridge: Cambridge University Press.

Bresson, A. 1993 Les cités grecques et leurs *emporia*. In A. Bresson and P. Rouillard (eds), *L'emporion*, 163–226. Paris: De Boccard.

—— 2000 *La cité marchande*. Paris: De Boccard.

Camporeale, G. 2006 Gli Etruschi in Provenza e in Linguadoca. In S. Gori and M.C. Bettini (eds), *Gli Etruschi da Genova ad Ampurias. Atti del XXIV Convegno di Studi Etruschi ed Italici, Marseille, Lattes, 26 settembre–1 ottobre 2002*, 13–20. Pisa: Istituti Editoriali e Poligrafici Internazionali.

Carraro, F. 2007 The 'speaking objects' of Archaic Greece: writing and speech in the first complete alphabetic documents. In K. Lomas, R.D. Whitehouse and J.B. Wilkins (eds), *Literacy and the State in the Ancient Mediterranean*, 65–80. London: Accordia Research Institute.

Cartledge, P. 1983 'Trade and politics' revisited: Archaic Greece. In P. Garnsey, K. Hopkins and C.R. Whittaker (eds), *Trade in the Ancient Economy*, 1–15. London: Chatto and Windus.

Colonna, G. 1983 Identità come appartenenza nelle iscrizioni di possesso dell'Italia preromana. *Epigraphica* 45: 49–64.

Colonna, G. (ed.) 1985 *Santuari d'Etruria*. Milan: Electa.

—— 1991 Le iscrizioni votive etrusche. *Scienze dell'Antichità* 3–4 (1989–90): 875–903.

—— 2000a Il santuario di Pyrgi dalle origini mitistoriche agli altorilievi frontonali dei Sette e di Leucotea. *Scienze dell'Antichità* 10: 251–336.

Colonna, G. 2000b I Tyrrenòi e la battaglia del Mare Sardonio. In P. Bernardini, P.G. Spanu and R. Zucca (eds), *Μάχη. La battaglia del Mare Sardonio. Studi e ricerche*, 47–56. Oristano: La Memoria Storica, Mythos.

—— 2004 I greci di Caere. In G.M. Della Fina (ed.), *I Greci in Etruria. Atti dell'XI Convegno Internazionale di Studi sulla Storia e l'Archeologia dell'Etruria*. Annali Fondazione Faina 11: 69–93. Rome: Quasar.

Columeau, P. 2000 La faune archéologique des Pistoles, témin d'un culte? In A. Hermary and H. Tréziny (eds), *Les cultes des cités Phocéennes. Actes du Colloque International Aix-en-Provence 4–5 juin 1999*, 114–17. Aix-en-Provence: Édisud.

Cristofani, M. 1975 Il 'dono' nell'Etruria arcaica. *Parola del Passato* 161: 132–52.

—— 1976 Storia dell'arte e acculturazione: le pitture tombali arcaiche di Tarquinia. *Prospettiva* 7: 2–10.

—— 1989 Ripensando Pyrgi. In *Miscellanea Ceretana* I. Quaderni del Centro di Studio per l'Archeologia Etrusco-italica 17: 85–93. Rome: Consiglio Nazionale delle Ricerche.

—— 1995 Novità sul commercio etrusco arcaico: dal relitto del Giglio al contratto di Pech Maho. In J. Swaddling, S. Walker and P. Roberts (eds), *Italy in Europe: Economic Relations 700 BC–AD 50*, 131–7. London: British Museum.

—— 1996 *Etruschi e altre genti nell'Italia preromana. Mobilità in età arcaica*. Rome: Giorgio Bretschneider Editore.

Dedet, B., and M. Py 2006 Chronologie et diffusion des importations étrusques en Languedoc Oriental. In S. Gori and M.C. Bettini (eds), *Gli Etruschi da Genova ad Ampurias. Atti del XXIV Convegno di Studi Etruschi ed Italici, Marseille, Lattes, 26 settembre–1 ottobre 2002*, 121–44. Pisa: Istituti Editoriali e Poligrafici Internazionali.

Dietler, M. 1990 Driven by drink: The role of drinking in the political economy and the case of early Iron Age France. *Journal of Anthropological Archaeology* 9: 352–406.

—— 1995 Early 'Celtic' socio-political relations: ideological representation and social competition in dynamic comparative perspective. In B. Arnold and D.B. Gibson (eds), *Celtic Chiefdom, Celtic State: The Evolution of Complex Social Systems in Prehistoric Europe*, 64–71. Cambridge: Cambridge University Press.

—— 1996 Feasts and commensal politics in the political economy: food, power, and status in prehistoric Europe. In P. Wiessner and W. Schiefenhövel (eds), *Food and the Status Quest: An Interdisciplinary Perspective*, 87–125. Oxford: Berghahn Books.

—— 1997 The Iron Age in Mediterranean France: colonial encounters, entanglements, transformations. *Journal of World Prehistory* 11 (3): 269–358.

—— 2005 *Consumption and Colonial Encounters in the Rhône Basin of France. A Study of Early Iron Age Political Economy*. Lattes: Édition de l'Association pour le Développement de l'Archéologie en Languedoc-Roussillon.

—— 2006 Culinary encounters: food, identity and colonialism. In K.C. Twiss (ed.), *The Archaeology of Food and Identity*. Center for Archaeological Investigations Occasional Paper 35: 218–41. Carbondale: Southern Illinois University.

Duval, S. 1998 L'habitat côtier de Tamaris (B. du Rhône). Bilan de recherches et études du mobilier des fouilles de Ch. Lagrand. *Documents d'Archéologie Méridionale* 21: 133–80.

Duval, S. 2006 Mobilier céramique et commerce à destination d'habitats indigènes en Provence occidentale, du VIe s. au debut du Ve s. av. J.-C. In S. Gori and M.C. Bettini (eds), *Gli Etruschi da Genova ad Ampurias. Atti del XXIV Convegno di Studi Etruschi ed Italici, Marseilles, Lattes, 26 settembre–1 ottobre 2002*, 103–20. Pisa: Istituti Editoriali e Poligrafici Internazionali.

Fiorini, L. 2005 *Topografia Generale e Storia del Santuario. Analisi dei Contesti e delle Stratigrafie. Gravisca. Scavi nel Santuario Greco 1, 1*. Bari: Edipuglia.

Gantés, L.-F. 1999 La physionomie de la vaisselle tournée importée à Marseille au VIe siècle av. J.-C. In M.-C. Villanueva Puig, F. Lissarrague, P. Rouillard and A. Rouveret (eds), *Céramique et peinture grecques. Modes d'emploi. Actes du colloque international, École du Louvre, 26–27–28 avril 1995*, 365–81. Paris: Documentation Française.

—— 2002 Les fouilles de l'ilot de la Cathédrale ou îlot. In L. Long, P. Pomey and J.-C. Sourisseau (eds), *Étrusques en mer. Épaves d'Antibes à Marseilles*, 104–5. Aix-en-Provence: Musée de Marseille, Édisud.

Given, M. 2004 *The Archaeology of the Colonized*. London: Routledge.

Glinister, F. 2000 The Rapino bronze, the Touta Marouca, and sacred prostitution in early Central Italy. In A. Cooley (ed.), *The Epigraphic Landscape of Roman Italy*, 19–38. London: Institute of Classical Studies.

Gori, S. and M.C. Bettini (eds) 2006 *Gli Etruschi da Genova ad Ampurias. Atti del XXIV Convegno di Studi Etruschi ed Italici, Marseille-Lattes, 26 settembre–1 ottobre 2002*. Pisa: Istituti Editoriali e Poligrafici Internazionali.

Gosden, C., and Y. Marshall 1999 The cultural biography of objects. In Y. Marshall and C. Gosden (eds), *The Cultural Biography of Objects. World Archaeology* 31 (2): 169–78.

Gran-Aymerich, J. 2006 La diffusion des vases étrusques en Mediterranée nord-occidentale: l'exception gauloise. In S. Gori and M.C. Bettini (eds), *Gli Etruschi da Genova ad Ampurias. Atti del XXIV Convegno di Studi Etruschi ed Italici, Marseille, Lattes, 26 settembre–1 ottobre 2002*, 205–19. Pisa: Istituti Editoriali e Poligrafici Internazionali.

Gras, M. 1986 La coupe et l'échange dans la Mediterranèe archaïque. In *Hommages à François Daumas*, 351–9. Montpellier: Institut d'Egyptologie, Université Paul Valery.

—— 1993 Pour un Méditerranée des *emporia*. In A. Bresson and P. Rouillard (eds), *L'emporion*, 103–12. Paris: De Boccard.

—— 2000 La battaglia del Mare Sardonio. In P. Bernardini, P.G. Spanu and R. Zucca (eds), *Μάχη. La battaglia del Mare Sardonio. Studi e ricerche*, 37–46. Oristano: La Memoria Storica, Mythos.

Haak, M.L. 2007 Phocéens et Samiens à Gravisca. *Bulletin Antieke Beschaving* 82 (1): 29–40.

Hannestad, L. 1974 *The Paris Painter. An Etruscan Vase-Painter*. Copenhagen: Det Kongelige Danske Videnskabernes Selskab, Kommissionaer Munksgaard.

—— 1976 *The Followers of the Paris Painter*. Copenhagen: Det Kongelige Danske Videnskabernes Selskab, Kommissionaer Munksgaard.

Hemelrijk, J.M. 1984 *Caeretan Hydriae*. Mainz: P. von Zabern.

Horden, P., and N. Purcell 2000 *The Corrupting Sea. A Study of Mediterranean History*. Oxford: Blackwell.

Izzet, V. 2004 Purloined letters: the Aristhonotos inscription and krater. In K. Lomas (ed.), *Greek Identity in the Western Mediterranean*, 191–210. Leiden: Brill.

Janin, T. 2006 Systèmes chronologiques et groupes culturels dans le Midi de la France de la fin de l'âge du Bronze à la fondation de Marseille: communautés indigènes et premières importations. In S. Gori and M.C. Bettini (eds) *Gli Etruschi da Genova ad Ampurias. Atti del XXIV Convegno di Studi Etruschi ed Italici, Marseille-Lattes, 26 settembre–1 ottobre 2002*, 93–102. Pisa: Istituti Editoriali e Poligrafici Internazionali.

Jehasse, J., and L. Jehasse 1973 *La nécropole préromaine d'Aléria (1960–1968)*. Paris: Éditions du Centre National de la Recherche Scientifique.

—— 1979 The Etruscans and Corsica. In D. Ridgway and F.R. Ridgway (eds), *Italy before the Romans. The Iron Age, Orientalizing and Etruscan Periods*, 313–51. London: Academic Press.

—— 2001 *Aléria. Nouvelles données sur la nécropole*. Lyons: Maison de l'Orient Méditerranéen.

Johnston, A. 1979 *Trademarks on Greek Vases*. Warminster: Aris and Philips.

—— 1985 Etruscans in the Greek vase trade? In M. Cristofani (ed.), *Il Commercio Etrusco Arcaico. Atti dell'Incontro di Studio, 5–7 dicembre, 1983*, 248–55. Rome: Consiglio Nazionale delle Ricerche.

—— 2000 Greek and Latin inscriptions. In A. Johnston and M. Pandolfini, *Le Iscrizioni. Gravisca. Scavi nel Santuario Greco 15*, 1–66. Bari: Edipuglia.

Johnston, A., and M. Pandolfini 2000 *Le iscrizioni. Gravisca. Scavi nel Santuario Greco 15*. Bari: Edipuglia.

Lagrand, C. 1986 Les habitats de Tamaris, l'Arquet et Saint-Pierre à Martigues. In M. Bats and H. Tréziny (eds), *Le territoire de Marseille grecque. Actes de la Table-ronde d'Aix-en-Provence, 16 mars 1985*. Études Massaliètes 1: 127–35. Aix-en-Provence: Université de Provence.

Landes, C. 2003 Lattes étrusque. In C. Landes (ed.), *Les Étrusques en France. Archéologie et Collections. Catalogue de l'exposition*, 129–39. Lattes: Imago, Musée de Lattes.

Lulof, P. 2005 Una bottega tettoia-ionica a Caere. In A.M. Sgubini Moretti (ed.), *Dinamiche di Sviluppo delle Città nell'Etruria Meridionale. Veio, Caere, Tarquinia, Vulci. Atti del XXIII Convegno di Studi Etruschi ed Italici, Roma, Veio, Cerveteri/Pyrgi, Tarquinia, Tuscania, Vulci, Viterbo, 1–6 ottobre 2001*, 209–13. Pisa: Istituti Editoriali e Poligrafici Internazionali.

Marchesini, S. 1997 *Studi onomastici e sociolinguistici sull'Etruria arcaica: il caso di Caere*. Florence: L.S. Olschki Editore.

Martelli, M. 1981 Un askos del Museo di Tarquinia e il problema delle presenze nord-ioniche in Etruria. *Prospettiva* 27: 2–13.

Martelli, M. 1989 La ceramica greca in Etruria: problemi e prospettive di ricerca. In G. Maetzke (ed.), *Atti Secondo Congresso Internazionale Etrusco Firenze 26 maggio–2 giugno 1985*. Supplemento di Studi Etruschi: 781–811. Rome: Giorgio Bretschneider Editore.

Mele, A. 1979 *Il commercio greco arcaico. Prexis ed emporie*. Naples: Institut Français de Naples.

—— 1986 Pirateria, commercio e aristocrazia: replica a Benedetto Bravo. *Dialogues d'Histoire Ancienne* 12: 67–209.

—— 1988 Il Tirreno tra commercio eroico ed emporia classica. In T. Hackens (ed.), *Navies and Commerce of the Greeks, the Carthaginians and the Etruscans in the Tyrrhenian Sea = Flotte e Commercio Greco, Cartaginese ed Etrusco nel Mar Tirreno = Flotte et Commerce Grecs, Carthaginois et Étrusques en Mer Tyrrhénienne. Proceedings of the European symposium held at Ravello, January 1987*, 57–68. Strasbourg: Conseil de l'Europe, Division de la Coóperation Scientifique.

Meskell, L. 2004 *Object Worlds in Ancient Egypt. Material Biographies Past and Present.* Oxford: Berg.

Meskell, L. (ed.) 2006 *Archaeologies of Materiality.* Oxford: Blackwell.

Miller, D. 2005 Introduction. In D. Miller (ed.), *Materiality*, 1–50. Durham, NC and London: Duke University Press.

—— 2006 Consumption. In C. Tilley, W. Keane, S. Kuechler, M. Rowlands and P. Spyer (eds), *Handbook of Material Culture*, 341–54. London: Sage.

Moliner, M. 2000 Les niveaux archaïques de la Place des Pistoles à Marseille: un espace cultuel? In A. Hermary and H. Tréziny (eds), *Les Cultes des Cités Phocéennes. Actes du Colloque International Aix-en-Provence 4–5 juin 1999*, 101–17. Aix-en-Provence: Édisud.

Morel, J.P. 2006 Les Étrusques en Méditerranée nord-occidentale: résultats et tendances des recherches récentes. In S. Gori and M.C. Bettini (eds), *Gli Etruschi da Genova ad Ampurias. Atti del XXIV Convegno di Studi Etruschi ed Italici, Marseille, Lattes, 26 settembre–1 ottobre 2002*, 23–45. Pisa: Istituti Editoriali e Poligrafici Internazionali .

Morselli, C., and E. Tortorici 1985 La situazione di Regisvilla. In M. Cristofani (ed.), *Il Commercio Etrusco Arcaico. Atti dell'Incontro di Studio, 5–7 dicembre, 1983*, 27–40. Rome: Consiglio Nazionale delle Ricerche.

Neppi Modona, A., and F. Prayon (eds) 1981 *Die Göttin von Pyrgi. Archäologische, Linguistiche und Religionsgeschichtliche Aspekte. Tübingen, 16–27 Januar 1979.* Florence: Leo Olschki Editore.

Osborne, R. 2006 W(h)ither Orientalization? In C. Riva and N. Vella (eds), *Debating Orientalization. Multidisciplinary Approaches to Change in the Ancient Mediterranean*, 153–8. London: Equinox.

Pandolfini, M. 2000 Le iscrizioni etrusche. In A. Johnston and M. Pandolfini *Le iscrizioni. Gravisca. Scavi nel Santuario Greco 15*, 69–132. Bari: Edipuglia.

Parise, N. 1985 La prima monetazione Etrusca. In M. Cristofani (ed.), *Il commercio etrusco arcaico. Atti dell'Incontro di Studio, 5–7 dicembre, 1983*, 257–62. Rome: Consiglio Nazionale delle Ricerche.

Pianu, G. 2000 *Il bucchero. Gravisca. Scavi nel Santuario Greco 10.* Bari: Edipuglia.

Polanyi, K. 1963 Ports of trade in early societies. *Journal of Economic History* 23 (1): 30–45.

Purcell, N. 2005a The ancient Mediterranean: the view from the customs house. In W.V. Harris (ed.), *Rethinking the Mediterranean*, 200–32. Oxford: Oxford University Press.

Purcell, N. 2005b Colonization and Mediterranean history. In H. Hurst and S. Owen (eds), *Ancient Colonizations. Analogy, Similarity and Difference*, 115–39. London: Duckworth.

Py, M. 1985 Sauvetage programmé sur le gisement de Tonnerre I (Mauguio, Hérault). In B. Dedet and M. Py (eds), *L'occupation des rivages de l'Etang de Mauguio (Hérault) au Bronze Final et au Premier Age du Fer*, vol. 2. Cahier de l'ARALO 12: 49–120. Caveirac: Association pour la Recherche Archéologique en Languedoc Oriental.

—— 1988 Sondages dans l'habitat antique de Lattes: le fouilles d'Henri Prades et du Groupe Archéologique Painlevé (1963–1985). In G. Barruol, C. Landes, A. Nickels, M. Py and J. Roux (eds), *Lattara 1*, 65–146. Lattes: Association pour la Recherche Archéologique en Languedoc Oriental.

—— 1995 Les Étrusques, le Grecs et la foundation de Lattes. In P. Arcelin, M. Bats, D. Garcia, G. Marchand and M. Schwaller (eds), *Sur les pas des Grecs en Occident. Hommage à André Nickels*, 262–75. Paris: A.D.A.M. Éditions.

Py, M., F. Py, P. Sauzet and C. Tardille 1984 *La Liquière, village du Ier Âge du Fer en Languedoc oriental.* Revue Archéologique de Narbonnaise Supplément 11. Paris: Centre National de la Recherche Scientifique.

Py, M., D. Lebeaupin, P. Séjalon and R. Roure 2006 Les étrusques et Lattara: nouvelles données. In S. Gori and M.C. Bettini (eds), *Gli Etruschi da Genova ad Ampurias. Atti del XXIV Convegno di Studi Etruschi ed Italici, Marseille, Lattes, 26 settembre–1 ottobre 2002*, 583–603. Pisa: Istituti Editoriali e Poligrafici Internazionali.

Rasmussen, T. 1985 Etruscan shapes in Attic pottery. *Antike Kunst* 28: 33–9.

Riva, C. 2010 *The Urbanization of Etruria. Funerary Practices and Social Change, 700–600 BC.* Cambridge: Cambridge University Press.

Rizzo, M.A. 1990 *Le anfore da trasporto e il commercio etrusco arcaico.* Rome: De Luca.

Rouillard, P. 1995 Les *emporia* dans la Méditerranée occidentale aux époques archaïque et classique. In G. Vallet (ed.), *Les Grecs et l'Occident. Actes du Colloque de la Villa 'Kérylos' (1991).* Collection de l'École Française de Rome 208. Cahiers de la villa 'Kérylos': 295–108. Rome: École Française de Rome.

Sciacca, F. 2003 La tomba Calabresi. In F. Sciacca and L. Di Blasi (eds), *La tomba Calabresi e la Tomba del Tripode di Cerveteri*, 11–199. Città del Vaticano: Musei Vaticani, Museo Gregoriano Etrusco.

—— 2006–7 La circolazione dei doni nell'aristocrazia tirrenica: esempi dall'archeologia. *Revista d'Arqueologia de Ponent* 16–17: 280–92.

Serra Ridgway, F.R. 1990 Etruscans, Greeks, Carthaginians: the sanctuary at Pyrgi. In J.P. Descoeudres (ed.), *Greek Colonists and Native Populations. Proceedings of the First Australian Congress of Classical Archaeology*, 512–30. Oxford: Clarendon Press.

Shefton, B. 1994 Massalia and colonization in the north-western Mediterranean. In G. R. Tsetskhladze and F. De Angelis (eds), *The Archaeology of Greek Colonization.*

Essays Dedicated to Sir John Boardman. Oxford University Committee for Archaeology, Monograph 40: 61–86. Oxford: Oxbow Books.

—— 1995 Leaven in the dough: Greek and Etruscan imports north of the Alps – the Classical period. In J. Swaddling, S. Walker and P. Roberts (eds), *Italy in Europe: Economic Relations 700 BC–AD 50*, 9–36. London: British Museum, Department of Greek and Roman Antiquities.

Slaska, M. 1982 Anfore marsigliesi a Gravisca. *Parola del Passato* 37: 356–9.

Sourrisseau, J.-C. 2002 Les importations étrusque à Marseille, de Gaston Vasseur aux grandes interventions d'archéologie preventive: une découverte progressive, des problématiques renouvellées. In L. Long, P. Pomey and J.-C. Sourrisseau (eds), *Les Étrusques en Mer. Épaves d'Antibes à Marseille*, 89–95. Aix-en-Provence: Musée de Marseille, Édisud.

—— 2003 Saint-Blaise. In C. Landes (ed.), *Les Étrusques en France. Archéologie et Collections. Catalogue de l'exposition*, 61–79. Lattes: Imago, Musée de Lattes.

Strathern, M. 1988 *The Gender of the Gift. Problems with Women and Problems with Society in Melanesia.* Berkeley: University of California Press.

Torelli, M. 1982 Per la definizione del commercio greco-orientale: il caso di Gravisca. *Parola del Passato* 37: 305–25.

—— 1997 *Storia degli Etruschi.* Bari: Laterza.

—— 2004 Quali greci a Gravisca? In G.M. Della Fina (ed.), *I greci in Etruria. Atti dell'XI Convegno Internazionale di Studi sulla Storia e l'Archeologia dell'Etruria.* Annali Fondazione Faina 11: 119–47. Rome: Quasar.

Tosto, V. 1999 *The Black-Figure Pottery Signed ΝΙΚΟΣΘΕΝΕΣΕΠΟΙΕΣΕΝ.* Amsterdam: Allan Pierson Series.

van Dommelen, P. 1997 Colonial constructs: colonialism and archaeology in the Mediterranean. *World Archaeology* 28: 305–23.

Villard, F., and G. Vallet 1955 Megara Hyblaea V. Lampes du VIIe siècle et chronologie de coupes ioniennes. *Mélanges de l'École Française de Rome, Archéologie et Histoire* 65: 7–34.

12

CONCLUDING THOUGHTS

Michael Rowlands

I think all the contributors to this volume would agree that the theoretical thread that has linked Mediterranean studies for much of the twentieth century is now in pressing need of revision. Regardless of the problems still remaining over the concept of the Mediterranean itself, for much of this period the idea has been accepted that academic specialisation should continue to focus on constituent regions, each defined by historical and cultural singularity, and the encounters and interactions between them. What the editors in the Introduction describe, quoting Cherry (2004), as hyper-specialisation in the study of regions has been to the detriment of examining flows and movements of peoples and things except in the language of encounter between fixed localities or regions. The editors have described this as the 'fundamental paradox' that 'while islands in general serve as essentialising metaphors for isolation (e.g. Kirch 1986; Rainbird 1999), in the Mediterranean they are more often than not interconnected through much broader social, cultural and politico-economic interaction spheres' (this volume: p. 10). While the isolationist language of 'cultures' and 'peoples' has been avoided for some time in archaeology, words such as 'identity', 'locality' or 'ethnicity' have been substituted instead, without perhaps a significant development in conceptualisation or empirical investigation.

It would be widely acknowledged in archaeology that since the impact of Frederik Barth (1969) on studies of ethnicity, identities have been seen as constituted rather than essentialised and to varying degrees open to transitory movements and change. As the editors say:

> The lesson that archaeologists can learn from the social sciences is that self-ascribed identities, whether individual or collective, are not primordial and fixed, but emerge and change in diverse circumstances: socio-political, historical, economic, contextual and – in the case of the Mediterranean's seas and mountainous islands – geographical. (this volume: p. 4)

Dissatisfaction with how the local has been conceptualised is in part due to the looseness of the term 'Mediterranean' and the loss of a sense of unity that has taken place since the distancing from Braudel's writing on the Mediterranean as a 'civilisation'. But it has also been a response to the changing realities of understanding the present response of Mediterranean societies to the impact of globalisation and postcoloni-alism. The recognition that 'societies' are constituted and reconstituted over long periods of time is complemented by the knowledge that this has not been *sui generis* with each in possession of its own unique history but through the flows, movements and connectivities that have constituted them in difference (Figure 12.1). So, in terms of archaeological theory, the turn away from the study of autonomous locali-ties has, as in this volume, resulted in the reverse perspective; the study of flows and connectivities as the basis for understanding the production of localities.

At present, when cultural difference is increasingly becoming deterritorialised because of the mass migrations and transnational/transcultural flows of the late capi-talist, postcolonial world (Appadurai 1996; Hannerz 1992; Gupta and Ferguson 1997: 5), there is obviously a special interest in understanding how questions of identity and cultural differences are spatialised in new ways and may have been so over long periods of time. The idea of the Mediterranean as a 'cultural ecumene' or having been constituted as 'a world in creolisation' for a very long time (Hannerz 1987) may therefore be apposite. Beginning in the 1970s with the various influ-ences from political economy and world systems theory insisting on foregrounding

Figure 12.1   The Bronze Age *navetas* of Mallorca and Menorca, like the two at S'Hospitalet Vell (nos. 1 and 2) in Mallorca, embody both long-term and widely connected developments (see also Ramis, this volume: figure 4.1; photo Museum of Manacor).

regional and global forms of connectedness (Gunder Frank 1967; Mintz 1985; Wallerstein 1974; Wolf 1982), several authors linked ideas of the Mediterranean in prehistory as a core to various identifications of semi-periphery and periphery within what we might call a Greater Mediterranean (Fynn-Paul 2009), usually with some conception of unequal exchange and differential wealth accumulation as the links between them (Kohl 1978; Frankenstein and Rowlands 1978; Sherratt 1995). The work of the late Andrew Sherratt is certainly the most salutary here as a consistent and immensely learned and influential argument for the case that the local was always constituted through the role it played within inter-regional flows and connectivities of material lives (Sherratt 1993). While strong criticisms were made of the determinism of world systems theory, it is indisputable that it created a focus on the large-scale movements of persons and things that has been beneficial in showing how archaeology is unique in its capacity to provide large ranging patterns in the material culture data at its disposal.

A second critique that has helped to move discussion of difference beyond the idea of autonomous localities or 'cultures' has been the focus on hybridity. A Hobbesian view of society and culture as order emerging from a primordial state of original chaos has its own Judaeo-Christian roots which, of course, are not unrelated to the long-term history of the Mediterranean. But whereas the secular version of a *telos* of order achieved through social solidarity has been described as a Western cosmology (Sahlins 1996), the elevation of ethnic and cultural hybridity aims to look at alternative versions of chaos and order that relate broadly to postcolonial experiences concerned with the 'provincialising' of a European-led view of World History (Chakrabarty 2000). Our present fascination with hybridity is not only a conceptual response to understanding current global shifts in geo-political and historical relations but also to its use as a metaphor to grasp very different efforts towards differentiation, classification and hierarchisation that are occurring now and have occurred in the past (Scott 2005). If order means the creation of difference, the categories that impose order are themselves products of differentiation – the blending or reblending of differences as part of the praxis of connectivity. It is understandable that theorists of hybridity have explored the processes that erode and destabilise boundaries; hence interstitial zones and borderlands, non-places and fuzzy zones, mobility, migration, transnational movements and flows and technologies of mass communication have been emphasised in new research mainly because the formerly naturalised limits of nations, cultures and ethnicities had become blurred in forms of and spaces of hybridity, flux, liminality and uncertainty (Brightman 1995; Scott 2005: 194). The power holders of old orders are, of course, concerned to limit these tendencies for dichotomies to disintegrate and chaos to ensue before new ones can be established (Bhabha 1989; Gupta and Ferguson 1997). The recognition that all differences are constructed, negotiable and transient and yet will always be with us encourages hybridity theorists to argue that sites of original chaos (i.e. culturally homogenous units where no difference is recognised or allowed) are brief and insubstantial moments in long-term historical processes. We do, after all, make meaning by making order, and we make order by cognising and recognising categories (Douglas 1966).

No doubt, as this volume's editors and many of the contributors argue, the key empirical focus for such processes lies in the local investigation of the effects of long-term processes of migration and mobility by investigating the 'co-presence' of diasporic peoples and object diasporas. Studying material traces of movement will focus on how factors such as materiality, mobility, hybridisation, co-presence and conflict impact(ed) on the formation of identity and subjectivity, whether past or present. Hence islands or localities become the material base for studying the consequences of processes of interaction and hybridity and different forms of mobility and connectivity and their resolutions over long time periods. Hence the need for 'concept metaphors' like hybridity or connectivity to form necessary rubrics for comparative study and to facilitate the linkage between theory and particular case studies. The chapters in this volume are unified around the shaping of concept metaphors, in particular materiality, mobility (which I also take to cover hybridity, which is the well-known concept from postcolonial theory), contact and identity. Moreover the selection is for localities where the critical element of mobility resides in the co-presence of both people and objects in a specific context. 'In other words, the actual physical encounters that take place between different people, or between those people and objects old or new, oblige us to acknowledge the existence of these encounters and to come to terms with their significance' (Knapp and van Dommelen, this volume: p. 5). Since we are studying the results of mobility rather than the dynamics of flows as such, what do we learn from the contributions to this volume about the formation of the Mediterranean?

Material connectivities

The key concept of materiality is used in the volume not only because the data are principally archaeological but because we emphasise materiality as an avenue giving us independent access to the ordinariness of migration and mobility. While we cannot proceed with assumptions of persons and things as separate without qualification over their interrelations, even so there is a straightforward assumption that we refer to the physical natures of objects and how migrant worlds are created through the intersections of persons and things in motion.

Corinna Riva sums up the problem very well in her critical take on the way classical studies have either been concerned with the arduous task of linking material culture with specific ethnic carriers and consumers of that culture or with understanding the 'colonial' relationships of an assumed dichotomy between Greek and Etruscan outsiders and indigenous communities. If you look instead at how things create subjectivities then the relation is inverted and discrete identities with entangled objects become more a pattern of interacting flows of things and entangled identities. By not starting with 'ethnic identities' and exploring instead what kinds of identities are shaped by material culture we are in a better position, she argues, to see how simple bipolar categories like colonial and indigenous or being 'Greek' or 'Etruscan' do not tie in with the complexity of the material worlds of interaction and encounter that she is dealing with. Hybrid identities create a challenge to material culture studies since it is not as if there is great theoretical literature on migration and material culture to draw upon to explain the Mediterranean situation (Basu and Coleman 2008). Instead she, like Vives-Ferrándiz and others, shows that ethnic categories that are later, even modernist, inventions have consistently distorted the realities of the complexity of entangled identities. We are used to names and things being mutually constitutive as part of a modern nationalist ideology, but contributors to this volume show that the Mediterranean world is very different. What is needed, of course, is much more systematic mapping and super-positioning of typologies of material culture and typologies of migration and mobility. Riva, for example, denies that there is a special 'Etruscan exchange' associated with colonial motives. Trade in wine is for export and is very different from internal political economic relations within and between Etruscan cities. But the motives of Etruscans for external trade interact with those of Phocaeans, who are concerned with the use of military force to establish trade mercantile monopolies but not necessarily to enforce colonial relations. In both cases, it remains unclear who has these motives and whether they are unified under ethnic labels. We are left questioning whether or when separate ethnic identities of the Etruscan, Greek, Phocaean, Punic or whatever kind came into being through these different interactions rather than acting as timeless categories. Even more significantly, when was this 'reality' of ethnic difference described in a literate sense, i.e. when was it described as such, against perhaps other realities of material flows suggesting the co-presence of other more fluid and perhaps hybrid identities, more dangerous to certain power holders?

The need for rigorous mapping of migration patterns, flows of material goods and patterns in material culture is made especially pertinent by Ramis's study of the Balearic islands. An initial 'colonisation' of the Balearics by populations from south-western France is succeeded, he argues, by a break in continuity, isolation and long-term divergence from developments on other islands. What he calls the 'Hawaiian model' may or may not be a useful analogue, since the motives to migrate seem to be an extension of what was already moving people around on the adjacent mainland. Some special purpose, something to do with a preoccupation with exploiting mountain resources but which did not lead to the development of some kind of long-term flows of materials and populations over the area; instead it resulted in isolation and implosion. But the evidence is of wholesale population movement and migration as an 'event', without any long-term relations to a homeland being established. In Sardinia, on the other hand, Hayne provides us with a rigorous mapping of the island relating the *nuraghi* to localised indigenous settlement, only to show that the material culture patternings suggest more entangled acceptance of foreign materials being absorbed into indigenous rituals on a gradient from the northwest to the southeast of the island.

Since it is argued that the study of material connections and flows is required prior to locality, we are justified in asking what conclusions can be drawn as to what characterises the nature of these flows in the most general sense. If we thought of Europe north of the Alps in the same periods, we would probably say trade in metals. If we were researchers in the Pacific, we would stress the organic and plant-based nature of material flows, seen particularly in Damon's (2008) work on trees and canoes, or Strathern's on net-bags (Küchler and Were 2005); if we were thinking of West Africa, it would be a toss-up between textiles and pottery (Picton and Mack 1989). From the contributions amassed here, it is undoubtedly the flows of cult materials, from containers to oils, unguents and the paraphernalia of sacrifice and commensality that are striking. Russell's rejection of *ex oriente lux*-type colonisation of Sardinia in the Late Helladic III period proposes instead a more localised idea of elites in control of trading resources. Moreover, the evidence for hierarchy seems to decrease with the evidence of the rising importance of copper production in the LBA and some forms of connectivity with groups in southern Italy. While we may use the language of trade and exchange as a gloss for such movements, it is quite striking that the key elements are rarely mundane and often transcendental in value. In an area of the world that has spawned much discussion of 'Axial Ages' and seen the separation of the transcendental from the mundane in ancient Greece and ancient Israel, it may not be entirely wrong to consider when and where the separation of cosmos from society may have occurred (Eisenstadt 1986). It is clearly difficult to generalise, but at some point the main characteristics of what connects and binds has to be summarised in order to get to grips with the conceptual problems this involves.

Contact and encounters

The complexity of flows and mobility in the case studies establishes what we also gain from a sense of contemporary processes of cultural globalisation. Rather than opposing the existence of autonomous local cultures confronting homogenising and more powerful colonising or imperialising movements, contributors to the volume insist on 'contact zones' where complex borrowings and imitations can take place. Their attention to 'reading' and borrowing cultural products, the power to appropriate and to resist are all fashioned into arguments that show the transformation and mutations of populations into 'hybrid localities'.

Alicia Jiménez's contribution is the most theoretically developed, with the explicit reference to a theory of mimesis. Copying or imitation, she argues, has been the basic assumption behind the historical formation of the unity of a Mediterranean world, assuming the desire in peripheral regions to emulate the symbolic power of imperialising or colonising centres. The desire to become Roman or to stay 'native' has been one example of the general tendency to study 'contact' as principally either the shallow mimicry of the powerful by the weak or as imperfect copying leading to decline or a kind of 'false consciousness' of the 'native' (Figure 12.2). The 'Bhabha thesis' on mimicry – the 'almost but not quite' inferiority of the 'uncivilised' catching up (Bhabha 1985: 107–8) – is part of the rejection of the binary coloniser/colonised model in postcolonial theory. Yet she takes up the implicit point that emulation is not 'copying' but reinterpretation and transformation of the meaning of the appropriated idea by the subjugated. If there is no 'original' to copy then mimicry, as she argues, becomes a process of creative appropriation and reinterpretation that, widely shared, helps understand the desire for the wider sense of unity that becomes, in our case, the formation of a Mediterranean world. But as she also points out, this creativity can only be legitimised through claiming an original unity with what is being copied; difference, in other words, takes place under the false shadow of a claim to unity.

We have in Jiménez's case the particular issue of Romanisation to explain – which in turn has its own problems of relating authenticity to copying Greek models. But the more important issue raised by the mimesis thesis is whether it allows a much broader understanding of the spread of difference in unity as a Mediterreanising identity. What is most striking here is that many of the contributions suggest that such a widespread process is contextualised within the spread of cults – ritual, imperial and personal – and strongly connected to forms of commensality, libation and sacrifice. This suggests that mimesis is not so much an emulation of physical appearance, dress and manner in an everyday sense but of ritual power through imposition of cults.

Vives-Ferrándiz's description of Phoenician settlement in southeast Iberia illustrates many of these arguments in a novel and insightful way. Starting with the premise shared by Riva and others that the ethnic label 'Phoenician' is more an obscurantism than a help, what is striking in his account is the extent to which, although of Levantine origin, these settlements were themselves opportunistic and integrative within local settings already assimilated into extensive trade networks and

Figure 12.2   View of the *forum* at *Baelo Claudia*, which offers a typical example of mimesis in a Roman provincial small town (Andalusia, Spain; photo F. Prados Martínez).

material exchanges. Varying from area to area, newcomers assimilated or integrated to varying degrees in terms of their basic material culture of consumption, architecture and domestic goods. On these grounds, it would be questionable whether terms like Phoenician were more than a later 'ethnic label' attached to an increasingly disparate and heterogeneous pattern of settlement. In the absence of monopolistic conditions imposed by force, mercantile competition, promoted by comparative advantage in the development of entrepôts and cosmopolitan networks, mixed shrewd recognition of the special advantages of siting settlements with access to trading networks. The question of language is quite important here, and the fact that at La Fonteta evidence of inscriptions suggests use of texts and a Levantine language code of some sort is also a pretty sure indication of some means of excluding others from a trading privilege (Figure 12.3). All this adaptation and negotiation seems very lively and opportunistic, except when it comes to funerary rites, where the evidence instead suggests conservative adherence to ritual through absorbing novel elements from outside; the introduction of the 'new' confirms the 'old' by appearing to enhance a certain technical efficacy in the rites.

Vives-Ferrándiz's use of the continuity and change metaphor implies the role of collective memory as a powerful force of duration that domesticates and integrates new practices into long-term patterns of funerary ritual. Marina Gkiasta's discussion of Early Bronze Age Crete raises even more strongly the question of the dialectical relation between localised duration or continuity taking place within larger regional and inter-regional ideologies of mixing, mimetic rivalries and change. Localisation suggests that contact promoted at some levels heterogeneity and hybridity, but at others encouraged purification and isolation and a strong sense of past, a point already made for modern Crete by the anthropologist Michael Herzfeld (1991). Sarah Janes in her discussion of Late Bronze and Early Iron Age Cyprus also concludes that large-scale and complex inter-regional and island connectivities in trading and diplomacy,

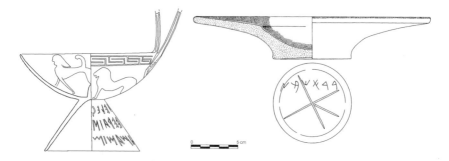

Figure 12.3 These inscribed bowls from Cerveteri (Etruria, Italy) and Peña Negra (Alicante, Spain) demonstrate the close links between food and wine consumption, naming and local identities (see Riva: figure 11.2 and Vives-Ferrándiz: figure 10.7, both this volume).

presumably also implying access to wealth and accumulation, produce locality at home with a strong focus on maintaining identity through funerary ritual. Whatever its origins, Kostoglou also ends up arguing that local preferences and tastes determine the acceptance and development of iron technology in her case study in northern Greece.

These contributions bring out a more wide-ranging theoretical question with long-term implications for understanding cosmopolitanism as characteristic of Mediterranean identities. Globalisation theorists, for example, have stressed that current, apparently undisciplined flows of finance capital, media and consumption that threaten to dissolve local identities into a culturally homogenised landscape have done nothing of the kind (Appadurai 1996; Meyer and Geschiere 1999). The rise of cultural heritage debates in archaeology (whether as an industry or not: Lowenthal 1996) since the 1970s is said to be linked to the need to preserve identities in the face of dissolving, mainly Americanised, global culture. Such new productions of locality may be a response to late capitalism, but others, even here, would say the local is a great deal more resistant, and that the excesses of globalisation have been greatly exaggerated (e.g. Butler 2006). Our Mediterranean cases suggest the latter may not only be part of a more general theoretical recognition of the power of the local, in particular its long-term duration, but also of how a more dialectical approach that entangles both perspectives may be needed. Some of the characteristics of a Mediterranean identity about which Braudel was so insistent may be worth revisiting here, in particular the stress on early urbanism, cosmopolitanism and the mixing or hybridising of populations, as well as the fact that ethnicity as a fixed and purified category is not a particularly helpful concept, at least for understanding the formation of communities in later prehistory. Marcel Mauss, writing on the concept of civilisation in 1920, summarised the issue rather well:

> The history of civilisation, from the point of view that concerns us, is the history of the circulation between societies of the various goods and achievements of each. ... Societies live by borrowing from each other, but they define themselves rather by the refusal of borrowing rather than by its acceptance. (Mauss 1920; translation Schlanger 2006: 44)

If the local survives by refusing to accept the reality of external dependence, then we have more complex issues to resolve than a simple inside or outside dichotomy will reveal.

Materiality and identity

Identity is one of the sub-themes organising the volume, and yet it is probably the most difficult to detect what is meant by the use of this term in the various contributions. The editors are clear that we have to be aware that a modern 'naturalist' idea of the person separate from others with a self-absorbed conscience and 'soul' – a mind separate from body, etc. – is not to be projected back into Mediterranean prehistory. What takes its place? Gkiasta takes a relational view; the person is a construct of their social and political relationships and as a 'dividual' is the sum of all these social contexts. This rather 'Melanesian' view of identity as constituted through exchange relations is perhaps more widely shared in the volume, but the other is more 'naturalist', that 'groups' form through the interaction of inside and outside or through the experience of encounter and contact. Hybridity of persons is the path taken to understand the creation of new identities as being more complex than the meeting of indigenous and foreign bodies. Hayne, for example, focuses on growing 'individualisation' as a product of foreign interaction and 'growing awareness of status differentials'; yet the examples of statuettes and the askoid pottery suggest identification with shared substances or ideas of shared essence, perhaps literally experienced through acts of commensality and ritual performance, since the actual contexts of finds are often sacred or ritual sites (Figure 12.4). Games, martial arts, offerings, stylised forms of body behaviour and the like may all be better understood as phenomenal aspects of shared embodied experience than self-realisations of the individualising kind. This in turn questions whether it is so obvious to distinguish between 'foreign' and 'indigenous' bodies rather than perceptions of how 'relationality' implies recognition, particularly in the formation of elites, of acquired body substances or a sense of shared essence through tracking heroic genealogies and such-like in widely dispersed networks and as agents of material connectivities. Kostoglou's argument that iron was a localised and elite phenomenon in the early Iron Age also suggests that innovation in the supply of a new material relates to specialised use and consumption rather than utility. It may be quite wrong here to separate person from thing, and instead the idea of bodies literally made of bronze or iron may not be an impossible idea.

The fact that it may not be so easy to distinguish indigenous from foreign is also brought into question by the assumed human/non-human distinction made to create an identity. A notion of the person that distinguishes a clearly human from non-human essence is actually quite a novel modernist phenomenon (e.g. Descola 2005). In fact we know from various Mediterranean contexts that human/non-human forms – the Medusa effect or the Minotaur creation, etc. – are quite prevalent, and we can assume that in different contexts human and animal forms can be shared or transformed (Napier 1986). Whether we can call this animism, totemism or something still to be conceptualised is less important than grasping the fact that even when we move from 'monsters' to singular human forms, we cannot assume that individuals exist, nor that this is the purpose of representation. If and when we can say individuals are represented, it is because we are interested in understanding when the autonomous human form emerges and with it the focus on the internalised spirit or conscience of the person, on which the classical Greek (and later Western) development of reason depends.

Civilisation

This brings us to the key issue of what contribution these new perspectives can make to understanding whether something more than the local exists that we can call the 'Mediterranean'. Cañete provides us with a revealing outline of how the

Figure 12.4 Sardinian bronze statuette of an Iron Age Nuragic woman that embodies both local individualisation and external connections (so-called 'Praying Lady' from the s'Arrideli hoard found outside Terralba; drawing by Erick van Driel, Leiden; see also Hayne, this volume: figure 8.2).

Mediterranean was constituted as a scientific category in nineteenth-century France. In the Introduction, the editors summarised their position as understanding the Mediterranean as an 'experience', presumably with definite limits as one moves to Europe or towards the Middle East. Experience is embedded in a particular material context and long-term historical dynamics.

As mentioned earlier, the contributors to this volume emphasise islands as products of the interactions between long-term durations in identity with the connectivities of mobility in peoples and things. The diversity-in-unity approach being sought touches all the contributions to the volume, and the overall argument is to understand the complex and detailed processes of encounter that occurred over time at many different island locations within the network. But this may not be enough to assess finally whether some kind of large-scale continuity exists that transcends notions of 'community', 'society' or 'region' and cannot, in Braudelian fashion, be associated with the experience of landscape in a vague ecological and geographical sense.

If we pursue the argument of this volume that the 'local' as island, identity, group (ethnic or otherwise) is constituted through interactions in wider fields of material connectivity and movement, then we also have to assume that this is an argument for the priority of the latter over the former in space-time (Figure 12.5). We do not have to assume a nineteenth-century 'unity of the Mediterranean' projected into prehistory but rather the idea of 'areas' of more or less interaction and shared material connections that constitute 'fields' in which local 'habituses' form and transform over time.

Many years ago, Mauss wrote on this theme in order to preserve the term 'civilisation' from the reductionism to 'society' that characterised the dominance of the Durkheim school in France.

Figure 12.5   View across the Stagnone lagoon towards the small island of Mozia off the Sicilian west coast that in many ways represents island interaction and material connections, as it hosted a Phoenician colonial settlement between the eighth and fifth centuries BC (photo P. van Dommelen).

There thus exist social phenomena that are not strictly attached to a determined social organism. They extend beyond the territory of any single nation, or they develop over periods of time exceeding the history of any single society. They lead a life which is in some ways supra national ... To these systems of facts, with their unity and their specific mode of existence, a special name should be given; the most appropriate seems to us to be that of 'civilisation'. (Durkheim and Mauss 1913; translation Schlanger 2006: 36–7)

This seems an eminently empirical approach to recognising large-scale distributions in the archaeological record that are genuinely prehistoric in terms of a problem for conceptualisation. The influence of social anthropologists criticising the unity of the Mediterranean as colonising or Hellenising models is relevant at a certain level of critique but is quite irrelevant as far as these empirical investigations are concerned. Generalising honour and shame to the Mediterranean, for example, only led to specific empirical refutation in particular circumstances. Bromberger's (2008) study of hair treatment as a series of transformations extending from Portugal to Afghanistan is very useful as an alternative method emphasising differentiation in space-time. It also illustrates that we may need to think in much broader regional terms than those shaped by later perceptions of the spread of Abrahamic religions. My earlier reference to Fynn-Paul's (2009)long-term definition of a 'Greater Mediterranean' by the expansion of zones of slave acquisition to Africa and Russia, as a consequence of monotheistic exclusion of their own populations from slave status, should remind us of an earlier argument from Eric Wolf, who pointed out some time ago that it was on the periphery rather than in the heartlands of the old centres of pre-axial civilisations that new heretical religions developed on which radical breaks in thought occurred, responding to organisational changes and cosmological disorders in the centres (Wolf 1967).

The chapters in this volume demonstrate without any equivocation that entities of shared essences and experiences existed in the *longue durée* of the Mediterranean 'worlds' that cannot be reduced to simple sociological categories such as society, ethnic group, community or region. What they are instead still remains an open question but, as the contributors to this volume show, they are the future of research.

References

Appadurai, A. 1996 *Modernity at Large: Cultural Dimensions of Globalization*. Public Worlds 1. Minneapolis: University of Minnesota Press.

Appadurai, A. (ed.) 1986 *The Social Life of Things: Commodities in Cultural Perspectives*. Cambridge: Cambridge University Press.

Barth, F. (ed.) 1969 *Ethnic Groups and Boundaries*. London: George Allen & Unwin.

Basu, P., and S. Coleman 2008 Migrant worlds, material cultures. *Mobilities* 3: 313–30.

Bhabha, H. 1985 Signs taken for wonders: questions of ambivalence and authority under a tree outside Delhi, May 1817. In H. Bhabha (ed.) 1994 *The Location of Culture*, 102–22. London: Routledge.

Bhabha, H. 1989 The commitment to theory. In H. Bhabha (ed.) 1994 *The Location of Culture*, 19–39. London: Routledge.

Brightman, R. 1995 Forget culture: replacement, transcendence, relexification. *Cultural Anthropology* 10: 509–46.

Bromberger, C. 2008 Hair: from the west to the Middle East through the Mediterranean. *Journal of American Folklore* 121 (482): 379–99.

Butler, J. 2006 *Precarious Life: The Powers of Mourning and Violence*. London and New York: Verso.

Chakrabarty, D. 2000 *Provincializing Europe: Postcolonial Thought and Historical Difference*. Princeton: Princeton University Press.

Cherry, J. 2004 Mediterranean island prehistory: what's different and what's new? In S. Fitzpatrick (ed.), *Voyages of Discovery: The Archaeology of Islands*, 233–48. New York and London: Praeger.

Damon, F. 2008 Apprehending the material and social world: rethinking 'religion' and 'production' along the south side of Monsoon Asia. *Chinese Review of Anthropology* 7: 181–99.

Descola, P. 2005 *Par-delà Nature et Culture*. Collection Bibliothèque des Sciences Humaines. Paris: Gallimard.

Douglas, M. 1966 *Purity and Danger: An Analysis of the Concepts of Pollution and Taboo*. London: Routledge.

Durkheim, E., and M. Mauss 1913 Note sur la notion de civilisation. *Année Sociologique* 12: 46–50.

Eisenstadt, S. (ed.) 1986 *The Origins and Diversity of Axial Age Civilizations*. Albany: State University of New York Press.

Frankenstein, S., and M. Rowlands 1978 The internal structure and regional context of early Iron Age society in south west Germany. *Bulletin of the Institute of Archaeology, London* 15: 73–112.

Fynn-Paul, J. 2009 Empire, monotheism and slavery in the greater Mediterranean region from antiquity to the early modern era. *Past and Present* 205: 3–40.

Gunder Frank, A. 1967 *Capitalism and Underdevelopment in Latin America: Historical Studies of Chile and Brazil*. New York: Monthly Review Press.

Gupta, A., and J. Ferguson (eds) 1997 *Culture, Power, Place: Explorations in Critical Anthropology*. Durham, NC and New York: Duke University Press.

Hannerz, U. 1987 The world in creolization. *Africa* 57: 546–59.

—— 1992 *Cultural Complexity. Studies in the Social Organization of Meaning*. New York: Columbia University Press.

Herzfeld, M. 1991 *A Place in History: Social and Monumental Time in a Cretan Town*. Princeton: Princeton University Press.

Kirch, P. (ed.) 1986 *Island Societies: Archaeological Approaches to Evolution and Transformation*. Cambridge: Cambridge University Press.

Kohl, P. 1978 The balance of trade in Southwestern Asia in the mid-third millennium B.C. *Current Anthropology* 19: 463–92.

Küchler, S., and G. Were 2005 *Pacific Pattern*. London: Thames and Hudson.

Lowenthal, D. 1996 *The Heritage Crusade and the Spoils of History*. London: Viking.

Mauss, M. 1920 Les nations et l'internationalisme. *Proceedings of the Aristotelian Society* 20: 237–65.

Meyer, B., and P. Geschiere (eds) 1999 *Globalization and Identity: Dialectics of Flow and Closure*. Oxford and Malden, MA: Blackwell.

Mintz, S. 1985 *Sweetness and Power: The Place of Sugar in Modern History*. New York: Viking.

Napier, D. 1986 *Masks, Transformation, and Paradox*. Berkeley and Los Angeles: University of California Press.

Picton, J., and J. Mack 1989 *African Textiles: Looms, Weaving and Design*. London: British Museum Publications.

Rainbird, P. Islands out of time: towards a critique of island archaeology. *Journal of Mediterranean Archaeology* 12: 216–34, 59–60.

Sahlins, M. 1996 The sadness of sweetness: the native anthropology of western cosmology. *Current Anthropology* 37: 395–428.

Schlanger, N. (ed.) 2006 *Marcel Mauss. Techniques, Technology and Civilisation*. New York: Berghahn Books.

Scott, M.W. 2005 Hybridity, vacuity and blockage: visions of chaos from anthropological theory. *Comparative Studies in Society and History* 47: 190–216.

Sherratt, A. 1993 What would a Bronze Age world system look like? Relations between temperate Europe and the Mediterranean in later prehistory. *Journal of European Archaeology* 1: 1–57.

—— 1995 Reviving the grand narrative: archaeology and long-term change. *Journal of European Archaeology* 3: 1–32.

Wallerstein, I. 1974 *The Modern World System*. New York: Academic Press.

Wolf, E. 1967 Understanding civilisations: a review article. *Comparative Studies in Society and History* 9: 446–65

—— 1982 *Europe and the People without History*. Berkeley and Los Angeles: University of California Press.

INDEX